Configuration and Capacity Planning for Solaris™ Servers

Brian L. Wong

Sun Microsystems Press
A Prentice Hall Title

The publisher offers discounts on this book when ordered in bulk quantities. For more information, contact Corporate Sales Department, Prentice Hall PTR, One Lake Street, Upper Saddle River, NJ 07458. Phone: 800-382-3419; FAX: 201-236-7141. E-mail (Internet): corpsales@prenhall.com.

Editorial/production supervision: *Mary Sudul*
Cover designer: *Talar Agasyan*
Manufacturing manager: *Alexis R. Heydt*
Acquisitions editor: *Gregory G. Doench*
SunSoft Press publisher: *Rachel Borden*

10 9 8 7 6 5 4 3 2

ISBN 0–13–349952–9

Sun Microsystems Press
A Prentice Hall Title

Contents

≡

Contents

Contents

Configuration and Capacity Planning for Solaris Servers

Configuration and Capacity Planning for Solaris™ Servers

Preface

Configuration and Capacity Planning for Solaris Servers provides information about how to configure a Solaris–based system for use as a server in NFS, database management, Internet/intranet or general–purpose environments. In modern computing, systems are nearly always used in a networked context, so this book considers the impact of a server on its clients and networking infrastructure—and in turn how those components affect the server. This document concentrates on the load characteristics of each type of usage and how this usage interacts with the architecture of various Solaris–based servers to affect end-user performance.

Although the title might lead one to believe that this book is about Solaris, it is really about computer architecture—specifically, *applied* computer architecture. Solaris is certainly a topic, but more fundamentally the reader should take from this material an understanding of how to apply the principles of computer architecture to the solution of everyday configuration and usage problems.

One of the peculiarities of this book is its emphasis on understanding, configuring, and using I/O subsystems. Virtually every "server" system in the open computing era has an enormous interest in managing I/O. Modern server systems certainly have their share of central processing functions, but this topic is exhaustively covered in the literature and is relatively familiar to many readers. Much less well understood is the nature of I/O functions, and how to tailor usage, applications, software, and hardware to accommodate the realities of I/O.

Audience

This book aims to aid the reader in configuring a server for a given end-user requirement, whether that requirement is current or future. As such, it is oriented toward people who typically make this kind of recommendation or who are responsible for managing it once a

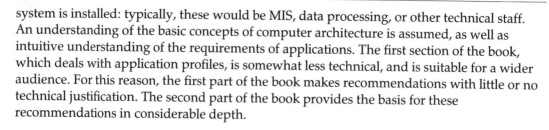

system is installed: typically, these would be MIS, data processing, or other technical staff. An understanding of the basic concepts of computer architecture is assumed, as well as intuitive understanding of the requirements of applications. The first section of the book, which deals with application profiles, is somewhat less technical, and is suitable for a wider audience. For this reason, the first part of the book makes recommendations with little or no technical justification. The second part of the book provides the basis for these recommendations in considerable depth.

How to Use This Book

This document consists of two very different sections. After introductory comments about methodology, the first four chapters—dealing with NFS servers, DBMS servers, Internet/intranet servers, and timesharing or general–purpose servers—are tutorial in nature. The categories are dealt with in order of increasing complexity. As a rule, DBMS servers are considerably more complex than NFS servers, and timesharing or general–purpose servers, especially ones with diverse user communities, are the most complex of all. These chapters are intended to be read in their entirety, rather than being used primarily as reference material. Because the topics are quite diverse and may not apply to every reader, each chapter is written to be independent of the others. Each chapter includes a number of case studies as well as explicit rules of thumb, along with questions to consider when analyzing real problems. As noted, in–depth technical explanations are often deferred. The case studies provide direct illustrations of the guidelines at work. Although the examples are designed to be representative, they are all completely fictional and do not represent any real site. Any resemblance between these case studies and actual sites is purely coincidental and unintentional.

The second section provides detailed technical material on a variety of subjects related to configuration planning. Technical bookstores carry a wide variety of excellent books on computer architecture, but most of them treat the subject in an abstract manner. The discussion provided in this text reflects the real–world concerns that are relevant in daily use. This section provides the technical justifications for the recommendations and rules of thumb provided in the first section. It is intended to serve primarily as reference material. There are chapters on each of the primary components of architecture: the basic system core (processors, memory hierarchy, and bus structures), storage systems (primarily disk), the backup and recovery process, and the Solaris 2 operating system. For the most part, this section is *not* specific to Sun products, since much of the architecture is a direct implementation or derivation from well-known industry standards such as SCSI.

Throughout the book, many sections conclude with a group of configuration recommendations that summarize the preceding text. These recommendations are marked with the ⇒ symbol.

Scope

This book addresses products announced by Sun Microsystems through December1996. Specifically included are various models of the Ultra–1, Ultra–2, SPARCstation 4, SPARCstation 5, SPARCstation 20, the SPARCserver 1000E, SPARCcenter 2000E and the Ultra Enterprise family, as well as Solaris 2 releases up to and including Solaris 2.5.1. Background information is provided about many earlier products such as the SPARCstation 2, the SPARCserver 600MP series, and previous releases of Solaris 1, including Solaris 1.1.1 (SunOS 4.1.3) and Solaris 1.1.2 (SunOS 4.1.4). To a degree that is feasible, Solaris running in Intel x86 and PowerPC systems is also covered, although the diversity of hardware platforms makes this task somewhat difficult.

Acknowledgments

The gestation period of an effort such as this is similar to that of multiple elephants, and over time, many people have contributed to this effort. Cheena Srinivasan provided the original motivation for this project several years ago. Tim Read wrote the ancestral first draft of the DBMS chapter and contributed many insights, especially on database management topics. Allan Packer also contributed parts of the DBMS chapter. (An early draft of the DBMS chapter was published on the World Wide Web and inappropriately credited to yet another author.) Shane Sigler taught me about the Internet and its servers. Jim Skeen, Allan Packer, Adrian Cockcroft, and Hal Stern provided a wide variety of suggestions and guidance on virtually every topic. The questions and requests from many Sun users and Sun systems engineers around the world, especially Dave Edstrom, Ken Rossman, John Meyer, Jim Alexander, and Jim Mauro, have motivated and shaped this work. Many thanks to all who have contributed. Finally, thank you to all who have kept me—and the project—moving in the right direction, especially my wife Jo.

Brian Wong
(brian.wong@sun.com)

November 1996

Methodology 1

Those people faced with the problem of making a configuration recommendation must begin with two sets of information: what service must be provided, and what service a given configuration can provide. Given a set of goals for end-user performance and cost constraints, one must forecast the ability of a specific set of components configured together. As anyone who has attempted such a forecast knows, such estimation is difficult and fraught with inaccuracies. Configuration estimation is hard. Some of the reasons are as follows:

- Configuration estimation is literally predicting the future—about the combination of products, about the deployment of the software system, and about the future users. *Estimating which configuration will satisfy a particular requirement requires gazing into a crystal ball and accurately gauging the future behavior of, and interaction between, user populations, application software, system software, networks, and hardware platforms.*

- Configurations are complex, involving many components, and complexity is increasing rapidly. Years ago exactly one computing paradigm was available: the mainframe with terminals. Now users are presented with a choice of several paradigms, with a wide variety of possible configurations in each. Each new generation of products provides so many more capabilities than the predecessor products that new ground is continually being broken.

- The rate of change in each of the technologies—applications, hardware, organization, operating systems, database management software, middleware—is already rapid and accelerating. By the time a product can be widely deployed and well understood, it is often obsolete!

- Information about systems, operating systems, infrastructure software such as database management systems, and transaction processing monitors is very generalized. The software infrastructure, like the hardware used to run it, has become so complex that experts in one domain are rarely experts in the other.

- Information about *usage* is rarely accurate; moreover, users always find new ways of using computation systems when new capabilities are made available. Systems are commonly procured for the purpose of running applications that are not yet developed, let alone well understood and fully characterized.

1.1 An Organized Approach

With all of these vagaries, estimated configurations are like the proverbial dancing bear: the amazing thing about a dancing bear is not how *well* it dances, but rather that it dances at all! It is amazing that most configurations work as well as they do. Unfortunately, also true is that the majority of installed systems that are performing acceptably are significantly over-configured in one or more dimensions.

Configuration estimation is still something of an art, but it *can* be approached scientifically. Although deciding with certainty that a particular configuration *will* meet a particular need is essentially impossible, safely arriving at the inverse conclusion that a particular configuration *cannot* handle a specific load is both possible and practical. Moreover, actual usage tends to expand to fill available resources; systems that are somewhat over-configured will inevitably absorb additional work.

To perform this sort of analysis, a system—meaning the entire complex of computers, peripherals, networks, software, operational staff, and policies—must be viewed as a series of connected components. Networks consist of clients, servers, and network infrastructure. The network infrastructure includes media—often multiple types—along with the bridges, routers, and network management that keep it running. Clients and especially servers consist of CPUs, memory hierarchies, busses, peripherals, and software. A configuration's performance limits in any dimension (for example, disk I/O) can usually be predicted from an analysis of the weakest components.

In more practical terms, data flows always move at the speed of the slowest component or subcomponent in the path. One very significant example is the rate at which an application obtains data from a storage system. The storage subsystem might be able to supply data at 4 MB/sec, but if the application reads a block of data, processes it, and then reads another block, the aggregate data rate experienced by the system may be significantly less than 4 MB/sec, since the storage system is likely to be idle while the application is processing each block of data.

Although this data flow model is valid for all computer systems, it is much more relevant to servers. To a large degree, server systems are conveyer belts for data, and estimating the speed of those data streams is a significant part of configuration estimation and planning.

Because modern application systems nearly always include many systems operating together, accurate configuration estimation requires consideration from macroscopic (network-wide) and microscopic (component or subsystem) perspectives. This discussion covers both.

This same methodology can be used to tune the system after it is installed: system and network tuning are largely after-the-fact estimation and bottleneck analysis. Tuning a configuration is most fundamentally the process of identifying the weakest component in the system and strengthening it, thereby removing a bottleneck.

The organization of the connected components, along with the capabilities and limitations of the components, is called the *system architecture*. This entire text is about identifying and solving architectural problems in large configurations, especially in servers and networks.

Removing the architectural obstacles to free the flow of data is the goal of a configuration plan. Sometimes this is just a matter of throwing enough resources (usually hardware) at the problem, but realistically most installations cannot afford to blindly proceed along such a path. Much of this book is devoted to helping the reader decide which bottleneck is the one to break, and which potential bottleneck really is not a problem at all.

1.2 The Virtual Storage Hierarchy

The most fundamental architectural notion in modern computer systems is that of the virtual storage hierarchy. Nearly every common computer, and certainly every system that runs Solaris, uses the same basic design: one or more main CPUs process data that reside in a hierarchy of memories. Every system has a number of different memories. In this context, the processors' caches, main memory, disk, optical storage, and even tapes are memories. The different levels of the hierarchy are characterized by the fact that the fastest ones are small and expensive, while the largest ones are much larger (in some cases measured in the terabyte range) and far less expensive. Even parallel systems, such as the SPARCcluster PDB and the IBM SP2 typically consist of a number of component systems that individually have virtual storage hierarchies.

The largest level stores all of the data that the system will use regularly ("regularly" may vary from site to site). Each of the other levels in the hierarchy caches the most frequently used portion of the next lower—and slower—level. The processors' cache stores the most frequently used portions of main memory, while main memory caches the more frequently used parts of the disk storage. Systems that have very large farms of optical disks or magnetic tape storage usually use standard magnetic disks as caches or staging areas for the most frequently used "near-line" storage.

This caching principle usually works well because of the principle of *locality of reference*. If a storage location is being referenced now, it will probably be referred to again in the near future. Furthermore, the next reference will probably be to a location that is nearby, and usually it will refer to the very next storage location. The term "usually" here often means "with a probability of over ninety percent"—in some cases, such as processor caches, hit rates are ideally in the vicinity of 98-99 percent.

Caches keep the most appropriate set of data at each level, but sometimes they are fooled, and the references fall into the ten percent category that is not cached at the current level. When the requested data cannot be found at the current level, the system must copy the referenced data from the nearest location in the underlying levels before processing can continue. Processing stops while the copy operation is performed (at least for the requesting process, and sometimes for the entire processor), so minimizing and accelerating the movement of data between storage levels is the central problem in the design and configuration of modern computer systems.

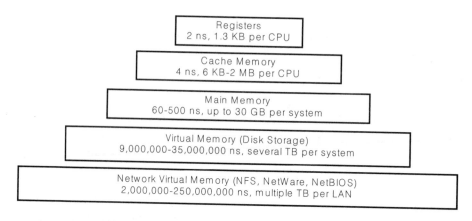

Figure 1. The virtual memory hierarchy. Every modern system implements this hierarchy in one form or another. Minimizing movement between levels and accelerating access at each level—is the central problem in capacity and configuration estimation.

In terms of configuration planning, optimizing the virtual storage hierarchy means sizing each of the caches appropriately, ensuring that the busses connecting the various components have sufficient bandwidth, and ensuring that the memories have the appropriate speed and capacity to handle the anticipated load.

1.3 Bottlenecks

Server systems, to a much greater degree than other systems, are in the business of transferring data from one place to another. Very often, the performance of the server is governed by the rate at which data flows through the system. (This notion is, of course, very generalized; thinking about any computer system this way at some abstract level is reasonable.) Accordingly, bottleneck analysis in a server consists largely of matching the speed of devices, busses, and processing capabilities.

Abstractly, data is transferred from a source via some pipe to a sink. Most people intuitively understand the notion of bottlenecks—if the pipe is not fast enough, it limits the speed of the data transfer. One pitfall that many users fall into is focusing on the speed of the pipe, and overlooking the speed of the source to provide the data, or the ability of the sink to consume it. A classic example is the rush to upgrade PC Ethernet boards from 8–bit to 32–bit implementations "to get off the slow ISA bus." The 32-bit boards certainly are better implementations than their 8-bit predecessors, but the 8.33 MB/sec ISA bus can never constrain the throughput of a 10 Mbit/sec (1.25 MB/sec) Ethernet, even when the latter runs at full bandwidth. In the other direction, PC Card (PCMCIA) FastEthernet cards are unlikely to deliver full 100 Mbit/sec throughput (12.5 Mbytes/sec), because the current PC Card bus is only capable of 4 Mbytes/sec.

A less theoretical example is the typical user benchmark that "measures " the performance of some network media implementation such as ATM. One approach is to put two systems on the network in question and use `ftp(1)` to transfer files from one to the other. This approach is certainly correct, but without some careful attention to detail, this benchmark can test quite a variety of different things. If the test transfers a batch of small files, the benchmark probably measures the speed that the receiving system can create files on disk— which is, in effect, the rotational speed of the target disk. If the systems are SPARCclassics or 90 MHz Pentiums, the benchmark probably tests the speed of the IP implementation on the receiving system, since these processors are not fast enough to drive an ATM network and `ftp(1)` tends to load the receiving system's processor more than the transmitter's. If the systems are faster and the files are larger, the next bottleneck is probably the speed that one system or the other can read or write disk files. Since an ATM network can actually transfer files at slightly more than 16 MB/sec, the network is not stressed unless transmitter and receiver have fast UltraSPARC or Pentium Pro processors and are equipped with four-way stripes to handle the files.

1.4 Performance Dimensions

Performance is a recurring topic throughout the book. Although the topic at hand is really configuring systems, this is fundamentally an exercise in performance estimation. There are several ways to measure performance, and they have different implications. Performance has many dimensions. Among them are throughput, latency, utilization, and efficiency.

1.4.1 Throughput

Most people think of performance in terms of *throughput*, which is the amount of "stuff" that is processed per unit of time. "MIPS," "megabytes per second," "NFSops/sec," and "transactions per minute" are all throughput metrics. For the most part, throughput measures apply to entire systems or subsystems. Throughput is a familiar notion to nearly everyone in the industry.

1.4.2 Latency

A much less familiar metric is a response–time or *latency* metric. This is the amount of time that an individual user or requester spends waiting for a result. For example, NFS benchmarks such as LADDIS always specify performance in a two-dimensional form, such as "4385 NFSops/sec at 40.4 ms response time." Although often mentioned in the context of an entire system, latency is primarily of interest to the *user* of the system. Most users are intuitively aware of latency issues, but latency is much less familiar than throughput.

Comparing throughput and latency is interesting and instructive. Although they both broadly address performance concerns, these metrics really have completely different meanings—and audiences. Throughput is primarily of interest to people who buy and manage systems. They are typically responsible for providing service or the mechanism for a user population to perform a specified amount of work. As long as the response time is "adequate," the primary consideration is whether or not the proposed system can get all the work done, that is, if the throughput is sufficient. Throughput in the context of configuration planning is thus a measure of *organizational* productivity.

On the other hand, latency is primarily of interest to the users. Most individual users do not care how many other people get to use the computer, as long as *their* work is done without undue interruption. They want the system to respond quickly and consistently. As such, latency measures are primarily measures of *individual* productivity.

The term "high performance" consequently means different things to different people. Although it is often true that a high-throughput system also delivers low latency, this far from necessarily so. Consider the busy people you know. They work hard all the time, and they usually have a long list of things to do. Because they are hard workers, the amount of work they accomplish per unit of time—their throughput—is high. Yet because their in– boxes are always full, getting such a person to take on a new task is usually hard, because your task has to get onto their to-do list and then make it to the top. Thus the latency of your request is high, even though the person is working at maximum throughput.

1.4.3 Utilization

Another dimension of performance is utilization. A system or component (such as a disk drive) is able to deliver a certain amount of throughput. At any level of performance, the system or component is working at some proportion of its capacity. That proportion is called the utilization. Utilization is interesting because it reflects how much of a resource remains, given a certain measure of performance in other dimensions. For example, a system that processes 110 jobs per hour at forty percent utilization is performing at a very different level than a system that processes the same throughput at 99 percent utilization.

By itself, high utilization is not necessarily a problem. Assuming that other performance goals are being attained, high utilization means that the system is not over-configured.

Unfortunately, many components behave differently at different levels of utilization. For example, disk drives respond to requests much more quickly at low utilization than at high utilization. Ethernets are particularly sensitive to high utilization, delivering both poor response time and substantially reduced throughput in such circumstances.

Utilization is one of the primary reasons that configuring for latency can be expensive: in order to ensure good response time for components such as Ethernets and disks, one must often configure many more of them than would appear necessary on first inspection.

1.4.4 Efficiency

Related to utilization is efficiency. A component that expends a great deal of effort to attain a given level of throughput is clearly not as desirable as one that expends less. However, efficiency is rarely considered in the configuration process. Although it is the dimension of performance that is the least controllable by users, it warrants attention in order to avoid surprises later. For example, the Solaris 2.3 version of telnet was fully configurable for 3,000 sessions, given sufficient memory. Unfortunately, that implementation used processor time so inefficiently that in practice, systems were unable to support more than 100–200 users— slightly more than six percent of the maximum theoretical capacity. (This particular problem is resolved in Solaris 2.4 and especially in Solaris 2.5. See Chapter 5, *Configuring Timeshare Servers*, for a much more extensive discussion of the issue.)

1.5 Units of Performance

Performance metrics are often quoted in many different units. They can be extremely confusing, and at best are often misleading. Converting all of the relevant statistics to the same units often helps avoid such problems. For example, network speeds are customarily expressed in terms of mega*bits* per second, while disk throughput is normally expressed in mega*bytes* per second. As a result, many people make a tacit assumption that network speeds are similar to disk speeds. When Ethernet's 10 megabits/sec speed is expressed as 1.25 megabytes/sec, though, it is clear that Ethernet is quite a bit slower than a typical disk, which transfers at about 4 megabytes/sec. Likewise, the perception of 115,200 BPS modems is "really fast," and indeed, this is a fast dialup modem. However, since there are 10 bits per byte (including start and stop bits), this rate corresponds to 11,520 bytes/sec, or 11.25 KB/sec, which is a more representative piece of information.

Sometimes this process takes more than one step. The term "NFSop" represents more than one kind of entity, so it does not translate directly into megabytes/sec. Fortunately, depending on the context, expressing NFSops/sec in terms of megabytes/sec is often reasonable. For example knowing that NFS data operations are 8 KB each, 320 NFSops/sec represents slightly more than 2.5 MB/sec.

1.6 Do the Math

An extension of this principle is "do the arithmetic," or what might also be described as "do not be intimidated or confused by different units." The first thing to do when faced with a configuration estimate is to get an idea of what is being requested. If a user asks to have 1 TB of data transferred to a client system each day, that task sounds impossible—1 TB is a lot of data. Upon closer analysis, this rate can be expressed as approximately 12.2 MB/sec. This is still considerable, but much less intimidating, since it is within the capacity of a 155 Mbit ATM network. Thirty frames of video per second sounds easily accomplishable, until this rate is quantified as 30 fps x 640x480 pixels x 24 bits/pixels, or about 26.4 MB/sec!

Configuring NFS Servers 2

The Network File System (NFS™) has been a part of the computing landscape for more than ten years. It is, by a considerable margin, the most popular facility for file sharing in the UNIX community. In addition, NFS has gained widespread popularity in nearly every other sphere of computing, because of its simplicity and availability on every major computing platform, from MS–DOS/Windows PCs and Macintoshes to IBM-compatible mainframes and Cray supercomputers. NFS provides the ability to transparently share data in heterogeneous networks. Servers and clients need not run the same operating system. In fact, configurations with widely varying types of NFS clients and servers are commonplace.

On Solaris-based systems, pure NFS servers are the easiest large-scale systems to configure, primarily because they exercise a single set of operating system code. Only one NFS server implementation is found on Solaris, since it is part of the operating system. Moreover, the NFS service itself is relatively simple. It provides only a few operations that are limited in semantic scope to locating remote files and providing unstructured access to them. This service is much less complex, for example, than a relational database, where upwards of 75 operations are defined in standard SQL. Moreover, SQL operations are applied to a complex set of data entities that include structural relationships. NFS has few of these issues and as such is much simpler[1].

2.1 The NFS Protocols

As with most standard protocols today, more than one version of NFS exists. Nearly all systems today use the traditional NFS Version 2 protocol, which has been in continuous use since 1985. To date, virtually all practical experience with NFS has been with Version 2. However, the NFS Version 3 specification has been available to the industry since 1993, and full-scale commercial implementations are expected from every major vendor by the end of 1996. The NFS implementation in Solaris 2.5 offers both Version 2 and Version 3. The default is to use Version 3 when both client and server implement the more advanced protocol.

---

[1] An excellent discussion of NFS can be found in *Managing NFS and NIS*, by Hal Stern. ISBN 0-937175-75-7.

2.1.1 NFS Version 2

The 18 NFS Version 2 operations appear in Table 1 below. They implement the fundamental operations necessary for file sharing: they permit clients to investigate the status of a remote file and file system, and access the data in them. Of significance is the *stateless* nature of the protocol: the operations are defined so that client and server need not maintain a continuous connection with its attendant bookkeeping. The server need not maintain any state about the client's connection. The client merely submits a request to the server, and the server processes it and replies. If the client gets a response, the transaction is guaranteed to be both complete and consistent. Without a response, the client resubmits its request until the server does respond. The server may have been shut down or even crashed between the original request and the response, and neither client nor server need ever know. The protocol is very simple, yet fully functional.

2.1.2 NFS Version 3

In response to a variety of technical requests from customers, the NFS protocol was revised in 1993, with the resulting protocol being designated Version 3. The new protocol is similar to its predecessor, but it makes improvements in several key areas. In particular, the new protocol implements the following changes:

- It permits write operations to be performed much more quickly through the use of a two–phase commit protocol, while still maintaining the server's stateless view of the protocol.

- It reduces the number of packets actually crossing the network by permitting file attributes to be returned on every operation, resulting in fewer operations to obtain attributes. All operations that modify a file's state now return the modified attributes, saving extra `getattr` requests. Furthermore, a new `readdirplus` operation permits the server to transfer information about multiple directory entries along with the attributes that would be returned by multiple `lookup` operations, for example, as would be used by a file manager.

- It extends the maximum size of files from 2^{32} bytes (4 gigabytes) to 2^{64} bytes. In addition, the size of data blocks to be exchanged is expanded, from a maximum of 8 KB to a maximum of 4 GB. Of course, the client and server must be prepared to handle such large files. Unfortunately, Solaris 2.5 does not support files larger than 2 GB. The maximum data block size is typically subject to restrictions imposed by underlying transport layers. For example, Solaris 2.5 supports block sizes up to 64 KB, since those are the largest blocks that can be handled by either the Solaris 2.5 TCP or UDP implementations.

- Support has been extended, permitting implementation of all common types of block and character special devices, sockets, named pipes, and FIFOs. These special devices are evaluated in the *client* context.

- Finally, Version 3 provides for the implementation of much more sophisticated file access controls, such as access control lists. The server is responsible for verifying specific kinds of access via an explicit `access` operation, and also for enforcing such access controls.

Naturally, both the client and server systems must implement these features; since many hosts do not, some of the new features are optional and are negotiated between client and server when a file system is mounted by the client. (For example, either a client or server may or may not support large files.)

Table 1. NFS operations as defined in Version 2 and updated in Version 3

Operation	Version 2	Changes in Version 3
null	Do nothing (used for testing and timing server response)	No change
root	Retrieve the root of the remote file system (carryover from V1, obsolete in V2)	Removed
lookup	Search directory for name and return file handle along with attributes	No change
access	—	Evaluate access permission to remote entity
readlink	Follow a symbolic link, and evaluate in client's namespace	No change
getattr	Obtain file/directory attributes such as type, size, permissions, access times	No change
setattr	Change file/directory attributes	No change
read	Read one data block (up to 8 KB)	Data block size up to 4 GB
write	Write one data block (up to 8 KB)	Data block size up to 4 GB
commit	—	Commit previously written data to stable storage
wrcache	Write data block to the cache (carryover from V1, obsolete in V2)	Removed
create	Create a file	No change
mknod	—	Create UNIX-style device files, pipes, and FIFOs
remove	Remove a directory entry	No change
rename	Change the entry's name entry	No change
link	Create a hard link	No change
symlink	Create a symbolic link	No change

Table 1. NFS operations as defined in Version 2 and updated in Version 3

Operation	Version 2	Changes in Version 3
mkdir	Create a directory	No change
rmdir	Remove a directory	No change
readdir	Obtain (multiple) directory entries	No change
readdir+	—	Obtain directory entries along with their attributes
pathconf	—	Obtain system configurable attributes of a POSIX file system
statfs	Obtain static and dynamic file system	Replaced by fsstat
fsstat	—	Obtain static file system information such as read size, max file size, etc.
fsinfo	—	Obtain dynamic info about the mounted file system such as free space count

2.1.2.1 NFS Interoperability

Although they are quite similar, NFS Version 2 and Version 3 are different protocols, and they are *not* directly interoperable. Solaris servers offer both protocols and respond correctly regardless of which protocol the client requests. Servers are able to handle V2 and V3 simultaneously, and no special issues are associated with configuring such a system. This fact also applies to clients; clients are free to request both V2 and V3 services from either the same or different servers.

Client and server decide which protocol to use during the mount process. Solaris 2.5 clients request V3 services by default; if the server is not able to honor the V3 request, V2 is used instead[2]. Not all clients capable of V3 operation default to V3; for example, SGI workstations running Irix 5.3 default to NFS V2 although the V3 option is available.

One area of common concern is interoperability between a client that may not support large files or file systems and a server that does. Large files are problematic, because NFS Version 2 has an inherent 2 GB addressability limit. NFS files are addressed symbolically (initially by name, and by a name–equivalent file handle once opened), while data within the remote file is addressed by offset within the file. NFS Version 2 uses a 31–bit offset, limiting those files to 2 GB. Large file *systems*, however, are not much of a problem, even for

---

[2]   A user can discover what NFS and transport protocols are in use on a *client* system with the nfsstat(1m) command.

NFS Version 2. The size of the file system is reported to the client only for purposes of determining the amount of free space in the file system. In particular, the size of the file system is *not* important to manipulating files. In these cases, file access works as always, but a client might be confused about the amount of space that is used or free in the file system. Most often this confusion happens when the client is running Solaris 1, which can report a negative number for free or allocated space[3]. Solaris 2 clients are prepared for remote file systems up to 1 TB in size and so are unaffected by these considerations.

For NFS Version 3, the picture is slightly different. The over–the–wire protocol removes the 31–bit limitation, using 64–bit offsets. Of course, both client and server must support files larger than 2 GB for this new limit to be useful. Unfortunately, neither Solaris 1 nor Solaris 2 support large files yet[4]. As a result, attempts to open files that are larger than the supported maximum are rejected, in order to prevent problems with file pointers after the file is opened. As with Version 2, no problems with large file *systems*, even when large *files* are not supported.

2.1.2.2 Media Interoperability

In the eight-layer OSI networking model, NFS is a level–6 presentation protocol. As such, it requires the use of lower–level transport, network, and physical protocols. Figure 2 shows the relationships between the various protocol layers. The NFS protocol is transport–independent. Virtually all current implementations use the UDP/IP Internet protocol suite for transport, although network and physical protocols vary widely and the use of TCP/IP is increasing in popularity. NFS is commonly used on Ethernet, Token Ring, FDDI, FastEthernet (100baseT), and ATM, in addition to a variety of wide-area network media. In the Solaris implementation, no special programming or configuration is needed to switch physical media or even to use multiple physical media simultaneously. With the currently available media spanning an incredible 22000:1 performance range (from 56 Kbit/sec WANs to full-duplex 622 Mbit/sec ATM), selection of the appropriate physical media is the most crucial decision when configuring for an NFS application.

A few implementations permit the use of the TCP/IP Internet protocol suite for transport. Although TCP represents slightly more work for the server than the equivalent traffic transported via UDP, TCP can be instrumental in making NFS a viable application over noisy and relatively low–performance networks—especially WANs that cross one or more satellite links. Solaris 2.5 uses TCP/IP by default, but uses UDP/IP when necessary (for example, when the partner does not support NFS over TCP).

---

[3] If the site has a copy of Solstice:DiskSuite 1.0, the licensing terms of that product permit the use of the client software at that site simply by copying them to the clients. In this case, the important program is df(1).

[4] Large (1 TB) files will be supported for both local and remote (NFS) access in Solaris 2.6.

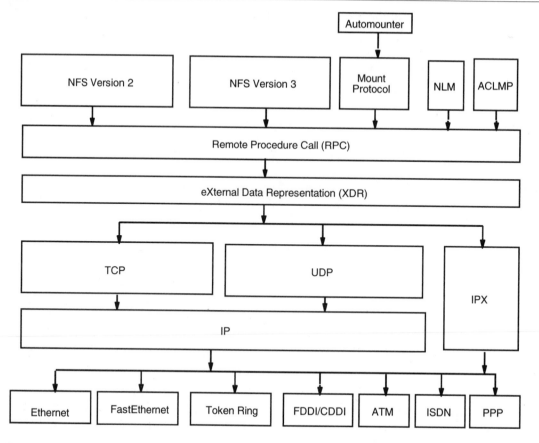

Figure 2. The NFS protocol stack, showing NFS and its supporting protocols

2.1.3 Associated Protocols

The NFS protocols always operate within a framework of other protocols and services. These facilities implement a mechanism to initiate service (the mount protocol), a layered automated name–lookup mount protocol (the automounter) , and file lock management (the Network Lock Manager). With the advent of access control lists, Solaris 2.5 also provides a Solaris–private protocol for managing remote access control lists (ACLs). The Solaris implementation of access control lists is discussed more completely in section 9.2, *UFS and UFS+ File Systems*.

2.1.3.1 Mount Protocol and the Automounter

The most basic adjunct protocol is the mount protocol, used to initiate remote file system access. The mount protocol itself is not interesting, except to note that negotiation between client and server is done at mount time. For example, selection of block sizes, local attribute management, and transport protocol are all chosen at mount time. The `mount_nfs` command also implements the selection of the NFS version protocol by probing a server for NFS Version 3. If the server transmits a negative response (or no response at all), the mount is retried using NFS Version 2.

The automounter is a client–side facility that is layered on top of the mount protocol. The automount daemon interposes itself between applications and the regular NFS mount protocol: remote file systems are assigned locations within the file system namespace, and all references to those locations are trapped by the automounter. If the remote file system is not mounted, the automounter consults the name service, finds the remote file system, and mounts the file system in the assigned location. Once the file system is mounted, the automounter's only task is to unmount the file system after a period of inactivity.

Combined with name services such as NIS+ or NIS (or higher–level services such as *xfn* federated naming services), the automounter can be used to define a consistent enterprise–wide file system. Only the referenced portions are visible on any given client system, but users and administrators can have a single namespace to understand, rather than having to know how to find the path to files relative to each client's mount points or server's exported file systems.

From a capacity planning perspective, the use of the automounter creates no additional load on client, server, or network. The only incremental traffic imposed by the automounter is the occasional unmount and mount of file systems that are infrequently used. Experience shows that this load is negligible.

2.1.3.2 Lock Daemon and Status Protocols

File locking poses something of a problem for a stateless file sharing protocol such as NFS, in that locks are inherently stateful. To circumvent this problem, file locking is handled by a separate protocol, known as the Network Lock Manager (NLM) protocol. The `lockd` protocol relies on a related status protocol called *status monitor*. (The status monitor is implemented by the `rpc.statd` daemon.) The locking subsystem maintains a table of locks that are pending against all opened files, and the server is responsible for propagating these to its clients. Because NFS itself is a stateless protocol, the server and client need some mechanism to find out each other's state, and they use the `statd` protocol for this purpose. `Statd` determines when to reacquire locks (for example, when the server crashes) and when to invalidate client locks that it determines to be invalid (such as when the client reboots or unmounts the file system).

2.1.3.3 Access Control List Management Protocol

Solaris 2.5 utilizes the V3 access procedure to reliably determine access to remote files, even when those files are protected by access control lists. The access procedure is called by a client with a file handle, a proposed access type, and the caller's identity. The server evaluates the permissions and returns an indication of whether or not the access would be permitted if submitted in the same context. This is sufficient to determine whether or not the proposed access will succeed or fail, but it provides no mechanism for manipulating advanced access control functions from a client. No mechanisms are defined for discovering why a proposed access type would fail, nor is any provision made for changing the configured access controls. This omission was a conscious decision on the part of the protocol designers, since no widely agreed upon standard exists for defining extended access controls.

To work around these problems, Solaris 2.5 implements a sideband protocol for manipulating access control lists. The protocol permits clients to obtain ACLs from the server and to set them from the client. (Obviously, the protocol respects permissions on the containing directory.) Because the implementation of ACLs is private to Solaris, the ACL protocol is also private to Solaris. The ACL protocol is used in conjunction with both NFS Version 2 and Version 3, since either can be used between Solaris 2.5 systems. The protocol can be extended to accommodate future industry–standard access protocols. Without the ACL management protocol, the server enforces all ACLs, but clients would not be able to view or change ACL entries. In some cases, this restriction can lead to the disturbing—but appropriate—situation in which a user on a non-ACL system appears to have access to a remote file, but that access is denied by the server because the invisible access control list excludes the proposed access. This case applies, for example, to Solaris 1 clients, which have no notion of ACLs or the ACL management protocol.

2.2 NFS Usage

Every file system entry has a number of characteristics that describe the file or access to it, such as the type of entry (file, symbolic link, directory), the size, access times, permission masks, and the like. Manipulation of these file attributes constitutes the majority of NFS operations.

Of the 18 NFS Version 2 operations, six operations represent the vast majority of the operations, both by count and by resource consumption: `getattr`, `setattr`, `lookup`, `readlink`, `read`, and `write`. These operations implement file attribute retrieval and modification, file name lookup, symbolic link resolution, and data read and write. The operations fall clearly into two distinct sets of operations: `read` and `write` manipulate the file's actual contents, while the others manipulate the file's attributes (see Table 2). The distinction is drawn primarily upon the type of load each request places on server and network resources.

Table 2. Classification of NFS operations

Data Operations	Attribute Operations
`Read`, `Write`	`Null`, `lookup`, `access`, `readlink`, `getattr`, `setattr`, `create`, `mknod`, `remove`, `rename`, `link`, `symlink`, `mkdir`, `rmdir`, `readdir`, `statfs`

2.2.1 NFS Attribute Operations

Attribute operations are much lighter weight than data operations. Because they are very small (normally much less than a few hundred bytes per file), most of the file system attributes associated with active files will be cached in the server's memory. Even if they are not cached, they are easily found and read from disk. Once the attributes are obtained by the server on behalf of any client, servicing any request made against those attributes involves only bit-wise manipulation of the cached attributes and the usual network protocol processing. The networking overhead of processing these operations is relatively high, since the proportion of useful data bytes in the actually transmitted packet is low. Attribute requests are transmitted in small packets (most are 64-128 bytes). As a result, attribute operations consume relatively little network bandwidth.

2.2.2 NFS Data Operations

By contrast, data operations in NFS Version 2 are nearly always 8 KB in size[5], and under NFS Version 3 they can be *much* larger. Whereas each file has just one set of file attributes, it may have many data blocks, potentially millions. For most kinds of NFS use, data blocks are not usually cached on the server, and thus servicing them represents a significant investment in resources: in addition to the usual network protocol operations, the server must locate and retrieve the data, possibly through several indirect blocks. On the network, data operations consume much more bandwidth: each 8 KB data operation involves the transfer of six large packets (on Ethernet, two on FDDI or one on ATM). As a result, network congestion is much more of a factor when considering data operations.

Despite the fact that the manifest purpose for using NFS is to provide access to the *contents* of remote files, most NFS servers spend the vast majority of their time servicing attribute operations, rather than data operations. When an NFS client system wants to use a file stored on a remote file server, it issues a series of `lookup` operations to locate the file within the remote directory hierarchy, followed by a `getattr` operation to obtain the file's

---

[5] Early versions of PC-NFS—5.0 and earlier—limited requests to just 1 KB.

permission mask and other attributes; finally, a `read` operation obtains the first block of data.

Consider the common process of reading a user's `.cshrc` file. This file usually resides in a remote file system, something like `/export/server/home/user/.cshrc`. To read the `.cshrc` file, the client system must be able to access all four of the remote directories in the path to the file. Verifying this capability means looking up each entry in the containing directory, and then obtaining the permission mask to determine that the user has sufficient access to proceed, a total of four `lookup` operations. Next the file itself must be looked up, and finally the first data block is read. Since only a rare `.cshrc` file is larger than a single data block, this process takes six NFS operations—only one of which moves any of the file's data.

Most files are quite short, averaging much less than 64 KB in most environments. Fewer data operations are required to read the entire file than to locate it and open it! A 1992 study at Sun revealed that the average file size had increased since the days of BSD 4.1, from about 1 KB to slightly more than 8 KB. Less thorough studies in 1994 seem to indicate that file sizes seem to be rising again, to about 50 KB. Even so, the proportion of work associated with the data retrieval is quite small.

The classification of proposed NFS service into categories dominated by attribute operations or dominated by data operations is the basis for determining correct NFS server configurations.

2.2.3 Attribute–Intensive vs. Data–Intensive NFS

Applications that access many small files can be characterized as being attribute-intensive. Perhaps the best example is the classical software development shop. Large software systems normally consist of thousands of small modules; each module often has an include file, a source file, an object file, and some sort of archive control file (such as SCCS or RCS). Most of the files are small—often just 4 KB to 100 KB in size. Because NFS transactions normally block the requester while the transaction is being serviced, the processing time in such applications is usually dominated by the speed at which the server handles the lightweight attribute requests. Data operations typically make up less than forty percent of the operations by count. In all but the most extreme attribute-intensive servers, only moderate network bandwidth is required—10 Mbit Ethernet is usually adequate, although other traffic may cause overall congestion when switched networks are not used.

Most home directory servers fall into the attribute-intensive category: most files are small. In addition to being small relative to the attribute size, small files also give the client systems an opportunity to cache the file data, eliminating the need to retrieve it again from the server. The server caches data also, but because of the large number of files handled by the server— with little interclient locality—the server is much less likely to retain the data in cache.

At the other end of the spectrum are applications that access very large files; these fall into the data-intensive category. Geophysics, image processing, and ECAD all fit into this category. In these applications, typical NFS usage is for a workstation or compute engine to read a very large file into memory, process it for a long time (minutes, or even hours), and finally write back a result file. In these application domains, files often reach 1 GB in size, and files larger than 200 MB are the rule rather than the exception. With large files, the expense of servicing data requests dominates processing. Significantly, having sufficient network bandwidth is *always* crucial to data-intensive applications.

For example, Ethernet's media speed is 10 Mbit/sec. This sounds fast, but 10 Mbit/sec is 1.25 Mbytes/sec, and this speed cannot be achieved in practice due to protocol overhead and the finite speed of processing at each end of the two-way conversation. The net usable speed of an Ethernet is approximately 1 MB/sec, achievable only in ideal circumstances: it can only be attained by dedicating an Ethernet to the conversation. Traditionally this has been practical only in rare instances. (Today, switched Ethernet hubs are making this much more cost–effective.) When multiple clients are active on the network, the maximum tolerable sustained network utilization is approximately 35 percent, which corresponds to an aggregate data rate of 440 KB/sec. Running an Ethernet at nearly 100 percent utilization is certainly possible (and occasionally useful), but because of its arbitration scheme, users perceive that Ethernets are sluggish at utilization over about 35 percent.

The data-intensive nature of this type of client dominates the configuration planning process for this type of client, dictating the networking media and often the type of server involved. In many cases, implementation of data-intensive applications mandates the rewiring of networks.

Environments are considered data-intensive if more than about half of the NFS operations move user data. The classical Legato mix is representative of attribute-intensive environments. In this reference environment, 22 percent of operations are reads and fifteen percent are writes. The Legato mix is derived from measurements taken in 1987 of diskless Sun-3/50 clients running software development tools under SunOS 3.5. Although clients, servers, software development tools, files, and networks are all very different from their 1987 counterparts, the Legato mix is still remarkably representative of many environments.

2.2.4 Bursty Nature of NFS Loads

If NFS clients made uniform demands upon servers (or networks), we would often arrive at configurations with huge numbers of dedicated Ethernets or large numbers of high-speed networking media such as FDDI. Fortunately, NFS traffic is normally quite bursty; clients can make extensive demands of file servers and networks, but they do so only on a sporadic and relatively infrequent basis.

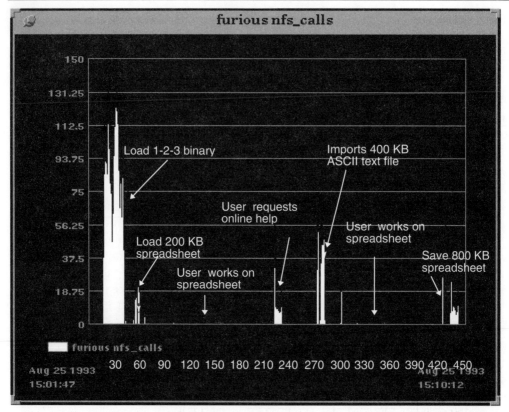

Figure 3. SunNet Manager log of NFS traffic generated by a 486DX2-66 PC-NFS 5.0 client using Lotus 1-2-3W. Sample granularity is one second.

At most other times, clients generate little or no demand. For the remainder of this chapter we will refer to a client that is actively making demands as a *fully active client*. For a variety of reasons, many clients (in some environments, most clients) are often idle, imposing little or no load on their servers. For example, some clients are large enough that they can cache most or all of their data; other systems are only used part-time; and even heavily used clients are often left completely idle while their owners are at lunch or in meetings.

Finally, the usage pattern of most applications causes clients to impose load very unevenly. Consider a typical application. Under typical use, the system will read in the application binary, executing the code pages leading up to a user dialog that specifies a data set to operate on. The application then reads the data set from the (probably remote) disk. The user interacts with the application, manipulating the *in-memory* representation of the data. This phase continues for most of the runtime of the application, until the modified dataset is saved to disk near the end of the run. Most, but not all, applications fit this general profile, often in repeating phases. The following series of figures illustrate the nature of typical NFS load.

Figure 3 shows a SunNet Manager log of a 486/DX2–66 MS-DOS PC under normal use. The bursty nature of clients is very clear: peaks of up to 100 ops/sec occur for short periods of time, but the average is much lower—7 ops/sec, and the typical sample about 1 op/sec. Over time, this system averages about 0.1 NFSops/sec during working hours.

Figure 4 shows the NFS traffic generated by an Ultra–2 running various data analysis tools and high–end publishing software. The relatively even load displayed by this graph is typical of most clients. Although up to 400 ops/sec are demanded at times, these are for short duration (1-5 seconds). The resulting overall load, averaged over time, is much lower—in this case, below five ops/sec, even excluding the idle nighttime hours. In this graph, the sample interval is one second.

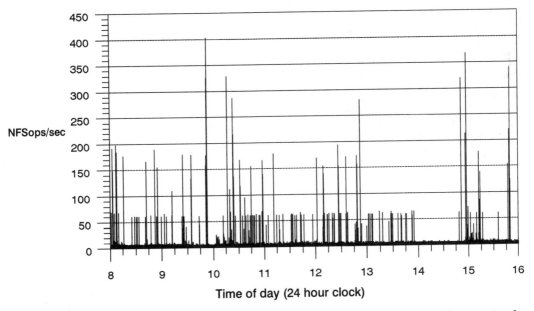

Figure 4. The NFS client load generated by an Ultra–2 running Solaris 2.5.1. The sustained load is 4.8 NFSops/sec, despite bursts of over 400 NFSops/sec.

2.2.5 NFS and PC/Mac Clients

The dominant PC operating systems, MS-DOS, Microsoft Windows, and Apple's Macintosh System 7.x, do not use single-level virtual memory for disk or virtual disk I/O operations as do workstations running UNIX or VMS. Single-level VM systems such as Solaris treat all disk and virtual disk I/O as an extension of memory. The result is a tendency to defer disk or network access until absolutely necessary; normally this strategy results in more uniform I/O demand. In small-memory systems it sometimes results in *more* I/O activity, although in systems configured with typical-sized memories, it usually results in much less I/O activity overall. Workstations tend to be configured with *much* more memory than PCs, resulting in minimal NFS overhead. SPARCstation 20s average well over 100 MB per system, while average memory size for PCs is less than 16 MB.

2.2.5.1 Real-Memory Operating Systems

Personal computer operating systems use the simpler two-level I/O model, in which memory is managed separately from file I/O. The practical result is a less even I/O load. For example, when a Windows PC invokes 1-2-3, *all* of 123.EXE is copied into the system's memory. The entire 1.5 MB of code is copied to memory, even if the user then quits, without performing any other function. This client will not issue *any* additional I/O against this file while the application is running, because the entire binary is resident in memory. Even if it is swapped out by Windows, it will be swapped to a local disk, resulting in no network traffic.

By contrast, a Solaris-based system would have copied into memory only the functions necessary to execute initialization and the quit function. Other functions are paged in later upon actual use, a substantial initial saving that also spreads the I/O load out over time. If the client is short of memory, pages may be thrown out and reloaded from the original source—the network server—resulting in additional server load. For the server, the end result is that the I/O load from PC and Mac clients is much less even than for workstation clients running the same type of applications.

2.2.5.2 Smaller Files

Another characteristic of the PC user base is that the files used by these clients are considerably smaller than those typically found in the workstation community. Very few PC communities are characterized by the description "data-intensive," primarily because memory management in PC operating systems is complex and limited in capability. The attribute-intensive nature of these environments structures configurations around solving random-access problems.

2.2.5.3 Less Demanding Clients

Although the fastest PCs challenge workstations in raw CPU performance, the typical PC is still a much less demanding network client than a typical workstation. Part of this differential is due to the fact that the vast majority of existing PCs are based on the slower Pentium and 486 processors; the slower processors attract less demanding applications and users. At full speed these slower processors simply generate requests less quickly than workstations because the internal busses and network adapters are not as highly optimized as those found in larger systems. For example, the typical ISA Ethernet adapters available in

1991 were capable of sustaining only about 700 KB/sec (compared to over 1 MB/sec in all 1991 workstations). Some PCs, especially portables, utilize "Ethernet" interfaces that connect through a parallel port. Although this arrangement saves a bus slot and is very convenient, these are often the slowest of all Ethernet interfaces, because many parallel port implementations are limited to 60-100 KB/sec. Of course, as more powerful PCs with 32-bit DMA-capable network adapters become more prevalent, the margin will close, but the vast majority of PC-NFS clients fall into the older, *much* less demanding category. The ability of a 66 MHz 486 DX2 PC equipped with a 32-bit EISA Ethernet interface is demonstrated in Figure 3. With extremely few exceptions, PC and Mac clients use NFS Version 2.

2.3 The NFS Client

The NFS server seems to get the most attention when people are deciding upon NFS configurations, but the clients are at least as important. Judicious use of the features of many client operating systems can significantly reduce the requested load on NFS servers, effectively increasing their capacity.

2.3.1 Interaction with the Virtual Memory System

In a UNIX-based system such as Solaris, the NFS client subsystem is a peer of the disk subsystem. That is, it provides services to the virtual memory manager and to the file system in particular on the same basis as disk services, except that these services are fulfilled with the involvement of the network. This statement may seem obvious, but it has specific implications on the operation of the NFS client/server system. In particular, the virtual memory manager is interposed between applications and the NFS client. File system accesses made by applications are cached in the *client's* VM system, reducing the client's requirements for NFS I/O.

The caching activity of the virtual memory system delays and sometimes completely avoids NFS activity. For most applications, large memory configurations *on the client* lead to less load imposed on the server and higher overall (i.e., client/server) system performance. This situation is particularly true of diskless clients, which must use NFS as backing store for anonymous memory. For example, consider a diskless workstation running Lotus 1-2-3. If both data and application binaries are located remotely, the system will have to page in the 1-2-3 executables via NFS as required. The text pages are cached in main memory. Then the data will be loaded into memory via NFS; for most 1-2-3 files on typically configured workstations, the data will be cached in memory and will stay there for a considerable time (minutes rather than seconds).

If a temporary file is created and kept open, the file's creation is performed immediately in both the client and the server, but updates to the file contents are normally cached on the client for some time ("written behind") before transmission to the server. In accordance with UNIX file semantics, updates to it are flushed to the backing store when the file is closed, in this case to the NFS server. Alternatively, cached writes may be flushed to the backing store by the `fsflush` (Solaris 2.x) or `updated` (Solaris 1.x) daemons. As with normal disk I/O, cached NFS I/O data stays in memory until the memory is required for some other purpose.

When the write operation is issued, the server must commit the data to stable storage before the operation is acknowledged, but this requirement does *not* hold on the client. If cached data is referenced again, for example, if some text pages of 1-2-3 are executed again, the reference is satisfied directly from the client's virtual memory rather than issuing requests to the server. Of course, when the client is short of memory, modified pages are written back to the server quickly, and unmodified pages are simply discarded to make room for new data.

2.3.2 Cache File System (CacheFS)

Solaris 2.3 introduced a new feature, called the *Cache File System*. Under the standard NFS protocol, files are obtained directly from the server, block by block, to the client's memory and manipulated directly. Data is written back to the server's disk. The CacheFS interposes itself between the application and the NFS client code. When blocks of data are obtained by the NFS client code, they are cached in a dedicated area on a local disk. The local copy is known as the *front file*, while the server copy is called the *back file*. Any subsequent access to a cached file is made to the copy in the local disk cache, rather than to the copy that resides on the server. For obvious reasons, this technique can substantially reduce the NFS load demanded of a server. One of the features of CacheFS is that it is a completely client-side technology. The server does not know of the client's internal caching; this arrangement permits Solaris 2 clients to reduce load for non-Solaris servers.

Unfortunately, the CacheFS is not a complete answer to reducing server load. First, because it makes copies of data blocks, the system must make arrangements to keep the copies consistent. Specifically, the CacheFS subsystem periodically inspects the attributes of the back file (the time-out period is user configurable); if the back file has been modified, the front file is purged from the cache and the next access to the (logical) file will cause the file to be obtained and cached again. Unfortunately, most programs continue to operate on entire files, rather than on specific data blocks. For example `vi`, 1-2-3 and *ProEngineer* read and write their data files in their entirety, regardless of the user's actual intent, although `dtpad(1)`, `textedit(1)` and *AnswerBook* do not. Programs that utilize `mmap(2)` to access files usually do not access the entire file, while programs that utilize the `read(2)` and `write(2)` system calls usually do. As a result, the CacheFS usually ends up caching whole files. NFS file systems that are frequently modified are not good candidates for CacheFS: files would be continually cached and purged, eventually resulting in *more* overall traffic than simply operating over NFS.

The problem of keeping cached data consistent among clients and the server also results in another twist: when a client modifies a file, the front file is invalidated and the back file is updated accordingly. The next read reference to the file will obtain and cache the file again. This process results in more traffic than standard NFS if file updates are common.

Because the CacheFS is a relatively new feature, few measurements have been made of its behavior in actual use. Most of the measurements that have been done are found in the context of the CacheOS administrative feature (discussed below). In software development environments, CacheFS is able to reduce NFS traffic by about 85 percent when it caches relatively static read-mostly data such as include files and reference object libraries such as `libXm` and `libX`. Application binaries are also excellent candidates for cached file systems.

An example of an application that does *not* lend itself to CacheFS is `/var/mail`. The author naively discovered this by trial-and-error! With about one email arriving per minute, combined with a mail spool file about 60 MB in size, the network was constantly being thrashed as the spool file was transferred over and over again, once per minute. Since the network was a standard Ethernet, the maximum throughput of the transfer was about 1 MB/sec—taking about 1 minute to transfer. Since the file was being updated once per minute, the entire network was continuously consumed!

For clients running Solaris 2.5 or later, the `cachefsstat(1m)`, `cachefswssize(1m)` and `cachefslog(1m)` commands help administrators evaluate the value of a CacheFS installation. Hit rates for a given file system should normally be higher than about thirty percent. Hit rates lower than this level mean that the access pattern on the file system is widely randomized, or that the cache is too small. The latter can be deduced by comparing the size of the cache with the file system working set as reported by `cachefswssize(1m)`. Realize that a CacheFS cache hit rate does not need to be particularly high to be useful, especially compared to the hit rates normally associated with CPU caches. Usually the cache disk is an inexpensive model that is quite large compared to the size of the back file system, and virtually any network access that is avoided through the use of the cache is a fairly large overall benefit.

The `cachefsstat(1m)` command also provides an indication of how write-intensive the back file system is, via the consistency check statistics. High rates of consistency failure (say, over about 15-20 percent) are an indication that the cache may be updated more quickly than appropriate for a cached file system.

The following rules summarize the use of CacheFS:

⇒ Use the CacheFS for file systems that are read-mostly, such as shared application file systems.

⇒ Do *not* use the CacheFS for file systems that are written frequently, either by the client or by some process running on the server.

⇒ CacheFS is especially useful for sharing data across relatively slow networks, such as WANs connected by less-than-T1 lines.

⇒ CacheFS is useful for high-speed networks interconnected by routers that introduce latency.

⇒ On Solaris 2.5 and later, use `cachefsstat(1m)` to monitor the effectiveness of cached file systems.

2.3.3 Diskless Clients

Years ago, disk drives were quite expensive, and providing every desktop workstation with its own local disk was not cost-effective. The diskless client model was developed as a way of providing much less expensive workstations that were still capable of delivering workstation performance. In 1986, the speed of networks (1 MB/sec Ethernet) was similar to that of low-cost disks (about 1.2 MB/sec), and this arrangement was quite successful.

Since 1995, the disk drive industry has become *incredibly* competitive, and even high-performance 2 GB disks are inexpensive—and provide far more sto rage than required for the basic operating system and swap space. Only two reasons remain for using the diskless client model. A few users are required to operate their systems without local storage for security reasons, but the primary reason for using diskless clients is that this model is much more convenient to administer centrally.

Diskless clients have acquired a bad reputation for being much slower than their diskfull cousins, but in fact this is only partly true. Certainly with fast, inexpensive disks commonly available, local disk access is quick. But with modern servers and high speed networks, NFS activity is also very fast. In most installations, the primary reason that diskless clients perform poorly is a lack of main memory. When the client system is short on memory, it is forced to swap processes out to the backing store—which is the file server for diskless clients. Unfortunately, the low price points made possible by diskless configurations encouraged diskless systems to be installed in large numbers, and with minimal memory. The result was often memory-starved systems, exacerbated by a jammed network. However, when configured with adequate memory, the practical performance of diskless clients is almost always nearly indistinguishable from that of diskfull clients, even in large communities.

Because diskless clients concentrate all of their configuration information on a server shared with many other clients, the administration of the group is markedly easier—only a single system need be backed up, and recovering from administrative mistakes that make the client unbootable is much easier than on stand-alone systems. Furthermore, since most clients can share most of their operating systems (e.g., `/usr`), cumulative disk space can be considerably reduced in large workgroups. Finally, and most importantly, the diskless client model permits the desktop workstation to be a field-replaceable unit with no state to preserve. For some organizations this capability is crucially important, because it permits the virtually instantaneous replacement of a failed desktop system.

2.3.4 Diskless Boots, JumpStart™, and Network Installation

The diskless boot process is used in several different circumstances, including CacheOS ™ bootup and most types of installation of operating installation, notably including JumpStart. JumpStart is a mechanism used for using templates to describe the required installation process for client systems. The installation process is thus customized to recognizable classes of client; for example, all SPARCstation 5's with 535 MB disks on a given network branch might be set up as CacheOS clients, while Ultra–1's on the same network branch might be configured to use a different set of file servers and mount different applications.

In addition, the most effective mechanism for installing operating systems on client systems is via a network. Network installation via regular Ethernet is about three times as fast as installation via a double–speed CDROM. Even compared to the latest 6X and 8X CDROMs, network installation is likely to be much faster, because all currently available CDROMs suffer from extremely slow seek times. (Most CDROMs take on the order of 100 ms to seek, and sometimes as much as 330 ms.) The installation process refers to many files, causing many CDROM seeks; network installations almost always use disk-based reference sources, and disk seeks are far faster.

Many administrators seem to be fearful of diskless boot procedures, even for functions such as operating system installation, usually related to the performance stigma of diskless clients. The diskless boot process involves fairly intensive NFS activity for a few minutes. A typical diskless boot on a SPARCstation 20 Model 71 generates about 50 NFSops/sec for about two minutes. Network installations take rather longer—about 9–15 minutes depending on which packages are installed and the configuration of the boot server. These rates are for installation onto a standard 5,400 rpm disk via standard Ethernet, but installation onto faster clients such as the Ultra–1/170 over more capable networks such as FastEthernet are only marginally faster. The rotational speed of the target disk is usually the limiting factor when network media speed exceeds 10-15 Mbits/sec. When faster 7,200 rpm disks are used, peak NFS demand approaches 70 NFSops/sec.

2.3.4.1 CacheOS Clients

A related topic is CacheOS, an unbundled package sold by SunSoft that leverages the diskless client model. The CacheOS is set of modules that permit the client's kernel to be operated as a diskless client—except that instead of being a pure diskless client, the operating system maintains a local cache via CacheFS. The CacheOS boot process differs from the standard diskless boot process in that it locates or creates a file system on a local disk for use as a cached file system. Once the cache is established, the diskless root and /usr are mounted from the boot server, and operation proceeds normally.

The largest proportion of network traffic associated with diskless clients is virtual memory traffic accessing remote swap space. CacheOS clients avoid most of this traffic by placing a swap file in the file system used for the cache, rather than using a remote swap area. This avoids the most onerous performance problem arising from diskless client operation, excessive network swapping. The crucial point of the CacheOS is that although it uses local disk resources, no persistent data is kept on that disk—only cached copies of NFS file systems and swap space(which is volatile storage anyway) reside on the local disk. From a capacity planning perspective, a CacheOS client is a diskless client during bootup and a dataless or standalone client thereafter.

2.3.4.2 Configuring CacheOS Boot Servers

For most installations using CacheOS, the requirements for a boot server are surprisingly small. Most administrators are inclined to provide a large server, but such a configuration misses the point of a CacheOS installation. In practice, a minimal file server such as a SPARCstation 4 or SPARCstation 5 is more than adequate. CacheOS clients are only active in an NFS sense during their bootup stage, something that normally happens very rarely. Moreover, rebooting more than one or two clients simultaneously is a rare occurrence, except in the case where all clients in a given location reboot due to a widespread power failure.

Once the clients have booted, the use of local swap space and the local CacheFS cache for the root and /usr file systems keeps the clients from generating network overhead. Using the guidelines associated with the LADDIS benchmark, a disk drive is usually adequate for handling about 60 NFSops/sec, and 10baseT networks are sufficient for 250-300 NFSops/sec. Accordingly, a two-disk, single-network low end server such as a SPARCserver 4 or 90 MHz Pentium server is entirely adequate for booting three or four simultaneous CacheOS clients (40-50 NFSops/sec). Users have reported that even a SPARCclassic server is a reasonable CacheOS server for as many as 20-25 clients under normal circumstances.

Given sufficient networks, the Ultra–1/170 can handle 65-70 clients even in the worst case of all booting simultaneously, and Ultra–2/2200s are more than twice as capable. These are more optimistic than one might expect from a comparison with LADDIS scores, because that benchmark uses a relatively large file set. In the "power-fail-and-reboot" scenario, all of the clients use the attributes of previously cached files, representing a small set of file attributes on the server. This access pattern dramatically reduces disk drive requirements, because the data for most clients is mostly shared and therefore cached on the server.

The primary drawback to the CacheOS arrangement is that it makes the entire client population dependent on the availability of the "diskless" boot server. Failure of the server not only stops clients from booting, but because CacheFS must occasionally check the consistency of the remote file caches, normal client operation also eventually grinds to a halt. The best way out of this dilemma is the use of a highly available server such as that offered by Open Vision, Tidal Wave Technologies or Solstice HA-NFS. When NFS services are made available via redundant hardware and operating systems, CacheOS becomes the preferred client organization for large installations.

2.4 The SPEC SFS Benchmark

NFS servers are compared using their scores on the SPEC SFS benchmark, otherwise known as LADDIS, because the benchmark has been transferred to the SPEC consortium. The LADDIS name is a historical acronym for the six vendors who participated in the original specification of the benchmark: Legato (originator of the PrestoServe concept), Auspex, Data General, Digital, Interphase, and Sun. The current workload is known as 097.LADDIS.

2.4.1 What Is SPEC SFS?

SPEC SFS is a benchmark that attempts to emulate the usage pattern of a large number of NFS clients. It is descended from the `nhfsstone` benchmark originated by Legato. A group of client systems makes NFS service calls to the server under test, and both throughput and operation latency as perceived by client processes are measured. One of the clients, known as the *prime client*, collects all of the statistics, validates the results, and coordinates and controls the client network.

In order to minimize the impact of varying the clients on the server (after all, the *server* is under test), the 097.LADDIS code does not rely upon the NFS implementation of the client. Instead of making calls to the local NFS client service, the 097.LADDIS programs make direct remote procedure calls (RPC) to the server. As noted later, this approach has both advantages and disadvantages. It does eliminate the differences between NFS client implementations, but often those differences are significant. For example, it discounts the use of CacheFS and local virtual memory caching, both of which are instrumental in reducing the requested load on the NFS server in real environments.

2.4.2 Guidelines for Optimizing SFS

As with other standardized benchmarks, the run and reporting rules for SPEC SFS strongly influence the configurations tested. More or less, the run rules tell the vendors "get the biggest number you can." As a result, vendors normally build bigger and bigger configurations until some part of the system becomes a bottleneck and can no longer be expanded. Guidelines for optimizing SFS are provided here so that users can get a perspective on what is required in an SFS configuration and what is not. In particular, cost, manageability, and reliability are not mentioned at all in the SFS run rules—so reported configurations do not account for these crucial factors.

In most Solaris–based systems, the processor complex is the least expandable system component; it is nearly always less configurable than most of the I/O peripherals. (This expression is: a 24-CPU configuration is still a *very* flexible system, despite the fact that it is still less configurable than the thousands of disks and hundreds of networks that can be configured or controlled in a maximally configured Ultra Enterprise 6000 system.) Among Sun systems, the largest tested system is the 24–processor Ultra Enterprise 6000, equipped with 20 Ethernets and upwards of 500 GB of disk. When reading a vendor's full disclosure report, the following maxima should be kept in mind:

- Each Ethernet handles 250–300 NFSops/sec; 300 is the absolute maximum before utilization and collisions overwhelm response time. A reasonable upper bound on a given system's 097.LADDIS score is the number of configured Ethernets x 250.

- FastEthernets can handle at least 3,000 NFSops/sec under 097.LADDIS conditions. When fully standardized and implemented, full-duplex FastEthernets should handle considerably more than 3,000 LADDIS NFSops/sec.

- FDDI networks can handle at least 3,500 NFSops/sec; they impose no congestion problems.

- As yet no vendors have published results with ATM, but with triple FDDI's bandwidth and somewhat higher processor efficiency, the sky is the limit.

- Each data disk in the configuration is good for about 60 NFSops/sec; a reasonable upper bound for a given system's SFS score is thus bound by the number of disks in the configuration. (This limiting rate assumes typical 1995 disks with 5,400 rpm rotational speed and approximately 10 ms average seek time; 7,200 rpm disks are about thirty percent more capable.) This limitation has some elasticity, because maximum performance involves a delicate tradeoff between throughput and latency. The SFS run rules invalidate any result with an operation latency in excess of 50 ms. To avoid excessive NFS latency, disk utilization must be kept at a minimal level—usually under fifty percent. The use of NVRAM write acceleration helps this situation by reducing disk utilization.

- One consequence of these two facts, combined with the SFS run rules, is that a typical 097.LADDIS configuration has *many* more networks and disks than the typical NFS server installation. The tested configuration of the SPARCcenter 2000E involves 20 Ethernets and well over a hundred disk drives.

- A single 60 MHz SuperSPARC processor is capable of delivering about 700–800 NFSops/sec (depending on platform), while an 85 MHz SuperSPARC is capable of approximately 1,100 NFSops/sec, and a 167 MHz UltraSPARC–I can handle about 2,200 NFSops/sec as shown in Figure 5. Solaris 2.5.1 scaling is approximately 87 percent, through at least 24 processors.

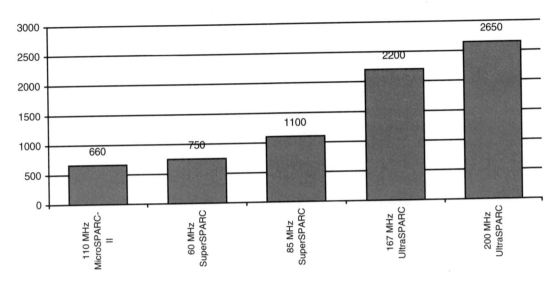

Figure 5. Per-processor LADDIS capability, given sufficient network and disk subsystems.

- Pentium processors running at 133 MHz are faster than a 60 MHz SuperSPARC, but are normally coupled to much slower memory systems; typically they do not have server-oriented architecture features such as very low-latency memory access, multiple I/O busses and hardware `bcopy(3)`. Consequently, they are capable of only about 500-700 NFSops/sec in uniprocessor configurations and 1,000-1,200 NFSops/sec in dual–processor configurations. The same relative strengths apply when comparing the 200 MHz Pentium Pro and the 167 MHz UltraSPARC. Combined with the limited configurability of most Solaris x86 systems (typically a maximum of three ISA and three PCI slots), these systems are usually confined to fairly small applications.

- At least two clients must be configured on each network; for a large configuration such as that for the Ultra Enterprise 6000; at least 40 clients must be in use. One of the practical implications for users is that they are unlikely to have the configuration necessary to replicate current vendor results.

Estimating a particular configuration's 097.LADDIS score is reasonably easy given these boundaries. For example:

- A SPARCstation 20 Model 712 with four Ethernets and 12 GB of disk storage as six disks (each with 2.1 GB capacity) will be unlikely to exceed 360 NFSops/sec, due to its disk limitations. If configured with 24 disks (say, 535 MB each), its four Ethernets would then limit it to less than 1,000 NFSops/sec.

- A dual-processor Compaq *ProLiant* with 120 MHz Pentium processors, two Ethernets, and two caching RAID-5 disk arrays, each consisting of five 1 GB disks (8 GB of data storage), will deliver about 500 NFSops/sec, because it does not have enough network bandwidth.

- A SPARCcenter 2000E with ten 85 MHz processors, 4 GB memory, ten FDDI networks, and 300 GB of disk will be limited to less than 2,000 NFSops/sec if configured with the typical 35 x 9 GB disk drives; however, if configured with five disk arrays containing 150 x 2 GB disks, the same storage capacity is available, but the full capacity of the system (over 6,000 NFSops/sec) can be delivered. The same would be true of an Ultra Enterprise 4000 with three UltraSPARC processors.

Each of these systems was over configured in the processor department and under configured for I/O. In every case except the SPARCcenter 2000E, a single processor would have been more than adequate for the I/O subsystems configured. Unfortunately, this situation is more the rule than the exception in existing NFS installations.

2.4.3 SPEC SFS Strengths and Weaknesses

SFS is useful for comparing platforms and classifying them into major groupings. Clearly the Ultra Enterprise 6000 (about 24,000 NFSops/sec) and the Auspex NS 7000 (about 11,000 NFSops/sec) are in a completely different category than other platforms that are offered as high-end NFS servers by most other vendors (generally in the vicinity of 4,000-6,000 NFSops/sec). In addition, the benchmark can be used in some specialized cases as a way to size an application with relatively little data. The run and reporting rules specified and enforced by SPEC make the results directly comparable and generally reliable. Finally, SFS has evolved into a benchmark that is relatively easy to run correctly, if not necessarily optimally. Nonetheless, the benchmark has some significant weaknesses.

Probably the worst thing about SFS results has nothing at all to do with the results themselves, but rather with the marketing of those results. Because they are the only "NFSops/sec" data in common circulation, these results strongly influence perceptions about what "conventional" load is. Current NFS servers are able to outperform typical loads by an astonishing margin. In a marketing environment where a high-end server with a 097.LADDIS score of 4,000 NFSops/sec is considered completely uncompetitive, the typical NFS client population demands less than 500 NFSops/sec, and even the largest sites demand instantaneous peaks well under 2,000 NFSops/sec. As a result, a surprising number of installations have servers capable of delivering 10-20 times their typical load.

Another issue with 097.LADDIS is that although it can be configured to test operation mixes other than the default Legato mix, in practice, this configuration option is never exercised. As a result, SFS results are not useful for comparing servers for a data-intensive environment. (Even running 097.LADDIS with a strongly read- or write-oriented mix would not simulate the requirements of data-intensive sites, since its disk access patterns are *much* more randomized than typical data-intensive work.) SPEC does not permit reporting results with other than the default Legato mix, because vendors have been unable to agree on guidelines for reporting such results.

As previously noted, because 097.LADDIS makes direct RPC calls to the NFS server under test, it fails to consider the impact clients will have on the entire NFS environment. Client-side caching such as provided by UNIX virtual memory systems, and facilities such as CacheFS can influence the load on an NFS server by as much as 85 percent in some applications. Workload reduction is fifty percent in many cases, and in these cases sizing "by LADDIS" obviously results in a significant—and costly—overestimate.

Finally, the current 097.LADDIS benchmark utilizes *only* the NFS Version 2 protocol. As NFS Version 3 becomes more prevalent, Version 2 results will become less relevant, especially for data-intensive sites. The SPEC consortium is developing a Version 3 benchmark, but it is not expected to be adopted before late 1996 or early 1997. At that time, two new workloads will be introduced, to be known as SPECnfs96.v2 and SPECnfs96.v3.

2.5 NFS Server Configuration Guidelines

The following questions should be answered in order to provide sufficient information to accurately size an NFS server configuration. The discussion that follows this checklist describes how to estimate a configuration from the information.

2.5.1 Checklist

- Is the load attribute-intensive or data-intensive?
- Will clients be using the Cache File System to reduce requests?
- Are the clients able to cache a significant proportion of their NFS–mounted data, thus avoiding server requests?
- On the average, how many fully active clients must be supported?
- What kinds of client systems are involved, and what kind of operating system are they running?
- How big are the file systems that must be shared?
- Are the NFS requests directed at the same files over and over again by different clients (e.g., include files), or are they for different files?
- How many and what kind of networks are feasible? Is this network configuration appropriate to the anticipated kind of traffic?
- Are the CPUs in the configuration sufficient to manage the traffic associated with the anticipated networks?

- If WANs are involved, are the media and routers sufficiently low-latency and high-throughput to make NFS practical?

- Are the disk drives and host adapters sufficient to achieve the required performance?

- Is striping or other RAID functionality required to adequately spread the disk access load across the available disk drives?

- If NFS write operations are common, is some sort of NVRAM write acceleration configured?

- Is the intended backup strategy consistent with the type, number, and architectural location of the backup devices?

2.5.2 Network Configuration

The most important configuration requirement for NFS servers is not the ability or configuration of the server, but rather provision for sufficient network bandwidth and availability. This translates into configuration of appropriate number and type of networks and interfaces.

2.5.2.1 The Application Profile Determines Network Media

The most important factor governing network configuration is the dominant type of NFS operation used by the applications. Data-intensive applications demand relatively few networks, but these networks must be high-bandwidth such as FDDI or ATM. Most attribute-intensive applications are easily handled with less expensive infrastructure such as Ethernet or Token Ring, although many networks may be required to avoid excessive response time.

Making this decision is relatively simple: if individual clients require aggregate data rates in excess of 1 MB/sec, or if more than one client must be able to simultaneously consume 1 MB/sec of network bandwidth, the applications require high-speed networking. The 1 MB/sec dividing line is actually artificially high, as it represents the speed you are *guaranteed* not to exceed. Under typical conditions, the speed of an Ethernet is effectively about 440 KB/sec rather than 1 MB/sec due to response time considerations.

Switched Ethernet and full-duplex Ethernet both reduce the problems, but do not really resolve the issue for data-intensive environments. Both technologies require new networking hubs and network interface cards, and provide only moderate improvements in available bandwidth. Switched Ethernets are most commonly found in configurations that use a single 100 Mbit/sec interface into the server and a switching hub that fans the single fast network into a large number of 10baseT spines. The 10baseT branches can be connected to individual clients or may be shared. This topology is useful for avoiding congestion in attribute environments, but does *not* address the primary problem in data–intensive applications: the interface into the client system throttles overall throughput to less than 1 MB/sec.

Full-duplex Ethernet is another technology sometimes offered for purposes of improving network throughput. However, given existing applications and protocols, full-duplex Ethernet does not address real-world problems. It is usually touted as being "20 Mbits/sec—twice as fast as Ethernet" but this rate is only achievable when traffic is perfectly balanced in each direction. Especially for NFS, such balance is rare, and for most such applications, full-duplex Ethernet is indistinguishable from standard half-duplex Ethernet.

The most significant argument against deployment of full-duplex Ethernet is expense. It requires new network interfaces for both client and server, and new network hubs. Full-duplex operation requires two twisted pairs compared to one for regular Ethernet, often necessitating rewiring. Justifying this level of effort and expense is difficult without also moving to a much faster technology such as FastEthernet or ATM. Full-duplex wiring is not a bad idea, since the new FastEthernet standard defines a full-duplex option. New installations should certainly install multiple pairs per drop—but NFS applications should not be the primary motivator for full-duplex wiring.

If the application does not require high sustained data bandwidth, lower-speed networking media such as Ethernet or Token Ring will probably suffice. These media offer sufficient speed for the small `lookup` and `getattr` operations that dominate attribute-intensive activity, as well as the relatively light data traffic associated with such usage. FastEthernet is of course suitable for this application. The primary advantage of FastEthernet over traditional Ethernet is that its superior bandwidth permits many more clients to be configured on a single network without fear of "meltdown" under heavy load situations.

2.5.2.2 Use High-Speed Networks to Avoid Congestion

High-speed networks are most useful for providing service to large data-intensive client populations, possibly with lower infrastructure costs, rather than offering maximum throughput on system-to-system conversations. The reason for this limit is the current state of NFS Version 2 implementations, which operate on 8 KB blocks of data with only a single 8 KB of prefetch (i.e., a maximum of 16 KB of data can be identified to the server in a single operation).

The practical effect is that a client and server that communicate over a fast network can transfer data at a peak rate of approximately 4 MB/sec[6]. This is more than four times as fast as the peak rate available over Ethernet, despite ten (or more) times greater media speed.

---

[6] This rate is only achieved by adding the statement `set nfs:nfs_async_threads = 16` to the `/etc/system` file *on Solaris 2.3 clients.* Solaris 2.4 clients need to add `set nfs_max_threads = 16` to their `/etc/system` file. SunOS 4.1.x clients should start 12 `biod` daemons rather than the default 8. The tuning mechanism is not expected to change in the future.

(NFS is a presentation–level protocol. Lower-level transport protocols such as TCP and UDP are capable of higher speeds using the same hardware. Most of the time in NFS is spent waiting for replies and other application-level processing. Other application-level protocols that do not rely upon immediate replies and acknowledgments can also utilize the higher media speeds.) New features in Solaris 2.5 permit the user to request the use of additional readahead blocks. The peak rate on a 16 Mbit/sec Token Ring is about 1.1 MB/sec.

The major advantage of high–speed networks in NFS Version 2 environments is that these networks can sustain multiple full-speed simultaneous conversations without degradation. When a server transfers 1 MB/sec of data to a client on an Ethernet, this conversation consumes 100 percent of the network's available bandwidth. Attempts to transfer more data on this network result in lower throughput for all users. The same client and server can transfer about 4 MB/sec on an FDDI ring, but on the higher-speed network this transaction consumes only 33 percent of the available bandwidth. The network can sustain three or four other such transfers simultaneously without serious degradation.

This situation can best be compared to highways. When traffic is light, a two–lane road with a 55 MPH speed limit is nearly as fast as an eight–lane motorway with a 65 MPH speed limit. However, when traffic is heavy, the motorway is much less sensitive to congestion.

Although 100 Mbit/sec FastEthernet appears to be the equivalent of 100 Mbit/sec FDDI, it is not, especially in situations where network utilization is very high. Because FastEthernet is literally Ethernet running at a higher speed, it is subject to the same issues when operating at high utilization: collisions result in lower throughput as utilization increases (Figure 6). In data–intensive environments, FDDI and ATM are greatly superior to FastEthernet except when dedicated FastEthernets are allocated to each client.

FDDI is also slightly—about five percent—more efficient than Ethernet and Token Ring in data-intensive environments because it uses a large maximum transfer unit (MTU)—4,500 bytes vs. 1,500 bytes for Ethernet and 2,048 bytes for Token Ring. For 8 KB data transfers, this requires processing only two packets, rather than five or six on Token Ring or Ethernet. This differential is of interest only in data-intensive environments, because attribute requests are so small (80-140 bytes) that they always fit in a single packet.

ATM networks share this packet-size advantage with FDDI; most current ATM implementations use a maximum transmission unit (MTU) of 9 KB, specifically in order to accommodate an entire 8 KB data packet with its associated TCP or UDP, IP, and media overhead. Early results with NFS over ATM show that the MTU advantage is approximately 6.5 percent over Ethernet. Although ATM technology is still somewhat immature, it seems destined to become the networking medium of choice in data-intensive environments, because of its high speed (presently defined at 155 Mbit/sec, 622 Mbit/sec, and 2.4 Gbit/sec, all full-duplex) and because it uses a point-to-point topology in which client-server connections are able to allocate media bandwidth to specific clients .

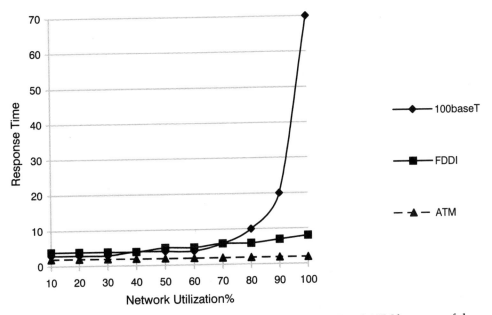

Figure 6. The effect of utilization on response time of requests. FDDI and ATM have graceful degradation curves, whereas collision-based FastEthernet degrades rapidly as utilization increases.

When existing wiring precludes the use of fiber media, consider using FDDI or ATM on twisted pair wiring. Most vendors now offer some sort of FDDI or ATM on Category-5 shielded twisted pair cabling, and some vendors also offer options for running on *unshielded* cabling, albeit at reduced speed.

⇒ For attribute-intensive NFS, 10 Mbit/sec Ethernet or 16 Mbit/sec Token Ring is quite sufficient. The use of 4 Mbit/sec Token Ring is not recommended.

⇒ For data-intensive NFS, use 10 Mbit/sec Ethernet only when existing coax cabling precludes the use of higher–speed media.

⇒ FDDI and ATM are preferred over FastEthernet in data–intensive environments for their much more graceful degradation characteristics under load.

2.5.2.3 NFS Version 3

NFS Version 3 improves substantially on the point–to–point throughput of NFS V2 clients. Given fast processors on client and server systems, Solaris 2.5 provides client–to–server throughput in excess of 11 MB/sec for both reads and writes. (This rate is obtainable with a 200 MHz Ultra–2 server and client using a high-speed network.) The increase in performance is attributable to much larger data block sizes (64 KB) and larger readahead, combined with some judicious tuning[7]. Of course, this level of performance is only available when the source file system is configured on a disk subsystem capable of operating at this speed—and when the client application actually requests data at this rate.

In data–intensive environments with fast clients (i.e., UltraSPARC), the extremely high bandwidth demand suggests quite a different networking strategy than recommended for NFS V2. UltraSPARC–based clients can fully utilize a 100 Mbit/sec network, and the most appropriate strategies are either dedicated 100 Mbit networks (for example, switched 100baseT) or ATM networks shared with a few other clients.

2.5.2.4 NFS and Full–Duplex Networking

ATM networks are always full-duplex; 155 Mbit/sec ATM networks can thus yield about 310 Mbits/sec theoretical bandwidth. If the application is evenly balanced for reads and writes (for example, a batch–style application that writes an old master file, processes it, and writes a new master file), a full–duplex network can be treated as effectively double the bandwidth. Applications that are strongly read– or write–biased will not benefit from full–duplex networking. An application in this category might be one that reads a model description from a file, computes a stress model, and displays the results graphically. The I/O of many applications, such as simulations, are heavily biased in one direction. In these circumstances, full-duplex networking is of use only when the overall network load is produced by a large number of clients. Most installations that have the necessary client load on a network are attribute–intensive, but due to their nature, these loads are not normally network–constrained. Data–intensive applications are network constrained, but these are configured with many fewer clients and often do not benefit from full-duplex networking. Certainly no issues arise with installing full–duplex networking, but NFS applications do not themselves justify the expense of installing full–duplex networks.

2.5.2.5 NFS Over Wide-Area Networks

The network topology can affect the perceived performance of an NFS server and the service provided. NFS clients and servers are often located on different networks joined by a router. Although provision of NFS service over complex networks must be carefully considered, it is possible to successful configuration of networks and applications in wide-area NFS topologies is possible.

The most important issue in this situation is operation latency: the time that elapses between the issuance of a request and the receipt of the response. Latency is not as critical in local area networks since the short distances associated with LANs do not impose significant media delays, and because LANs typically operate at high speed. Wider-area networks

---

[7] Solaris 2.5 *clients* should add `set  nfs:nfsv3_nra=6` to their `/etc/system` file. This configures the client to request six readahead blocks from the server.

impose operational delays simply to transport packets from site to site. Packet latency increases for a wide variety of reasons:

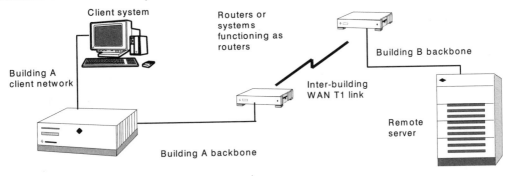

Figure 7. Typical inter-building networking topology puts three routers between clients and servers

- Router latency: Routers take finite—and often significant—time to route packets from one network to another. Most wide-area networks (even short ones between two adjacent buildings) use at least two routers. The typical campus-style topology often puts three or even four routers between client and server (Figure 7).

- Network transmission latency: The physical media used to transfer packets over wide-areas can often inject significant latency of their own, over and above that of their routers . For example, satellite bridges are often associated with very high latencies.

- Erroneous transmissions: Wide-area networks are approximately an order of magnitude more susceptible to transmission errors than most local-area networks. When errors cause significant retransmissions, both latency and throughput are adversely affected.

2.5.2.5.1 WAN Latency

The effect of network transmission latency can be dramatic. Application–to–application transmission in a LAN is typically 1 ms or less. Similar figures in world–wide WANs can easily amount to 500 ms! The response time of the *server* itself is 50 ms or less—usually in the vicinity of 5-10 ms for the throughput normally associated with WAN requirements. Adding moderate delays of 20-50 ms results in a user perception that the server is responding in 50-110 ms. The server is still able to deliver its full throughput in these circumstances, but users have a very different perception.

Latency is important to NFS activity because of the request-response nature of most attribute-intensive loads. Each request-response pair is subject to transmission latency in each direction, and perceived end-user response is directly affected. The process of looking up remote path names involves a `readdir`, `lookup`, and `getattr` operation for each part of the path. A minimum of 1,500 milliseconds—a second and a half!—is required to just to open a file buried five levels into a directory structure if the end-to-end network latency is 100 ms.

2.5.2.5.2 WAN Throughput

Given low latency and reasonably error-free transmission, wide-area file service *is* feasible. The most common configurations utilize high-speed point-to-point synchronous serial links that are connected to one or more local area networks at each end. In the U.S., these serial links typically offer T1 (1.544 Mbit/sec) or 56 Kbit/sec lines; European carriers offer slightly higher speeds: 2.048 Mbit/sec (known as E1) or 64 Kbit/sec, respectively. To put these speeds in perspective, expressing them as 197 Kbytes/sec (T1) and 7 Kbytes/sec (56 Kbit/sec) is useful. At 7+ Kbytes/sec, most leased–line WANs are not fast enough to operate useful NFS services. (Another way to express this speed is "about 2 NFSops/sec," since an 8 KB data operation will take almost a full second to transmit on the WAN.) Fortunately, T1 speeds do offer an opportunity for certain classes of applications that require sharing of consistent files across long distances, and higher-speed lines are available. Usually known as T3 , these leased lines permit speeds up to 45 Mbits/sec (5.6 Mbytes/sec). Most T3 lines are usually allocated to data in fractional form (i.e., half of the line is allocated to voice and half to data).

These lines appear to be much slower than the local area networks to which they are connected, but fast serial lines (T1 or better) offer throughput much closer to that of local area networks. Serial links can be used at near 100 percent utilization without undue overhead, while Ethernets typically saturate at approximately 440 Kbytes/sec (3.5 Mbits/sec, 35 percent network utilization), about twice the throughput of a T1 line . For this reason, file service over high-speed serial lines can move data at useful speeds. This is capability particularly useful for transferring bulk data from site to site. Wide-area NFS dominated by attribute processing can be successful if latency is not critical. But in a wide-area environment, the short packets are transferred quickly (i.e., at high throughput) over each segment, although routing and media delays often impose significant latency.

2.5.2.5.3 TCP Transport

One way to ensure that data is not retransmitted extensively is to use the TCP protocol for transport, rather than UDP. This is not available in many implementations, but when both client and server are running Solaris 2.5 and later, this is an option. TCP is a heavier-weight protocol than UDP, resulting in higher CPU overhead per packet, which is why it has not been used traditionally in LAN environments. Despite this overhead, TCP is useful for controlling transmission costs in error–prone environments, especially in WAN environments where the cost of retransmission can be substantial. When the TCP protocol is not available, the NFS block size can be set to 1 KB instead of the normal 8 KB, in order to minimize the amount of data that must be retransmitted in the event of an error.

The NFS client service caches the attributes of files that it acquires from the server, and attributes are aged to ensure that the client reacquires attributes at intervals. Attributes are reacquired if the file is accessed after the attributes have expired. For remote files that are held open, this causes occasional traffic as the clients update their cached attributes. In a typical LAN environment, the traffic associated with a few `getattr` operations is insignificant, but on a WAN, when bandwidth is at a premium, administrators may also consider increasing the attribute cache time-out mount (`actimeo`) parameter to reduce the number of times remote clients must reacquire attributes.

⇒ 56 Kbit/sec or 64 Kb/sec lines are usually *not* fast enough for most NFS use.

⇒ T1, E1, or fractional T3 serial lines *are* often suitable for wide-area NFS.

⇒ NFS over WANs is dominated by network and router latency; throughput is not usually a problem. Use the Cache File System (CacheFS) on clients to substantially reduce wide-area network traffic, unless the traffic is dominated by NFS writes.

⇒ Adjust NFS mount parameters in WAN configurations to use the TCP protocol, reduce the read and write block sizes, and consider increasing the attribute cache time-out.

2.5.2.6 Determine Clients-per-Network Ratio

With these considerations in mind, the following rules of thumb can be used to determine the proper type and number of networks:

⇒ If the application is data-intensive, configure FDDI or ATM networks. If fiber cabling is not feasible for logistical reasons, consider operating FDDI or ATM over implementations. New installations should consider that ATM uses the same 62.5 micron multimode fiber cabling as FDDI. (In fact, adapters are available to permit the use of installed FDDI cabling to implement ATM networks.)

⇒ When NFS Version 2 is used, configure one FDDI ring for every five to seven simultaneously active data-intensive clients. Despite maximum NFS V2 point–to–point throughput of about 4 MB/sec (a third of the throughput of an FDDI ring), very few applications make continuous NFS demands, and the degradation character of FDDI prevents worst–case meltdowns. In data–intensive EDA and earth resources applications, this often works out to 25-40 clients per ring.

⇒ Configure one FastEthernet for every three to five fully active V2 data–intensive clients. Normally this calculation works out to a total of 10-15 clients per FastEthernet. FDDI and ATM are generally recommended over FastEthernet when configuring for data–intensive applications.

⇒ If NFS Version 3 is used, clients can consume far more network bandwidth (as much as 11 Mbytes/sec), and only one or two active clients can share a 100 Mbit/sec network.

⇒ In data-intensive installations where an existing cabling plant mandates the use of 10 Mbit/sec Ethernet, configure one Ethernet for every two active clients, with a maximum of four to six clients per network.

⇒ If the application is attribute-intensive, configuration of Ethernet or Token Ring networks is sufficient.

⇒ Configure one Ethernet per eight to ten *fully active clients* in an attribute-intensive environment. It is unwise to exceed 20-25 clients per Ethernet regardless of demand because of the severe degradation experienced when many clients are active . An Ethernet is able to sustain about 250-300 NFSops/sec on the 097.LADDIS benchmark at high collision rates. Exceeding 200 NFSops/sec per Ethernet on a sustained basis is unwise.

⇒ A branch of a switched Ethernet is treated as a full Ethernet, but the 100 Mbit server interface must not be overloaded.

⇒ Configure one Token Ring network per ten to fifteen fully active clients in an attribute-intensive environment. If necessary, 50-80 total clients per network are feasible on Token Rings due to their superior degradation characteristics under heavy load (compared to Ethernet).

⇒ Mixing network types is reasonable for systems that provide service to more than one class of users. For example, both FDDI and Token Ring are appropriate for a server that supports both a document imaging application (data-intensive) and a group of PCs running a financial analysis application (attribute-intensive).

These rules of thumb are summarized below in Table 3.

Table 3. Per–network configuration capacity

Network Media	Attribute–Intensive	Data–Intensive	
	Clients/Net	Clients/Net	Max Throughput
10baseT	20-25	Not recommended	1 MB/sec
16 Mb Token Ring	50-80	Not recommended	1.1 MB/sec
100baseT	120-200	7-12	11 MB/sec
FDDI	250+	12-18	11 MB/sec

2.5.3 Network Topology Considerations

One consideration that is often overlooked in the process of sizing NFS servers is that NFS is rarely the only traffic on the network. Networks support a wide variety of other services, and some of them can consume significant network bandwidth. Other traffic affects the sizing of NFS servers in several ways.

First, non-NFS traffic can consume network bandwidth, resulting in poor performance from an otherwise reasonable configuration. This situation is of particular concern in data-intensive environments, where network bandwidth is already at a premium. The best solution is to ensure that network utilization stays at an acceptable level, usually by configuring more or faster networks. If ATM is in use, it may be possible to guarantee response time by dedicating bandwidth to each client/server connection, although this mechanism is presently somewhat inflexible and only a partial solution in this environment.

Perhaps more important, non-NFS traffic often uses the network in very different ways than NFS. Most NFS servers provide service to clients attached to networks local to the server, typically in a star configuration as seen in Figure 8.

This topology works well for NFS because clients rarely generate much interclient NFS traffic. As a result, the server is called upon to do relatively little routing—perhaps none at all. Non–NFS traffic, though, can impose a very different type of load. Consider the same NFS configuration, but with a database server (perhaps owned by a different group) located on one of the segments. The desktop systems are clients of both the NFS server and the database server, meaning that NFS traffic normally travels over a single segment to the server, whereas database traffic would normally cross two segments. This load impacts the traffic level on the segment hosting the database server and also adds loading to the NFS server, because it is then asked to service routing load in addition to its normal duties. Routing is not a major concern for a server where two or three segments are in use, but it can be for large systems, which might be configured with 100 or more segments. Under such circumstances, dedicated routers permit the server to devote its efforts to its real work.

⇒ Use dedicated purpose-designed routers when network traffic has a significant component that is client-to-client, rather than client-to-server.

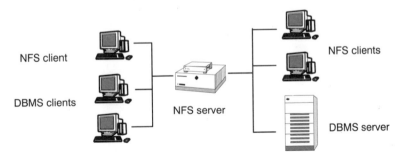

Figure 8. A routing topology problem. When an NFS (or DBMS) server is called upon to route substantial unrelated traffic, file service may be degraded. This degradation is especially likely with pre-UltraSPARC systems, when a dedicated router should be considered.

2.5.4 Processor Consumption

Because nearly all Solaris-based systems are designed as general-purpose systems with extensive peripheral expansion, it is possible to configure a Sun system so that the processor becomes the limiting factor in the system. In NFS environments, processor power is used to process the IP, TCP or UDP, RPC, and NFS protocols (in roughly this order), as well as device management for both disk and network interfaces.

Although Pentium- and Pentium Pro-based servers are attractively priced and seem to have the raw processor power to match many SPARC–based systems, the internal architecture of most of them limits their performance. In particular, slow memory systems, few and slow I/O busses, and lack of specific support for server applications (such as DVMA acceleration and streamlined interrupt processing, as discussed in Chapter 6.1 *System Architecture*) result in lower performance from Solaris x86 systems than from SPARC systems with equivalent processor power. Particularly for NFS service, x86 systems are recommended primarily for attribute-intensive workgroup systems. Few are suitable for data–intensive applications.

The following rules of thumb apply to configuring NFS servers:

⇒ If the environment is predominantly attribute-intensive and involves fewer than four to six Ethernet or Token Ring networks, a uniprocessor system such as a SPARCstation 5 or a Pentium-based PC is quite sufficient. For large attribute-intensive environments with many networks, dual processor SPARCstation 20s or fast uniprocessors such as the Ultra–1 are recommended. Larger platforms such as the SPARCserver 1000E or Ultra–2 are very capable in such applications.

⇒ If the environment is data-intensive, configure processors based upon the amount of network bandwidth configured in the server according to Table 4:

Table 4. CPU configuration per network bandwidth for data–intensive NFS servers

Processor	Solaris 2.3	Solaris 2.4	Solaris 2.5
MicroSPARC, MicroSPARC–II, Pentium, or SuperSPARC w/o external cache	Not recommended	Not recommended	Not recommended
40 MHz SuperSPARC	17 Mbits/sec	19 Mbits/sec	23 Mbits/sec
50 MHz SuperSPARC	25 Mbits/sec	28 Mbits/sec	34 Mbits/sec
60 MHz SuperSPARC	30 Mbits/sec	34 Mbits/sec	41 Mbits/sec
75 MHz SuperSPARC	38 Mbits/sec	42 Mbits/sec	51 Mbits/sec
85 MHz SuperSPARC	43 Mbits/sec	48 Mbits/sec	57 Mbits/sec

| 167 MHz UltraSPARC | Not supported | Not supported | 100 Mbits/sec |
| 200 MHz UltraSPARC | Not supported | Not supported | 125 Mbits/sec |

2.5.5 Solaris SMP Scalability

Solaris 2.5 shows scalability of about 87 percent, meaning that doubling the number of processors results in 87 percent more performance. Figure 9 shows operating system scalability for data–intensive applications in terms of overall network throughput available for given processor configurations. Because the machine–dependent layer of the kernel often governs scalability of NFS, these numbers apply only to SuperSPARC –based systems. In particular, these are unlikely to represent the actual capability of either x86 or UltraSPARC systems, which may be more or less scalable than SuperSPARC.

Scalability of 87 percent is nearly a worst–case for Solaris, because NFS service runs *entirely* in the kernel, where internal locking strategy is most heavily stressed. Most applications execute primarily in user space, where kernel locking is not an issue, and scalability in user code exceeds 95 percent in almost all cases.

For data-intensive applications, the combining scalability rules with processor consumption rules results in the processor configurations shown in Table 5. Larger caches (1 MB on UltraSPARC, 2 MB on SuperSPARC) deliver about ten percent additional performance when available.

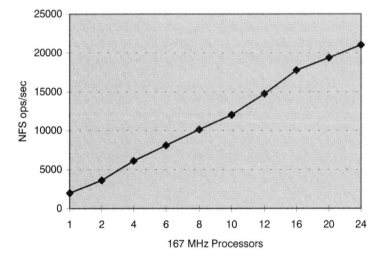

Figure 9. NFS multiprocessor scalability on the Ultra Enterprise x000 family. Scalability as processors are brought online is excellent. Response time remains constant, never exceeding 24.2 ms or under 18.7ms at any load level. The corresponding curve for the SPARCcenter 2000E has similar characteristics.

Table 5. System–wide data–intensive throughput for given CPU configurations, assuming Solaris 2.5.1. UltraSPARC processors are configured with 512 KB caches, SuperSPARC with 1 MB caches.

CPUs	50 MHz SuperSPARC	85 MHz SuperSPARC	167 MHz UltraSPARC
1	35 Mbits/sec	60 Mbits/sec	100 Mbits/sec
2	65 Mbits/sec	110 Mbits/sec	195 Mbits/sec
4	120 Mbits/sec	210 Mbits/sec	390 Mbits/sec
8	200 Mbits/sec	400 Mbits/sec	750 Mbits/sec
16	400 Mbits/sec	700 Mbits/sec	1200+ Mbits/sec

2.5.6 Disk Configuration and Load Balancing

Like network configuration, disk configuration is governed by the type of client. The performance of disk drives varies widely according to the access pattern requested of them. Random access is by its nature not cacheable and requires the disk arm to seek for virtually each I/O operation—a mechanical motion that lowers performance. Sequential access, especially sequential read access, requires many fewer disk seeks per operation (usually once per cylinder, about 1 MB), leading to *much* higher throughput rates. (In 1996, a fast disk drive delivers almost 6 Mbytes/sec in sequential conditions, but about 950 Kbytes/sec under random access.)

2.5.6.1 Random Access Pattern for Attribute–Intensive NFS

Unlike data-intensive environments, nearly *all* file access in an attribute-intensive environment that requires disk access results in random access patterns to the disk subsystems. When files are small, access to data is dominated by retrieval of the directory entries, inode entries, and the first few indirect blocks—a disk seek is required to obtain file/directory metainformation as well as each block of user data. Thus the disk arm spends much more time seeking among the various pieces of file system information than it spends retrieving user data.

As a result, the configuration criteria for attribute-intensive NFS differs substantially from data-intensive environments. Because the overall time required to process a random I/O operation is dominated by the disk arm seek, the overall throughput of a disk is *much* lower in random mode than in sequential mode. Under these conditions, the SCSI bus is much less busy, permitting many more disks to be configured onto a SCSI bus before bus utilization becomes an issue.

For the typical attribute–intensive NFS server, the configuration goal is to provide the largest reasonable number of disk drives, since disk arms are the limiting factor in the disk subsystem. The nature of attribute-intensive applications means that storage requirements are relatively small compared to the density of modern disks. Under these circumstances configuring four (or even eight or nine) smaller disks is much better than operating with a single large disk. Although this typically costs more per megabyte of storage, the performance benefits are substantial. For example, two 1 GB disks cost about fifteen percent more than one 2 GB disk, but they provide more than twice the random I/O capability. (Refer to Table 12 on page 116.)

Attribute-intensive environments are best configured with a large number of small disks connected to a moderate number of SCSI host adapters, ideally through some sort of disk array. The recommended configuration is four to five fully active disks on a typical fast SCSI bus or 8-10 fully active drives on a fast/wide bus. Normally, this means that the bus can be fully configured—access is rarely balanced evenly across all disks. Most disk arrays configure their disks on multiple internal SCSI busses. The ability of the array controller to handle such a workload is usually not a factor, although some of the slower disk arrays might be saturated under very heavy loads. (Some array controllers—like some early models of the Data General Clariion—saturate at around 450-500 I/Os per second. Most modern controllers, including later models of the same family, are able to handle far more.) The peripheral bus connecting the disk array to the host is unlikely to be a bottleneck, because attribute-intensive loads are dominated by small random I/O. For example, a fast/wide SCSI-2 bus can deliver more than 4,000 I/Os per second. Since even fast disk drives deliver about 100 I/Os per second in random-access environments, even very dense disk arrays with 30-40 disks can be configured on a single host adapter.

Making a more accurate recommendation on the number of disk arms that are required in an attribute-intensive environment is difficult, because loads vary widely. The response time of the server is governed by how quickly attributes can be looked up and returned. Configuring least one disk drive for every two fully active clients is a reasonable rule of thumb, in order to minimize latency. Alternatively, this latency might be reduced by configuring additional main memory, permitting the dominant attributes to be cached. For attribute environments that have a high proportion of writes, the use of either host–based or array controller–based NVRAM can reduce disk utilization, but does not affect the primary disk load (which is read–oriented).

> Caution: For typical attribute–oriented NFS servers with storage capacities in the 5-20 GB range, configuring a few very large disks such as the 9 GB models currently available is nearly always a *serious* mistake.

2.5.6.2 Sequential Access Pattern for Data–Intensive NFS

Because data–intensive environments have fewer simultaneously active clients than attribute–intensive environments, most file access is sequential, even on file servers that provide data to many clients. Solaris does a good job organizing its device access under these circumstances. Configure for a sequential environment when providing service to data-intensive applications.

Configuring for this type of load is straightforward: use the disks with fastest internal transfer speeds, preferably in stripes. The internal transfer speed is *much* lower than the burst-transfer speed quoted for most SCSI disks. See section 7.1.1.4, *Decoding the Specifications*.

In a serial-access environment, computing the number of disks required to service the peak load is relatively easy. Each fully active client can demand up to 5.4 MB/sec from the disk subsystems when using NFS Version 2, and fast clients running Version 3 can demand almost 10 MB/sec. Because fast disks transfer less than 7 MB/sec (often much less), striping or some form of RAID is required to deliver this level of performance (see section 7.5 *Berkeley RAID Concepts*). Even when the disks can deliver the necessary throughput, substantial headroom is required, because multiple clients accessing the same RAID device can substantially degrade sequential throughput. Fortunately, data–intensive environments typically have relatively few clients, and those clients tend to be extremely bursty; the result is unhindered access to the disk subsystems.

A good first estimate is one RAID device for every three fully active V3 clients, or one device for every four to five V2 clients (in this context, "device" means a logical volume or metadisk, rather than necessarily a physical device). This ratio is suggested, even though each RAID device should be able to deliver over 15 MB/sec and clients request less than 10 MB/sec, because of the possibility of multiple active clients. Given the high data rates associated with data–intensive NFS, use caution when configuring disk arrays—many common disk array controllers are unable to transfer sequential data faster than 12-15 MB/sec. If the chosen network media is 10 Mbit Ethernet or 16 Mbit Token Ring, one disk per fully active client is sufficient, since the clients will be throttled at about 1 Mbyte/sec anyway.

2.5.6.3 Use RAID to Spread Disk Access Load

Even when transfer rates do not exceed the abilities of individual disks, some form of RAID is usually required to balance disk *activity* across multiple disk drives as well as accelerate the transfers. A common problem in NFS servers is poor load balancing across disk drives and disk controllers (unfortunately, the problem is all too common, and is not limited to NFS servers). For example, one common configuration uses three disks to support a population of diskless clients. The first disk holds the server's operating system and application binaries, the second disk holds the root and swap file systems for all of the diskless clients, and the third disk contains the home directories for users of the diskless clients. This configuration is logically balanced across disk drives, although balancing the configuration by physical usage would be far more effective. In such an environment, the disk that holds swap for the diskless clients is usually *far* busier than either of the other two disks—many times this disk is seen at 100 percent utilization while the others average less than five percent—and often zero percent! A much better arrangement is to spread the very busy swap areas across all the disks (this would also mean spreading the home directories across all the disks).

RAID methods transparently spread disk access across a number of disk drives, using any of the striping, mirroring, or RAID-3/5 organizations. (Disk concatenation, achieves a minimal amount of load balancing, but only when disks are relatively full.) Disk striping substantially improves serial read and write performance, useful in data–intensive environments. A good starting point for stripe chunk size (interlace size) is:

$$Chunk\ Size = \frac{File\ System\ Cluster\ Size}{Number\ of\ Data\ Disks\ in\ RAID\ Volume}$$

The default file system cluster size is 56 KB, but data–intensive sites should use a larger value as discussed in *UFS and UFS+ Parameters* (section 9.2.3). If the underlying disk is a RAID–5 volume, the file system cluster size should be configured to match the stripe width of the RAID–5 volume. Usually the cluster size (*maxcontig*) and stripe width should be configured to be some multiple of 32 KB. In attribute-intensive environments where random access dominates disk utilization, both a large chunk size and the default cluster size are quite suitable.

Although disk mirroring is primarily intended to promote fault-resilience, mirroring has the side effect of improving disk access time and reducing disk utilization by providing read access to two or more copies of the same data. This optimization is particularly effective in environments dominated by read operations, such as most attribute systems. Write operations normally are slightly slower on a mirrored disk since multiple actual writes must be accomplished for each logical operation requested.

Industry consensus recommends a target maximum utilization of 60-65 percent for each disk drive[8] (drive utilization is reported by the `iostat(1)` command). In practice planning a data layout in advance to yield this level of utilization is difficult or impossible. Usually, attainment of evenly balanced disk utilization takes some iterations of monitoring and data reorganization. Moreover, usage patterns change over time, sometimes radically, so the data layout that works well at installation may perform very poorly a year later. There are also a variety of other second-order considerations when optimizing data layout on a given set of disk drives. For further information, consult section 7.6.2, *Data Layout Optimization*.

2.5.6.4 Logging File System

The UFS+ logging file system provides two important features for NFS servers: safe, two–phase updates to the file system, and greatly accelerated file system consistency checking upon reboot. Rather than committing writes directly into the file system, log structure file

---

[8] Patterson and Hennesey, *Computer Architecture: A Quantitative Approach.*, First Edition (Kaufman & Broad, 1990) p. 545.

systems such as UFS+ put changed data into a separate log (or journal), and *then* modify the file system itself. This arrangement permits the file system to be recovered to a consistent state even if the operation is interrupted by a catastrophe.

The preceding discussion should make it obvious that in most cases, writes to a logging file system will not be as fast as direct operation on the file system—the operation must be applied first to the log, then to the file system, and finally removed from the log. This degradation is most noticeable in situations that are dominated by writes, especially large writes. For small (8-16 KB) operations, writing to a remote UFS + file system is about the same speed as writing on a normal file system. In situations where many writes are being committed to the file system at once, UFS+ is slightly faster than UFS, because seek distances are minimized. Unfortunately, large writes onto a remote UFS+ file system can be noticeably slower than writing on a standard file system. For the trivial operation of writing 100 MB remotely, UFS+ is typically 15-20 percent slower. The difference can be significant in data–intensive environments.

Apart from the outright performance deltas, the primary impact on configuration is that UFS+ file systems require space on an additional disk drive. This space must reside on a disk drive separate from the drives that host the file system itself, both because the log is the insurance against catastrophe and because placing the log on the same disk as the file system proper would result in substantially degraded typical seek distances. Fortunately putting every log on a separate disk drive is *not* necessary. There is little point in a log larger than 128 MB, since the kernel maintains a log-rolling thread that keeps the log contents small. Most file systems will never fill even a 32 MB log. (User data is not placed in the log; only directory modifications are transacted—see section 9.2, *UFS and UFS+ File Systems*.) Given the density of most modern disk drives, concentrating several file system logs into a small region of a disk drive is a reasonable strategy. This provides reasonable density without causing long disk seeks back and forth across the log disk. A major consideration is that this strategy concentrates the recovery of several file systems into a single disk, so any such configuration *must* mirror the log disks.

The use of a UFS+ log is incompatible with the use of host–based non-volatile memory (NVRAM) or PrestoServe write acceleration. (Currently, UFS+ logs cannot be write– accelerated with this mechanism, but there are no problems with the two products coexisting on the same system. Controller-based NVRAM easily interoperates with UFS+ logs.) For further discussion, particularly configuration of UFS+ disk subsystems, see section 9.2.1.3, *Configuring UFS+ Log Devices*.

2.5.6.5 Disk Configuration Summary

Disk configuration rules can be summarized as follows:

⇒ In data-intensive environments, configure at least one RAID device for every three active clients on high–speed networks, or one disk drive for every client on Ethernet or

Token Ring. ("RAID device" in this context means a single volume such as a RAID–5 or RAID–1, rather than a physical RAID controller.)

⇒ In attribute-intensive environments, configure at least one disk drive for every two fully active clients (on any network medium).

⇒ In attribute–intensive environments, the number of disks that can be configured on a SCSI or FibreChannel bus is effectively unlimited, and only the slowest disk arrays will be saturated by typical loads.

⇒ In data–intensive environments, pay close attention to throughput limitations of SCSI busses and disk array controllers.

⇒ Use some form of RAID such as striping, RAID-1+0, or RAID-5 to spread the disk access load across many disks. Solstice:DiskSuite, SPARCstorage Volume Manager, or some sort of RAID controller are all useful alternatives.

2.5.7 Unusual Memory Requirements

Because Solaris implements virtual memory file caching, most users are inclined to configure NFS servers with very large memory subsystems. However, the typical file usage pattern of NFS clients means that data is retrieved from the buffer cache only in rare circumstances; this memory is usually not necessary.

In typical servers, the size of the disk area provided to the client population greatly exceeds the size of main memory. Most clients do not share the majority of their files, and most applications typically read an entire data file into memory and then close it. As a result, the client rarely accesses the original file again. If no other client uses the same file before the cache is overwritten, the cached data is never used again, and the pages are overwritten with new data when memory is required to cache something else. Flushing the page to disk is not necessary, because the memory image being overwritten is already on disk. Nothing is gained by having the old page in memory if it will not be used again. When free memory drops below a configurable threshold, pages not recently used are made available for reuse.

The largest class of exceptions to this rule of thumb is the temporary work file, which often is opened at the beginning of processing and closed at the end. Because the file remains open on the client, the data pages associated with the file continue to be mapped (and cached) in the client's memory. The client's virtual memory subsystem uses the server as a backing store for the temporary file. If the client does not have physical memory sufficient to keep these pages in cache, some or all of the data pages will be paged out or overwritten during subsequent operation, and references to that data will then cause an NFS read to be issued to retrieve the data. In this case, the server would benefit from being able to cache such data; adding the equivalent amount of memory to the clients is likely to improve performance even more. This class of temporary data is the most convenient to store on a workstation's local disk, since its temporary nature means that it need not be backed up.

The behavior of write operations is widely misunderstood. The problem is that two different subtasks are being performed on behalf of a single logical write operation. When a process writes on a standard UNIX file, UFS buffers the written data in memory for normal lazy write–behind. Some time later, the system actually flushes the written data to the backing store, which is NFS in this case. When the write is actually performed, it is sent to the server in standard—safe—NFS form. Because the write is not effected until the usual buffering mechanism is exhausted, reducing server load is quite possible, simply by increasing the client's ability to cache writes.

2.5.7.1 Main Memory Configuration

Probably the simplest and most useful rule of thumb is the "five-minute rule." This rule is used in database systems where the greater complexity makes sizing caches very difficult. The current relationship between the price of memory and disk subsystems means that caching data that will be referred to more than once every five minutes is an economically feasible proposition. Size server memory at about 16 MB plus the data anticipated to be referenced every five minutes. The principle behind the five-minute rule is discussed in detail in section 3.5.2.1, *Sizing the DBMS I/O Cache.*

In the end, several simple rules of thumb govern the configuration of memory in NFS servers:

$\Rightarrow$ If the server provides primarily user data for many clients, configure minimal memory. For small communities this usually means 32 MB, and for large communities about 128 MB. In multiprocessor configurations, always provide at least 64 MB per SuperSPARC processor or 128 MB per UltraSPARC processor. Attribute-intensive applications normally benefit slightly more from memory than data-intensive applications.

$\Rightarrow$ If the server normally provides *temporary file space* for applications that utilize those files heavily (Cadence's *Verilog* is a good example), configure server memory equal to about 75 percent of the size of the active temporary files in use on the server. For example, if each client's temporary file is about 5 MB, and the server is expected to handle 20 fully active clients, configure (20 clients $\times$ 5 MB) $\div$ 75% = 133 MB of memory. (Of course, 128 MB is the most appropriate easily configured increment.) Scratch files can often be directed to a local directory (on the client system) such as /tmp, resulting in much higher client performance as well as substantially decreased network traffic.

$\Rightarrow$ If the server's primary responsibility is to provide only executable images, configure server memory equal to approximately the combined size of the heavily used binary files, including libraries! For example, a server expected to provide /usr/openwin to a community should have enough memory to cache Xsun, cmdtool, libX11.so, libxview.so, and libXt.so. This particular NFS application is quite different from the more typical NFS application in that it normally provides the same files over and over to all of its clients. As a result, this type of server *is* able to effectively cache most of its active data. Clients will not normally use every page of all of the binaries, so configuring only enough memory to hold the frequently used programs and libraries is reasonable.

⇒ Memory can be sized on the five-minute rule: memory is sized at 32 MB plus memory to cache the data accessed more often than once in five minutes.

2.5.7.2 Swap Space

Because NFS servers do not run user processes, the need for swap space is practically nil. The only real requirement for swap space on a pure NFS server is as emergency space to save a crash dump in the event of a system panic. Configuration of swap space at approximately fifty percent of main memory size is more than adequate for such servers. (A pure NFS server could be configured with literally no swap space at all. The recommendation for half of main memory is only for saving a crash dump.) Note that most of these rules are the opposite of common expectations!

2.5.8 PrestoServe/NVSIMM and NFS Version 2

Disk operations are mechanical, so they are slow; normally UNIX buffers file system writes in memory, and permits the issuing process to proceed while the operating system arranges for the data to be physically written on the disk. The synchronous nature of NFS Version 2 writes means that they are typically *very* slow—much slower than local disk writes. When a client issues a write request, the server is required to update the data on disk, as well as the associated file system metadata. For a typical file, this process means *four* disk writes. Each operation must update the actual data, the file's directory information indicating the time of last modification, and an indirect block; if the file is large it also requires updating a double-indirect block. The server must execute all of these disk updates and ensure that they are complete on disk before it can acknowledge the completion of an NFS write request. An NFS write can take 150-200 milliseconds (three or four synchronous writes at 40+ milliseconds each), compared to the normal 15-20 milliseconds for a local disk write.

NFS V2 servers can use non-volatile memory (NVRAM) to greatly accelerate NFS writes. These options take advantage of the fact that the NFS protocol merely requires an NFS write to be committed to non-volatile storage, rather than specifically requiring it to be on disk. As long as the server always returns the data that is acknowledged from previous write operations, the server is free to save the data in any manner available.

PrestoServe and NVSIMM implement precisely these semantics. With one of these options configured, the NVRAM device driver intercepts requests for synchronous disk writes. Instead of permitting them to be sent directly to the disk device, the writes are committed instead to non-volatile memory and acknowledged as complete. This arrangement is *much* faster than waiting for the mechanical operation of writing the data onto disk. Eventually, the data is committed to disk.

Because a single logical NFS write involves three or four synchronous disk operations , the use of NVRAM significantly accelerates the throughput of NFS write operation. Depending upon conditions (such as file system state, other demands on the disk, the size of and location of the writes, etc.), the use of NVRAM accelerates NFS writes by two to four times. For example, typical NFS V2 write throughput under Solaris 2 is approximately 450 KB/sec; with NVRAM, the rate is approximately 950 KB/sec, and somewhat higher when using faster media. Read operations do not benefit to any material degree.

Unfortunately, NVRAM is not available on Solaris x86 systems, making them much less suitable for most kinds of NFS service involving NFS V2.

2.5.8.1 NVSIMM vs. PrestoServe

From a disk subsystem or NFS client's perspective, the PrestoServe and NVSIMM options are functionally equivalent. The primary difference is that the NVSIMM is slightly more efficient, because it requires less manipulation of the data. Because the PrestoServe board is physically resident in the SBus, its use requires that data be copied to it across a peripheral bus. By contrast, the NVSIMM resides directly in the main memory. Data bound for disk is not copied to the NVSIMM over a peripheral bus; a much faster memory–bus copy can be used instead. For these reasons, NVSIMM is preferred in situations where both NVSIMM and SBus PrestoServe are available.

2.5.8.2 Restrictions

Because of the magnitude of the acceleration involved, NFS V2 servers should *always* use NVRAM in any system that provides general NFS service. Two exceptions exist: servers that provide read-only service, and servers operated in redundant high–availability configurations that share disk drives. The most common example in the former category is a server that provides binaries to a large community of clients. Shared–disk systems such as high availability cluster nodes *cannot* use host–based NVRAM because they cannot maintain a consistent view of the contents of each other's accelerator memory.

Because the NVSIMM/PrestoServe device driver must reside on disk in the root file system, NVRAM acceleration cannot be applied to the root file system. The NVRAM driver must flush dirty buffers to the disk before any other processes become active. If the root file system were accelerated, it might be dirty after a system crash, and the NVRAM driver might not be loadable. Ordinarily this issue does not arise except for servers that export the /var file system tree—for the purpose of exporting /var/spool/mail or /var/spool/mqueue. These trees must be placed in a separate file system if they are to be accelerated by NVRAM.

The use of host-based NVRAM lowers the maximum throughput of a system by as much as 5-10 percent. Maximum throughput degrades because the system must use processor power to manage the NVRAM cache, and to keep the cached and disk copies consistent. However, the *response time* of the system is improved by as much as forty percent. For example, the 50 MHz SPARCserver 1000's maximum throughput on the LADDIS benchmark without NVSIMM is 2,108 NFSops/sec at 49.4 ms response (using Solaris 2.3; Solaris 2.4 and Solaris 2.5 numbers are much higher on the same platform). The same system configured with NVSIMM delivers only 1,928 NFSops/sec, but the average response time is reduced to about 32 ms. As a result, users of NFS clients perceive a server equipped with NVRAM to be *much* faster than one not so equipped, even though the overall system throughput is slightly reduced. (This differential is a classic tradeoff between throughput and latency.) Fortunately, the lost throughput is rarely an issue because maximum throughput capacity of most systems is much greater than typical loads, which are in the range of 50-250 NFSops/sec per network.

⇒ Always configure host-based NVRAM in NFS Version 2 servers unless the disks are shared with another system or the system is configured with a disk subsystem that includes extensive caching.

⇒ If disk drives are shared with another system, *do not* configure host–based NVRAM write acceleration.

⇒ NVSIMM is preferred over SBus PrestoServe.

⇒ NVSIMM/PrestoServe is incompatible with the use of the logging file system feature of Solstice: DiskSuite. (They can coexist on the same system, but they cannot be applied to the same file system.)

2.5.8.3 NVRAM Acceleration and NFS Version 3

One of the primary goals of the NFS Version 3 protocol revision was the elimination of the synchronous writes and the need for NVRAM acceleration. The new protocol succeeds in this regard. Tests show that although NVRAM acceleration is compatible with NFS Version 3, the performance improvement is marginal—less than five percent in all cases, although it never hurts performance. There is no reason to configure NVRAM acceleration for servers that offer only NFS Version 3 services.

Most NFS Version 3 servers must also support NFS Version 2. Clients are free to use either protocol, and only Solaris 2.5 and some DEC clients default to Version 3[9]. PC-NFS, Solaris 1 Solaris 2 previous to Solaris 2.5, HP-UX, and AIX represent the vast majority of installed clients, and none of these support Version 3. For the foreseeable future, Version 2 is likely to remain the majority NFS client.

---

[9] SGI's Irix operating system supports NFS Version 3, but the default protocol is Version 2.

⇒ Servers that use *only* the NFS Version 3 protocol do not need write acceleration.

2.5.9 Caching Disk Subsystems

Developed in 1990, host–based NVRAM write acceleration is still a useful tactic. However, this organization pre–dates the common availability of disk arrays with extensive caching capabilities. Most server–class disk arrays can be configured with 16-128 MB of memory and use sophisticated algorithms to manage them.

Because the disk array has no connection to file systems—it accepts read and write requests without regard to file semantics—it is able to accelerate more than just synchronous file system writes. In the NFS context, this means that the synchronous writes issued by NFS are accelerated, with the same impact as host–based NVRAM acceleration. If faced with an exclusive choice between configuring host–based NVRAM and a caching disk subsystem, the latter is preferable, especially if the system may have non–NFS requirements. The effects of host–based acceleration and subsystem–based acceleration are complementary and do offer some additive acceleration when configured together. Caching disk subsystems also have the advantage of being immune to conflicts with host–based volume management, such as the problems of interoperating UFS + logs with host–based NVRAM acceleration.

2.5.10 Provisions for Backup and Failure-Resistance

File system backup and failure resistance is the same for NFS servers as it is for any other system. An extensive discussion of the details of providing for file system backup, recovery, and failure-resistance is in Chapter 8, *Backup and Recovery*. The recommendations about backup and fault resistance can be summarized as follows:

⇒ Simple, relatively small backups can be handled with one or two tape drives. Tape drive location on SCSI busses is not important if the drives are not active during the client systems' working hours.

⇒ Fully consistent backups require the locking of the file system against modifications. This requires Solstice Backup (Legato Networker) or similar products. Again, configuration of the backup devices on the SCSI busses is not especially important if backups are normally run during off hours.

⇒ Mirrored file systems provide the ability to survive complete disk failures, and additionally provide the opportunity to provide continuous access even during fully consistent backups. Mirroring imposes a small penalty in disk write throughput (the penalty is a maximum of about seven to eight percent in random access, 15-20 percent in serial access; in most cases the degradation is about half these figures). Mirroring configurations substantially improve read throughput in multi-user environments.

⇒ For reliability reasons (rather than performance considerations), mirrored file systems should be configured with each submirror on a separate SCSI bus.

⇒ If backups are to be performed during normal system operation, the backup device should either be configured on its own SCSI bus, or on the same SCSI bus as an *off-line* (detached and inactive) mirror, to avoid severe response time problems.

⇒ Configure NVRAM when rapid file system recovery is required in an attribute-intensive environment. Even if the system shares disks with another system in a high–availability configuration, the NVRAM can be disabled during normal operation and used only for recovery, which is inherently a single-system operation.

⇒ Data-intensive environments may require high-speed, mechanically assisted schemes, such as 3490E-compatible tape transports, and mass storage units such as stacking units or robotic libraries.

2.6 Load Estimation

Estimating the load to be placed upon a new system is an imprecise task, but a reasonable estimate can often be produced in advance using one of two basic approaches. The preferred method is to measure existing systems. This method provides some assurance of the accuracy of the baseline, although future usage is often not equivalent to the existing load. The alternate method is a rough computation; this is useful when systems to measure do not exist.

Two separate metrics must be known to accurately arrive at a configuration: the NFS operation mix, and the overall system throughput. The operation mix indicates whether the system is attribute-intensive or data-intensive.

2.6.1 Measuring Existing Systems

A wide variety of mechanisms is available for measuring existing systems. The simplest is simply to use nfsstat(8), which provides the operation mix. Since these statistics can be reset to zero with the -z flag, nfsstat can also be used to measure system throughput in a shell script such as this:

```
#!/bin/sh
nfsstat -z >/dev/null        # zero initial counters
while true
do
    sleep 10
    nfsstat -z -s            # show the statistics
done
```

The output shows how many NFS calls were serviced in the sampling interval, and hence the rate at which NFS operations are being handled. If the system is under heavy load CPU, whether from excessive NFS service queues or other processing demand, sleep(1) can actually sleep for much longer than the requested ten seconds, overestimating the demand.

If the existing server is so overloaded, a more accurate tool must be used to measure the load. There are many such tools, among them are SunNet Manager , NetMetrix from HP, and SharpShooter from AIM Technologies. All of these tools permit capture of actual load throughput and operation mix by monitoring the network interfaces in promiscuous mode. Post-processing of the data is usually required to calculate average throughput; a variety of methods can be used to do this (`awk(1)`, or a spreadsheet such as *WingZ* or *1-2-3*).

Either method is accurate as long as the peak resource utilization on the network and server being monitored stays below approximately 95 percent. If the processor is saturated, this method shows only the load that the server is able to *handle*, rather than the load that would be demanded if the server had more capacity.

The author once naively upgraded an old, overworked file server that was clearly the primary bottleneck in the network. The new machine was more than ten times as capable and was expected to remove the problems. The old server was already running the networks at 35-40 percent utilization (i.e., 100 percent of the usable facility), a fact that is obvious when viewed with 20-20 hindsight. When the new server was installed, the file server bottleneck was removed—and the networks melted down under 550 percent collision rates! The new server was processing many more requests far more quickly, resulting in drastically more network traffic on an already overloaded network. In the end, the new server was able to fill four networks. The moral of the story: consider all of the resources, even those that are not yet causing problems.

2.6.2 Estimation without Existing Systems

If no existing system is available to measure, a "ballpark" estimate based upon the anticipated usage is often possible. Making such an estimate requires an understanding of how much data is being manipulated by the client. This method is quite accurate if the application falls into the data-intensive category. A reasonable estimate can also be made for attribute-intensive environments, but a variety of factors make such an estimate less accurate.

2.6.2.1 Estimating Data-Intensive Environments

The first step is to arrive at an estimate of the fully active demand of a typical client. This can be approximated from an understanding of client behavior. If the load is data-intensive, aggregate the anticipated reads and writes and use this figure as the per-client estimate. Attribute operations are normally insignificant in a workload dominated by data operations—they comprise a small percentage of the total operations, imposing a trivial amount of work on the server when compared to the work necessary to provide the data.

For example, consider a client workstation that runs an application to search for patterns in thermal sensor data via NFS Version 2. The typical data set is 400 MB, and is read in chunks of about 50 MB, processing each completely before continuing to the next. Processing each chunk takes about five minutes of CPU time, and the result files written out are 1 MB in size. Assuming that the networking medium will be FDDI, the peak NFS demand will happen when the client reads a chunk of 50 MB. At the maximum rate of about 3.3 MB/sec, the client will be fully active for about fifteen seconds, at a rate of 420 read ops/sec. Since each run takes about thirty minutes of elapsed time, or 1,800 seconds, and (400 + 1) MB × 125 ops/MB = 50,125 ops are required per run, the average rate is 28 ops/sec. The server will be required to service the peak demand rate—420 ops/sec—for approximately 15 seconds every five minutes, or about five percent of the time. Three pieces of useful information result from this exercise: the average active demand rate (28 ops/sec), the peak demand rate (420 ops/sec), and the frequency that the peak rate is required. From this information, an estimate of the overall demand rate can be formed. If ten clients are to be configured, the average demand rate will be 280 ops/sec (this rate is *not* comparable to a LADDIS result, because the operation mix is *very* different). The chance that two clients will demand the peak rate simultaneously is about $0.05 \times 0.05 = 0.025$ or under three percent, and three clients will simultaneously require peak service even less frequently. The following conclusions can be drawn from this information:

- Since the probability of having three clients active is far less than one percent, even worst case sustained demand will always be less than about triple the instantaneous peak.

- Two FDDI networks are required, since the maximum anticipated demand is just 3×3.3 MB/sec = 10 MB/sec, the theoretical bandwidth of an FDDI network (12.5 MB/sec before accounting for UDP and IP overhead). Alternatively, a single ATM network could be used.

- Since only two or three clients will be fully active at any moment, one RAID device is required.

- With only three clients likely to be active (at 3.3 MB/sec), only one fast/wide SCSI host adapter is required.

- Network demand will be 3 x 3.3 MB/sec = 10 MB/sec ≈ 80 Mbits/sec. With Solaris 2.5, one 75 MHz SuperSPARC processor (or better) is required.

- Because the server is unlikely to benefit from a large file cache, minimal memory is required—128 MB memory is plenty ("minimal" is a relative term; most data–intensive NFS servers have 500-1,000 MB of memory installed, an unnecessary luxury).

- NVSIMMs can be configured without consuming SBus slots, which many of the Sun multiprocessor older platforms can support. NVSIMM is not essential, because the proportion of writes is likely to be very small (less than 1:400, or 0.25 percent). NVRAM write acceleration is only required if the disk array does not perform write caching.

Note that when configuring for data-intensive applications, comparing the anticipated demand rates with a server's 097.LADDIS score is not generally useful because the operation mixes are so different that the loads are not comparable. Fortunately, this estimate is normally quite accurate.

2.6.2.2 Estimating Attribute-Intensive Environments

The preceding example assumed that the NFS attribute load was negligible compared to data operations. If this assumption does not hold, for example, in a software development environment, a guess must be made as to the anticipated NFS mix. In the absence of other information, the Legato mix can be assumed. The 097.LADDIS benchmark uses this mix; data operations include 22 percent reads and 15 percent writes.

Consider a client workstation whose most intensive work is to recompile a software system consisting of 25 MB of source code. The workstations can compile the system in about 30 minutes; the compilation processes generate 18 MB of intermediate object code and binaries. From this information the client system will write 18 MB to the server, and read at least 25 MB (possibly more, since a third of the source code consists of header files included by a multitude of source modules). The cache file system can be used to prevent the re-reading of the include files. Assuming that CacheFS is used, 33 MB of actual data must be transferred during a build, or 33 MB × 125 data ops per MB[10] = 4125 data operations in 30 minutes (1,800 seconds), a rate of about 2.3 ops/sec. Because this is application is attribute-intensive, the missing attribute operations must be estimated. Assuming the Legato mix, the overall rate is approximately:

$$NFS\ Read\ Ops\ Rate = \frac{Read\ Data\ Size \times 125}{22\%}$$

for NFS V2 read operations, and:

$$NFS\ Write\ Ops\ Rate = \frac{Write\ Data\ Size \times 125}{15\%}$$

for NFS V2 write operations. In this case, the rate is (25 MB of reads × 125 ops/MB) ÷ 22% = 1,800 seconds, or 7.89 ops/sec. At the same time, the clients also generate (18 MB of writes × 125 ops/MB) ÷ 15% = 1,800 seconds, or 8.33 ops/sec. With no additional information, there is no certain way to estimate the peak load; taking the higher of the loads resulting from estimating via reads and writes is a reasonable approach. In this example, the ratio of reads to writes is very similar to the Legato mix. This might not be the case, for example, if source browser files were being created (source browser files are often four to six times the size of the source code).

If 20 workstations of this description are on the network, and the clients use NFS Version 2, the following conclusions can be drawn:

---

[10] NFS V2 data operations are 8 KB each, so 125 operations are required to move 1 MB.

- Even in the unlikely event that all 20 workstations are fully active all the time, the combined demand rate is 8.33 ops/sec × 20 clients or 166 ops/sec, below the maximum of 200 ops/sec sustainable by an Ethernet. The cautious configuration would include two networks for this load, but if logistical considerations preclude two networks, one will probably suffice.

- Since the load is very light, a SPARCstation 5 or a Pentium–based PC is more than adequate (even in the worst case, only two networks must be configured). A system with three free PCI slots (for two Ethernets and a SCSI host adapter) is required.

- Although the aggregate amount of data is very small (25 MB of source code and 18 MB of object code; even 20 complete copies only total 660 MB), the recommended disk configuration is at least two 535 MB disks. Assuming that CacheFS is in use, a single disk *might* be sufficient, since the header files will not be read frequently (they will be cached on the clients).

- The volume of data is small, and much of it will be read and sent to many clients on a repeated basis, so configuring enough memory to cache all of it is worthwhile: 16 MB of basic memory, plus 25 MB to cache the source code results in a 64 MB configuration. Additional memory is required, since the source code will have to compete with other data for the available memory in the server.

- With just one or two data disks, a single SCSI bus is completely adequate, and disk arrays are not required for either disk capacity or I/O throughput reasons.

- Because writes will be common in this environment, NVRAM write acceleration is essential (unless the clients use NFS Version 3), eliminating most Solaris x86 systems unless equipped with a disk array that includes NVRAM buffering.

- The final system is a choice between a low-end SPARCstation 5 or a well-configured Pentium PC. The maximum computed 166 ops/sec demand rate is less than half of the SPARCstation 5's LADDIS score of 460 ops/sec. The check against the 097.LADDIS score is appropriate for attribute-intensive situations because 097.LADDIS scores are reported using such a mix.

Table 6. LADDIS scores for various Sun NFS servers. Network media is 10baseT for systems not using UltraSPARC, and 100baseT for UltraSPARC systems. Slightly (5%) higher rates are available from FDDI; slightly (5-8%), slightly lower rates are available from 16 Mbit Token Ring.

Platform	LADDIS score	Configuration Notes
SPARCstation 10 Model 40	411 ops/sec at 49 ms	Solaris 2.3
SPARCstation 10 Model 51	472 ops/sec at 49 ms	Solaris 2.4, 1 x 50 MHz CPU
SPARCstation 10 Model 512	741 ops/sec at 48 ms	Solaris 2.4, 2 x 50 MHz CPUs
SPARCstation 20 Model 71	850 ops/sec at 41 ms	Solaris 2.4, 75 MHz CPU
SPARCserver 1000 Model 1104	1,410 ops/sec at 41 ms	Solaris 2.4, 4 x 50 MHz CPUs
SPARCserver 1000 Model 1108	1,928 ops/sec at 42 ms	Solaris 2.4, 8 x 50 MHz CPUs
SPARCcenter 2000 Model 2208	2,575 ops/sec at 49 ms	Solaris 2.4, 8 x 50 MHz CPUs
SPARCcenter 2000E	6,000 ops/sec at 39 ms	Solaris 2.4, 10 x 85 MHz CPUs
Ultra–1/170	2,200 ops/sec at 31 ms	Solaris 2.5
Ultra–2/2200	4,583 ops/sec at 38 ms	Solaris 2.5.1, 2 x 200 MHz CPUs
UE 3000/4000/5000/6000	3,629 ops/sec at 28 ms	Solaris 2.5.1, 2 x 167 MHz CPUs
UE 3000/4000/5000/6000	6,113 ops/sec at 22 ms	Solaris 2.5.1, 4 x 167 MHz CPUs
UE 4000/5000/6000	10,151 ops/sec at 19 ms	Solaris 2.5.1, 8 x 167 MHz CPUs
Ultra Enterprise 6000	17,747 ops/sec at 21 ms	Solaris 2.5.1, 16 x 167 MHz CPUs
Ultra Enterprise 6000	21,014 ops/sec at 18 ms	Solaris 2.5.1, 24 x 167 MHz CPUs

2.6.2.3 Last Resort: Using a Similar Load

If no existing system is available for measurement, and the behavior of the application is not well understood, making an estimate based on Table 7 may be possible. This data is intended to provide some sample measured NFS loads in order to offer some guideposts for estimating load. Table 7 is *not* meant to provide a definitive picture of how much load can be expected from specific tasks. Of course, these figures are subject to variation by individual user and application.

Table 7. *Average* sustained NFS usage rates during working hours

Platform	Version 2		Version 3
	Attribute–Intensive	Data–Intensive	Data–Intensive
Windows PC or Macintosh	0.1 ops/sec	-	-
SPARCstation 2	0.5-1 ops/sec	-	-
SPARCstation 10/20	1-2 ops/sec	3.3 MB/sec	5 MB/sec
Ultra–1	2-4 ops/sec	5 MB/sec	9 MB/sec
Ultra–2/SS1000 compute engine	—	5 MB/sec	9 MB/sec
250 user SPARCcenter 2000 timesharing	50 ops/sec	—	—

2.6.3 Case Study 1—File Service for a Small Office

The law firm of Dewey, Cheetham & Howe has just purchased six new PCs. In the process of having them installed, the senior partner who manages the internal organization, Ms. Anne Howe, realized that installing all of the software on each of the new PCs consumed significant staff time. Installation and upgrade of software for the existing 22 PCs and Macintoshes had become unmanageable. Also, the process of transferring lengthy legal briefs between systems on floppy disks warranted a new solution. In addition, a policy requiring each user to do backups is routinely ignored, with predictable consequences. Finally, Anne is considering moving all of the firm's paper documentation (from past briefs, correspondence, etc.) to a document imaging system in the near future. Anne would like to install a central file server to address several separate requirements:

- Centralized software installation, so that either installing or upgrading software is done only once, rather than dozens of times.

- Consolidated backup of user files, permitting a regular, reliable mechanism to provide disaster recovery.

- A "bulletin-board" service where user files can be posted for easy sharing.

- A temporary holding area for scanned-image documents. Anne would like to begin scanning documents as soon as possible in order to reduce the time between selection of the vendor and initial.

The first issue is that two very different kinds of services are required. The provision of application software and user files is clearly dominated by attribute operations: as with nearly all sites dominated by PCs, user files are relatively small, and binaries are virtually always attribute-intensive. On the other hand, the scanned-image documents are clearly dominated by large files, and this process is data-intensive. The requirements for these services are broken down separately; in the final analysis, a single system to provide all services may or may not be feasible.

The various staff groups estimate that the disk space required to handle these disparate functions is about 700 MB for software distribution, and about 400 MB per user[11] for centralized file storage (since the files will *all* be stored centrally, there is no real notion of a "bulletin-board", but this strategy has been approved by the customer). With 28 users, this amounts to about 12 GB of storage. The amount of storage required for the scanned images has not been determined yet. The image size can be estimated, though, since legal pages are 8.5" x 14". At 150 x 150 dpi resolution, a monochrome image is thus about 325 KB, and half that (175 KB) after lossless compression. Accordingly, a library of 100,000 pages results in storage requirements of at least 17.5 GB. If the images are scanned at 300 x 300 dpi, the resulting files are four times the size, totaling 70 GB. For the moment, assume that the images will be scanned at 150 dpi. (Processing the scanned images through an optical character recognition process would result in far more drastic compression, because only ASCII text would be saved, but in this case the nature of legal documents mandates that the actual photographic image be stored.)

2.6.3.1 Configuring the Attribute–Intensive Server

Anne's staff is not sure how much of the 700 MB of software distribution space will be used frequently; nearly half of the space represents working areas for upgrades. Additional space is consumed by storing multiple software versions such as Windows 3.1 and Windows 95, of which nearly all users use just one version. A rough estimate of the applications to be used frequently is about 50 MB. This represents the entire directory trees of the applications; a cursory inspection reveals that the popularly used executables and startup files are about 20 percent of this, meaning that 10 MB of memory should be reserved.

Because the primary file service is attribute-intensive, Ethernet is an appropriate network media. The network must support 28 clients, the upper end of the recommendation for a single network. The clients are all PCs and Macintoshes running real-memory operating systems, so they are lighter-weight than typical workstations, and the clients can be configured on a single network, although a second network is a good idea.

Only one processor is required to handle the attribute-intensive part of this load. Any current processor is clearly sufficient because the 28 clients will average less than 30 NFSops/sec, a small proportion of the capacity of an entry–level Pentium–based PC server. The load will probably average *much* less than 30 ops/sec, and may be as low as 5 ops/sec. Refer to *NFS and PC/Mac Clients*, section 2.2.5. A SPARCstation 5 is also a good choice for this application.

---

[11] Legal services generate a great deal of paperwork and use many documents. Disk storage of 400 MB per user is quite a bit more than average in attribute-intensive environments.

Disk storage requirements amount to 12 GB. The server must handle 28 clients, but casual observation suggests that only four or five of them will be active (in an NFS sense) under normal circumstances, so two or three file system disks are sufficient. The light nature of the workload (30 NFSops/sec) means that this load can be served by six 2 GB disks or even three 4 GB disks. In addition, a boot disk is required, and the UFS+ file system logs can be placed on this disk; the file system logs should be mirrored, so one additional disk should be configured.

Because this environment is attribute-intensive, the system needs 16 MB plus 10 MB for the executables (discussed above), plus some additional memory for caching attributes. Although 64 MB would permit caching additional binaries, 32 MB is adequate.

Anne has specified that backups must be run every day, but full backups will be done weekly. Normally, incremental backups are smaller, typically less than ten percent of the volume of the full backup. Daily incremental backups are often less than one percent of the total file system size. In this case, the system will be required to backup less than 1.2 GB per day, so a single 4 mm DDS–1 tape drive (2 GB native capacity, 4-5 GB with compression) is sufficient for this task. Full backups are to be run unattended on the weekends, so a 4 mm stacker is a more suitable solution. Because little active usage occurs over the weekends or at night when the backups will be run, configuring separate SCSI busses for the backup processes is unnecessary. Attaching the CDROM and tape stacker to the built-in SCSI host adapter will work well. Solstice Backup (bundled with the Solaris workgroup server license) can be used to schedule and perform the backups.

The final configuration for the attribute-intensive work is a 133 MHz Pentium PC or SPARCstation 5 with 32–64 MB memory; two small (1 GB) disks for the operating system and UFS+ logs and three 4 GB disks for storage; a CDROM; and a 4 mm tape stacker are configured on the built-in SCSI host adapter with the boot disk and the UFS+ logs. A second network interface is also required; on Sun systems the second SCSI host adapter and second network interface can be combined on a single SBus board, but a PCI system would probably require two slots, and might require as many as four. In a SPARCstation 5, NVRAM takes the form of an SBus PrestoServe, leaving only one of the three SBus slots available.

2.6.3.2 Configuring the Data–Intensive Server

The data-intensive workload is much lighter than normal, since for now the system must server only one client: the scanner system. The scanner can scan two pages per minute; assuming the images are 150 dpi, 700 KB of data are written to the server every minute, or 700 KB/minute ÷ 60 seconds/minute = 12 KB/sec on average. The load will be very bursty, though, because the scanner creates a 325 KB image once every 30 seconds and writes it all at once. Unlike most data-intensive environments, this data rate is easily handled by one 10baseT Ethernet. Because of the minimal network traffic, a uniprocessor is more than adequate. The scanner system should be configured on a dedicated Ethernet, requiring the system to be configured on three networks.

Ordinarily, data–intensive servers configure one disk for every three clients. During the data acquisition phase, only one client generates load, but after the retrieval system comes online, the staff estimates that as many as four clients will be simultaneously active. Four active clients requires that slightly more than one disk drive to deliver sufficient disk access capacity. The raw data requirements of 17.5 GB, combined with default 21 percent overhead for UFS file systems means that 22.2 GB of disk storage must be configured. After accounting for the 4.9 percent differential between disk specifications (see section 7.1.1.4.1, *Millions of Bytes vs. Megabytes*), 23.3 GB of disk drives are required. This capacity can be achieved with six 4 GB disks, and the low overall data transfer requirements permit configuring all six on a single SCSI host adapter. NVRAM write acceleration should be configured, especially because the initial load is *all* writes.

Backing up the system in an unattended fashion is not completely straightforward. The DDS–1 tape drive in the 4 mm stacker unit is rated at 5 GB capacity (using typical compression) and transfers at 1 MB/sec. At these specifications, backing up the system should take 17.5 GB × 1024 MB/GB ÷ 1 MB/sec × 3600 secs/hour = 5 hours, using four tapes. However, the data is already fully compressed, so the tape drive will not be able to compress the data at all. Tape capacity is therefore only 2 GB and transport speed is about 550 KB/sec. The backup will use nine tapes and will take more than nine hours. Two stackers with four tapes each are required to achieve the required capacity. If the data is broken down into two file systems, the backup can be completed in about half the time, and disaster recovery time will be correspondingly shortened. With only about 1 MB/sec being transferred on the SCSI bus, the two stackers can be configured on a single SCSI bus. Furthermore, the I/O load offers no compelling reason to configure an additional SCSI bus—the tapes can be put on the internal SCSI bus along with the boot disk and the UFS + log, as those disk functions do not demand high throughput.

The data–intensive configuration requires a SPARCstation 20 Model 71 (the minimum processor configuration for any data–intensive application). The base memory of 64 MB meets the minimum requirements for data–intensive systems. NVRAM can be configured with NVSIMM. I/O expansion requires one SunSwift SBus card for SCSI and the second Ethernet, as is a third Ethernet interface. The six 4 GB data disks can be configured in an outboard multidisk enclosure, and UFS + logs and the operating system can be stored on the system's internal disks. Two of the system's four SBus slots remain available.

2.6.3.3 Combining Data–Intensive and Attribute–Intensive

The combined data-intensive and attribute-intensive loads are light enough that the two servers can be combined into a single machine. The networks and disk subsystems for each server were sized independently, and combining them in one system would have no material impact. Combining the memory is a simple matter, so the potential trouble areas are the backup arrangements and especially the processor. The primary (attribute–intensive) load is very light; at 30 NFSops/sec, it represents less than five percent of the processor capacity of a SPARCstation 20 Model 71. At the same time, the 75 MHz CPU is rated to handle 51 Mbits/sec of network (see Table 4). Only 30 Mbits/sec are configured, so almost half the processor should be available to handle the attribute load, while less than five percent is required.

Combining the backup devices is more difficult. The attribute load requires a single 4 mm stacker, while the data–intensive load requires two, and both were originally configured on their respective system's internal SCSI busses. With three tape drives on a single bus— combined with mirrored UFS+ log traffic—the utilization of the SCSI bus *could* become an issue. Another SCSI bus dedicated to the tape drives is the safest course.

2.6.4 Case Study 2—File Service for Software Development

Certified Computer Consultants does a burgeoning business in for-hire software development. Because they specialize in the production of object-oriented modules, their software library contains what their chief librarian describes as "an incredible number" of source files along with related files such as Interleaf documents and Cadre Teamwork collections. CCC would like to replace their four aging Sun–4/280s with faster equipment, preferably with a single system. As CCC's business is essentially the creation and maintenance of source code, their development environment includes a wide variety of systems, from current UNIX platforms such as SPARCstations, HP, and IBM workstations, to a variety of older platforms.

The file server's primary responsibilities will be as follows:

- Primary storage of both reference (production) libraries and shared development trees. Technical writers also will use this system for their primary file storage.

- Management of backup functions; because each development architecture builds and runs a current test environment every night, most of the file systems must be available on a full-time basis.

The software development lab is the quintessential attribute-intensive environment; there is little debate as to which category of server this is. CCC's system administration department requests that the new server be capable of maintaining at least 21 GB of fully mirrored online storage. Fifty-five software developers are physically located in the building, along with 11 technical writers and eight secretaries. The other administrative users (in Finance and Sales) will continue using their own facilities. In addition, a number of contract developers and writers are not provided with offices. Instead, they are connected to the network via dialup asynchronous PPP links running at 28.8 Kbits/sec. At various times, between six and 12 contractors are supported. The remote users will be upgraded to ISDN connections in the near future.

The total of 74 local users is currently located on a single logical Ethernet network, along with the four servers. This load is made tolerable by the use of smart bridges to isolate traffic onto several segments. The existing network and servers are completely saturated, so measuring the entire existing server is unlikely to yield a very accurate indication of the overall load. Measurement of a single client system on a Saturday reveals the typical active load for the developer workstations to be approximately 5 NFSops/sec per seat, alternately very intense (120-200 ops/sec) during builds and very quiet (0-0.5 ops/sec) at most other times. (Measuring a single client and multiplying is more accurate than measuring the server, because of the overload condition on the server.) The average load for 74 users is 370 ops/sec. The remote users are much less intense, because they use CacheFS to reduce their NFS traffic to an absolute minimum. At any rate, the 3 KB/sec PPP links drastically restrict the load that these users can generate. When the remote users are upgraded to ISDN , they will each have two basic rate circuits, or 2 x 64 Kbits/sec = 32 Kbytes/sec, permitting 3–4 NFSops/sec.

A new network topology should be installed, dividing the client systems into multiple subnets. With attribute–intensive work dominating the load, Ethernet is acceptable. Eight 10baseT networks should be able to accommodate all 75 users active simultaneously—even under the most pessimistic assumptions. Configuring for this worst–case condition would permit room for growth. If growth is neglected, as few as four networks could be used. Eight nets can be configured using two SQEC/S SBus quad-port Ethernet interfaces. An alternative is to use a single 100baseT FastEthernet connection to the server and switched Ethernet hubs to provide 10baseT connectivity to client systems. An even better solution is the use of 100baseT throughout, although this involves upgrading the network interfaces for each client. In this case, a single 100baseT network can be shared among all the client systems.

If the average load is 225 ops/sec, most load peaks will be about double this, 450 -500 ops/sec. Checking the LADDIS scores in Table 6 (page 68), the Ultra–1/170 clearly has sufficient capacity (2,200 ops/sec) to handle the peaks. A more expensive but much more flexible host system is the SPARCserver 1000E. With two 85 MHz processors, this system can handle "only" 1,800 NFSops/sec, but the system can accommodate much more CPU and peripheral expansion. With only two SBus slots, the Ultra–1 does not have sufficient I/O expansion to handle this workload.

Assuming that half of the 75 users actively make NFS demands, the network has about 40 active users. The recommendation is to have one disk for every two active users, requiring 20 disk drives. The storage is to be fully mirrored, so read capacity is doubled (twice as many disks are available to satisfy the request) while write capacity remains approximately the same. The Legato mix is 22 percent reads and 15 percent writes, about 60 percent/40 percent, so for this application a mirrored disk subsystem has about 60 percent more access capacity than a non–mirrored configuration. Thirteen disks (20 ÷ 1.6) are required to handle the storage access requirements.

The raw storage requirement is for 21 GB, and with default UFS parameters (21 percent overhead), this translates to 26.6 GB of disk space. After accounting for 4.9 percent for the difference between millions of bytes and megabytes, 27.9 GB of disk drives are required. This requirement can be accomplished with fourteen 2.1 GB disks, seven 4.3 GB disks, or four 9 GB disks. After mirroring, the configurations use 28 x 2.1 GB, 14 x 4.3 GB, or 8 x 9 GB disks. The last configuration is the least expensive, but since at least thirteen disks are required, the best configuration is the use of fourteen 4.3 GB disks, seven in each submirror. Fourteen drives is an inconvenient quantity from a packaging perspective, because it would require at least three six–disk enclosures, and a disk array is more appropriate. Additionally, another disk is required for UFS+ logs, along with a mirror for the log disk; a boot disk is also required, a total of three small disks (1 GB today) in addition to the data spaces.

The normal recommendation is to provide 64 MB memory per processor, and this case is no exception; the two processor system should have 128 MB. With many active clients and the high percentage of NFS writes associated with the operation mix found in software development work (the Legato mix has 15 percent writes), NVRAM write acceleration must be used. The use of UFS+ logs eliminates host–based NVRAM, so the configuration will rely on the 16 MB NVRAM in the SPARCstorage Array.

With the requirement for full-time availability, combined with substantial overnight processing load, care must be taken to configure the backup subsystems to minimize impact on processing. Because the disks are all mirrored, it is possible to lock the file systems against writes, sync them to disk, and then offline the submirrors for unimpeded backup [12]. The relatively low transfer speed of 4 mm helical-scan drives (500 KB/sec) means that at least two drives are required, and the data volume requires the use of the 4 mm stacker unit. Two tape backup devices can be configured on a single SCSI bus; the stackers do not require a dedicated SCSI bus, so they can be configured with the three internal disks, CDROM, and the built–in tape drive. Solstice: Backup or a similar facility is required to provide the ability to lock the file system against modifications while the mirrors are synchronized into a consistent state (i.e., the bundled `ufsdump(1m)` is not sufficient).

The dialup PPP links require the use of relatively high speed serial links, and these are best connected to a terminal server. The terminal server is used to process the many interrupts associated with serial traffic at these speeds, permitting the server itself to concentrate on NFS service. When the remote users are upgraded to ISDN circuits, they should be connected to a router. As with the terminal server, the router would shield the server from having to manage the interrupts and other overhead from as many as 12 ISDN circuits.

---

[12] For Solstice:DiskSuite, offlining the submirror rather than simply detaching it permits an optimized resync to be effected upon completion.

Furthermore, since the only SBus ISDN boards handle only a single circuit, 12 circuits would require 12 SBus slots at a significant cost.

The final configuration is a SPARCserver 1000E with two 85 MHz processors, 128 MB of memory, and three internal 1 GB disks; a SPARCstorage Array with fourteen 4.3 GB disks; and two 4 mm DAT stacker units. With two CPUs, this system has three SBus slots. One slot is used for the FibreChannel interface to the SPARCstorage Array. Another slot is configured with a SunSwift SBus card connecting to the FastEthernet. Even if the clients continue to use 10baseT, the best server configuration uses 100baseT to connect to a switched Ethernet hub. Failing that, the server must be configured with two quad–Ethernet SBus boards instead of the SunSwift. The configuration still fits into three SBus slots, although virtually any expansion will require a second system board for the purpose of obtaining three more SBus slots.

2.6.5 Case Study 3—File Service for Integrated Circuit Development

Central Silicon Casting specializes in rapid development of custom integrated circuits. The company has sixty design engineers who run a variety of electronic computer-aided design (ECAD) tools, both off-the-shelf and custom-designed. Like nearly all ECAD shops, CSC has a large data management problem: the design engineer's working environment is dominated by the need to process very large files. Typical circuit description files are 70-100 MB in size.

The designers, who normally work in teams of three or four, frequently need access to all of the files associated with a project. A centralized file service is thus required. Each designer has a powerful workstation—each desktop has either an HP 9000/735 or a SPARCstation 20 Model 152. Although not an issue with CSC's own software, the high licensing costs for some off–the–shelf software aggravate the data-sharing problem by strongly motivating CSC to purchase a few very large compute servers to provide shared simulation power, rather than purchasing licenses for every desktop system. At present three compute servers are installed, and a fourth one is expected within the next few months. Even with the new server fully operational, the simulation backlog is expected to run approximately 18 hours per day (CSC has a policy of running end-to-end simulations at every development checkpoint, resulting in a very heavy simulation load). Compounding the heavy load is CSC's policy of operating continuous incremental backups.

The file server must provide three general classes of files: large circuit description files (these average approximately 100 MB each), library description files, which are much smaller (3–5 MB each), and typical home directories. Current data storage requirements are 310 GB of circuit description files; all other files consume approximately 25 GB. CSC anticipates that data storage requirements will expand to 600 GB of circuitry and 40 GB of miscellaneous files within the next 12–18 months. All storage must be protected, although mirroring is not required.

The primary file service is the provision of circuit description files. This environment is clearly data-intensive, requiring high–speed networking. Unfortunately, the expense of rewiring with fiber is prohibitive, so the existing twisted pair wiring must be used. The wiring restriction can be handled by using 100baseT, CDDI[13], or twisted-pair ATM. CSC specifies CDDI. CSC estimates that of the 60 clients, at most 25 of them would be active at the same time.

2.6.5.1 Networking Requirements

The HP workstations are running HP–UX 9.01, and the Sun workstations are running Solaris 2.4; neither are expected to be upgraded within the next year due to application software considerations. Neither operating system supports NFS Version 3, so the maximum point–to–point throughput demanded by a workstation will be the 4 MB/sec provided by NFS V2. At 4 MB/sec, five to seven active clients can be supported per 100 Mbit/sec network. About 40 percent of the clients are active, so five to seven active clients represents about 15 total clients per CDDI network. Four CDDI networks are required for the 60 users.

Each of the four compute engines represent about four active clients, if they handle four to eight simultaneous simulation jobs. Such a load is easily possible given CSC's simulation policy. The compute servers are treated as 16 active clients, and they require another three CDDI rings. With this many networks, ATM might be a better choice than CDDI, given its substantial bandwidth advantage, especially between the compute servers and the file server. A single 155 Mbit ATM interface can handle the compute server load.

2.6.5.2 Disk Subsystem Requirements

The workstations and the compute servers combined to total about 40 active clients; 13–14 RAID metadevices are required if one is provided for every three clients. These probably should be RAID–5, as CSC has specified fully protected storage. Typical 5+1 RAID–5 devices (meaning five data disks plus one parity disk) yields a requirement for 14 x 6 = 84 disk drives, and this can be configured in three SPARCstorage Arrays (each can configure 30 disk drives). However, 40 clients demanding 4 MB/sec represent a disk data rate of 160 MB/sec, but each disk array is capable of only 22 MB/sec (see section 7.5.12, *SPARCstorage Array*), so at least eight arrays are required to sustain the data rate.

The server is required to provide storage for 310 + 25 = 335 GB of storage. The default UFS parameters consume 21 percent overhead, which is excessive for applications such as this one with very large data files. Accordingly, the inode density and minimum free space

---

[13] CDDI networks run the standard FDDI half-duplex protocol but on twisted-pair copper media. The primary advantage to CDDI is its ability to use existing wiring; performance is identical to FDDI.

threshold should be substantially reduced, to one inode per megabyte and one percent `minfree` (see section 9.2.3, UFS and UFS+ *File System Parameters*). The modified parameters consume about two percent of the raw data space, so the file system must be built on metadevices amounting to 335 GB + 2% = 342 GB. Each RAID–5 device consists of five data disks, and with 14 RAID devices, the system has 70 data disks. This requires about 4.8 GB per disk, slightly more than available from current 3.5″ 4.3 GB disks and much less than 5.25″ 9 GB disks. These disks are actually only 4.0 GB or 8.5 GB after accounting for notational differences (see section 7.1.1.4, *Decoding the Specifications*), so the file system data needs 86 of the smaller disks or 41 large ones. Because the disks are configured into 5+1 RAID–5 metadevices, the total disk requirement is for 90 + 18 = 108 of the 4.3 GB disks or 45 + 9 = 54 of the 9 GB disks. The former meets the data access requirement for at least 84 disk drives, but the latter does not. Configuring 84 of the large disks yields a storage capacity of 70 x 8.5 GB = 595 GB, conveniently matching storage requirements a year out. If this configuration is selected, the users must consider that while there is plenty of disk *storage* expansion capacity, but no excess disk *access* capacity has been configured. More disks should be added to the configuration as clients are added to the network.

In addition to the data storage itself, each of the file systems requires a UFS + log. Because this system will handle very large files, each file system should configure the maximum recommended UFS+ log, 128 MB. Any number of file systems is reasonable, but because of the logistical problems associated with manipulating very large file systems, the 335 GB of storage should broken down into 5–10 individual file systems. If the system is configured with ten file systems, ten UFS+ logs are required; at 128 MB each, the logs consume only 1.3 GB of storage space, but the heavy write activity expected on the disks me ans that each file system should have an independent log, to avoid bottlenecking a 33 GB file system by saving a couple of disk drives. If each file system is given its own log—that should be mirrored—five 67 GB file systems should be configured. This requires ten disk drives of arbitrary capacity. The least expensive suitable disks are 2 GB 7,200 rpm disks. There is plenty of room to configure them in the SPARCstorage Arrays.

2.6.5.3 Backups

CSC mandates continuous incremental backups, meaning that when one incremental dump is completed, the system goes back and runs another incremental. Complete dumps are done every weekend. The data volume clearly rules out most commodity backup devices: an 8 mm drive would take over 19 hours to dump even a single 67 GB file system, and even a DLT–7000 takes over four hours to dump a file system. The fact that virtually all of the files are very large makes speedy backups more feasible, because the backup process will spend almost all of its time reading large files sequentially rather than jumping the disk arms around to follow directory structures. Solstice:Backup can dump large files at approximately 13 MB/sec; at that rate a complete dump of a 67 GB file system takes about two hours. Other backup software can operate even faster; Open Vision's Net Backup has been demonstrated to deliver data streams to tape at over 15 MB/sec each.

Only a few tape drives are capable of accepting 13-15 MB/sec; the only one directly supported by Solaris 2.5 is the StorageTEK SD-3 Redwood, a high–end helical scan unit capable of approximately 15 MB/sec transfers and 50 GB per tape capacity. The device requires a differential fast/wide SCSI bus; given its 15 MB/sec transfer rate, each drive needs a dedicated bus. The continuous incremental backup policy means that at least one tape drive is always busy, so a minimum of two Redwood tape drives (and two SCSI host adapters) is required.

2.6.5.4 Core System

The large configuration dictates an Ultra Enterprise server, for the purposes of obtaining enough SBus slots for four CDDI and one ATM-155 network interfaces, eight disk arrays, two differential fast/wide SCSI host adapters for the tape drives, and a single–ended SCSI host adapter for the built–in CDROM. Four CDDI rings and one ATM-155 network are configured in the system, a total of 710 Mbits/sec of network bandwidth recall that ATM is a full-duplex media). Table 4 (page 50) indicates that 750 Mbits/sec of networking requires eight UltraSPARC CPUs after accounting for Solaris scalability. With eight CPUs, memory should be configured at about 1 GB. Eight processors require four CPU/memory boards.

Excluding the disk arrays, seven SBus slots are required to accommodate five network interfaces and two differential host adapters. The single-ended host adapter is already available on the SBus I/O board. Eight SPARCstorage Arrays require as many FibreChannel interfaces. Each Ultra Enterprise SBus I/O board provides for two FibreChannel interfaces in addition to three SBus slots; the three I/O boards required to handle the seven SBus cards thus can connect six of the eight SPARCstorage Arrays. Another SBus slot is required to handle the last two disk arrays, since the SBus FibreChannel interface also accommodates two ports.

The requirement is for four CPU/memory boards, and three SBus I/O boards, a total of seven boards. The Ultra Enterprise 4000 and 5000 each can handle eight boards, while the Ultra Enterprise 6000 provides for up to sixteen. Any of the systems can handle the required configuration. The proposed system is physically very large, requiring the controlled environment provided by a data center, so the UE5000 or UE6000 are preferred. Performance of the two systems is identical if configured identically.

The final configuration is an eight-processor Ultra Enterprise 5000 or 6000 with 1 GB memory, eight SPARCstorage Arrays with 108 x 4.3 GB disks, and twelve 1 GB disks. Four CDDI interfaces are required for clients and an ATM interface for the compute servers. Backup is accomplished via two StorageTEK Redwood helical-scan tape drives connected via dedicated fast/wide SCSI busses. No host–based NVRAM is configured; the system relies upon the 128 MB of NVRAM cache in the disk arrays.

Configuring DBMS Servers 3 ≡

The most common single class of applications for Solaris–based server systems is database management systems. Unfortunately, DBMS servers are more complex and more generalized than NFS file servers. The *lingua franca* of relational DBMS systems, Structured Query Language (SQL), is much richer than the basic operation set of NFS. Moreover, many DBMS implementations are available on Solaris, each with different characteristics. As a result, the discussion that follows is necessarily of a very generalized nature. It is impossible to provide a correct answer to the question "How many of *these* users will *this* system support?".

Given the diversity of applications, DBMS implementations, workloads, users, and requirements, any vendor willing to provide a firm answer to "how many of my users will it support?" is either guessing, or has made a detailed, in-depth analysis of an actual implementation. It is easy to tell the difference.

Determining that a particular configuration *cannot* accomplish a given task is almost always far easier than conclusively determining that a given configuration *can* accomplish a specific task. For example, it is easy to determine that a system with a single disk drive cannot achieve random-access throughput rates associated with 500 disk accesses per second: even the fastest disks can handle only about 100. However, a system with five or six such disks may or may not be able to handle the same load, because the bottleneck may not be in the disk subsystem. The system may not be able to process the data quickly enough to request the 500 disk accesses per second, even if the storage subsystem is sufficient to deliver them.

This chapter primarily addresses systems that serve as DBMS service providers in client/server mode, in an attempt to reduce the level of complexity to a comprehensible level. Treatment of systems that provide both DBMS services *and* run the applications that use the DBMS service is deferred until Chapter 5, *Configuring Timeshare Systems*. Such systems are timesharing systems in the truest sense of the term.

3.1 All DBMS Systems Are Different

Both database-oriented applications and DBMS systems themselves vary widely in nature. They cannot be as easily classified as NFS usage is divided into "attribute-intensive" and "data-intensive""

A number of fundamentally different database architectures are available in the market, but the UNIX marketplace seems to have settled primarily on the relational model. Most systems being installed today are relational, the architecture chosen by Oracle , Sybase, Ingres, DB2, Informix, Progress, Empress, and dBase. Software AG's ADABAS is a hierarchical system , although it is able to process standard SQL .

3.2 DBMS Architectures

Even with the overwhelming majority of systems operating under the same broad conceptual framework, there are large architectural differences between the various products. The most significant configuration consideration is often the implementation of the DBMS itself.

DBMS systems fall into two major classes, referred to as "2N" and "multithreaded"" The two architectures are diagrammed in Figure 10 Figure 11. The older 2N implementations run a process on the server for *each* client, even if the client is actually running on a physically separate system. Each client application thus uses two processes—one on the server and one the client system.

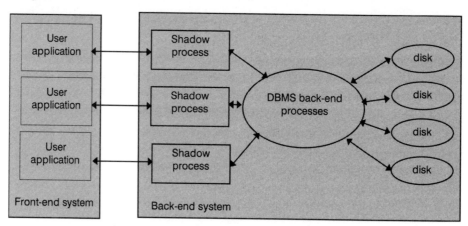

Figure 10. "2N" DBMS architecture. Although the application (front-end) and server (back-end) are shown here on different systems, they can be operated together on a single system.

Configuration and Capacity Planning for Solaris Servers

Multithreaded implementations are designed to avoid the extra expense of managing so many processes, and typically have a single cluster of a few processes running on the server system (generally one per physical CPU). These processes are internally multithreaded so that they service requests from multiple clients. Most of the major vendors use a multithreaded implementation or are moving in that direction.

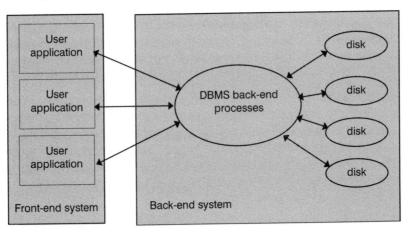

Figure 11. Multithreaded DBMS architecture. As with 2N systems, nothing prevents front-end and back-end processes from running on the same system.

Although the multithreaded model seems conceptually more appealing, in practice it is not necessarily the most efficient or highest–performing solution, despite having the advantage of less context-switching. In particular, 2N implementations seem to scale better on multiprocessors, possibly because they place greater reliance on the operating system's scalability. These 2N implementations are also more susceptible to optimization through the use of transaction monitors. Nothing inherent to multithreaded implementations causes them to run more slowly or to scale more poorly than 2N systems; the current situation probably reflects development history more than technical necessity.

Table 8. DBMS server architectures by vendor and version

Multithreaded	2N
Oracle Version 7 (optional)	Oracle Version 6, default in Oracle Version 7
Sybase v4.9.x, System 10, System 11	Informix v5.x and v6.x
Ingres v6.x, v7.x	Ingres v5.x
Progress version 7, version 8	Progress version 6
ADABAS version 2.1	DB2 version 2.1

3.3 DBMS Implementations

Even when two DBMS engines share basic system architecture, they often choose to implement that architecture in different ways. One notable example is how the engines store data on disk. Some, such as Ingres, choose to store database files in the standard UNIX file system, while others can bypass the operating systems' file system and operate directly on the raw disk devices. Each strategy has advantages and disadvantages. Although they have little impact on the services provided to end users, the differences are germane to configuring the system (the particulars of choosing between raw and file system database storage are discussed in section 3.5.4, *Disk I/O Subsystems* later in this chapter).

Sometimes options that appear to be the same are implemented differently. Good examples are *disk striping* and *mirroring*. For example, Oracle offers disk *concatenation*, although it is commonly referred to as striping. For many purposes, the two are equivalent, but for a serial table scan, they perform quite differently, because the Oracle concatenation only involves one disk at a time, whereas lower–level disk striping can activate multiple disk arms. The mirroring offered by Informix 5.1 and Sybase System 10 correctly and completely implement the availability features normally associated with disk mirroring, but they do not offer disk load balancing across submirrors, a feature that can have a dramatic effect on disk performance.

Another area that distinguishes database implementations is their internal locking strategy. Higher algebra shows that a specific order for locking data can guarantees adequate lock coverage without deadlocks. Unfortunately, this safe locking order is one of the least efficient strategies in a multi-user environment, and DBMS vendors spend considerable time optimizing their locking strategies. Many different tradeoffs are available to the developers, and their choices can result in very different performance for a given task, even if overall performance between implementations does not differ very much.

Of significance at other times are a DBMS's internal latching strategy and execution, which vary widely between DBMS implementations. (*Locks* and *latches* are often confused. Users can manipulate locks to some degree, because they apply to user–created entities. Latches are entities that are internal to the DBMS itself, and are used to control access to components within the DBMS, such as its internal tables; latches are analogous to *mutexes* within Solaris. The user has no control over latching behavior.)

Another area where the various engines differ widely is in their query optimizers. Most simple SQL statements have only one execution strategy, but complex queries may be executed in many semantically equivalent ways, with performance varying over an astonishing range. This situation is particularly true of statements that use the `join` operator, which requests that the DBMS combine two or more tables together in a cross–product. Different optimizers are able to take advantage of specific implementation information that may not be available or that might mean something quite different in another implementation.

All query optimizers have internal rules that govern their behavior. Sometimes these rules can cause apparently identical systems to behave completely differently. For example, one benchmark ran six times slower when moved to a much larger platform, although the disk layout was identical. Days of debugging eventually revealed that the query optimizer had come to a decision point while executing a join between two tables. With no meaningful information as to which table to select from first, it chose the table that appeared in the system catalog first—i.e., the table that had been created earlier in time. Because the database had been created by hand, the tables had been created in different orders. Because the size of the selected portions of the two joined tables differed by a factor of more than 10,000, constraining first by the table with less relevant information caused the benchmark to run *much* faster! This particular problem has been corrected by the vendor, but it illustrates the complexity associated with these systems.

3.4 Application Load Characterization

As if having all of the underlying DBMS engines be completely different were not complex enough, sizing a system for the purpose of solving a specific business problem is even harder. Applications are even more diverse than the database engines, partly because the DBMS is a functional kernel that forms the basis for applications, and partly because of the sheer number and diversity of problems that need to be solved. Even the protocol exchanged between the client application and the DBMS service provider is not universal. Although all of the popular packages implement some form of the Structure Query Language (SQL), each implementation has its own extensions and peculiarities. Most software developers host their applications on more than one DBMS platform, and the applications take on a sort of skewed behavior as they adapt to the strengths and weaknesses of their host DBMS. A package that operates very efficiently on a given hardware platform with one DBMS may perform much better or much worse on identical hardware and another DBMS.

Unlike NFS, where it *is* possible to understand the load imposed on a server without knowing the details of an application, characterizing the load generated by a database application is impossible without detailed information about what the application actually does. Even with this knowledge, many assumptions must be made as to how the DBMS system will access data, which strategy the DBMS's query optimizer will take on a given SQL statement, how effective the DBMS's disk cache might be on specific transactions, or even what the mix of transactions might be.

3.4.1 Application Categories

DBMS applications can be divided into three broad categories: online transaction processing (OLTP), batch processing, and decision support systems (DSS). Applications in these three categories usually make completely different kinds of demands on their host systems.

In this context, the term "application" really means a single program, rather than the typical application suite. Most DBMS applications are really suites of applications, and often the various members of the suite fall into different categories. An order–entry application has the characteristics of OLTP, yet the reports that describe periodic performance or that perform internal reorganization or consistency checking fall clearly into the batch processing category. At the same time, the database may be occasionally searched on an ad-hoc basis to support decision makers.

Classifying a candidate application makes it possible to get an idea of what sort of system components will be required to support that application.

3.4.1.1 Online Transaction Processing (OLTP)

Online transaction processing systems typically support standardized queries, usually for many users whose only interaction with the system is through a single application. Examples are customer–service or customer–order applications in which operators answer phone calls and place orders or query order status via a computer system. Users of such systems run only stored queries created by knowledgeable application developers. Furthermore, and probably more relevant for configuration purposes, queries are nearly always keyed; the queries can be satisfied using a few random–access disk operations. For example, a call to your bank to ascertain the status of a check is unlikely to result in the bank retrieving anyone's records besides yours.

OLTP applications often spend as much time formatting and presenting the data they spend retrieving the data. Many OLTP applications are read–only; for example, order–status applications retrieve a customer's record, and both the customer table and the transaction table are normally indexed by customer name or id. The DBMS is able to retrieve the desired records without having to search the entire table. In addition, the amount of data that is handled is relatively small, because the vast majority of queries return only a handful of records. Because the queries are known in advance, they can be pre-compiled and stored in the DBMS's data dictionary, minimizing the overhead of running the query. Finally, the database administrator can easily optimize the database layout to accommodate the well-known queries.

3.4.1.2 Batch Processing

The traditional "data processing" application is a batch–oriented system. The typical company's payroll processing system is a classic batch application. For each pay cycle, the system goes through the entire list of employees, computing the relevant payroll amounts and printing checks and other associated reports as it updates each record with a "check issued" field. As with an OLTP application, accesses to the databases are created by application programmers, and the database administrator can account for their characteristics well in advance.

Unlike OLTP applications, batch processing is dominated by long sequential table scans and sometimes by frequent updates to the database. Batch applications rarely have a user interface, and the effort of formatting the data is nearly always dwarfed by the business of finding, processing, and updating the data. Note that these requirements are diametrically opposite to the requirements of OLTP applications!

3.4.1.3 Decision Support Systems (DSS)

Decision support systems, the third primary category of applications is, by a wide margin, the hardest to characterize. Decision–support applications are semantically extremely diverse. Many of them are simply interfaces for ad-hoc queries; all of them provide users with the ability to create and execute complex new queries that were not pre–compiled. Because the queries can only be estimated in advance, the database administrator can only guess as to what queries will be demanded of the system.

Furthermore, experience indicates that the typical decision support query is six orders of magnitude—a million times!—more resource-intensive than typical queries in OLTP environments. Because of the very diverse and ad–hoc nature of decision support queries, it is very difficult for database administrators or the DBMS itself to provide extensive, useful optimization. Nearly all DSS queries involve some sort of aggregation and sort criteria, and quite possibly one or more multi–way joins.

Perhaps the most volatile element in the DSS application is the user. Most users of decision support systems are not database engineers or administrators; they have little or no understanding of the relationship between a particular query and the amount of work that query might generate on the host system. DSS users also tend to be relatively highly placed in the organizational structure, and tend to have responsibility for many functional areas. Compare this situation with the telephone operator's responsibility to a single customer at time. As a result of their wider organizational responsibilities, DSS users often use data from disparate organizations and information sources; often the various tables were not expected to be used together, with predictable negative consequences.

The author has seen queries that can be expressed very reasonably in human terms turn into essentially impossible SQL queries. In one case, a user submitted a complex but perfectly ordinary-looking query that translated into a *thirteen* way join on tables consisting of tens of thousands of records, involving a—very theoretical—intermediate file of some 10^{30} records! The size of the intermediate table was theoretical because the server attempting to process this query had 32 MB of memory and 5 GB bytes of disk space.

A useful observation is that DSS and DSS-related applications—such as online analysis and data mining—are not merely quantitatively removed from traditional transaction processing schemes. They are *qualitatively* different. Traditional data processing is concerned with recording individual transactions and their direct results. In contrast, DSS applications are primarily concerned with the characterization of entire groups or classes of transactions. Because of the large number of transactions applicable to most businesses, the new domains are wholly different. In general, a decision-support application is about three orders of magnitude—a thousand times—more resource-intensive than the corresponding transaction processing application that produces its data. Table 9 summarizes the characteristics of the application classes.

Table 9. Characteristics of the Broad Application Classes

Application Class	DBMS Processing	Application Processing	Presentation or GUI	Dominant Disk Access Pattern
OLTP	light	light	moderate	random
Batch	moderate	moderate to heavy	nil	sequential
Decision support	heavy	light to heavy	light	sequential

3.4.1.4 Application Processing Weight

Although most users are aware of the issue, the extent of user processing bears a very large impact on the sizing of a system. For example, SAP/R3 is layered on various DBMS platforms, one of which is Oracle, and some of its modules perform functions such as General Ledger that are similar to what other applications packages offer. In this context, many users have asked, "How many Oracle users can I run on system X?" However, SAP/R3 is implemented in an internal interpreted language, primarily to accommodate the customization needed by the end user organization. Unfortunately, this technique can sometimes consume a great deal of processor time per unit of work—far more than otherwise seemingly equivalent traditional compiled–code applications.

Another example of application weight is the use of a non-traditional front–end interface. For example, one user discovered that the natural language interpreter that translated from English to SQL consumed as much processor time as the application and database combined. Furthermore, the natural-language processor was being front-ended by speech-recognition software, which also was equivalent in weight to the application!

3.4.2 The TPC Benchmarks

Just as the SPEC consortium provides specifications and run rules for the LADDIS NFS server benchmark, the Transaction Processing Performance Council (TPC) specifies the benchmarks that dominate the database world. To date, the TPC has specified four benchmarks, known as the TPC–A, TPC–B, TPC–C, and TPC–D. These are the primary ways that the performance and capacity of DBMS servers are compared. The benchmarks are described here because they are common yardsticks against which systems are measured—and sometimes sized. An understanding of what the benchmarks actually measure is crucial to their appropriate use.

The TPC specifies the actions that the benchmark program(s) must implement; for example, it specifies the generation of data to use in the database, the appearance of the user screens in the TPC–C, the response-time constraints in all of the benchmarks, and the size and logical layout of the databases. In order to avoid biasing any test results, the TPC provides only specifications rather than actual programs. Each vendor implements code that performs the specified actions; the actual program codes are normally considered proprietary to each vendor. However, the TPC imposes extremely strict rules for reporting results branded with the TPC label. Any result not fully audited by a TPC–approved auditor must be labeled something generic like "estimated tps" (meaning estimated transactions per second).

Each TPC benchmark results in some throughput metric, such as "TPC–C transactions per minute." Vendors must provide a price/performance metric with every throughput score, preventing a vendor from overwhelming a benchmark through the sheer application of hardware. Vendors must price the entire configuration, including hardware (even terminals), software, and middleware. Pricing must be "publicly available."

The benchmark specifications mandate maximum response time for each transaction type, meaning that for practical purposes transaction latency is fixed for all vendors. None of the benchmark standards specify criteria for manageability, ease–of–use, or practicality. For example, very few DBMS systems should be implemented without some form of RAID storage protection. Yet no results have yet been published with protected storage, since storage protection obviously costs both money and performance, while not fulfilling any requirements specified in the benchmark definition.

3.4.3 TPC-A and TPC–B

Both the TPC–A and TPC–B benchmarks descended from a pre–TPC benchmark known as Debit/Credit or TP1. All of these benchmarks emulate the actions of a bank handling automatic teller transactions. The primary difference between the TPC benchmarks and their predecessors is the *much* tighter rules on database scaling and especially on the reporting of results.

The TPC–A version of this benchmark requires that the tested system deliver its results to terminals, and thus must at least perform the presentation. Note that the term "tested system" typically refers to an entire complex of systems operating in a client/server configuration, even though the result is normally associated with the machine that runs the database engine. The benchmark specification mandates both think time and guaranteed response time. The TPC–B version of the benchmark does away with the terminals and presentation services and tests only a back-end database engine with no think time.

3.4.3.1 The TPC–A/B Transaction

The TPC-A and TPC-B benchmarks specify a single transaction simple enough to quote:

```
void TPC_A ()
{
    scanf("%ld %ld %ld %ld", &branch, &teller, &acct, &delta);
    BEGIN TRANSACTION
    UPDATE account
        SET balance = balance + @delta
        WHERE number = @acct
    SELECT @balance = balance
        from account
        where number = @acct
    UPDATE  teller
      SET  balance = balance + @delta
      WHERE number = @teller
    UPDATE  branch
      SET  balance = balance + @delta
      WHERE number = @branch
    INSERT history
      (account, teller, branch, amount, amounti,
       timestmp, location, other)
    VALUES
      (@acct, @teller, @branch, @delta, 0, getdate(), @location, "null")
    COMMIT TRANSACTION
    printf (%ld %ld %ld %ld\n", balance, teller, acct);
}
```

This transaction simulates the handling of automatic teller transactions that withdraw amounts from various accounts. The most useful piece of information is that the transaction merely moves the account balances around, doing absolutely no verification of input, balances, or output.

The table sizes are scaled by the reported transaction rate, in order to prevent a very fast processor from reporting a very high transaction rate by simply caching a small database entirely in memory. In a real application, demand for a larger transaction rate is virtually always accompanied by a larger user population—and a much larger database. The three tables are:

- a small one containing branch information (100 bytes/transaction/ sec),
- one for teller information (1 Kbytes/transaction/sec), and
- a fairly large one for customer accounts (10 Mbytes/transactions/sec).

Transaction histories must be maintained to the tune of 130 Mbytes/transactions/sec.

3.4.3.2 The TPC–A "Application"

The TPC-A transaction itself is quite simple: presentation services are nearly non–existent, and application processing is almost completely absent. As can be seen from the listing above, the entire "application" consists of exactly one call to `scanf(3)` and one call to `printf(3)`! Few applications have lower processing requirements.

3.4.3.3 I/O Requirements

The I/O requirements for TPC–A are quite interesting. If the host DBMS system has been well tuned, the TPC–A/B transaction requires the I/O system to do approximately 1.0 reads and about 1.1 writes to disk for each transaction. Each transaction reads once, writes once, and posts an update to the log. Many transactions happen very quickly, so the log process is able to batch log requests together. These disk I/O operations move 4.5 Kbytes of data per transaction. A server that delivers about 1,000 transactions per second on TPC–A thus consumes less than 5 Mbytes/sec of disk I/O bandwidth. Both the data rates and the amount of data moved are much lower than those found in virtually any real applications.

3.4.3.4 Using TPC–A Results

As with the LADDIS benchmark, systems and tuning for TPC–A have overtaken the relevance of the benchmark results themselves. For example, at this writing (mid 1996), mid–range systems would be regarded as "completely uncompetitive" if they delivered "only" 10,000 tps–A. However, banks that actually run automatic teller networks report that sustained transaction rates are typically less than *one* transaction per second, and peak rates never exceed 100 transactions per second, even in large state-wide networks. One bank, which operates a state-wide teller network, reported that its peak instantaneous transaction rate for 1991 was *seven* transactions per second. Even five years late, real transaction rates are well under 100 transactions per second.

Of course, a real ATM must do much more work than simply manage the balances, since it must also validate the user's card and also enforce other kinds of security (such as ensuring that a card cannot be used at two machines fifty miles apart within five minutes). In practice these "peripheral" activities consume many more resources than the actual task of managing the customer account. The point here is not to criticize the design of the benchmark, but rather to illustrate how representative of real applications it is (not).

> Caution: Many users, faced with the problem of sizing and configuring a
> system for their own business, attempt to size their purchase by counting
> their transactions and then selecting a system whose TPC–A score is similar.
> *because of the lightweight nature of the TPC-A design, this is always a serious
> mistake.*

3.4.4 TPC-B

The TPC-B benchmark was intended to test the server portion of a client/server configuration. Accordingly, it is a less-elaborate version of the TPC-A . It uses the same database schema and runs the same transaction, but it eliminates the already trivial application processing, as well as user think time. Transactions requests are transmitted to the server from client systems, which are presumed to have performed all of the transaction preprocessing and presentation services. Because think time is eliminated, reported TPC-B transaction rates are much higher than for TPC-A running on the same platform. For obvious reasons, the TPC-B suffers from the same problems that afflict the TPC-A.

Although TPC–A is somewhat useful as an "apples–to–apples" comparison, its single transaction, light I/O demand, and nearly non–existent application processing render it irrelevant for sizing real systems. Because of these issues and others, the TPC has now withdrawn the TPC–A and TPC–B benchmarks. The Council prohibits publication of new results on either of the old benchmarks.

3.4.5 TPC–C

Because the TPC–A has so many shortcomings, the TPC created a new benchmark, which was approved in 1992. Called TPC–C, this code is *much* more complex than its predecessor, and as a result it accurately represents at least one class of real OLTP applications.

Although not all of the various proposals were accepted, many details were changed in TPC–C to make the benchmark more representative of real applications. Instead of a single transaction, the newer benchmark uses five different types of transactions. Some of the transactions are direct responses to user requests, while others are absentee batch requests. The TPC-C transactions are far more diversified than TPC -A. Some of the TPC-C transactions require deletes and inserts in addition to the updates used in TPC–A. Serial table scans are required to support the batch transactions, and the indexed transactions have skew in the retrievals; furthermore, the tables are multiply indexed. Many more data types are exercised; in particular, variable length character strings and time data types are used extensively.

The TPC–C score is reported in transactions per *minute*, and is abbreviated "tpm-C." Note that the time units are quite different from TPC–A, which are reported in transactions per *second*. The substantial variance in units reflects the relative weight and sophistication of the two benchmarks.

3.4.5.1 The TPC–C Model

The benchmark simulates the functional core processing associated with a large retailer's warehousing activity. The warehouse has a stock (30 MB), item descriptions (8 MB), customers (20 MB), a number of geographic districts for such things as local tax rates (1 KB), and orders. Each order has summary information and line items; the order information is about 7 MB, and the line items are an additional 16 MB. These sizes are raw data sizes, so each warehouse will normally consume about 180 MB of disk space after accounting for indexing and other overhead. The database is scaled with the delivered transaction rate by using multiple warehouses. Since each warehouse has ten terminals and a reported transaction rate of approximately one transaction per terminal per minute, one warehouse is required for every reported 10 tpm–C.

3.4.5.2 The TPC–C Transactions

Instead of a single transaction that retrieves and updates individual previously existing records via an index, the TPC–C defines five different transactions:

- New Order—create a delivery order; all of the items must be valid. Stocking levels are updated, reflecting stock that is reserved for the order. Parts are not uniformly ordered, and order frequency varies widely. One of the significant but often overlooked characteristics of the TPC-C reporting rules is that only new order transactions are reported in the score; the others are only present to generate load. Note that the *other* transactions are defined to be 57 percent of the overall workload. Ordinarily the new orders represent 43 percent of the workload, but if the host system is short of resources, new orders can represent far less than 43 percent of all transactions.
- Order Status—retrieve an order by either customer id number or by customer name. Some customer names are duplicated in the database, and handling this is sometimes non–trivial. This transaction is 4 percent of the load.
- Payment—record payment of invoice against the associated order. This transaction is a direct descendent of the TPC–A transaction, although it specifies customers by either id or name. Payments represent 44 percent of the transactions.

- Delivery—update the database to reflect orders that have been delivered. The delivery transaction is a small batch operation; it updates 10 orders. Four percent of the workload are delivery transactions.

- Stock–Level—inquire how many items that were recently ordered have a stocking level below a threshold. Although this transaction is easily described in human terms, it is surprisingly I/O–intensive, because it is a statistical query that requires reading many candidate records. Unlike the other transactions, the stock-level transaction requires significant I/O as a result of a tablescan operation. Although stock-level is numerically only four percent of the transactions in the overall workload, this transaction consumes system resources disproportionate to its apparent frequency.

Each transaction has specific rules, such as think time, keying time, required response time, how to pick among duplicate customer names, etc. For obvious reasons, the TPC –C represents a much more intensive load than its predecessor.

3.4.5.3 The TPC–C Application

Unlike the TPC–A, a significant proportion of the TPC–C test is presentation. Real users must be emulated with a remote terminal emulator (RTE), and each transaction has a complex screen with a defined format. Input must be validated, status must be updated, etc.—all things that real applications must do to be considered viable. As a result, presentation is a lot of work, and most vendors have been forced to optimize code in the presentation path that the TPC–A completely ignored.

Although accurately comparing the five TPC–C transactions with the single TPC–A transaction is difficult, studies at Sun have shown that the TPC–C application consumes about *thirty* times more processor power per reported transaction than TPC–A.

3.4.5.4 TPC-C I/O Requirements

As could be expected from such a large change in the benchmark, TPC –C requirements place much more stress on the I/O subsystems than TPC–A. Gray and Reuter reported the following typical I/O rates[14]:

---

[14] Gray and Reuter, *Transaction Processing: Concepts and Principles.*

Table 10. I/O requirements for TPC transactions

Transaction	Reads	Writes
New Order	23	23
Payment	4	4
Order Status	14	0
Delivery	130	130
Stock Level	410	0
TPC–A	1	1.1

Studies at Sun show that the I/O rates associated with reported TPC–C transactions are more than 15 times those seen with TPC–A (70 KB/sec compared to 4.5 KB/sec). This corresponds to an aggregate I/O rate of slightly more than 24 MB/sec of I/O for a system that delivers slightly over 21,000 transactions per minute and supports thousands of users. This figure undoubtedly seems absurdly low in an age where individual disk drives can deliver up to 9 MB/sec, but it is representative of most OLTP-style applications. Note that even this figure requires over 120 disk drives running at full utilization, because nearly all of the I/O is random-access, limiting each disk to about 800-950 KB/sec throughput (refer to section 7.1.2, *Disk Access Patterns* for a more complete discussion).

3.4.5.5 Using TPC–C Results

Because of the complexity of the TPC–C benchmark, users who have relatively simple OLTP requirements can use it the way people would like to use TPC–A results. Compute the number of similar transactions required and find a system with a TPC–C score that is similar. However, bear in mind that 57 percent of the TPC–C transactions are *not* reported in the score, and that some or all of these might be more important than the 43 percent of new orders that are reported.

For larger concerns, consider that even the TPC–C benchmark does not address more complex components of a real application. In particular, the specification does not include requirements for performing referential integrity checks. Modern applications use this feature to help ensure that the database stays consistent. The function is extremely useful, but it can be costly. A relatively simple transaction such as deleting a customer name may cause the firing of a long cascade of referential integrity triggers. This can turn a seemingly simple transaction into a very complex one. Naturally, the complexity of the integrity checks increases rapidly as the database itself gets more and more complex.

3.4.6 TPC–D

The TPC has recognized that even the much more rigorous TPC–C does not even begin to address decision support applications. To better quantify performance in this area, as well as to spur vendors to do additional development and testing in related areas, the TPC has defined a new benchmark, known as "TPC–D." This benchmark was approved in April 1995, and a few vendors—including Sun—have published results. TPC -D scores are reported as a *power metric* and a price/performance metric. The power metric is a direct indication of how fast the set of queries are completed; larger power metrics reflect shorter run times.

3.4.6.1 The TPC–D Model

The new benchmark consists of 17 different retrieval queries and two update queries, operating on a nominal database of about 650 MB of data. The queries are oriented toward the *ad–hoc* reporting characteristic of decision support applications. The 650 MB of raw data requires about 400 MB of indexes, and efficient operation requires about 400 MB of temporary space! The TPC–D defines a data generator program, because a 650 MB database is unrealistically small (virtually all decision support databases hosted on Solaris systems presently occupy in excess of 60 GB, and 600 GB-1.5 TB is becoming common). The generator is able to create correctly scaled databases of arbitrary size. A TPC–D database consisting of 1 TB of raw data is said to be of *scale factor* 1,000 (written SF1000) because it is 1,000 times the size of the reference data set. Implementing a SF1000 database requires at least 1.6 TB of actual disk space after accounting for indexing and temporary space. In practice, access capacity considerations and protected storage (e.g., mirroring or RAID -5) are factored in, most SF1000 databases occupy in excess of 3 TB of disk drives.

3.4.6.2 TPC–D I/O Requirements

The TPC–D benchmark uses full–table scans, multi–way joins, sorting, aggregation, and statistical queries, many of which are extremely I/O–intensive. During Sun's first audited TPC-D run, researchers at Sun observed sustained disk I/O transfer rates in excess of 170 MB/sec, even when operating on behalf of only a single query stream [15]. To put this workload in perspective, an NFS server delivering 21,000 NFSops/sec has to move data at about 62 MB/sec, but this workload represents support for 2,100 users! Likewise, the TPC -C requires about 24 MB/sec to handle something over 20,000 users. These I/O r ates helped deliver a TPC-D power metric of 625 on an Ultra Enterprise 6000 using a scale 100 database.

---

[15] More recent studies at Sun suggest that the maximum aggregate disk-to-host throughput on Solaris 2.5.1 is on the order of 875 MB/sec. This requires a fully-configured Ultra Enterprise 6000 system and hundreds of disk drives.

3.4.6.3 TPC-D Processor Requirements

One of the key characteristics of the TPC-D benchmark is that it consumes an astonishing amount of processor time. The TPC-D makes extensive use of parallel queries. This in turn places enormous demands on the system's processing capability. As with other operating system functions, initiating and processing disk I/O operations consumes a finite, non-zero amount of processor time. At these sustained rates, even the relatively efficient Solaris kernel async I/O subsystem consumes significant processor power.

The largest demand on the processor, though, is servicing the higher-order DBMS logic required to process the complex TPC-D queries. Much of the processor time is devoted to handling things like type conversions (for example from integer to date) and internal sorting and query optimization algorithms. Sun's Ultra Enterprise 6000 required 24 167 MHz/512 KB UltraSPARC processors to attain the 625 power metric.

3.4.7 Client/Server Computing

Probably the most controversial topic in configuring for large DBMS applications today is whether or not to "go client/server," and if so, how to do it. Two basic computing models are available today: *client/server* and *host–based* (often called timesharing). The host–based model is easy to describe and understand: a computer system runs the application and all of the services it relies upon. User interaction is handled with a terminal or X-terminal (or a PC emulating a terminal). The client/server model runs the application on more than one computer—on *many* computers, in some complex cases.

3.4.7.1 What Is Client/Server Computing?

A great deal of confusion exists in the industry about just what client/server computing is. Some vendors promote the use of a server with X-terminals as "client/server," while others insist that client/server computing can only be accomplished in peer–to–peer configurations with high–powered workstations. Naturally, as with any controversial debate, the most useful position is somewhere between the two.

A surprising proportion of users equate client/server computing with the use of a graphical user interface (GUI). Undoubtedly this perception is due to the client/server terminology used in the X11 environment. However, for the purposes of achieving high performance, redeployable, and particularly highly–available database systems, graphical user interfaces are orthogonal to the issue at hand: they are not required, nor are they out of place.

Client/server is also often equated with "rightsizing a mainframe," but this association has more to do with the typical application environment than any particular association with mainframes. In fact, a common scenario leaves the database engine on a mainframe, while running application business logic on open system servers and presentation logic on workstations or PCs. In such scenarios, client/server is often a strategy for relieving the pressure for expansion of an existing mainframe, by moving some proportion of the processing load (the application itself) off the mainframe onto less expensive hardware.

For our purposes, client/server means a configuration in which a single application is divided into two or more components operating on fully functional different computer systems. It does *not* refer to the use of any sort of display terminal that cannot run applications—that is, an X-terminal falls into the same category as a traditional ASCII terminal. All of the following arrangements are client/server operations:

- a system running the DBMS server, with each instance of the actual user application(s) running on a PC with Windows;
- a system running the DBMS server, with all instances of the user application(s) running on a single time–shared system that is a different system than the DBMS server;
- a system running the DBMS server and a transaction processing monitor, with instances of the user application running on workstations; and
- a system running instances of the application, with several systems running DBMS servers and the GUI being displayed on X-terminals.

On the other hand, *none* of the following configurations are client/server:

- a system running the DBMS server *and* the user applications, with the GUI being displayed on X-terminals;
- a system running the DBMS, with the users accessing the DBMS system by `telnet`'ing from PCs running X-windows; and
- a system running the DBMS and the application programs; the applications are separate programs and access the DBMS via a transaction monitor.

The essential difference between these two categories is that in the first category, the application is divided onto two (or more) systems that are independent. In the second category, the application processing is being hosted on a single system. For a variety of reasons, the client/server organization is the superior architecture from a performance and flexibility standpoint.

This particular organization is common primarily because database access is the best developed service; at least fifteen different DBMS implementations are available today. Currently available technologies such as automatic RPC program generators, along with Sun's ToolTalk registry system, make it easier to create other services. Products such as the various object services (SunSoft's NEO, HP's ObjectBroker, NeXTstep, etc.) will provide an even more flexible approach to creating client/server applications.

3.4.8 Why Client/Server?

On the face of it, it is hard to understand why one might want to take something that may work well on a single system and make it work on multiple systems. Clearly it involves additional complexity, in terms of initial estimation, ongoing operational management, and capacity planning in the future. But a number of factors mean that some form of client/server will be the preferred computing architecture. They have to do with the economics of building large computers and its consequent impact on overall scalability, the almost overwhelming amount of available computing cycles in already–installed desktop computers, high–availability concerns, and the ability to manage change in large application environments.

3.4.8.1 Computer Architecture and Microcomputer Economics

The economics of computer and operating system design are such that it is *much* easier and less expensive to build a hundred small computers than a single system that is a hundred times as powerful as one of the smaller ones. Building a system backplane capable of transferring 1 GB/sec is straightforward using 1996 technology. At the same time, building a backplane capable of transferring 1 TB/sec is far more complex and expensive; it is definitely not straightforward. One gigabyte/sec can be attained with easily obtainable commodity parts or at worst with application–specific integrated circuits (ASICs), whereas the much faster version must be completely custom designed. This disparity applies to far more than backplane busses; it applies to the design of processors, memory, I/O units, networks, operating systems, database management systems, and applications.

Many of the large applications now being developed or deployed in government and in large businesses are designed to service hundreds of users. Many are intended for user populations numbering in the thousands or even in the tens of thousands. For user populations of this size, designing and implementing single-system solutions is usually impractical and also economically unjustifiable if not technically impossible. The solution is to opt for client/server solutions that spread the work across multiple smaller systems in effective ways. The techniques used to construct these very large systems also apply to smaller applications meant for populations of 50-150 users.

3.4.8.1.1 Optimizing for Roles

Breaking an application into pieces and distributing the computation onto different computer systems provides the opportunity to more closely tailor the various computing elements to actual processing functions. Timesharing systems must be very generalized resources because they must potentially cater to any—or *every*—type of activity. In peer-to-peer installations, a database server can be configured and tuned to provide excellent database service, while client systems can be configured and tuned as application processors and/or display systems. Since the systems used as network components are generally smaller than a large timesharing system, they are less expensive and can be devoted to single classes of work.

One of the key factors is the relative scarcity of cache memory in all systems. Although current Solaris–based systems have caches ranging in size from 6 KB to 128 MB (64 processors, each with 2 MB caches), these are always very small compared to main memory sizes ranging from 16 MB to 30,720 MB. Cache is effectively the processor's gateway to memory. The size of the cache in a system is a fixed quantity, and preserving the cache's contents is a key factor in maintaining high performance (cache can be accessed in as little as one cycle, while main memory is 28-190 cycles away, depending on platform and circumstances). When a system must service a large number of functions, it is not able to consistently retain the relevant parts of any of those functions in cache. This limitation reduces the effectiveness of the processor, because a cache miss usually stalls the processor. When a new function is added to the system that causes the cache to miss much more frequently, that new function does not get the whole bill. The new function's code displaces other code or data in the cache, and in the process the system suffers high execution time because loads from memory take much longer than normal. Once the new function is in cache, it runs efficiently. Unfortunately, after the new function executes, the original owner of those cache lines will have to reload them—but because the original owner is now executing, the process that caused the original displacement is not charged for the increased. The original owner is the one that then sees much higher execution time!

3.4.8.1.2 Scalability

As application systems and user populations grow ever larger, the scalability of the processing systems becomes more and more important. Large user communities require correspondingly greater resources, and constructing monolithic systems to support them is both difficult and expensive. Client/server systems are usually easier to "scale up" than more traditional computing models. Part of the reason is that systems can be dedicated to service provision. If the load requires it, the biggest available (or affordable) system can be applied solely to the single task of providing the required service. The same system applied in a timesharing configuration will necessarily support fewer users, since it must carry the additional burden of application processing.

As the application approaches the limits of available or affordable technology, vendors must provide ever-larger systems. The finite ability of processor caches mentioned earlier is one example of how multiple systems scale better than large monolithic systems. Most current enterprise–class servers use symmetric multiprocessing (SMP) operating systems. Although symmetric multiprocessing is a well-known technology, and most vendors are now able to deliver SMP systems that scale to relatively large numbers of users, the technique appears to reach a point of diminishing returns. For example, Solaris 2.5 is able to scale to 20-24 processors even in unfavorable circumstances[16], and to 40–50 processors for more common types of applications. However, as applications grow, even 64–processor systems may become insufficient. Client/server configurations are one form of clustered computing, the next logical step for applying increased processing power to applications.

One of the primary reasons why client/server configurations are highly scalable is that they usually provide individual users with some dedicated processing capability. For example, in most client/server configurations, the user's desktop system executes the code that provides presentation services. The server system executes only logically shared services such as the database back-end. Because of the complete isolation of the front–end code on what amounts to a dedicated system, the front–end portion of the application is completely scalable. Additionally, this arrangement has the significant benefit of isolating users from each other; one user's activity has much less impact on other users than if they all share a single system.

3.4.8.1.3 Reuse of Existing Desktops

Modern desktop workstations and fast PCs are easily powerful enough (and expensive enough) to take on a large share of application processing. Furthermore, most users of major applications now already have desktop computers. Since these systems have a great deal of processing power, especially when considered as a group, and taking advantage of this large pool of already-available computing resources makes sense.

3.4.8.2 Reliability and Availability Considerations

Client/server configurations also provide opportunities for making the overall application system more reliable. This capability is especially valuable in the large user communities where client/server configurations are already more attractive for scalability reasons.

In a monolithic system, if a part of the system goes down, the entire system goes down—the application processors, the DBMS, etc. are all subject to the same constraint. The system cannot recover from such disasters because the entire computing resource fails. At best, failover to a secondary system requires the user to reestablish connection, restarting the application, even if a viable backup copy of the database is available. Without extensive preparation, such as the use of a fault-tolerant system or at least checkpointing to a multiported disk facility, a service interruption loses the user's application context.

In a peer-to-peer arrangement, the developer can take relatively simple precautions against the failure of a centralized resource and to ensure that application service continues

---

[16] Such as NFS, which executes *entirely* in kernel space. The primary factor determining scalability of SMP implementations is the locking strategy in the kernel. User applications are not subject to these restrictions except to the degree that they request kernel services.

uninterrupted. Because the application itself runs in the distributed desktops, failure of any one of the desktops does not affect the others. More important, if a service provider such as the DBMS fails, the application program is still running—it is not directly affected by the loss of the service provider. The user's application context is completely valid, allowing the developer to make arrangements to use an alternate service. If the secondary service is brought online quickly, the user may not even know that a failure has occurred. This capability is even more useful and flexible with the advent of the ftSPARC ™ fault-tolerant systems. Using a relatively small fault-tolerant system as a front-end to a highly-available cluster, processing can be made extremely resistant to failures, even if the workload demands more capability than can be economically provided in a single system.

3.4.8.3 Configuration Management Issues

One of the significant benefits of the client/server architecture is that the division of labor provides very clean ways to distribute the application across many systems. In most such cases, all access to the facility is directed through a single application programming interface that provides the ability to make connections to both local and remote servers. Once the application uses a client/server architecture, the overall system configuration can be modified in a relatively transparent fashion. Such reconfiguration is nearly impossible in a more traditional architecture when only one system is available.

Disruption of the user and application environment is thus held to a minimum. The ability to easily relocate data and services is one of the key advantages of peer -to-peer configurations.

3.4.8.4 Candidates for Client/Server

Client/server solutions are more attractive for some applications than others. Small applications by their nature generally do not encounter scaling problems, and often such applications often address a business problem of limited scope or importance. An infrastructure failure might disable the application without crippling the business.

The applications that most often require the unique abilities of client/server configurations are those that already pose some of the biggest challenges. Mission-critical applications that must remain available will rely upon the ability of application programs to gracefully survive the failure of one or more support services. Applications with large user communities often require the superior scalability offered by peer -to-peer configurations. Peer–to–peer solutions will lend themselves to businesses that have applications that use or acquire data that is partitioned into multiple domains, either literally (geographically) or logically for other business reasons.

In order to operate in a client/server configuration, the application must be suitably coded. The most important criterion is that the application be composed of logically separate functional units with relatively easily decomposed services. Additionally, the application cannot depend upon use of features that are inherently single-system, for example, shared memory. Most client/server applications rely upon an application programming interface that is network–transparent. For example, DBMS systems all have a way of transmitting an SQL statement from the client system to the server for processing, along with a defined mechanism for retrieving the results of the query.

Client/server is not mutually exclusive with traditional timesharing. If the client and server are binary compatible, they can feasibly and reasonably run a client/server application in a completely timesharing fashion under the right circumstances. Moreover, an application that is normally operated in client/server mode might be run in both client/server and timesharing configurations. For example, the accounting department might support its own users with individual systems in client/server mode, but casual users from outside the organization might timeshare a single client system. Of course, many of the advantages of the peer-to-peer arrangements are lost for those users who are supported via timesharing mode. This hybrid arrangement may also be useful during the development of the application.

3.4.8.5 Client/Server Performance

Most DBMS application systems consist of three logical parts: a user interface, some application processing, and a back-end DBMS service provider. The user interface and application processing are usually combined in a single executable program. Some sophisticated applications provide multithreaded front-end processing that is disconnected from presentation services. Increasingly, the back-end DBMS server is provided with a dedicated system, in order to provide as little interference as possible.

When feasible, use of the client/server model separating the front-end processing and presentation services from the DBMS provider provides a substantial improvement in overall system performance. This permits the critical resource—the DBMS provider—to operate undisturbed on its host system. This division of labor is particularly effective for systems that are dominated by presentation activities such as driving hundreds or thousands of terminals in `cbreak` mode. Most `curses-` (screen-) based programs use `cbreak` terminal handling today.

The opposite of client/server mode, "timesharing" mode, usually delivers higher performance only when the presentation requirements are *very* lightweight, or when the concurrent user load is light. Applications that have forms-based presentation are essentially never lightweight. Even applications that operate in a conversational `printf/gets` mode are sometimes sufficiently heavyweight to justify the use of client/server configurations. The difference between client/server and timesharing configurations is illustrated in Figure 12.

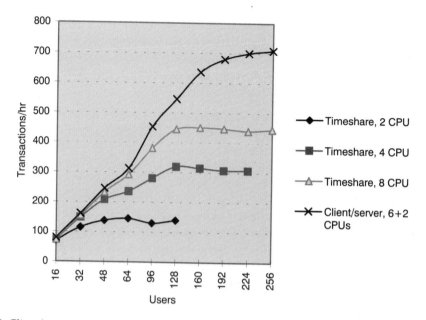

Figure 12. Client/server vs. timesharing models. The client/server configuration uses the same memory and processors as the single 8-CPU timesharing system. The timesharing system is an 8-CPU SPARCserver 1000E with 1 GB memory, while the client/server configuration has a 6-CPU SPARCserver 1000E with 768 MB and a 2-CPU SPARCserver 1000E with 256 MB memory.

A configuration that is becoming increasingly popular is the "three–tiered" model. In this arrangement, a dedicated server handles database services. Typically the DBMS requires a rather large system such as a SPARCcenter 2000E, Ultra Enterprise 5000, or HP9000/T520. Most application code runs on one of a few application servers in timesharing mode; in particular, each application server runs code on behalf of many users. Presentation services, and some of the application code runs on front–end systems, usually Wintel PCs. The application servers act as servers to the front–end PCs while simultaneously acting as clients of the DBMS server. The best–known application that is customarily deployed in three–tiered configurations is SAP/R3, but many application vendors are adopting the model. This general architecture is likely to increase in popularity in the future.

⇒ Configure in client/server mode where possible, unless front-end *and* presentation load are unusually light.
⇒ Back-end DBMS service providers should run on a dedicated system where this is possible.

3.4.8.6 Transaction Processing Monitors

The use of a transaction processing monitor is one method of achieving higher performance from a given configuration, especially in client/server mode. Transaction monitors are also sometimes useful for constructing heterogeneous logical databases from diverse, independent physical databases. For example, some data might be in one format (e.g., Oracle on a Sun) and other data in quite different form (perhaps Ingres on a VAX or IMS on an IBM mainframe). In addition, some TP monitors provide lightweight presentation services. The best-known TP monitor is IBM's Customer Information Control System (CICS) ; several CICS implementations (from IBM, MicroFocus, XDB, VI Systems, and Integris) are now available on Solaris platforms. Other TP monitors are Tuxedo/T from Bea, TopEnd from AT&T/NCR, and Encina from Transarc.

TP monitors achieve these results by interposing themselves between an application and the DBMS system or systems. The application must be modified to issue *transactions*, written in the TP monitor's language, rather than directly accessing the database through the usual mechanisms (such as various forms of embedded SQL). The application programmer is also responsible for writing a description file that maps transactions into specific database access in the native access language of the underlying DBMS system (SQL for nearly all UNIX DBMS systems).

Transaction monitors were originally developed on mainframes to avoid problems with communications and presentation overhead. When the first transaction monitors were developed (in the late 50s and early 60s), virtually any code for formatting output and handling remote terminals represented a substantial amount of overhead. Transaction monitors were designed to offload the formatting and other presentation services into a communications processor. This arrangement also reduced context switching overhead. Although these particular issues are not usually problematic today, the programming model created to solve these issues has been adapted to other applications.

3.4.8.6.1 Data Access Flexibility

TP monitors place few restrictions on the richness or complexity of the access to the underlying DBMS.A single transaction may issue a request for one set of data from a DB2 database on an IBM mainframe running MVS, another piece of data from a local Sybase database, and then merge the two data sets together for presentation to the application. The result can be the illusion that the data is stored in a unified database under control of a single DBMS system.

Because many existing legacy installations use CICS, migrating part or all of the databases associated with these systems can be accomplished with little disruption of the existing applications. All that is required is to physically migrate the data to the new platform and to modify the transaction description to use the data in the new location. The complexity of such migrations should not be underestimated, since they often require changes in data representation. One example might be translating from COBOL "PIC S9(12)V99" to C++ float, or from integer or floating point numbers to a DBMS "date" or money type. Some applications (perhaps most) may require changes in fundamental data organization, for example from IMS's network architecture to the relational architecture used by UNIX DBMS systems. However, the ability to preserve the processing and presentation sections of existing applications greatly reduces the complexity and risk associated with rehosting such applications.

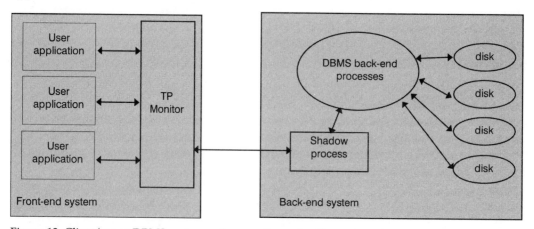

Figure 13. Client/server DBMS systems when configured with a transaction monitor. The shadow process on the back-end system only appears when the DBMS uses the "2N" architecture. Compare with Figure 10.

3.4.8.6.2 Performance Implications

In addition to the access flexibility afforded by the use of a TP monitor, performance benefits accrue from this arrangement. The TP monitor is always multithreaded. Because the TP monitor interposes itself between the application and the DBMS, it substantially reduces the number of concurrent DBMS processes actively accessing the database. Under most circumstances the DBMS services just a single "user"—the TP monitor. This function is particularly important when the DBMS is of the "2N" variety, because only one shadow process is used (to connect to the TP monitor), rather than one for each end-user process [17]. Compare the TP monitor configuration in Figure 13 with the equivalent 2N configuration in Figure 10 (page 82). This reduces the context switching overhead on the DBMS back-end system.

---

[17] The term "shadow process" is peculiar to Oracle. Informix calls the corresponding entity a "virtual processor."

TP monitors can also improve performance by reducing the amount of information transferred between the DBMS system and the application process. Because only the required data is made part of each transaction, data transfer can be reduced. This possibility is of particular importance when client and server are connected by a busy and/or low-bandwidth network, such as a wide-area network on satellite lines.

⇒ TP monitors can be considered when the application source code is available. Use TP monitors to integrate disparate sources of database information.

⇒ TP monitors are particularly useful for reducing client/server traffic on low-bandwidth or wide-area networks.

⇒ Consider a TP monitor when large user populations must be serviced and the DBMS in use prefers or requires the "2N" architecture.

3.5 Configuration Guidelines for DBMS Servers

Although this section offers configuration recommendations, the usefulness of these recommendations is strongly affected by application considerations. This fact cannot be overemphasized! The efficiency of the application and DBMS system are much more important than host configuration. There are hundreds of examples of small changes in applications or database schema making 100- or 1000-fold (or even greater!) improvements in performance. For example, a `select` statement that requests one specific record might cause the DBMS system to read one record from the tables or *every* record in the table, which might be 100 GB of data, depending upon whether or not the table is indexed by the lookup key. Often a table must be indexed by several keys to accommodate different access patterns generated by applications. Judicious indexing can have very dramatic effects on overall system performance. After systems are installed, they should be monitored to see if changes should be made to the database, even for internally developed or off-the-shelf third-party applications. Improving the performance of an application can often be accomplished simply by reorganizing the database, even without access to the application's source code.

Another consideration that receives little notice but that often has a dramatic effect on delivered performance is internal lock contention. The DBMS system must lock data against conflicting simultaneous access; any other process that requires access to this data will be unable to proceed until the holder of the lock releases it. Many times a system performs very poorly when locking strategy is less than optimal.

Each of the DBMS systems has a large number of tunable parameters, some of which can have dramatic effects on overall system performance. The recommendations provided here are predicated upon reasonably tuned applications and DBMS systems.

3.5.1 Checklist

The following questions summarize the process of arriving at a reasonably accurate DBMS configuration. The following sections describe how to determine configurations based upon this information.

- Which DBMS product is being used? Is it a "2N" or multithreaded implementation?
- What transaction processing monitors, if any, are being used?
- Can the application be operated in a client/server configuration?
- How many users will be simultaneously active?
- What is the basic or dominant disk access pattern?
- Which queries dominate the load?
- What is the indexing strategy? Which queries can be optimized by indexing (i.e. , are converted from serial access to random access) and which queries *must* be implemented by full- or partial-table scans?
- How big is the raw size of the database?
- Are the disk drives sufficient and properly organized to accommodate the anticipated *access* load? Are separate disk resources allocated for the various DBMS storage functions, such as logs, temporary tables, etc.?
- Is sufficient disk storage capacity configured to accommodate the raw data, the indexes, temporary table spaces, as well as room for data growth?
- Are sufficient processors configured to handle the anticipated users?
- Is a dedicated network between client and server systems required?
- If the anticipated load is heavily oriented toward updates, does the configuration have room for some sort of NVRAM write acceleration?
- Is the anticipated backup policy consistent with the type, number, and location of the backup devices?

3.5.2 Memory

Memory configuration usually has the largest impact of the various components of the DBMS server hardware. Although most people think of memory as storage for program execution, the majority of main memory in DBMS systems is used as a data cache to avoid doing physical disk I/O. Because access to memory is approximately 30,000 times faster than access to disk, minimization of disk I/O is of paramount importance [18]. Tinkering with other configuration parameters is futile if insufficient memory is available. If a configuration must be proposed without sufficient information—often the case—overestimating memory size is

---

[18] Memory can be accessed in about 500 ns, even under pessimistic conditions (a cache miss requiring a dirty line flush), whereas access to a disk takes about 15 milliseconds, or 15,000,000 nanoseconds. Even assuming that every byte on a page is accessed, this is still a factor of 2,000 slower.

much safer than underestimation. Fortunately, recovering from memory configuration mistakes is usually easy.

3.5.2.1 Sizing the DBMS I/O Cache

Each DBMS system names its data cache differently, but they all perform the same function. Oracle calls this memory the System Global Area (SGA), while Sybase calls it the Shared Data Cache. Informix refers to this entity as resident and virtual shared memory. Usually the cache is implemented as a large area of shared memory and is sized by a parameter in the DBMS's control files or tables. The size necessary for the DBMS disk cache varies widely by application, but the following rules of thumb can be used to arrive at a useful approximate size.

Practical experience with Oracle and Sybase has shown that cache areas can be productively sized anywhere from 4 MB to more than a gigabyte or even larger. As with any cache, increasing the cache size eventually reaches a point of diminishing returns. A *very* rough estimate of data cache size might be 50 KB to 300 KB per user. Each of the DBMS systems has a mechanism for reporting the efficiency of the shared data cache; most also can provide estimates as to what effects increasing or decreasing the cache size will have. One rule is sometimes called the "five-minute" rule, derived from the equation[19]:

$$Frequency = \frac{(Memory\ Cost\ per\ Byte - Disk\ Cost\ per\ Byte) \times Object\ Size}{Object\ Access\ per\ Second\ Cost}$$

Given current prices for memory, disks, and SCSI or FibreChannel subsystems, the break-even point works out to approximately five minutes, meaning that data that are accessed more frequently than about once every five minutes should be cached in memory. Accordingly, an estimate of the data cache size is the size of the total data that the application expects to use more frequently than once very five minutes *on a system-wide basis*. Allow at least this much space for the data cache. Additionally, reserve another 5-10 percent for storing the top levels of B-tree indexes, stored procedure code, and other DBMS control information.

Dramatically increasing the size of the cache usually results in diminishing returns. For example, experimental data suggests that sizing the DBMS cache larger than 2 GB pays almost no dividends in typical transaction processing environments, other than permitting support for more client connections. The sole exception to this rule of thumb is the case where the *entire* useful dataset can be cached, a technique known as *supercaching*. The supercaching technique is discussed extensively in section 9.1.5.3.

---

[19] Gray and Reuter, *Transaction Processing: Techniques and Concepts*, p. 56.

Each of the DBMS systems provides a mechanism for determining the cost or benefit of resizing the various DBMS caches. Once the system begins operation, use these mechanisms to explore the effects of changing the size of the DBMS I/O cache. The results can often be surprising! For example, dedicating too much memory to the shared data cache can deprive shadow processes of the memory required to operate normally. Memory might also be traded off between the shared data cache and the virtual memory pool used by Solaris to buffer UFS operations.

Although the macroscopic purpose of a DBMS system is to manage volumes of data that are by definition very large (and that will inevitably be many times larger than main memory), research has repeatedly shown that access to data generally follows a 90/10 rule: 90 percent of all accesses are to 10 percent of the data. Furthermore, more recent research shows that this 90/10 rule follows a fractal pattern: within the "hot" data referenced by 90 percent of the accesses, a further 90/10 rule applies[20]. Thus about 80 percent of all data accesses refer to about one percent of the aggregate data. Note that this reference rate accounts for DBMS internal data such as B-tree indexes, whose access is normally invisible to the application programmer. Although cache hit rates of approximately 95 percent are desirable, blindly providing an in-memory cache of ten percent of the data is not economically justifiable. Even for small 5 GB databases this requires 500 MB of main memory. However, providing a cache for 1 percent of the data usually *is* feasible, even for very large databases. The same 500 MB of main memory thus serves a 50 GB database, and the 30 GB maximum memory size of the Ultra Enterprise 6000 is sufficient to support databases up to about 3 TB in size.

⇒ Size the DBMS data cache so that data accessed more frequently than once in five minutes can be kept in the cache; additionally, add 5-10 percent.
⇒ If the access pattern cannot be determined, provide *at least* one percent of the DBMS's raw data size (excluding indexes and overhead).
⇒ At a minimum, configure 200 KB per user.

3.5.2.2 DBMS I/O Cache and Decision Support

The preceding memory sizing discussion applies to "traditional" DBMS applications, which fall into the online transaction processing category. Transaction processing applications usually benefit from caching strategies because they manipulate relatively small amounts of data, following relatively repetitive access patterns. Although the same data is not usually being retrieved over and over again, the same tables are accessed over and over again. In this environment, caching the table access structures (such as B-tree nodes and index hash keys) is a productive strategy. Accordingly, the DBMS and host server are configured to provide the caching services.

---

[20] *Ibid.*

Decision support applications have distinctly different access patterns. Typical accesses are very large—often involving several entire tables—and most queries share little or no information. Caching the data is pointless, because it will not be accessed again quickly and thus every access would be satisfied from disk, rather than from memory. In fact, caching this data would actually be counterproductive, because the effort expended to manage the I/O cache would be wasted in almost every instance. To avoid this problem, the DBMS vendors implement heuristics in their query optimizers that dynamically change the behavior of the caching mechanisms based on the amount of data that the query is expected to manipulate. Caching is not used for most DSS–style queries, and consequently, the I/O cache is not important for this function.

The shared memory region used by the DBMS systems is *not* exclusively used for I/O buffering. It is also used for holding sort areas and temporary table space during merge operations and a variety of other functions. While the I/O cache itself is not important to most DSS applications, the size of sort areas can have a significant impact on overall performance. Consider the sort requirements of typical queries if such a query can be identified (for DSS applications, identifying these requirements in advance is often impossible).

⇒ For DSS applications, size the shared memory region according to sort requirements, if these can be identified.
⇒ In the absence of sort requirements, configure about 1 GB for databases up to 100 GB, 2 GB for databases 100 GB–500 GB.

3.5.2.3 Other Memory Requirements

Naturally, the system must also provide space for the traditional uses of memory as well. In a DBMS server, always provide at least 32 MB for the base operating system, and most DBMS systems require more. Next, provide 16-32 MB for the DBMS's executables (log writers, consistency checkers, archivers, etc.) and sufficient space to keep the application binaries in memory. These binaries are usually 1-2 MB, but occasionally they can reach 15-50 MB. The operating system shares binaries when they are used by multiple processes, so space for only a single copy must be reserved. Allocate space for the DBMS server code itself, depending upon the general architecture of the server. For 2N architectures, configure 200 KB–500 KB per user; multithreaded architectures require only 60 KB–300 KB since they have many fewer processes and much lower memory overhead.

⇒ Even for small systems, always configure at least 64 MB per SuperSPARC processor or 128 MB per UltraSPARC. Corresponding figures are 48 MB per Pentium and 96 MB per Pentium Pro. The additional information processed by each CPU requires memory to avoid excessive paging.

3.5.3 Processors

Processor consumption will vary enormously between applications, DBMS systems, individual users, and even times of day. For example, the TPC–A results show that a ten–processor SPARCcenter 2000 (rather than the newer SPARCcenter 2000E) is capable of handling the requests from nearly 10,000 users, or 1,000 users per processor [21]. This is achieved with an application that is essentially non–existent, combined with *extensive* tuning in Solaris, Oracle, and the benchmark—considerably in excess of the tuning effort made by most users. Numerous SPARCcenter 2000's and SPARCcenter 2000E's are known to handle the back–end DBMS work for 3,000–5,000 users using 12-15 processors. A more realistic upper bound on the users-per-processor ratio is probably on the order of 300 per 85 MHz SuperSPARC processor. Larger applications naturally result in fewer users per processor.

As noted previously, Oracle Financials represents a much heavier workload than TPC–A, or even TPC–C. Financials is a heavier weight measure for a variety of reasons. Financials uses many different transactions, rather than just one as in the TPC–A; a non-trivial amount of application processing must be done on the DBMS host itself after the data is retrieved from the DBMS; and Financials cannot be operated with a transaction processing monitor. Experience with Financials has shown that a 60 MHz SuperSPARC processor can handle about 50 fully active users in timeshare mode and 80–100 fully active users in client/server mode, even with short think times. (The time between the system's response and the user's next request is called the think time. As far as the system is concerned, this is idle time, and it permits the system to devote its attention to requests from other users.)

Even within a single processor family, such as the SuperSPARC, performance does not necessarily scale directly with clock rate, due to considerations such as backplane bus speed and features that may be added to the processor between versions. For example, the 85 MHz SuperSPARC-II is 41 percent faster in clock rate, but delivers only 30–35 percent higher performance than the 60 MHz SuperSPARC, because both run on the same 50 MHz system backplane. In this case, the performance improvement due to the raw clock rate differential is only about 25-28 percent. The additional improvement is due to implementation of a faster cache controller and more sophisticated memory interface (s ee *SuperCache Latency Considerations*, section 6.2.1.2).

---

[21] This result is achieved with the multithreaded Oracle Version 7 database server operating in client/server mode, front-ended by the Tuxedo/T transaction-processing monitor. For full details on the entire configuration, consult the Full Disclosure Report (FDR), available from *http://www.tpc.org*. (The FDRs for all official TPC results are available at this address.)

Table 11. *Approximate* number of supportable users per processor, including think time and idle users

Application Type		85 MHz SuperSPARC Processors				
		1	2	4	8	16
TP Monitor	Client/Server	320	620	1,200	> 2,000	>4,000
Lightweight	Client/Server	220	400	800	1,500	>2,500
	Timeshare	150	300	570	1,000	2,000
Heavyweight	Client/Server	100	200	350	700	1,300
	Timeshare	75	140	260	500	1,000

		167 MHz/1 MB UltraSPARC Processors				
		1	2	4	8	16
TP Monitor	Client/Server	500	1,000	2,000	> 4,000	many
Lightweight	Client/Server	400	800	1,500	2,500	many
	Timeshare	250	450	700	1,200	3,000+[22]
Heavyweight	Client/Server	140	270	450	850	2,000
	Timeshare	100	180	320	600	1,100

In this context, 167 MHz UltraSPARC processors with 512 KB of cache are capable of at least twice the processing ability of an 85 MHz SuperSPARC with 2 MB cache. The faster processor's relatively small cache is offset by the SPARC V9 trap definition, causing context switches and interrupts to be substantially more efficient. In most DBMS applications running on SuperSPARC processors, the operating system's handling of context switching and related traps represents a significant proportion of the overall operating system overhead (see section 6.2.5.1, *Register Sets and System Interface*).

These numbers are predicated upon an entirely interactive user load. In reality, workloads such as those indicated here rarely if ever occur without batch processing. In general, configure additional processors to handle the batch jobs. The rules of thumb provided here should be used *only* as a first estimate! Finally, the estimates shown in Table 11 take into consideration the nature of very large workloads: very large populations tend to be

---

[22] SunSoft does not test or support more than 3,000 timesharing users on a single system, regardless of workload.

somewhat irregular in their user behavior. When many users share a single pool of resources, the probability that a number of users request significant resources at approximately the same time increases greatly, and the system must handle a very large peak workload. In effect, the user population itself scales non-linearly.

3.5.4 Disk I/O Subsystems

As noted in the discussion about memory, disk accesses are about 30,000 times slower than memory. As a result, the best way to optimize disk I/O is not to do it at all! Unfortunately, this approach is economically impractical, at least in a complete fashion. Providing sufficient I/O capacity is thus crucial to sustaining DBMS performance. A variety of technical considerations lead to some surprising conclusions.

3.5.4.1 Query/Index/Disk Relationship

Without understanding the customer application, the database administrator's indexing strategy, and the DBMS's storage and search mechanisms, making an accurate statement about what type of disk access a given transaction will impose on the system can be difficult. Quantifying the I/O behavior of complex transactions issued from a third party application can be especially difficult. However, in the absence of firm information, it is reasonable to assume that a transaction that retrieves a small number of specifically named records from an indexed table *by the index key* will be a random access operation. For example,

```
select name, salary from employee
    where phone-number = "555-1212" or
        ssn = "111-111-1111";
```

will almost certainly be a random access lookup if the employee table is indexed by `phone-number` and `ssn`. However, if the table is indexed only by name and employee number, this query will be executed as a serial table scan, involving every record in the table.

Queries that involve a range of key values may generate a combination of random and serial access, again depending upon the indexing in place. Consider the query

```
select part_no, description, num-on-hand from stock
    where (part_no > 2000 and part_no < 24000);
```

If the stock table is indexed by `part_no`, this query will probably generate a serial scan of the index, followed by random retrievals of the matching rows from the data table. The scan might be further reduced if the index is physically stored in some kind of sorted order. However, if for some reason this table were *not* indexed by `part_no`, the query would almost certainly result in a full table scan.

Sometimes a query can be satisfied entirely from the index, completely avoiding access to the actual tablespace. For example, the `part_no` query can be satisfied entirely from an index if `description` and `num-on-hand` are not requested. For some queries, construction of the right indexes can yield a substantial reduction in I/O requirements.

Updates to the database will cause updates in all of the affected indexes, and the log will be written accordingly. Detailed coverage of this process goes far beyond the scope of this text, requiring a thorough understanding of the individual DBMS involved, the complex nature of queries, and query optimization. Estimating the disk access requirements is imprecise without knowing the details of how the DBMS stores data, for even the simple transactions shown here. Computing the disk access requirements for a five-way outer join constrained by a correlated subquery would be difficult even for application authors!

> Note: In cases where queries of such complexity are expected to govern the overall performance of an application system, *insist upon consulting experts* with experience tuning your DBMS system. The margin for error with this kind of query is often 1000:1!

3.5.4.2 Storage Capacity vs. Access Capacity

One of the most common problems in DBMS systems is the provision of ample disk storage capacity without sufficient *access* capacity. The disk processing on most servers is dominated by random-access activity. Vendors offer disk drives in many different capacities, especially in mid-range configurations, but their random access performance is nearly the same, as shown in Figure 44 (page 273).

Although the 9 GB disk has more than four times the storage capacity of a 5,400 rpm 2.1 GB disk available at the same time, it actually provides six percent *less* accessibility, due to differences in SCSI firmware. The larger disk delivers 72 I/Os per second (2 KB), whereas the smaller one delivers 77 I/Os per second. Even when the larger capacity drive is as fast as or faster than a smaller one, it is never two or three times faster. Four small disks with the same storage capacity as one large disk will *dramatically* outperform the large disk. For this reason, the greatest I/O access capability is nearly always achieved by using the *smallest* feasible disk, rather than the largest, even when the larger disk may have superior specifications in every way. For a given amount of storage, the access capacity is dramatically greater—more than six times greater, in fact—when using the 1 GB disk compared to the 9 GB model, as shown Table 12.

Table 12. I/O Capacity for 190 GB of storage (1995 street pricing). Note that the 2 GB and 4 GB models spin at 7,200 rpm, while the others spin at 5,400 rpm.

Disk	# Req'd	ops/disk	SCSI strings	Cost	Price/MB	Price/op	IOPS	MB/sec
1.05 GB	186	78	16	$400	$0.47	$6.34	14,508	320
2.1 GB	93	105	8	$1,020	$0.53	$10.65	9,765	160
4.3 GB	46	108	4	$1,480	$0.37	$14.69	4,968	80
9 GB	22	85	2	$2,245	$0.26	$27.81	1,870	40

Although using such small disks is not always practical (capacity restrictions may require the use of larger disks, or perhaps not enough SBus or PCI slots are available to configure the necessary host adapters), the higher access capacity subsystems should always be considered. I/O access capacity is especially important when configuring systems whose actual I/O load is either known to be bursty or is completely unknown, or in the case that the data is relatively small in comparison to the number of users accessing it.

Configuring disks solely on storage capacity it is likely to be a serious mistake to. Although the disk accessibility problem is not a new one, it is getting more serious with time: disk storage capacities are increasing much more rapidly than access capacity, and will continue to do so for the foreseeable future. On the other hand, configuring entire systems to optimize disk I/O performance is not cost-effective. Most disk systems store data of widely varying importance. Typically some data is very important and is accessed frequently and at high speed; other data is often archival in nature and need not be placed on the highest-speed (and most costly) storage subsystems.

⇒ For maximum overall performance, configure the smallest feasible disk drives.
⇒ For maximum overall performance, configure as many SCSI busses as possible within other constraints. (Disk arrays typically configure their disks on many internal SCSI busses, while connecting to the host via a single, separate SCSI bus or FibreChannel . These count as multiple busses.) This consideration is secondary to having as many disk drives as feasible.
⇒ Configure moderate numbers of disks (five or six) per fast (10 MB/sec) SCSI bus. About twice as many are feasible on a fast/wide (20 MB/sec) SCSI bus: ten to twelve disks unless the disks in question are expected to experience significant periods of sustained sequential I/O.
⇒ Use disk striping to improve disk drive response time and increase effective throughput (Solstice:DiskSuite, Volume Manager, or hardware RAID are equivalent for this purpose).

⇒ Remember that disk capacity specifications normally are in units of 1,000,000 bytes, rather than units of 1024 KB as more often reported by software.

⇒ To minimize the cost of disk subsystems, configure very dense disk drives such as the current 9 GB models; as noted above, this tactic can have a severe adverse impact on overall performance, but can be as much as 60 percent less expensive.

3.5.4.3 Platform RAID vs. DBMS Facilities

RAID facilities have become cost–effective in the past several years, but DBMS systems have been having to manipulate much larger units of data for quite some time (much more complete discussion of RAID can be found in *Berkeley RAID Concepts,* section 7.5). Most DBMS systems have some RAID functionality built into them. For example, Sybase System 10 has provisions for mirroring, while Oracle 7 has a facility for spreading table spaces across multiple disks in a form of striping.

System–level or subsystem–level RAID implementations are usually much more complete than their DBMS counterparts. For example, Informix 6 and Sybase System 10 implement mirroring, in that logical writes are committed to two independent places on the disk subsystem. However, neither offers read balancing: All reads are directed to the primary mirror, resulting in imbalanced I/O load. Oracle 7 implements disk concatenation but not actual disk striping. As a result, sequential table scan performance is limited to the speed of a single disk drive, far less than that available from a lower–level striping implementation.

Even when the DBMS provides the desired functionality, it is not normally integrated with other functions such as hot sparing or with higher–order RAID functions such as RAID–1+0. Finally, lower–level RAID implementations can usually take much better advantage of hardware–specific optimizations such as NVRAM caches.

3.5.4.4 File Systems vs. Raw Disks

Most DBMS systems permit the database administrator to choose to place the DBMS files either in raw disks or in standard UNIX file systems. A few, notably Progress, Ingres , and Interbase, *require* the use of UNIX file system storage (interestingly, Ingres requires the use of raw disks for its logs, but places the tables and indices in the file system). For systems that permit a choice, the tradeoffs involve a number of very different criteria.

3.5.4.4.1 Processing Efficiency

Storage in the file system is somewhat less efficient—the differential is usually 5 percent but always less than 15 percent—since an additional layer of system software must be traversed for every DBMS disk access. When processor power is the limiting resource in large DBMS systems, the use of raw partitions improves performance at peak load because it frees processor power for other purposes. For this reason alone, most database administrators normally opt for storage on raw disk partitions. If the system is expected to be pressed to its limits, especially in terms of processor utilization, this choice may be the most appropriate. However, processor efficiency becomes an issue only under peak load; most systems experience peak demand only on an occasional basis.

3.5.4.4.2 Minimizing Storage Capacity Overhead

File system storage also extracts a price in terms of storage capacity. When using the default file system parameters, the Berkeley Fast File System organization consumes approximately 10 percent of the formatted disk's capacity with metainformation about the files and file system. However, when a file system is used to store files for a database, the default inode density parameter is overly conservative. The default parameters cause the creation of one inode for every 2 KB of storage space, in anticipation of typical files that are quite small. Because DBMS systems create a few very large files, the default parameters consume considerable storage space needlessly. An Oracle database stored in a file system will typically require only 100-200 files, and Ingres databases usually use fewer than 2,000. Using the defaults, a 4 GB file system will normally have 2.4 million inodes! If the file system is to store DBMS files, it should be created with inode density of at least 1 MB/inode. This configuration reduces inode overhead by 99.9 percent at no performance penalty! (In theory, performance could be degraded if the file system fills completely and the system is forced to hunt for free blocks, but DBMS systems preallocate disk space, so this problem does not occur in practice.)

In addition to inode overhead, the file system reserves 10 percent of the remaining space in order to permit free space to be found quickly when extending files. As with inode overhead, reservation of this much space is overly conservative, particularly in the DBMS environment. For a variety of reasons, DBMS systems pre–allocate their storage within the file system, and never extend these files. In this circumstance, reservation of 10 percent of a file system is inappropriate, and a 1 percent free space reservation is much more reasonable. Solaris 2.5 implements these recommendations as their default, except for the 1 MB/inode specification.

The disk's capacity is reduced by a total of 21 percent when the file system is built with default parameters, but when constructed with 1 MB/inode density and one percent free space, the file system overhead is reduced to just over one percent of the disk, a much more acceptable level (see section 9.2.3, *UFS and UFS+ Parameters*, for further discussion).

3.5.4.5 Why Store DBMSes in File Systems?

Given that storage in the file system exacts a cost in terms of both processor power and storage capacity, it is reasonable to ask why anyone would bother. There are several good reasons why one might use file system storage instead of raw device storage. Most of them amount to flexibility and familiarity, although performance and capacity can also be considerations.

3.5.4.5.1 Ease of Access to File Systems

First, and perhaps most importantly, use of the file system permits standard UNIX utilities to operate on the storage. For example, the standard UNIX ufsdump(1m) and ufsrestore(1m) utilities can be used to reliably backup and recover DBMS storage. Unbundled backup tools such as Legato Networker or Open Vision Net Backup can also be used. Additionally, manipulation of sections of the database is much easier to accomplish. For example, moving a table from one disk or metadisk to another is straightforward, even if the disks are of different size and type. Although each of the DBMS vendors offers their own internal backup and recovery utilities, they are all different. Moreover, many of them are so slow that customers normally resort to the use of physical volume copying (i.e., use dd(1m)) with all of its attendant difficulties.

Although it is possible to use dd(1m) to backup databases, dd(1) is at best a blunt instrument that is best left for copying physical volumes with no hidden interrelationships. For example, dd(1m) has no notion of multiple volume tapes or tape stackers, whereas all of the file system backup utilities have already been modified to accommodate such devices. Storage in the file system permits uniform, reliable procedures to operate throughout the system or network; if appropriate, the DBMS vendor's tools can also be used.

Finally, because raw disks are not managed by the operating system at all, disk partitions (slices) committed to the database are nearly irretrievable, should disk space be required for a non-database purpose.

3.5.4.5.2 UFS Clustering for Sequential Throughput

In some circumstances, operation through the file system permits access to optimizations that the DBMS system may not implement. Specifically, the UNIX file system attempts to cluster together data into much larger physical entities than most DBMS systems. Because disk space for tables is typically pre-allocated, the file system is usually successful in aggregating data together in 56 KB blocks, while the DBMS storage managers typically operate only in 2 KB (or sometimes 8 KB) pages. Serial scans on tables or indexes stored this way will often be significantly more efficient than equivalent tables more conventionally stored. For example, current disks are capable of delivering 400-500 sequential disk I/O operations per second. When the blocks are 2 KB in size, 500 disk I/O operations move about 1 MB of data. However, through the file system, the disk's internal transfer speed limits access to somewhat over 5 MB/sec if the I/O is clustered into 56 KB units. If the system's operation is dominated by serial scans (or by joins, which often implicitly use serial table scans), file system storage nearly always provides higher performance (for further discussion about selection of maxcontig settings, refer to section 9.2.3, *UFS and UFS+ Parameters*).

3.5.4.5.3 UFS Buffer Cache

The use of the UFS file system also provides the opportunity for the operating system to use a large memory cache for the disk. Databases that operate on raw devices cache data in a DBMS–specific shared memory segment (the Oracle SGA, the Sybase Shared Data Cache, etc.). In some applications, having larger caches can provide a significant performance improvement. Rather than simply increasing the size of the shared data cache, the use of file system data storage permits the operating system to manage the cache in a different way from the way the DBMS cache is managed, in effect operating as a second-level cache. This can improve throughput, occasionally dramatically. Unfortunately no firm guidelines exist as to when this is appropriate (but see section 9.1.5.3, *Supercaching*, for additional discussion). When configuring DBMS file storage in the file system, increase main memory size by about 15 percent in order to avoid stealing memory from application or DBMS processes.

3.5.4.5.4 Raw vs. File System Configuration Summary

The selection of a DBMS file storage method can be summarized in these rules:

⇒ Configure raw disks for maximum peak performance in situations where the processor complex will already be under heavy load.
⇒ Configure DBMS tables in file systems for maximum flexibility.
⇒ When placing DBMS tables within a UNIX file system, allow a maximum of one percent additional space for file system overhead. Use non-default file system parameters: inode density = one inode per megabyte and free space = one percent.
⇒ Configure 15 percent additional memory (or a correspondingly smaller shared data cache) if the DBMS stores tables in a UNIX file system.

3.5.4.6 DBMS Metadata

Users usually think of the DBMS as storing and retrieving their data without considering what is actually stored on the disk. In practice, a considerable amount of additional information is maintained by the DBMS software. As a result, a given amount of user data will *not* fit into that amount of disk space. The database schema, table indexes , B-tree directory nodes, temporary tables, pre-allocated space for hash tables and indexes, sort space, log files, archives, and a myriad of other functions all consume disk space.

Unless more accurate information is available, configure approximately twice as much disk space as raw data. This configuration provides some flexibility for creating indexes to improve application performance. Although a factor of two seems excessive, consider that the indexing mandated by the proposed TPC–D benchmark consumes over 400 MB; the raw data occupies about 650 MB. Using the default Oracle storage parameters, the raw data used for the TPC–C benchmark expands by 30 percent when stored in an Oracle database, even without indexing Requiring much more than 100 percent additional space is easily possible.

⇒ Configure *at least* 50 percent more disk space (plus file system overhead if applicable) than raw data requirements; 100 percent additional is a much safer figure.

⇒ Space must also be allocated for temporary tables, transaction logs, and archives. These must be sized separately because they must be located on different physical disk drives from the database itself.

3.5.4.7 Data Distribution

Another factor that influences I/O subsystem configuration is the intended distribution of data across the disks, especially in smaller systems. DBMS systems all have at least six different storage functions:

- *data tables*, which hold the actual operational information;
- *indexes*, which overlay one or more alternate storage organizations onto the data tables, primarily for performance reasons;
- *temporary tables*, which provide storage for intermediate computations such as the results of a `join` operation; temporary tables are often used for performing sort operations;
- *transaction logs*, which record changes to the DBMS for recovery purposes;
- *rollback buffers*, which record the transitory impact of a pending transaction before it is committed to the database; and finally,
- *system definition*, which contains the data dictionary and other DBMS control information.

Even a minimal system should have at least four disks: one for the operating system and swap, one for the data, one for the log, and one for indexes. Contention for these resources in an I/O bound system is the largest single class of performance problems in environments where the application has been tuned to a reasonable degree (i.e., most production environments). Larger systems must take into account even more variables, such as mirrors, striping, and resource overlap. Providing all major logical entities with separate sets of disks is almost always productive and cost-effective..

3.5.4.7.1 Physical I/O Considerations

Although consolidating multiple functions onto single (physical or logical) disks is technically feasible, this is often very disruptive for the I/O subsystems and nearly always results in sub-par performance. Consider a database that consists of a 1.5 GB data table and 400 MB of indexes, and that requires a 40 MB log file. It is tempting to add these up and discover that they will all fit onto a single 2.1 GB disk (let alone on a 9 GB disk). If the application does any updates to the database, the disk arm is necessarily shuttled all the way across the disk for every transaction, because the updates will normally modify data in the raw tables, in the indexes, and finally in the log. In particular, the log—which must be written synchronously and slowly—has been effectively converted from a fast serial access process into a slow random access process. This will significantly delay every update transaction. Additionally, queries that select records from the data table by serially scanning the index will encounter greatly increased disk I/O wait time. In cases like this one, the index scan is done serially, but since the disk arm must be moved to retrieve each data record between index retrievals, the result is random access to the index that appears to be serialized! (In fact, the index may well have been created with the specific intent of serializing the scan.) If the data table, the index, and the log are on separate disks, only the table retrieval is a random access process, and delivered performance may be increased by a factor of two.

One last point about consolidating functions onto physical resources is that they often create situations in which disk seek times are *maximized!* Although the seek time of disk drives is quoted as a single number, in reality the length of the seek has a large impact on how long it takes. The quoted seek time is literally the sum of all possible seeks, divided by the number of possible seeks. It is *not* the time consumed by a "typical" seek. The physics of disk arm movement dictate that a short seek takes much less time than a long one. This characteristic is especially pertinent on physically large disks such as the 2.9 GB and 9 GB drives built in the 5.25" form factor. A seek to the adjacent cylinder takes a millisecond or two, but a full-stroke seek takes much longer than the quoted average seek. For example, the 2.9 GB disk typically seeks to an adjacent cylinder in 1.7 ms, but takes 23 ms for a full-stroke seek—13 times longer. Long seeks, such as those required by access to two distinct slices of the disk, are to be avoided if at all possible.

When a disk drive is overloaded with multiple functions, it is usually done by putting multiple slices onto the disk. This disk layout forces access to different functions to cross many cylinders, with consequent very long seek times.

Other situations arise that require separate disk drives, even if sufficient performance is available. In particular, log files are usually quite small (a few hundred megabytes). On the surface, dedicating a 2 GB disk for a 500 MB of log seems like a waste of good disk space. Logs for decision support systems are often much smaller, since these applications typically are not update–intensive. As a result, log files are often loaded onto disk drives with other functions. Aside from the performance considerations, this arrangement can be extremely unwise from a failure-resistance perspective. In a DBMS system, the log is *the* mechanism that is used to recover the database in the case of a catastrophic disk crash. Nonetheless, placement of the log files on the same disk as the database tables is a common occurrence. Users who make this mistake save the price of a disk drive but risk the loss of the entire database state with the crash of a single disk! Rather than placing the log on a disk with the data tables, users are advised to mirror the log disk.

3.5.4.7.2 Tradeoffs in DBMS Function Storage

Applications will stress the various parts of the DBMS storage system in very different ways, and a macroscopic analysis of the application can often point out which functions really must be segregated onto dedicated disks and which ones can be safely lumped onto disks with other functions. As noted, logical reasons dictate that logs must *always* be located on disks that do not hold data tables. Applications that perform extensive updates or which update very large data items may bottleneck on the log. One major consideration for applications that make very intensive use of DBMS functions is that they may have to trade off between retrievals and updates. Multiple complex retrievals are often accelerated by extensive indexing, but inserts and some kinds of updates may require updating many indexes, with consequent very low throughput. Queries that are dominated by read–only activity will not seriously stress the rollback buffers, since these are used by transactions that modify the database. Likewise, applications that do not perform extensive sorts or joins most likely do not require dedicated resources for temporary tables.

3.5.4.7.3 Data Distribution Summary

Summarizing the configuration rules for DBMS systems:

⇒ Segregate logical DBMS functions onto dedicated disk resources. At a minimum, put indexes, data tables, and logs on separate disks.
⇒ Plan data layout to minimize the number and length of seeks.

3.5.4.8 I/O Resource Utilization

In designing an I/O subsystem, attention must be paid not only to the maximum throughput capacity of the components, but also to the level of each resource's utilization. Most of the metrics used to describe the capacity of resources are oriented around throughput. For example, a typical SCSI bus is rated at 20 MB/sec. This speed is the rate at which the bits are transmitted across the bus. Such a metric provides no information about how busy the bus is, and consequently it also provides no information about how long it will take to service a given request. Providing the maximum throughput rating is like saying that the speed limit on the Interstate is 65 miles per hour: if the access ramps are so congested that getting on and off takes a long time, the overall speed is likely to be far below the posted speed limit.

Exactly the same principles apply to the various peripherals and peripheral busses, including both SCSI and FibreChannel. Experimental results indicate that SCSI bus utilization should be kept under 80 percent if peak performance is to be maintained. Likewise, disk utilization should be kept below 60 percent[23]. The SCSI bus can tolerate higher utilization than the disks themselves because of the buffering in the embedded disk controllers. This permits coordination of the track buffers, disk arm, and request queue in ways that are impossible on the unadorned SCSI host adapter.

Estimating average disk or SCSI bus utilization is usually impossible until the system becomes operational. As a result, the most appropriate configuration is one that spreads the

---

[23] Patterson and Hennesey, *Computer Architecture: A Quantitative Approach*, p. 545.

frequently used data and indexes across as many disks and SCSI busses as feasible within budgetary and technical constraints. For data that is infrequently accessed, for example, information used only during overnight batch processing (or other online semi-archival data such as year-old transactions) can be packed as tightly as feasible onto the drives.

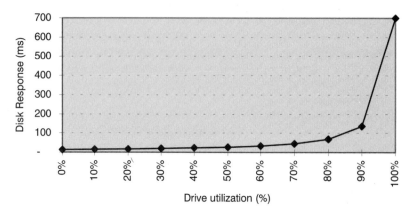

Figure 14. Disk response time as a function of disk utilization. Response time strongly impacts the user's perception of system performance.

3.5.4.8.1 Impact of Resource Utilization

To see how resource utilization impacts the overall system, consider that:

$$Response\ Time = Device\ Response\ Time \times (Length\ of\ Pending\ Queue - 1)$$

where $Device\ Response = \dfrac{Device\ Service\ Time}{(1 - utilization\%)}$.

So: $Response\ Time = \dfrac{Service\ Time \times (Length\ of\ Pending\ Queue - 1)}{1 - utilization\%}$.

This equation shows how the overall response time is dependent on the amount of work pending for the device, and on the utilization of the device. As the device utilization increases, the overall response time goes up quite dramatically (see Figure 14).

3.5.4.8.2 Reducing Utilization

Once the system has begun operation, the administrator and/or DBA can measure actual disk utilization and move data between disk resources accordingly. Data movement must be done with the other disk access parameters in mind as noted above—balance is the watchword.

Usually at least two mechanisms are available for spreading data across disk drives in the context of DBMS systems. Each of the DBMS systems has the ability to concatenate together multiple disk drives or UNIX files to effectively spread data access (only Ingres offers true striping, limited to a standard interlace size of 16 KB). Host- and subsystem-based RAID offers similar capabilities, in addition to RAID-5, hot sparing, and disk striping. If a table is I/O bound, investigate the queries causing the I/O activity. If they are random-access, for example, if many users are separately requesting individual records, the disk concatenation abilities native to the DBMS systems are completely adequate to spread the access load across multiple disks as long as the tablespaces are mostly full. If the accesses are serial in nature, for example, if one or a few users must scan every row in the table, true striping is more appropriate.

The primary benefit of striping is that the task of spreading data access is much simpler for the database administrator. With real striping, this task is trivial and yields optimal results in nearly every case. Logically dividing data across tablespaces using internal DBMS mechanisms is usually not so easy, but it can be done. The goal is to separate heavily used tables onto separate disk resources, resolving the conflicting requirements for combinations of access to those tables is often difficult, resulting in uneven loading. With lower-level RAID implementations, disk utilization will tend to level itself out naturally.

Given sufficient hardware, optimizing DBMS disk I/O performance by extremely careful hand–optimization of the disk layout is normally possible. However, such tuning *always* requires intimate analysis of the system in operation. Sun's experience has uniformly been that automated disk management through lower-level RAID has yielded better performance than all but the best hand-tuned configurations. Usually even the best hand-tuned configurations exceed automated stripes by only one to five percent.

DBMS systems divide a table into a few relatively large segments, placing the data uniformly onto those segments. The key differentiator between the DBMS systems' concatenation and low-level RAID striping function is the placement of adjacent data. When the disks are concatenated together, a serial scan uses each of the component disks heavily, but serially— only one disk is able to help service the query. True disk striping or RAID divides the data along much smaller boundaries, permitting all of the disks to help service a relatively small request. As a result, serial access is greatly improved by striping. Archive and log files are always accessed serially, and are good candidates for both striping and NVRAM acceleration if they constrict overall system performance.

In some cases, I/O bandwidth to temporary tables can constrain performance; this happens most often on key transactions that include multi-way joins. In these cases, the fastest configuration places the temporary tables in volatile or semi–volatile RAM–based storage. Various forms exist, ranging from a pure disk emulation physically stored in volatile RAM, to solid–state disks. Volatile–RAM systems usually are not necessary on Solaris–based systems because storing DBMS files in the UNIX file system is very simple. This scheme is successful because it is simple, and because it relies on the caching mechanism built into Solaris. Although some DBMS vendors (Sybase, in particular) do not support storage of tablespaces in the file system, temporary tables are a different matter, because their contents are by definition lost in the event of a system shutdown. Consider the use of NVRAM to accelerate access to temporary tables placed in the file system.

Some vendors offer small solid–state disks that plug into the EISA or SBus ; others are larger, full disk emulators that are external boxes connected to the host via SCSI. Because of the limited capacity and high price of this technology (20-50 times as much as rotating magnetic storage), resort to these devices only after solving the problem with standard magnetic disks proves impossible.

As databases continue to grow in size and importance, backup procedures that disable DBMS access become a practical impossibility. Online backups can pose significant configuration challenges since backup of the large volumes of data associated with databases involves I/O intensive activity. Online backups frequently drive disk and SCSI bus utilization to very high levels, with the resulting poor application performance. Pay special heed to the configuration of all devices involved in an online backup process.

⇒ After system installation, monitor and move data until utilization on each disk drive is less than 60-65 percent.
⇒ Use striping to spread serial disk access across multiple disks (use Solstice:DiskSuite , SPARCstorage Volume Manager, or a controller-based disk array).
⇒ Carefully investigate the *actual* properties of a DBMS's implementation of virtual disk functionality such as striping or mirroring.
⇒ Pay careful attention to the impact of online backup, especially in terms of SCSI bus utilization.

3.5.4.9 Network I/O Subsystems

Network I/O is a part of virtually every non-decision support DBMS system today. Most often the application operates in some form of client/server configuration, usually with a large centralized DBMS server combined with many PC or workstation client systems. This organization usually transfers a relatively small amount of data across networks, at least in typical OLTP applications. The amount of data transferred can often be minimized by running key parts of an application as stored procedures in the DBMS engine, rather than transferring the data to the client for processing. Of course, this transfers the processing requirement to the DBMS engine, where resources must be available to handle the work.

⇒ Minimize network transfer of data if necessary, possibly through the use of DBMS stored procedures.

3.5.4.9.1 Client/Server Considerations

If the DBMS operates in client/server mode, the network(s) connecting clients with the server must be adequately sized. Fortunately, most clients operate on specific pieces of data—individual accounts, stock items, the history of individual accounts, and the like. Under these circumstances, the speed of the network connecting clients and servers is rarely a problem. A single Ethernet or Token Ring is usually sufficient for 100-200 clients. In a test at Sun, a client/server configuration supporting more than 250 Oracle Financial users generated approximately 200 KB/sec of traffic between the front and back end systems. For obvious reasons closely monitor network utilization, especially as the number of clients exceeds approximately 20 per Ethernet or about 200 per FastEthernet. Token ring networks can sustain somewhat more load than 10 Mbit Ethernets, due to their superior degradation characteristics under high utilization.

Configuring a dedicated network between front-end systems and DBMS service providers is often useful for latency reasons, even when throughput is not a consideration. Building a dedicated Ethernet between client and server is as simple as plugging both into an inexpensive twisted pair transceiver hub. For situations where most or all of the client applications reside on a single system, pairs of systems can be connected with FastEthernet, FDDI, or ATM using only a cross-over cable. These configurations require only a single point–to–point connection and do not require a hub or switch.

3.5.4.9.2 Network Efficiency

Each of the different DBMS engines has different network I/O requirements. Oracle in particular uses a more straightforward but sometimes higher–overhead strategy for network transmission. SQL*Net transfers data between client and server using one TCP window for each column of each row. Because most columns are much smaller than a packet, each column of each row results in the transfer of a network packet. Sybase System 10 and Informix 6 consolidate entire rows into TCP windows. For some applications that are dominated by transfer of rows consisting of many columns, the Oracle approach can result in a surprising amount of overhead. TCP/IP packets incur an overhead of about 60 bytes per packet. When the number of packets is small, or when the payload is large, the overhead is inconsequential; however, in cases where rows consist of many small columns, the network overhead can be quite substantial. The sparse packaging of data on the network is most significant in wide-area network configurations, where the round-trip latency of each packet can be quite long.

This organization does have advantages. For applications that do not involve rows with many columns, the overhead required to encode and decode the TCP messages is avoided, resulting in less overall effort on the part of both client and server systems. In practice, the differential is not usually significant, and even when network utilization becomes an issue, more or faster networks can usually solve the problem (refer to Figure 15).

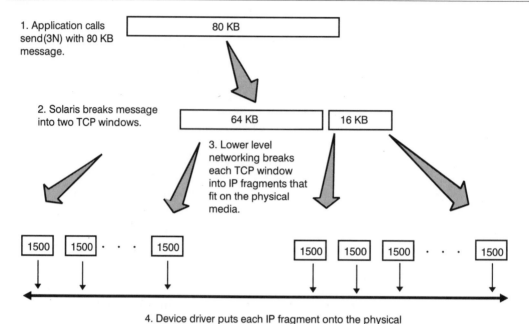

1. Application calls send(3N) with 80 KB message.

80 KB

2. Solaris breaks message into two TCP windows.

64 KB   16 KB

3. Lower level networking breaks each TCP window into IP fragments that fit on the physical media.

1500 1500 · · · 1500   1500 1500 1500 · · · 1500

4. Device driver puts each IP fragment onto the physical network (Ethernet or FastEthernet in this case).

Figure 15. The process of breaking messages into TCP windows, IP datagrams, and Ethernet packets

In some cases another solution to the network efficiency problem is the construction of the application using *stored procedures*. These are a mechanism for clients to specify entire DBMS–related actions for execution directly on the server. Stored procedures are essentially remote subroutine calls coded in SQL. The entire stored procedure executes on the server system, and only final results are sent back to the client system. For simple SQL statements, this arrangement is not much more efficient than the usual arrangement, but complex queries used by most applications involve multistatement SQL operations. For these applications, stored procedures can substantially reduce network traffic.

3.5.4.9.3 Large Data Objects

The most common circumstance in which Ethernet and Token Ring are not sufficient is when the units of data being stored in the database are very large. For example, X-ray images are often stored in DBMS systems, because they can be easily connected with other patient history data; these X-ray images are often 3-5 MB in size. Document storage/retrieval, mechanical CAD drawing storage, and multimedia are also data-intensive applications. In such cases, ATM is the most appropriate networking media, although FDDI may be used instead. FastEthernet is less suitable due to its degradation characteristics under heavy load.

3.5.4.9.4 Client/Server and Wide-Area Networks

For an increasing number of applications, front-end and back-end systems can or should be placed in geographically disparate locations, for business reasons, rather than technological reasons. Such systems must be connected by wide-area networks. Leased lines carrying synchronous serial networks are usually the media used for such networks. These lines are normally available in speeds of approximately 56 Kbit/sec, 1.5-2.0 Mbit/sec, and 45 Mbit/sec. Although the raw media speeds are considerably lower than typically found in local-area networks such as Ethernet, the nature of the serial lines is such that high utilization levels can be sustained. A T1 line offers 1.544 Mb/sec throughput (2,048 Kb/sec outside the U.S.). Compared to the 3.5 Mb/sec offered by Ethernet in normal environments, the T1 offers throughput that is not qualitatively different from Ethernet. Fractional T3 lines are often available in 10-20 Mb/sec, obviously rivaling Ethernet and Token Ring networks, albeit often with significantly higher latency. Quite a few applications can operate successfully in a client/server configuration over a 56 Kb/sec network, given careful attention to minimizing network traffic.

For traditional business applications, client/server traffic normally has low enough data volume between the front end and the back end that the somewhat lower network throughput is sufficient. In most cases, network latency is not an issue, but if the wide-area network is particularly long or if it is carried over very high-latency media (such as satellite links), the application should be tested to determine its sensitivity to packet delays.

Transaction processing monitors may be used to reduce client/server traffic to an absolute minimum.

3.5.4.9.5 Character Terminal Traffic

A common misconception is that the network traffic associated with terminal servers can overload an Ethernet. This is not true. Consider the 64-port Network Terminal Server, which can drive each port at 38,400 baud, or 3,840 characters per second[24]. If every port is operating at the full 38,400 baud, a total of 245,780 bytes (1.9 Mbits, approximately 20 percent utilization) of data will be sent from the host systems to the terminal server for distribution. Of course, some TCP/IP overhead is associated with this level of traffic, but it represents about 50 bytes per packet—about four percent at this level of traffic. This scenario represents a worst-case—for example, a situation involving 64 very busy printers. Typical traffic levels are much lower: one 2,000-character screen might be displayed once per minute. Under these conditions the 64-port terminal server handles approximately 35 bytes per second per port, or about 2 KB/sec aggregate.

---

[24] A byte consists of eight data bits, but baud ratings include start and stop bits. Occasionally, some networks use *two* stop bits.

Input characters need not be considered since even the fastest typists provide input at only 20 characters per second—1.0-1.5 cps is much more typical. Even when input is handled in cbreak mode, the most load that would be generated is about 1,300 cps (20 cps per port on 64 ports). This number represents 80 KB/sec after accounting for maximum TCP/IP overhead. Typical loads (64 ports at 1.5 cps) would be about 15 KB/sec after overhead.

3.5.4.9.6 Network I/O Configuration Summary

⇒ For client/server configurations where the clients run on remote PCs or workstations, configure 20-50 clients per Ethernet; as many as 100 clients can be configured on 16 Mb Token Rings due to that topology's superior degradation characteristics.

⇒ Configure a dedicated network between front-end and back-end DBMS systems if the front end handles many clients. If the data objects being manipulated are very large (more than 500 KB per object), configure FDDI instead of Ethernet or Token Ring.

⇒ DBMS front- and back-end systems may be configured separated by wide-area networks if "sufficient" bandwidth is provided. Ideally this minimum means at least a fractional T1 line. Such applications must be relatively insensitive to network latency.

⇒ Use stored procedures to reduce client/server traffic, especially when employing multistatement SQL programs.

⇒ When configuring client/server systems across wide-area networks, investigate the use of transaction monitors to reduce client/server traffic to a minimum.

⇒ Configure terminal servers on private networks only when shared networks are heavily utilized for other purposes.

3.5.4.10 PrestoServe/NVSIMM

The semantic definition of the SQL statement commit_work requires that the DBMS system be able to *guarantee* that updates to the database are dispatched and committed to stable storage (i.e., any storage that is persistent, even across system failures or power outages). In order for the DBMS system to meet this guarantee, it must issue at least some of its write operations synchronously. The operating system blocks the issuing process while such writes are being performed, and does not return control to the calling program until the data is committed to stable storage. Although this process is safe, it is also slow, since synchronous writes necessarily require the disk subsystem to physically place the data on the platters. A synchronous write to a raw disk takes approximately 20 ms, and a synchronous write to a file system can take several times as long (for example, if updates to the indirect or double-indirect blocks must be made).

Normally, DBMS systems write only their logs synchronously—the database can be reconstructed from the synchronously written log in the event of a system crash. Occasionally, the system as a whole can become bottlenecked on the logging process, usually in heavy transaction processing environments that make many updates (a read-only application, such as decision support, makes few entries to the log). The use of mirrored pairs for log disks exacerbates this situation. In such cases PrestoServe or NVSIMM may be able to accelerate the log process. By committing writes to the non-mechanical NVRAM instead of mechanical disk arms, the PrestoServe or NVSIMM can alleviate a substantial bottleneck in some systems[25].

One database, Progress, generates a substantial amount of synchronous UFS traffic (Progress mandates the use of UFS file systems for DBMS storage). As a result, *any* system running Progress should configure Presto/NVSIMM, unless the disks are configured in a dual-ported situation. The performance differential is dramatic: for most applications, overall performance improves by approximately 20 percent, and some applications have experienced considerably more.

⇒ Configure NVSIMM or PrestoServe when the application is log-bound or if the application is heavily oriented toward updates.
⇒ Configure maximum NVSIMM for any server that runs the Progress database engine.
⇒ Configure DBMS logs on mirrored disk pairs to ensure against data loss.
⇒ *Do not configure PrestoServe/NVSIMM in any system that shares its disks with another system, such as a dual-ported disk array or multi-initiator SCSI (see section 7.2.3.3,* Multi-initiator SCSI, *for a more complete discussion).*

3.5.5 Provisions for Backup

Because databases are typically both huge and critically important, backup is a crucial issue. The volume of data involved is usually immense, especially relative to the size and particularly speed of backup devices. Dumping a 20 GB database to a 4 mm tape drive at 500 KB/sec is virtually never practical—this will take nearly 12 hours.

3.5.6 Choosing When to Do Backup

Scheduling a backup for a system used primarily during normal office hours is relatively straightforward. Scripts are often used to carry out the backup procedure after close of business. Some sites run these scripts unattended; others use operators on overtime. Unattended backups will require sufficient backup capability online.

Planning and configuration are more difficult if the system must be online 24 hours, or if the time necessary to perform the backup is longer than the available window.

---

[25] Early editions of Solstice:DiskSuite did not support the combination of disk mirroring and PrestoServe/NVRAM. This limitation was removed with PrestoServe 2.4.1 and Solstice:DiskSuite 2.0 and subsequent releases. Early editions of the SPARCstorage Array Volume Manager also did not support the combination of Volume Manager and PrestoServe/NVRAM. This restriction has also been removed.

3.5.7 Online Backups

Some situations require an "online backup," i.e., carrying out a backup while the database is still active, with users still connected and operational.

Backing up a database presupposes that it is consistent—that all committed updates to the database have not only been logged, but have been written to the database tables as well. Online backups pose a challenge: after a consistency point has been reached and the backup commences, all database updates must be prevented from updating the database tables until after the full backup has completed, lest the backups become inconsistent. All major DBMS systems now provide an online backup capability.

The consistency problem is being overcome; most of the major DBMS vendors have implemented more sophisticated log mechanisms that allow all transactions to be in flight while backups are done. The database and the log are backed up together, and restored together. In the event of a crash recovery, the DBMS is able to inspect the log to determine which transactions in flight during the backup that subsequently committed.

Historically, online database backups were very slow, often taking an order of magnitude longer than offline backups. Recent studies with products such as Oracle's Enterprise Backup (OEUB) show that most of these performance problems have been resolved. Early results with OEBU version 2.1 suggest that suitably equipped systems can achieve online backups at rates in excess of 500 GB/hr, less than ten percent slower than fully offline backups[26].

3.5.8 Backup Duration

Backup duration is one of the most crucial issue for sites with large databases (50+ GB) and the choice of a backup methodology may be dictated by it. Small databases can readily be backed up using a single Exabyte or DAT tape drive. Although current tapes can back up data at roughly 1.25 GB per hour, this is clearly unacceptable for a large database. Mul tiple devices can be used in parallel to improve throughput, although kernel resource contention makes this approach less than fully effective for more than about forty tape drives.

Some 8 mm tape drives with hardware compression are capable of as much as 3 GB/hour, more than double that of the standard units. Some of these devices are rated at up to 25 GB capacity, but more typically they store 8-10 GB. IBM 3490-compatible drives can consume nearly 10 GB per hour, but their limited media size (200-400 MB before compression) means that they must be configured in mechanical stacker silos to be effective. Although the most–quoted specification for these devices is their media transfer speed, most users need to investigate media exchange time—400 MB can be written on a 3490E cartridge in slightly

---

[26] This study was ongoing as this text went to print. Results are preliminary.

over a minute. If media rewind and exchange takes just fifteen seconds, the overall throughput of the device drops by more than 25 percent. DLT-7000 is probably the most suitable format for systems with storage capacity in excess of 25 GB, since individual drives are capable of absorbing about 15 GB per hour.

For applications requiring very high performance tapes, the StorageTEK Redwood SD–3 helical–scan drive is able to sustain about 14.8 MB/sec transfers (about 50 GB per hour). As with backups on file systems, logical backups of databases are usually not able to sustain tape media speed, due to seek considerations (see section 8.2, *The Backup Process: Logical* vs. *Physical*).

Most backup media cite transfer speeds *after* accounting for lossless compression of approximately 2:1. However, experience with DBMS systems shows that more realistic compression ratios are in the range of 1.3–1.5:1, primarily because the data is often stored in some semi–compressed form on disk (for example, alphabetic index keys are often stored using some sort of difference coding; the two keys "White" and "Whiteside" might be stored as "White" and <cookie>"side", where the <cookie> represents "the previous key").

3.5.9 Using Disk Mirroring to Facilitate Backup

A simple but effective means of reducing backup times is to back up a detached disk mirror. Low-level RAID implementations offer disk mirroring with very little system overhead. If the mirror is detached immediately after a checkpoint, or after the database has been shut down, the mirror copy effectively becomes an online disk backup, which can be backed up whenever convenient. The database can even be restarted to allow normal processing to continue, albeit with reduced redundancy. Some DBMS implementations permit "freezing" the state of a table or tablespace to permit online backups[27].

If enough disk drives are available, a second set of mirrors can be used, allowing full mirroring to be retained even when one set of mirrors is detached (during normal operation, the disks would be three-way mirrored). In this case, the online disk backup can be kept intact after being copied to tape, allowing very fast recovery, should this prove necessary. This extra set of mirrors could be reattached just prior to the next checkpoint, providing enough time (about 30 minutes) is allowed for the mirror set to be resynced with the online mirrors.

---

[27] For example, Oracle extended their SQL language to permit "alter tablespace t for backup", instructing the engine to ensure that updates to the tablespace are retained in the logs during backup. The log is rolled forward later to retain consistency.

3.5.10 Backup Frequency

Most users carry out a full backup daily. Given that backups are carried out against the day when recovery will become necessary, considering recovery time is important. This includes restore time (usually from tape) and time taken to roll forward to incorporate the changes made to the database since the backup. Because of the importance of the roll-forward facility, mirroring the journals and archive logs that make it possible is crucial.

In an environment where a large number of transactions are being written to the database, the time required to perform a roll-forward from the most recent checkpoint may significantly increase the overall recovery time. This consideration alone may determine the frequency of backups. Each of the DBMS engines have a number of parameters that are used to control the frequency of checkpoints and the size of the logical differential between the log and the tables, and thus indirectly the roll–forward time. These parameters are normally expressed in units of time or transactions; because the recovery time is usually dependent more on the number of modified tables and indexes and the amount of modified data, checkpoint control is not precise. Some experimentation is usually required to achieve a balance between acceptable performance for database updates and potentially large differences between checkpoints and logs.

3.5.11 Backup Utilities

Two basic strategies underlie the backup process: copying the underlying operating system storage entities (meaning either the raw disks or metadisks, or the database's file system files), and copying the logical DBMS data. Copying the physical storage entities is *far* faster, because this process does not have to respect the DBMS's internal organization. The I/O is therefore able to operate serially, eliminating costly disk seeks.

When using raw partitions, the choice is simple: `dd(1m)` and `compress(1)` are really the only UNIX commands that operate on raw partitions. When storing the DBMS tables in UFS file systems, `tar(1)`, `cpio(1)`, and `ufsdump(1)` are the main choices. Most users prefer `ufsdump(1)` (or `dump(1)` for Solaris 1.x).

Most DBMS systems have utilities to extract raw data from the database and copy to external media, but these are typically much slower than simply copying the raw disk partitions, because they collect logical DBMS information, requiring many disk seeks. In addition, most DBMS vendors are now also offering backup utilities that are able to utilize internal information to provide backups that are faster than pure exportation of logical information, although they are still not as fast as copying the underlying storage. These utilities are usually also able to perform consistent online backups.

3.5.12 Recovering from Catastrophe

Nobody likes to think about disk crashes, application bugs, operator error, or other such problems. Yet they occur with sufficient frequency that every reader has at least one horror story about how difficult a catastrophe recovery scenario was—or was not. The time necessary to recover from backups is a function of the size and number of incremental backups. The cost of downtime must be carefully weighed against the expense of doing complete backups more or less frequently. Additionally, you can easily configure a backup device that is capable of performing a backup in the required nightly time window, but which performs recovery far too slowly—recovery typically takes three to five times as long as the original backup, depending on the physical organization of the data on the backup media. Less frequent complete backups mean more and larger incremental backups, lengthening the recovery time.

Consider a scenario in which a complete backup requires five 8 mm tapes—about 50 GB. Assuming that the tapes are loaded in an automatic stacking unit, this backup will take about 15 hours. Recovery from the single complete backup thus takes 40–65 hours—three days. However, most recoveries will not be from a single complete backup, but rather from a complete dump combined with several incremental backups. If the incremental backups are 10 percent of the size of the complete dump, and three of them are required to recover fully, the additional recovery time is 12-18 hours, a total of 52-83 hours. More frequent complete backups reduce the size and number of incremental backups, but they require more time, effort, and media in the ongoing operation.

This example presumes a single tape drive, but systems are fully capable of handling far more than the one tape transport. A system configured with multiple SCSI busses is able to handle many table spaces simultaneously. System backup and recovery performance scales nearly linearly as tape drives are added to the system *assuming that the disks are independent* (refer to Figure 52, page 297). When parallel backups or recoveries are applied to the same sets of disks, the disks usually become quite busy due to long and competitive seeks. In particularly bad circumstances, two parallel recoveries on a single set of disks can take more elapsed time than running the two recoveries one after the other.

⇒ Plan backup configurations based on *recovery time*, rather than on backup time.
⇒ Back up large data volumes in many small components to take advantage of backup scalability.

3.6 Putting It All Together—Case Studies

The case studies in this section are constructed to illustrate various configuration points outlined previously. Most actual situations will have most of these complexities, but especially in the DBMS category, many additional details will likely constrain configuration choices. Few large-scale applications are as simple (or as neat) as these.

3.6.1 Traditional IS Application—Oracle Financials

Murky Research is experiencing explosive growth, and the Finance department is being overrun with requests for status reports, forecasts, and overall requests for financial information. The Information Services department has decided to completely replace the badly overrun home-grown financial information system with Oracle Financials. The new system will have to handle 35-40 users. Provision is to be made for four Concurrent Manager (Oracle Financials batch processing) daemons. The existing database requires 900 MB of data storage; this number is expected to grow to about 1.5 GB of storage within a year.

3.6.1.1 Case Study 4—First Cut: "Mainframe Replacement" Style

The most obvious solution to this configuration is to construct a single system capable of handling all the users. This configuration is essentially the same as would have been proposed 20 years ago. In this case, because the key transactions are completely unknown, only a rough estimate can be made. Clearly the DBMS must be Oracle7, and Oracle Financials runs by default in 2N mode; no TP monitors are used. The existing database is 900 MB in size, and the system must be able to handle 1,500 MB. Accordingly, the SGA should be sized approximately 1.2-2 MB; with 40 users logged onto the system, the basic 32 MB of memory, plus 40×200 KB per user in the DBMS, plus 2 MB per user for the front-end processes, or 32 MB + 8 MB + 2 MB + 80 MB = 122 MB. In Table 11 (page 113) we see that for heavyweight 2N applications such as this one, operated in timesharing mode, a total of 40 users requires one 85 MHz processor.

The disk subsystem presents a quandary. Only 900 MB to 1,500 MB of data are required to store the actual data. When stored in a DBMS system, this amount of raw data corresponds to 1,800-3,000 MB of disk space after accounting for indexes, storage overhead, etc. This could be easily dealt with using three 1 GB disks or a single 4 GB disk, but clearly such configurations do not provide sufficient disk I/O capacity to handle 40 users. The most appropriate disk configuration readily available would be six 535 MB disks with fast/wide interfaces—but disks this small are no longer commonly available. Most likely this system must be configured with six 1 GB disks. Striping is used to balance disk access load. If the disk storage does not need to be fully available, mirroring and RAID–5 are not crucial: with just six disks, the reliability of the disk subsystem is expected to be about 83,000 hours (9.5 years). In addition, a disk is required to hold the system and application binaries, and two more are necessary for a mirrored log disk.

Forty users must be connected to the system in some way; the most efficient mechanism is the network terminal server. It supports 64 serial ports and connects to the main system via Ethernet. This system can easily be configured with an Ultra–1/140 with a SPARCstorage Array containing nine 1 GB disks. Some provision for backup is necessary, and this can be either a single 14 GB 8 mm drive or a 4 mm stacker with 20 GB capacity. Before the Ultra–1 was available, this configuration would have been handled by a SPARCstation 20 Model 612.

3.6.1.2 Case Study 5—Better Alternative: Client/Server Computing

A uniprocessor UltraSPARC is more than sufficient for this application, but in the era of the SPARCstation 20, a higher-performance alternate configuration for this task is a pair of uniprocessor SPARCstation 20 Model 61s in client/server configuration, rather than in the traditional timesharing mode. The disk configuration is the same, as is the use of the network terminal server. Instead of having a dual processor system handling the entire load, one SPARCstation 20 handles the front end (the actual user application programs), while the back-end DBMS code is handled by the other.

For a relatively small system supporting only 35-40 users, a timesharing system works about as well as a client/server system, and logistically may be easier to manage. However, consider a future Murky Research that is five times the size; with 200 users and 7.5 GB of raw data storage, this situation poses quite a different configuration problem. Not only is the sheer size of the system much larger, but also shutting down the database for the backups of 7-15 GB of database storage onto a 4 mm tape drive will not likely be an acceptable solution.

For the larger version of Murky Research, the raw data storage of 7.5 GB leads to configuration of at least 15 GB of database storage after accounting for indexing and other DBMS overhead. The recommended memory size is thus about 150 MB, plus the basic 32 MB, plus 150 KB per user or 30 MB, a total of 212 MB. The nearest available memory size is 256 MB. As shown in Table 11 (page 113), a dual–processor 85 MHz SPARCserver 1000E is sufficient for 200 users for the back-end system in client/server configurations.

To provide 15 GB of disk storage for as many as 200 users, the most effective configuration uses about 30 spindles, about the capacity of a single disk array. The smallest available disks—1 GB—are more than sufficient for this application, even after allowing for the various overheads. A single FibreChannel or fast/wide SCSI–2 bus is more than adequate to connect the disk array to the host. An SBus card is required for either host connection.

Oracle Financials deals with small data objects, so the client/server connection can be over Ethernet. A network can easily be dedicated to client/server communication.

While the smaller Murky Research could afford to stop the database for long periods of time during backups, this option is not feasible with such a large user population. If backups are to be done without taking the database down for extended periods of time, some mechanism must be found to dump the disk files rapidly. If it is feasible to take the database down for an hour each night, a very high-speed tape drive such as the StorageTEK Redwood. Capable of 10-15 MB/sec sustained throughput, these drives are capable of backing up the entire 15 GB database in about 30 minutes if the database is dumped physically. Tape units operating at this speed require dedicated SCSI busses; in this case, a fast/wide SCSI bus is needed, and this requires an SBus slot.

In the event that the office cannot make the database unavailable for the time required to dump it to tape, the only feasible solution is to mirror the database, detaching the mirror for backup after a checkpoint. The backup is a disk-to-disk copy, except that it is kept consistent during the dump. When the database is consistent, submirrors containing the archive, log, and the data tables can be detached for copying to tape. Once the submirror is detached for dumping, the system is able to proceed without interference, and the checkpointed data can be dumped at leisure. This approach attains the goal of keeping the database continuously online and available, but it poses significant configuration problems.

The most severe problem is the requirement for twice as much disk; an additional 15 GB of disk is required. The existing system has nearly 15 GB of available disk space, but the 200 users will saturate all of the disk access capacity. A second disk array is required, although it need not hold many disk drives: if the extra mirror will be used exclusively to perform an online backup, it does not have the access capacity requirements of the primary databases. Four 4 GB disks or eight 2 GB disks are quite sufficient.

With the time-critical backup being done on a continuous basis, the speed of the tape copy is much less important. The two 4 mm tape stackers have sufficient capacity and throughput to permit the off-line dumps to be completed in a reasonable amount of time; with two units online the dumps can be completed in approximately two hours with automatic tape changes handled by the stacker units. A single SCSI host adapter can be used to connect the two stackers.

The final back-end configuration for the larger Murky Research is a dual–processor 85 MHz SPARCserver 1000E with 256 MB memory. Two disk arrays are required, one with 30 small disks and one with an additional 15 GB of disk space. To accommodate online backups, one of the disks is used as a mirror; it is dumped to two 4 mm tape drives mounted in stacker units connected to the built-in SCSI busses located on the server's system boards. Even if the disk arrays provide data security in the face of disk failures, a software RAID implementation such as Solstice:DiskSuite or SPARCstorage Volume Manager is required to implement mirroring from one disk array to the other. A front-end system is also required.

The front-end system is much more a pure timesharing system than a DBMS server; accordingly, the rules for configuring timesharing systems are applied. The system must configure sufficient memory for 200 users. Experience has shown that Oracle Financials front ends consume about 1 MB per user; the front-end system needs 256 MB, since the Concurrent Managers (batch streams) will also require significant memory, and the system needs basic memory to function. For 200 users, Table 11 (page 113) indicates that 3–4 processors are required assuming that all users are fully active. This assumption is unlikely to hold; assuming that about half of the users are fully active, two or three 85 MHz processors are required. The terminals are connected to the systems via terminal servers.

The front-end system as specified has little use for extensive disk I/O subsystems. The application binaries can probably be obtained from the back-end system via NFS with little or no impact—the binaries will be shared by all users, and so will not likely ever be paged out. In fact, the only disk required on the front-end system is that needed to boot the system and supply it with swap space. Given the requirements, the most appropriate system is a SPARCserver 1000E with 256 MB memory and minimal disk.

The use of the terminal servers makes load balancing reasonably easy: the front-end systems can be classed in a rotary pool, and ports can be connected to alternating front-end systems. Rather than asking specifically for an individual front-end system, the users are instructed to request the name of the rotary pool, and the requests are spread across multiple front-end systems. The use of a name service such as NIS+ permits the various front-end systems to provide a community directory of users and access rights.

3.6.2 Minimal Sizing Based on Key Transactions

Normally, determining that a given system *will* be able to support a requested load is impossible, due to the complexity of the combination of hardware, operating system, DBMS system, and application. Nevertheless, one can make some reasonable assumptions, and then perform a rough analysis of the key transaction(s) to determine what configurations will *not* be able to handle the key transactions. Although this approach is a useful for relatively simple applications, especially those dominated by a single transaction or two, it is at best a vague approximation for larger and more complex applications.

The estimation process considers the known limitations of parts of the proposed system, and then compares these to the minimum estimated demand associated with the task at hand. For example, a 2.1 GB disk is capable of 62 random access I/O operations per second (8 KB each); each operation consumes about 2 ms of processor attention on a 50 MHz SuperSPARC running Solaris 2.3[28]. If an application requires about 700 random-access disk reads per second, a system with a single disk clearly cannot possibly perform the task in the required time; at least 12 drives are required. Furthermore, it is equally evident that a uniprocessor system cannot handle this problem, since the 700 disk operations per second necessitate 1,400 milliseconds of processor attention every second (i.e., 1,000 milliseconds). It is crucial to observe that although it is certain that a uniprocessor system with one disk will not be able to accomplish this application at the required speed, *it is far from certain that a 12-disk, dual-processor system will actually attain the required performance.* The uncertainty is due to the fact

---

[28] Solaris 2.5 is considerably more efficient, consuming about 0.7 ms on a 50 MHz SuperSPARC for the same task. Obviously, even less time is required on a 200 MHz UltraSPARC.

that so much of the application has been abstracted out of the calculations—in this case, the entire application computation has been simplified out!

3.6.3 Case Study 6—Loading a Database

As an example, consider an application that must be able to recreate a database within a four-hour window every night. The database consists of two tables, one with 10 million records of 2 KB each, the other with 40,000 records about 1 MB in size—40 GB. Assuming that the indexing is done in a separate operation, creating the first table requires completing 10 million 2 KB disk operations in the four hours, or 695 per second. As shown in Figure 44 (page 273), disks typically can achieve about 100 random-access operations per second (2KB) in raw mode, and about 400 ops/sec if the access is serial. Clearly, at least two disks must be used in parallel if the table creation is done serially, or twelve disks—in parallel—if the operation is done randomly. Usually the table itself is created serially, whereas indexes are often created randomly.

Creating the second table requires writing 40,000 records, 1 MB each in size (40 GB). Although DBMS systems differ in their treatment of large binary data (sometimes called "blobs"), they nearly always will write each data item in one place, and as a result this operation is performed serially. Since each record will consist of around 512 physical disk records, this operation will be dominated by serial disk access—even if each record is stored separately, less than one disk access in 500 will require a seek. This table creation requires 20,480,000 disk writes, or about 1,425 per second. At least four disks must be written simultaneously to achieve the required speeds. Since 40 GB must be stored, at least 14 disks must be used to store the data (two for the indexes and 12 for the data).

In order to achieve these disk I/O rates, the system must devote approximately 0.33 ms of CPU time on a 60 MHz SuperSPARC per disk operation. The first table requires 695 disk operations per second, or 230 ms/sec of processor attention. The second table requires 1,425 disk operations per second, or about 470 ms/sec of processor. Between them they require about 700 milliseconds per second, most of a 60 MHz SuperSPARC processor or about half of an 85 MHz CPU solely for manipulating the disk farms. In addition, all of that data has to come from someplace, and processing the incoming data requires processor time, too. The data arrives from an FDDI network utilizing TCP/IP. The system expects to receive a total of 60 GB of data in four hours, or about 4.27 MB/sec. A 75 MHz SuperSPARC can move about 10 MB/sec; the required data transfer rate consumes somewhat less than half of a 75 MHz processor. Given FDDI's maximum transfer size of 4,500 bytes, this rate is about 970 packets per second, and the 400 microseconds (0.4 ms, on 60 MHz SuperSPARC) per packet overhead costs 388 ms/sec of processor time (275 ms on 85 MHz). If the data does not arrive in full 4,500-byte packets, this overhead could well increase (for example, Oracle transmits a single field of a single record in a packet, regardless of size).

Between disk I/O and network I/O, we have consumed about 75 percent of an 85 MHz processor; at least one other processor must be configured in order to handle any other work. Notably, processor time must be available to run the database management system itself, as well as any other processing that must be handled during the nightly database reload. Furthermore, a moderate fudge factor must be provided, because this analysis presumes that the load can proceed at an average rate that will complete in exactly the specified time. This scenario is unlikely, so some additional resources must be configured against the inevitability that the average performance will be lower than computed and the inevitable bursty behavior.

The final estimated configuration requires a system with two 85 MHz processors; alternatively, a uniprocessor 167 MHz UltraSPARC can do the job. Twenty 2 GB disks are required to store the data and provide the required disk access, so at least 23 drives must be configured—the system and the DBMS log each require a disk, and the log should be mirrored. The overall data rate from the server to the disk subsystems totals about 12 MB/sec, suggesting that a single disk array and 25 MB/sec FibreChannel are sufficient to handle the serial transfer bandwidth requirements. About $1425 + 400 = 1825$ I/O operations must be processed each second, well below the capacity of a single SPARCstorage Array Model 112 (3,370 I/O ops/sec). An FDDI interface is required, and the system requires a single-ended SCSI interface for miscellaneous CDROM and a potential backup device. The FibreChannel interface and FDDI consume two SBus slots. The built–in SCSI is quite sufficient for the CDROM and any potential backup devices backup on this system is likely to be only a marginal requirement, because the data is continually refreshed from an external source). The DBMS load process itself does not require any particular amount of memory; only a few processes are running, and very little data can be cached, since this application is essentially write–only. Most two–CPU systems have 128 MB memory, and no particular requirement to have more or less.

Because requirements demand only two SBus slots with little prospect for many more, these requirements can be met with a dual–processor 85 MHz SPARCserver 1000E or some form of Ultra–1/170.

3.6.4 Case Study 7—Multi-User Query

Consider an application that provides order status information for a telephone-order service bureau. Although the application system supports a number of different types of users, only one key transaction is needed to size the system: account/order status query. During the day, the system must support 120 users running account/order queries with a maximum response time of two seconds. Typically, operators process about one call every two minutes (new orders are taken on a separate system and are posted to the query system nightly after the backups).

On the average, the system contains 7,000 active accounts and about 8,500 outstanding orders. All told, it currently retains record for 260,000 accounts (both active and historical) and 65,000 recent orders (orders older than three months are archived and removed from the outstanding order table). Rows in the account table are approximately 3 KB, and the account table is indexed by account number and last name. Rows in the outstanding order table are 90 bytes; each order refers to an average of six rows in the line item table; line items are 30 bytes each. The order table is indexed by account number. Finally, each line item refers to an item description; the system hold 1,050 current item descriptions, each 220 bytes long. These data sizes are summarized in Table 13.

Table 13. Data table sizes for the telephone-order application

Table	Number of Rows	Row Size	Raw Data Size
Accounts	260,000 (7,000 active)	3 KB	780 MB
Orders	65,000 (8,500 active)	90 bytes	5.9 MB
Line item	390,000	30 bytes	11.7 MB
Item descriptions	1,050	220 bytes	231 KB

From this data we know that the active data storage requirement is about 800 MB of raw data; after indexing and storage in the database, this probably represents 1.6-2.0 GB of disk storage.

In normal operation an operator receives a phone call from the customer, who provides either an order number or customer name. Occasionally the customer cannot be located directly by name, and the operator must query the account table by zip code. This situation occurs approximately five percent of the time. Once the order is located, the line items and their status are displayed on the screen. The vast majority of customer calls—over 99 percent—result in queries to only one order.

Described in terms of disk accesses, the typical transaction causes a keyed (random) read to the account index, followed by a keyed read to the account table, which reads 3 KB of data. The account record provides the index key to search the order table's index. Because there are 8,500 outstanding orders and only 7,000 active accounts, each access to the order index results in roughly 8,500 ÷ 7,000 = 1.21 disk accesses each to the order table and its index. Finally, each order refers to six line items; because these are very small and are written to the database at the same time, a reasonable presumption is that they will generate an access to the index and then just one access to the data (6 rows × 30 bytes per row is far less than a typical 2 KB DBMS data block). The last access is to the item description; ho wever, since this data is both very small (the entire table is just 230 KB) and very frequently accessed, it will usually be cached and probably not accessed from disk.

Given these figures, we can deduce that each customer call will probably generate a disk access for the account index, 1.5 to the account table (the row is 3 KB, but most data blocks are 2 KB), about 1.2 to the order table and 1.2 to the order table index, and one each to the line item table and its index—a total of about six disk reads, almost all random access.

Since each query is expected to take six disk reads, and 120 will demand 120 queries every two minutes, the average demand will be one query per second. Since six disk accesses are all that are required for each query, even a single-disk system will clearly be sufficient to handle the typical steady-state queries (recall that a separate disk is *always* recommended for the log disk, not for performance reasons, but rather for data security and survivability). Because a disk drive is capable of about 60 fully random I/O operations, a single-disk system is clearly capable of handling ten queries arriving at almost exactly the same time, so if the remainder of the system has sufficient resources, the disk subsystem can handle almost anything the users will request.

One further consideration remains, namely the five percent of transactions whose account records must be searched by zip code. Because the account table is not indexed by zip code, the search must be done serially! Therefore, to do *one* of these account queries, the system must read an average of 260,000 ÷ 2 = 130,000 rows to locate the right account record— within two seconds! Since each row is 3 KB, 1.5 I/O operations are required for each row, a total of 195,000 raw 2 KB I/Os. A 535 MB disk is capable of about 450 sequential I/O operations/sec, and four of them (i.e., 2.1 GB of storage) are thus capable of approximately 1,800 ops/sec. Even providing for 16 disks—four times the required storage capability—only 7,200 ops/sec are available. Configuring a disk subsystem that will provide the necessary disk access capacity is economically impractical. The only alternatives are to permit this transaction to take much longer than usual, or to index the account table by zip code. Indexing the account table is a simple matter that eliminates the problem with this transaction.

The best disk configuration uses four fast/wide disks; today this means 4 GB of disk capacity. The log file will be very small, and so can be placed on the system disk. Because the DBMS system was not specified, nor was any indication provided about the amount of application processing time associated with the application, estimating accurately how many processors are required is impossible. Each user performs one transaction every two minutes, and each transaction requires a trivial amount of processing: six disk operations at 0.23 ms each on an 85 MHz SuperSPARC, much less than one percent of a processor every other *minute*. The entire community will demand approximately 10 ms of processor time per query × 120 users ÷ 120 seconds = 10 ms of processor time per second. Clearly any of the processors will handle this load quite easily. Because of the 120 users, processors such as the 85 MHz, with large external caches, are recommended. With such low duty cycles, no other processors are required.

At least 128 MB is necessary, because 120 users will be logged in. If 1 MB is allocated to each user, 32 MB for the basic operating system, and 1 percent of the database yields 8 MB for the DBMS's shared data cache, the minimum memory size is 160 MB. Because the database is not updated, NVRAM acceleration for the log file is not needed.

Finally, the 120 terminals should be connected to terminal servers; no other demand competes for the Ethernet during the prime usage periods, there will be no other traffic will interfere with the minimal Ethernet bandwidth requirements of the terminal servers.

The final estimated configuration is a SPARCstation 20 Model 81 with 160 MB memory, an additional SCSI host adapter, four disks for the DBMS and a 1 GB internal disk for the operating system and miscellaneous DBMS functions. Two 64-port terminal servers are required.

3.6.5 Case Study 8—Online Status Query

The Last National Bank has decided to upgrade its status reporting system, primarily to offload the activity from its IBM ES/9000 mainframe. Marion Haist, the director of MIS for branch support, has already asked for a budget of $250,000 for the server required to support the upgrade (primarily because that was the entire amount available), but she needs some assurance that the upgrade can be accomplished within budget. The project looks daunting. After absorbing a number of local banks, LNB now has 214 branches, with each branch having an average of four customer service stations, resulting in a user population of nearly 850 users. The database must be downloaded every night from the mainframe.

Each station is equipped with a Windows PC. A Visual Basic application will be developed to submit queries to a centralized back-end database, meaning that the application will be run in pure client/server mode. Sybase System 10 is the bank's strategic DBMS system, and is to be used if feasible. The bank is concerned that a system sufficient to handle 850 users might cost far more than the $250K that is budgeted.

Marion indicates that slightly fewer than 400 users will be active simultaneously—each branch has more stations than qualified staff now. Of course, the system must be capable of handling all 850 users, should they all invoke the program, but planning for them all being active simultaneously is unnecessary. The users have specified that a three-second average response time is required, with a maximum (worst–case) response of five seconds. The response time requirement is one of the most troubling specifications, since the 1.7–2 GB main memory size estimated to be required to support 850 users is expected to cost nearly $100K by itself (the bank is expecting the configuration to look something like a quad–processor SPARCcenter 2000E with 2 GB memory).

Each active station averages about 70 customer requests per day. The branches are only open 9 AM to 6 PM in two time zones, suggesting that all of each day's queries will arrive within a ten–hour time window. The database, fortunately, is only 14 GB in size.

3.6.5.1 Configuring for the Daily Load

The first thing to do is to compute how much activity this workload generates. Some investigation reveals that average customer queries can be described with the following pseudo–code:

```
while (true) {
  GetCustomerName (name);
  LookupCustomerId (name, &customerId);
  while (!(lastXactFound=GetCustomerXact (customerId, xactRecord)))
      ShowXactRecord (customerId, xactRecord);
}
```

The master customer record is 1,060 bytes, while each transaction record is a 107 byte row in the database; the typical query returns "about" 50 transactions. With this information, we know that the workload consists of approximately 400 users x 70 queries = 28,000 queries per day. Averaged over the ten–hour workday, this is 28,000 queries / 36,000 seconds = 0.77 queries per second.

Assuming the customer table will be indexed by customer name, and that the transaction table will be indexed by customer ID, the typical query will require a random disk read to the index and a random disk read to the customer table to obtain the customer's master record. Then the DBMS needs to retrieve the 50 transactions from the transaction table. The transactions are logically linked together, so each query requires a random read from the index to find an entry in the list and then another read to obtain the transaction itself. All told, a single query will thus require about 104 random reads from the disk subsystem.

At the average transaction rate of 0.77 queries per second, the disks are required to supply 80 I/Os per second. Moreover, this rate is computed without relying upon a large in–memory cache. This is well within the capabilities of a single disk drive. In fact, this is about the random access capacity of a 7,200 rpm disk drive; a single disk arm is capable of delivering all of the required DBMS information for a single query in about one second (the query requires 104 reads, and a 7,200 rpm disk can deliver 100-110 2 KB I/Os per second). Clearly a 14 GB database for 850 users will not be stored on a single disk drive, so the chances of a $250K solution are looking much better. It's a good thing, too, since Marion gets word that she needs to reduce her capital equipment budget by about half.

The system must support 850 Sybase connections, each of which consumes about 60 KB, a total of 51 MB. Solaris 2.4 or Solaris 2.5 will consume at least 64 MB with this many connections, and Sybase requires another 32–64 MB for execution space for the database engines. A 1 GB shared data cache had been proposed, in consideration of the three-second response time requirement, but randomized nature of the access suggests that this is not necessary: no logical or physical relationship exists between successive queries, and a single customer's records will be retrieved more than once a day only on rare occasions. Accordingly, the five–minute rule suggests that the shared data cache should be about

1 percent of the 14 GB raw data size, or 143 MB. Total memory requirements are 322 MB, so a 320 MB configuration should fit nicely. Nothing points to a requirement for the 2 GB of memory as initially feared.

From the disk I/O requirements, the networking subsystem does not appear to be stressed, at least not in the vicinity of the server itself. A single query returns a master record (about 1 KB) and 50 transactions, 107 bytes each; the total data requirements for the query are slightly less than 7 KB. A 10baseT Ethernet can transfer this amount of data in about 5 milliseconds. However, the branch banks are remote, an d the leased lines from each branch to the central office are 448 Kbit/sec leased lines. This represents a raw data rate of about 56 Kbytes/sec, , transferring the data from the server to the PC will take about 1/8th of a second, assuming no contention for the network. Even if the WAN branches are congested and running at 80 percent utilization, transfer of the query data will still consume less than a second. N either the LAN nor the WAN will be overloaded.

The response time requirement seems easily achieved: even if the WAN is congested and remote traffic takes a full second to transfer, and even if a single disk drive is forced to supply all data with no help from the data cache, this transfer consumes only two seconds, much less than the allotted three seconds. Competition for the server's processor seems unlikely too, given the 0.77 queries per second average rate. Since a query takes on the order of one second to process (excluding WAN latency), with the average arrival rate of somewhat less than one query per second, the CPU will only rarely experience a load of more than one query at a time. A uniprocessor system will clearly handle the daily load.

3.6.5.2 Repopulating the DBMS

A backup strategy is unnecessary, because the database is recreated from scratch every night anyway. However, the database does have to be rebuilt between 6 PM and 9 AM, and preferably in much less time than 15 hours. The data is obtained from the ES/9000, and will be captured via a custom–developed program using SNA peer–to–peer protocols. The ES/9000 is already connected to a Token Ring, and the bank would like to use this as the mechanism for downloading the data if it is capable of doing so. If the download is to take two hours (a nice–to–have according to Marion), the system must transfer 14 GB in 2 x 3600 = 7200 seconds, a sustained transfer rate of slightly less than 2 MB/sec. This data rate is not extremely impressive, except that it is impossible to sustain on a 16 MB it/sec (i.e., maximum theoretical rate is 2 MB/sec) Token Ring network, even if the data can be retrieved from the mainframe and stored on the new server that quickly. If the download is only permitted to use half the network, the data rate is 1 MB/sec.

Given a 1 MB/sec input data rate, the disks must be configured to absorb it. This task is not as easy as it may appear. A single disk can handle 100-110 2 KB I/Os/sec, but this rate represents only 210 KB/sec. Furthermore, unless other arrangements are made, the straightforward approach of "read a record from the mainframe, insert a record in the

DBMS" will result in considerably more I/O than the obvious insertion into the table. The insert also causes a write to the log, in effect doubling the I/O load. Because the tables are indexed, the insert *also* causes a write to the index. This problem can be avoided by dropping the index before the load process begins, and then recreating the index after the data has been acquired from the mainframe.

Since the download mechanism must be created from scratch anyway, a better strategy is to break the download program into several processes. The basic strategy is for one process to obtain data from the mainframe and to create a scratch file in a way that makes efficient use of the disk drive. Whereas Sybase System 10 uses only 2 KB blocks, and may be required to do it in some form of random access, the download program can write a scratch file sequentially in relatively large blocks. Arranging to write the scratch file at the full 1 MB/sec obtainable from the network is straightforward—the data is buffered in memory until large blocks (say 128 KB or more) accumulate; the large blocks are written onto the disk periodically. At intervals, the scratch file is closed and a new scratch file is created to absorb the data stream. Meanwhile, the completed scratch file is used as input to the Sybase bcp bulk loading program, which bypasses the logging process and also makes much more efficient use of the disk drives. Before bcp runs, both the existing tables and indexes are dropped, and the tables are recreated in empty form; the indexes are to be recreated after the bcp completes.

3.6.5.3 Minimizing Cost

In view of the obviously lower than anticipated cost of the server, combined with the mandated budget cuts, the bank now would like to explore just how small a platform can be installed and still meet the requirements. The biggest problem seems to be the memory, which is larger than can be accommodated in most Pentium platforms—many can configure 256 MB, but few can manage 320 MB. The 320 MB configuration includes 51 MB of per–client connection information. However, fewer than half of the clients are expected to be active, and half of that memory can be reasonably permitted to be paged or swapped out. The inactive users will not be affected, except when they start up. Permitting the inactive connections to be swapped out saves half of the 51 MB. In fact, the system can permit virtually all of the 51 MB can be swapped out, with essentially no performance penalty. Even if the 60 KB per user is swapped out, just eight 8 KB disk I/Os are required to reload it from the swap area. Given a disk's ability to deliver 75-85 random 8 KB I/Os, the delay associated with swapping back in is 100 milliseconds. This amount of time is crucial when an application is swapped out *during* operation, but in this application, the swapouts will occur *between* usage periods for each user, configured memory is clearly sufficient to handle more than one user. Nonetheless, the analysis indicates that less than one query will be active on average, and even during periods of "heavy" usage, fewer than ten users will be active.

The largest consumer of memory is the shared data cache, at 143 MB. The SDC was sized at nearly 150 MB because of the five–minute rule, which suggests a data cache size of 1 percent of the raw data size. However, in this case, the five–minute rule is not particularly applicable. Only on rare occasions will almost any data except B–tree structures be cached and reused at all—all the requests will be for different accounts, and moreover, the database is rebuilt from scratch every night. Even if the cache were large enough and populated with data, it is extremely unlikely that the same account will be queried twice in the same day, let alone within five minutes. For these reasons, combined with budget–cutting pressure, it is reasonable to dispense with virtually all the shared data cache memory, limiting it to 10-20 MB. This leaves a 128 MB system, still large for what amounts to a single–user system, but justifiable given the large number of users who will depend on the system.

3.6.5.4 Final Configuration

The proposed configuration needs 14 GB of data storage. After accounting for the 5 percent margin caused by millions of bytes vs. megabytes, the data storage requires seven 2.1 GB 7,200 rpm data disks. Because one disk is sufficient to satisfy the requirements of the typical single query, spreading the disk load across more drives is unnecessary. Four 4.3 GB disks would probably suffice, but would not leave as much headroom in disk access capacity. Another disk is required for the operating system, Sybase executables, and the database log. Normally the log would require its own disk, but this application does not update the database, and so the log should be inactive. Finally, the log contents are not critical—the database can always be rebuilt from the mainframe should it be lost. Commit buffers are likewise not needed. One additional disk is required for the buffer space necessary for the downloading process, a total of eight drives.

The very low data rates found in this application make configuring all eight drives on a single fast/wide SCSI bus a viable configuration (putting them all in a disk array is also suitable). If the configuration does not use a disk array, Solstice:DiskSuite must be used to stripe the disk access across the database disks. The mainframe connection requires a Token Ring interface, consuming another I/O slot.

In the end, a 200 MHz Pentium with 128 MB is required. A slower processor would surely suffice, but in 1996 there is no economic incentive to choose a slower model. Only two PCI slots are required—one for a fast/wide SCSI host adapter, and one for a Token Ring interface. Solstice:DiskSuite is required, as is Solaris. The eight disk drives are the primary cost, probably amounting to less than $15K, and the entire system can probably be installed for less than $30K—about 85 percent below budget.

3.6.6 Cautions

This sort of analysis involves a number of inaccuracies. In particular, the technique neglects the efficiencies gained by caching various parts of the data; it does not take into account the overhead associated with logging or archiving; and it presumes that B-tree and other internal database access mechanisms are cost-free. It also does not take into consideration the amount of processing that may be done by the application, which is often substantial. However, this method does provide a baseline minimum configuration, and especially in the absence of more formal and/or complete analyses, it provides a reasonable starting configuration.

It is crucial to remember that although this kind of analysis is easily able to decide that a configuration is insufficient to meet the requirements, the method is not able to determine with any certainty that a proposed configuration *is* able to meet requirements.

Configuring Internet Servers 4 ≣

Internet servers provide a variety of services, including World Wide Web (WWW), electronic mail, `ftp` file transfer, Usenet news, and various types of firewall and network connectivity functions. Each function has characteristics that govern the sizing process. *Intra*net servers differ from *Inter*net servers only in their intended audience, but are usually isolated from the global Internet by a firewall. At the same time, because intranet systems provide service to internal users, intranet servers tend to have higher-bandwidth connections to their clients. For most configuration and system sizing purposes, Internet and intranet servers are equivalent.

Few Internet services require an entire system. The most useful way to size a full-service Internet or intranet server is to size the requirements for each service and simply add them up into a single system. Most sites have few enough requirements that individual systems can *easily* handle all of the tasks. Configuring independent systems for each service is certainly possible—and a few large sites need to adopt this strategy—but this practice leads to administrative overhead necessary only for the largest installations.

4.1 World Wide Web (WWW)

Probably the most visible type of Internet usage is the *hypertext transfer protocol* (`http`), the datatype manipulated by Web browsers. The `http` protocol is an application-level, object-oriented protocol that is normally carried by TCP/IP networks. Like the NFS protocol, `http` is stateless. The protocol is extensible, in the sense that the protocol can manipulate arbitrary objects that are not necessarily presently defined in the standard—new objects may be defined and carried within the existing protocol.

As is typical in object-oriented environments, objects in `http` are usually relatively small information. For example, the average object transmitted by `http` is certainly less than 15 KB[29], whereas the typical UNIX file size is approaching 100 KB.

---

[29] Current data is inconclusive. Some studies put the size around 7-8KB, others about 12 KB. The SPECweb96 benchmark uses a typical file size of 13 KB, although this is being reconsidered.

The practical impact of statelessness is that `http` transactions are short-lived and do not depend upon the uninterrupted operation of the server (that is, the server may cease operation and then return to service without the clients having to take special precautions against operating on stale data). However, the stateless nature of the protocol also has a cost: because the vast majority of `http` traffic carries small pieces of information, servers are required to handle many more connection setup and teardowns than one might expect.

Precisely because of its stateless, object-oriented nature, current `http` traffic is a poor technical fit for transportation over the TCP/IP protocol used to carry it. TCP is a connection-oriented transport, and as such is designed for relatively large data transfers, and its creators envisioned only a moderate connection rate to a service-providing host. The `ftp` protocol is part of the TCP/IP suite itself, and it typifies what TCP/IP was designed to do. An `ftp` client opens a connection to the server, and then transmits a small number of requests; the server responds by transmitting or accepting one or more complete files. Since files are relatively large, `ftp` service typically transmits hundreds of KB per connection, and the connection rate of incoming `ftp` requests is usually numbered in the thousands or tens of thousands per day, even on very busy servers. `Http` traffic represents quite a different load: requests rarely transmit more than a few KB, but the connection rate on busy sites may be in the tens of millions per day.

4.1.1 The Request-Response Paradigm

The `http` protocol as presently defined is strictly a request/response protocol: the client issues a request for an object and waits for the corresponding result. Neither the client nor the server begins processing the next request until the current one is processed completely. This lack of pipelining places a premium on transport and server processing latency. Any delays encountered become immediately apparent to the client, because it has no opportunities to amortize those delays across multiple request/response pairs. Large transfer sizes would help overall perceived performance, since they would minimize the number of request-response pairs; unfortunately, most `http` traffic consists of small transfers.

These same issues are present in NFS Version 2 and addressed in NFS Version 3. The request/response paradigm is simple, but it lacks the sophistication required to achieve high performance in large wide-area applications. The `http` 1.1 specification seems to be evolving in the same general direction as later versions of the NFS and SCSI protocols, specifically permitting multiple pending requests and pipelined transmissions.

4.1.2 HTML

The vast majority of `http` traffic consists of Web pages formatted in *hypertext markup language* (HTML). This is the formatting information that describes the appearance and location of Web pages. The nature of HTML descriptions contributes strongly to the character of `http` traffic. Specifically, it defines both the type of pages that can be described; it also dictates the transfer overhead and the mechanisms used to manipulate Web pages.

Each HTML page consists of many tags, each containing one piece of formatting information. Generally speaking, most pages consist of a small amount of text, combined with links to other pieces of information *not* stored in the page itself. For example, every image is stored independently of the pages that refer to it, as are video clips and stream audio. One of the important pieces of information is that HTML is interpreted *by the client*, meaning that references to externally stored information generate additional requests from the client. Many—and probably most—pages contain multiple images. A fairly typical commercial Web page consists of some text (generally 2-5 KB) and a few images (typically 5-10, ranging from about 2 KB for a "new" sticker to 50-100 KB for map and navigation images). Because each image is stored—and obtained from the server or servers—separately, a separate connection is required to transfer each component.

Web sites usually measure their load by how many "hits" they service per day. From a technical standpoint, one hit on a server refers to one `http` serviced connection. Thus the typical page is usually accounted as 5-15 hits—one for each of the images and one for the text itself (page counters actually count references to the page that contain them, but the counter for the server itself is maintained by the `http` server and is incremented for every reference to every object).

HTML objects fall two broad categories; like NFS files, they are distinguished primarily by their size. Text files are small; t is uncommon to find a Web page that contains even 10 KB of text. A page consisting of 10 KB of text would be seven or eight screens of information. All other files are considerably larger, ranging from small image files used to annotate text (for example, a "New" sticker) to much larger images such as map images and photographic content. Larger still are what might be called dynamic-content files, such as MPEG or QuickTime movies or audio streams such as RealAudio. Small image files may occupy only 4-5 KB, while large JPEG or GIF image files can easily consume 150-800 KB or even more. Audio streams are even larger; a one minute stereo recording in a format such as RealAudio is about 1 MB. Movies are presently the largest common file format. A one minute 320x200 movie stored in compressed MPEG format occupies about 5 MB. References to `ftp` downloads are even larger, frequently reaching into the tens and even hundreds of megabytes per file.

4.1.3 The Nature of `http` Processing

Although WWW usage is growing rapidly, actual per-server usage is not especially heavy and does not impose severe load. Most typical intranet sites handle a few thousand hits per day; busy ones handle about a million hits per day. For example, `www.sun.com` normally handles about 700,000 hits per day. On the day after a major announcement, the hit rate may be as high as a million hits. Under normal conditions, this server (an Ultra–1/140) is running at approximately five percent utilization. (This figure accounts only for `http` processing. Other processing, notably search engines, consumes considerably more processor power, as discussed in section 4.1.6, *Server-Side Processing*.) One of the busiest sites anywhere in the Internet is `home.netscape.com`, which averages about 85 million hits per day[30]. These numbers are impressive, but the corresponding average rates are mundane. Eighty-five million hits per day represents a sustained average of about 1,000 `http` connections per second. Current experience suggests that peak rates are about triple the sustained rate, so the maximum load is in the vicinity of 3,000 connections per second.

Well-known sites such as `www.sun.com` and `home.netscape.com` cater to global audiences, and their usage profiles show sustained activity at all hours. Intranet servers usually have a less diverse (and smaller!) user population, and they often handle the vast majority of their load in a period of eight to ten hours. Some of the busier Sun intranet servers handle about 10,000 connections per day[31]. This figure corresponds to an average rate during an eight-hour activity period of approximately 0.35 connections/sec and a peak rate of 1-2 connections/sec.

Ordinary `http` connections are short-lived: most are active for less than 200 milliseconds. Most browsers display the currently requested object in the lower-left footer of the browser window. Every time the footer flashes, a new connection has been initiated and processed. Because the processing of Web pages is a brief operation, combined with the human interaction required to "use" the resulting page, most "users" of a Web server are inactive virtually all of the time. Expressing Web server load in traditional terms such as "simultaneous users" rarely makes sense; the only useful metrics are hits per second and possibly hit latency.

4.1.4 `http` Servers

Many `http` servers are in operation, but for system sizing purposes they can be grouped into three categories: forking servers, threaded servers, and keep-alive servers. All categories handle the same protocols; the only differences are in implementation efficiency.

---

[30] Netscape Navigator uses `home.netscape.com` as its initial location unless users reconfigure the default. Since Navigator has about 85 percent market share, this practice generates a *lot* of hits!

[31] For example, one of Sun's intranet servers provides search engine services for about 2,000 engineers. This system sustains a fairly constant 100,000 hits per month, far less than one connection per second, even accounting for the fact that the vast majority of the queries are submitted within about twelve hours of each day.

4.1.4.1 Forking Servers

Forking servers are those that fork a server process for every incoming http request. This is implementation the most straightforward from a programmatic perspective, because it adheres strictly to the original Berkeley networking programming model. The original http servers, including the NCSA server through version 1.4 and the CERN server, were all forking implementations. Although straightforward to create and easy to understand, the forking design is ill-suited to commercial implementation because http requests are so short-lived and lightweight. When the WWW protocol first exploded onto the computing scene in 1993, Solaris servers spent about twice as much CPU time creating and destroying the daemon process than the daemon spent processing the actual request. Other UNIX implementations behaved similarly, since the UNIX process model is designed around long-lived processes.

These issues limited typical http servers to service rates of 10-20 connections per second, about 1.3 million hits per day. Although some leading-edge sites require higher throughput, even this unassuming capability is adequate to handle virtually all intranet sites. Practically speaking, the connection rate was not an issue for most sites using these servers. However, the processor consumption associated with these rates was such that it prohibited common servers such as uniprocessor SPARCstation 10s from running other tasks, for example local dynamic-content processing or other Internet services.

An intermediate evolution between a forking server and a true threaded server is called a *pre-forking* server. Instead of forking a server process upon receipt of an http request, a number of processes are created at startup time. After processing a fixed number of requests or some period of idle time, each server process exits; a new process is subsequently created upon demand. This arrangement often avoids the forking overhead, it does not solve the problem completely. The server processes are relatively large and consume memory, so they exit when no requests are arriving.

4.1.4.2 Threaded Servers

Most UNIX systems, including Solaris, offer an alternate programming model that accommodates this type of lightweight processing: the *threads* model. Threads provide a mechanism for managing multiple streams of execution within a single process. After the initial experience with forking servers, the implementers modified their code to use the threads model. Each process managed several threads, and was capable of processing multiple connections. On Solaris 2.4, thread_create(3) consumes about 90 percent less CPU time than fork(2)! Not surprisingly, threaded servers consume far less CPU time, permitting the server to process many more hits, or to handle dynamic content processing without having to resort to multiprocessor systems. Typical service rates for threaded servers on a SPARCstation 20 Model 71 (or the equivalent Netra *i*20) are about 100-150 connections/sec—about an order of magnitude better than their predecessors. If a server has responsibility only as an intranet Web site, a derived server such as the SPARCstation 20 or Ultra–1/140 running a threaded server is more than adequate.

4.1.4.3 Keep-Alive Servers

The World Wide Web and its related protocols and services continue to evolve at a frantic pace[32]. As usage increases, the `http` protocol is evolving to meet new requirements and to permit higher performance. One of the key performance-related changes in the `http` 1.1 specification is the transmission of multiple requests in a single connection, a feature called *keep-alive connections* (the RFC that defines the feature formally refers to it as a "persistent connection"). If the client browser requests that the server retain its connection [33], multiple transfers can be made over the single connection. Rather than sensing the termination of the connection, the client must rely on the indicated content length in the document header to determine the boundaries of each document. This arrangement reduces the requirement for threading and eliminates one of the fundamental problems with `http`, the high overhead rate associated with each request. Later versions of Netscape's server can handle the `http` 1.1 protocol, including keep-alive connections. Most current browsers (Netscape 1.1 and later, Microsoft Internet Explorer 2.0 and subsequent versions) generate `http` 1.1 requests when the server can service them. These so-called keep-alive servers are capable of handling about 250-300 connections/sec, nearly double the efficiency of their predecessors.

4.1.4.4 Proxy Servers

An important functional variant of `http` servers is the *proxy* server. As the name suggests, a proxy server is one that provides service on behalf of another server. Usually this arrangement arises because firewalls are used to restrict access to outside servers. Inside the firewall, clients send all requests to the proxy server. The proxy's job is to retrieve the requested objects from their external location and then provide them to the requesting client. This arrangement permits external traffic to be directed solely to the proxy system, rather than exposing every internal client to the hazards of global access. Proxy servers must handle more load than other servers, since they are both clients and servers. Given a threaded server, the cost of forwarding the client traffic is somewhat less than the cost of

---

[32] This result is largely due to the explosion in usage. At one time in 1994, traffic on the global Internet was increasing at the rate of ten percent *per week*, mostly attributed to the rapid acceptance and use of the World Wide Web. Even today (late-1996), a few of the largest sites continue to report usage increases of five percent per *week!*

[33] The term "keep-alive" is overloaded. In this context a keep-alive refers to a bit set in the `http` request header. It is different from, and unrelated to, the TCP protocol parameter by the same name.

providing the proxy server service itself. Although overhead approaching 100 percent is intimidating, the low cost of either part of the processing means that this is rarely a configuration issue.

Proxy servers often improve their performance by using caching techniques. By caching the requests and their replies, caching proxy servers are able to satisfy many internal requests without having to issue requests on the external Internet. Clients of most proxy servers have much better network connections to their proxy servers than to the global Internet. The caching proxy can satisfy cache hits without suffering the latency of accessing the Internet, savings that can be particularly useful when accessing slower sites.

4.1.5 Network Latency

The small size and request/response nature of host `http` requests place great emphasis on networking performance, but from a relatively unusual perspective. One of the largest determinants of perceived `http` performance is request latency, the round-trip time required to service an `http` request, including network transmission time to the server, server processing time, and return network transmission time. This issue is particularly relevant for users at large corporations, where complex network topologies are common. Each router in the client-server path injects latency in each direction, as does the use of a proxy server. For fast routers in simple networks, the overhead is negligible, but complex networks may have as many as ten or even 20 routers connecting a variety of networks between a client system on the user's desk and an Internet server in a remote location.

Fast routers add 1-2 ms of latency to each packet, whereas slow routers may add as much as 10 ms[34]! More complex networks may include wide-area links that are far slower (or more heavily utilized) than typical local area networks. The effect of latency is particularly acute in wide-area networks, because some long-haul network media can inject extremely high latency. Microwave relays are an excellent mechanism for bringing wide-area networks to remote offices at reasonable expense, but they are notorious for latency. For example, a typical T1 land-based transcontinental link injects about 7 ms of latency simply for the data to travel from one end of the link to the other. Wide-area networks can inject as much as 100-500 ms of latency, even when the link is not fully utilized! Bandwidth is not necessarily at issue here; a high bandwidth link may also have high (i.e., poor) latency.

Even for a relatively simple corporate intranet topology with five routers, 5-10 ms per operation are added, causing delays easily perceived by users. Another way to express this

---

[34] Older workstations have traditionally been used as routers near the end of their careers. For example, many sites use five-year-old SPARCstation 2s as routers as they are replaced on user desktops by more powerful models such as SPARCstation 20s and Ultra-based workstations. SPARCstation 2s have no problems keeping up with the throughput demands of slower networks such as Ethernet or T1, but they can inject significant packet latency.

situation is that a typical 5 KB `http` request takes about a millisecond to process in the server, meaning that even a fast router adds nearly 100 percent overhead! (A convenient way to measure network latency is to use "`ping -vs server`", which returns the round-trip latency of an ICMP echo request.)

Proxy servers also add latency, especially if the proxy does not cache requests or if the request does not hit the cache. Since proxies are both clients and servers, the overhead of a proxy server is about 200%, in addition to any other networking delays that the request may encounter. Sites that are very security-conscious often place a caching proxy server in a "demilitarized zone" consisting of two firewalls, such as Figure 16:

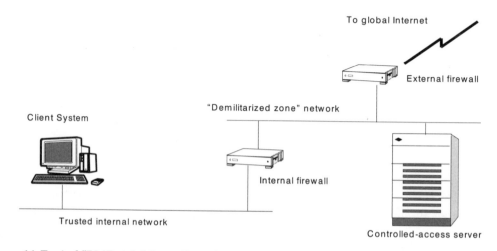

Figure 16. Typical "DMZ-style" firewall topology. The internal firewall permits controlled access to trusted hosts only from the controlled-access server such as a caching proxy Web server. Access to that server is restricted by the external firewall. This topology is safe, but it requires fast firewall servers to avoid noticeable latency penalties.

This arrangement is very secure, because clients are prevented from direct interaction with any external machine, but the latency associated with the arrangement warrants consideration. The security concerns that mandate such arrangements are often not negotiable, so the configuration planner may need to arrange to tolerate the overhead by reducing other latencies, for example by upgrading routers.

Network *latency* problems are often misdiagnosed as network *bandwidth* problems. Sometimes increasing the bandwidth does improve matters, but in most cases, improving the bandwidth only resolves a small part of the latency problem. Consider a corporate intranet in which a client in Los Angeles is browsing Web pages residing on a server in Boston. A typical network topology places a router between the client's network and the building backbone, and another between the building backbone and the external link; the situation is mirrored in the server's building. If the external link from Los Angeles to Boston is a direct T1 line, the transmission latency for a typical page is approximately 5 KB ÷ 1.5 Mbits/sec = 2.5 ms. Four routers are between the client and server; if they add 1.5 ms latency each, the router latency is 6 ms. The total network latency is 8.5 ms. Upgrading the external link to T3 speed (45 Mbits/sec) reduces the transmission latency to 0.83 ms, so overall latency is 6.83 ms—a 20 percent improvement, despite a 30,000 percent increase in bandwidth!

4.1.6 Server-Side Processing

Most of the resources used on Web servers are consumed not by the obvious http requests, but instead by various related server processing. Often the largest consumer is a search engine. Most Web servers that support search engines devote the majority of their CPU time to this service. The nature of both the search engine and the search criteria themselves varies widely, but searching a multi-megabyte database is a more demanding process than simply copying a 5 KB file back to the network.

In addition to CPU time, search engines consume substantial memory, often as much as 5-10 MB for a typical search. Memory consumption is relatively small because most search engines' indexing mechanisms successfully confine most search activity to the indices, avoiding access to the much larger pages themselves. Searches can be quite disk-intensive if the search criteria do not match well with the indexing strategy. Most searches are of fairly limited duration, and occur infrequently. Web servers with significant searching responsibilities should be sized around the search activities.

Search engines share many characteristics with database servers, and many of the same optimization tricks that apply to database engines apply to search engines. One effective but possibly expensive strategy is to use the file system as a virtual memory buffer to cache the entire search space (see section 9.1.5.3, *Supercaching*). This strategy is used on the AltaVista network search service: the site is designed to satisfy most searches from memory, instead of searching local disk or beginning a new search on the Internet. For obvious reasons, this technique substantially reduces search latency and improves the perceived speed of the search engine.

The supercaching technique is often much more cost-effective in intranet Web search applications than in most DBMS environments, because the amount of information managed (indexed) is often far smaller. Web search engines have a slightly different function than DBMSs. Requests to the latter usually use the indices as a method to retrieve transactional data stored in the same database. In contrast, the function of a Web search engine is to provide pointers to information that is usually stored elsewhere in the network. Combined with the impact of network latency, caching on the server can have a tremendous impact on client search performance— particularly for search engines that index data resident elsewhere on the network, rather than locally stored data.

4.1.6.1 `cgi-bin` Scripts

Search engines are usually a special case of generalized processing known as *Common Gateway Interface* (CGI). This mechanism is used to implement arbitrary server-side processing on behalf of `http` clients. Clients request processing by issuing requests for objects that are executable programs or scripts. Many common applications make use of this facility. For example, most mechanisms that show the number of times the containing page has been hit are implemented as `cgi-bin` scripts, as are most search engine requests and virtually all dynamic content Web pages. Applications such as MapQuest's Interactive Atlas or Data Broadcasting's stock quotations create the displayed Web page dynamically by executing binary programs on the server. The output of these programs is HTML code that is transmitted to the client for interpretation by the client Web browser.

In this scenario each request for dynamic content causes the `http` server to create a child process to create the content. Although this mechanism is sufficient and effective for many applications, it suffers from two fundamental limitations. First, communication between the client browser and the dynamic content is limited in extent and difficult to implement on an ongoing basis. The client can conveniently pass arguments to the `cgi-bin` script, but once the script creates the HTML output, communication between the `cgi-bin` executable program and the client becomes problematic. The other major issue with the `cgi-bin` model is that it is inherently server-biased. The limited functionality of most browsers makes it very difficult to organize client/server applications.

Sizing for Web servers that have significant `cgi-bin` activity is equivalent to sizing timesharing servers, albeit without the character-by-character overhead often associated with timesharing environments. The `cgi-bin` mechanism is often combined with shell scripts that perform the actual processing; this practice causes substantial overhead on the server because shell scripts typically consist of long sequences of invocations of programs, most of which perform relatively little work in proportion to the overhead of invoking them. Production servers should take care to invoke `cgi-bin` binaries directly. Scripts written in interpreted languages such as `Perl` or *TCL* are intermediate positions that are more easily developed and debugged than fully compiled C programs, but which nonetheless require the services of a language interpreter.

4.1.6.2 Java

One of the attributes of the Java language is that it can overcome the limitations of the `cgi-bin` model (as well as a variety of other problems). Java is a mechanism for embedding arbitrarily complex extensions into the `http` protocol—specifically, Java is an entire object-oriented language and environment. The most common examples of Java code (called *applets*) are Web pages that have moving content, such as a marquees or dancing figures. In reality, Java is far more useful: it creates programmability and extensibility in the remote client, but under the control of the server. The server provides the Java content upon demand. Because the Java content can be arbitrarily complex, it enables the creation of client-side applications that reside in the World Wide Web. Because the client is completely programmable, it is free to react to user or network input, and to initiate connections with objects residing elsewhere in the network. This organization is fundamentally different from the server-biased model of the `cgi-bin` script.

Java applets are simply textual objects that reside on the server. In their simplest form, they are merely additional `http` objects that are downloaded from the server upon demand. Used in this way, Java applets are simply more text, and sizing servers to handle such applets is trivial (and very lightweight). However, as client Java interpreters become more powerful, developers are creating much more complex applets that have all of the characteristics of standard object-oriented applications. Sizing systems for a client/server system built from fully general Java programs ceases to be an exercise in configuring Web servers; instead, the sizing must be based around the requests generated by the applets. For example, if the applet queries a database, the corresponding server is sized as a database server; the fact that the querying application is written in Java is irrelevant. Despite Java's class-oriented nature and the fact that the Java client requires a separate `http` operation for each class instantiation, the delivery of the applets themselves is trivial overhead compared to the processing of the application itself. The delivery overhead is similar in nature and extent to the linker/loader overhead found in classical operating systems.

4.1.7 Configuring WWW Servers

Configuring most Web servers is relatively simple, since most available servers can handle all but the heaviest peak loads. The most straightforward procedure is to begin with some targeted number of connections per day. For new Web servers with no past history, a conservative first target is about 10,000 connections per day for intranet servers or about 20,000 connections per day for servers catering to the global Internet. Adjust the daily rate to the service day of the intended users; for example, Web servers whose relevance is restricted to workers in a single office have a service day of eight to ten hours, whereas an international site with multilingual content probably has a 24-hour service day. Convert the adjusted daily rate to a connections/sec rate and multiply by a factor of three or four to obtain an estimate of peak instantaneous load. For example, 10,000 connections/day for a server catering only to the continental U.S. represents a peak rate of

$$\frac{10,000 \; connections \; per \; day}{8 \; hours} \times \frac{1 \; hour}{3,600 \; secs} \times 4x \; peak \; load = 1.4 \; connections \, / \, sec \, .$$

4.1.7.1 Network Capacity

The server (or server cluster) must have adequate network bandwidth. Alternatively, if network bandwidth is fixed, it may impose a ceiling on the service that the server must provide. Observations of http traffic suggest that peak loads are about three to four times as heavy as the sustained load, and network capacity should be planned accordingly (also permitting other traffic to share the network). The small size of typical requests means that the TCP/IP overhead amounts to 30 percent. Taken together, these factors suggest that the various network media can support average daily connection rates as shown in Table 14.

Table 14. Capacity of various network media in thousands of hits per day, after allowing for peak activity periods of three times the sustained rate. Typical hits transfer between 5 KB and 10 KB each.

Hit Size	28K Dialup	ISDN	56K	T1	10baseT	T3	100baseT
2 KB	28.4	64.5	56.4	1,593.7	12,902.4	58,060.8	129,024.0
5 KB	11.3	25.8	22.6	637.5	5,161.0	23,224.3	51,609.6
10 KB	5.7	12.9	11.3	318.7	2,580.5	11,612.2	25,804.8
15 KB	3.8	8.6	7.5	212.5	1,720.3	7,741.4	17,203.2
100 KB	0.6	1.3	1.1	31.9	258.0	1,161.2	2,580.5

For intranet servers, networking capacity is rarely an issue, because systems have at least 10baseT connectivity. Moreover, few intranet servers have large enough client populations to generate any significant load. Connections to the Internet can be problematic. Typical text Web pages are about 5 KB and since typical Web servers provide relatively few audio or movie files, the overall average is approximately 10 KB. A server with a 56 Kbit/sec leased line is capable of handling only about 11,300 hits/day.

Solaris scalability across networks is essentially linear, at least through the currently tested configurations up through 40-50 100baseT networks. Obtaining adequate capacity is a simple matter of providing enough network interfaces; for example, 100,000 hits per day requires about four T1 networks or 25-30 dialup lines.

4.1.7.2 Processor and Memory

Given a target peak transaction rate, select a suitable platform from Table 15. If the server is to operate as a proxy server, each request is effectively doubled. Most proxy servers are also caching proxies, helping reduce demand in some circumstances. Few Web servers are very demanding on processors, even pure proxy servers [35]. The rates shown in Table 15 are based on Solaris 2.5.1 with the Solaris Internet Server Supplement (2.5.1-SISS) and the Netscape

---

[35] Most proxy servers are I/O bound, not CPU-bound, but some of the reporting mechanisms (e.g., SunNet Manager) are misleading.

Enterprise Server. Stock Solaris 2.5.1 delivers about 20 percent lower throughput on equivalent hardware.

Memory is configured at 32 MB plus 2 MB per server process. Although non-essential, caching frequently-used pages in memory is a common goal. The Solaris virtual memory system arranges for this to happen without intervention on the part of the `http` server processes. (See section 9.1.5, *Caching File System I/O*.) Consider providing memory for everything that could reasonably be expected to be accessed more than about once every five minutes. (See section 3.5.2.1, *Sizing the DBMS I/O Cache*.) The effectiveness of caching depends on the diversity of the pages provided by the server. For systems that provide primarily static content for a single logical site, caching may be very effective. On the other hand, it is pointless to try to cache a large proportion of a system that operates as many different logical sites, since they will tend to direct their requests to widely scattered parts of the file system.

Memory should always be configured with at least 64 MB per SuperSPARC or Pentium processor or 128 MB per UltraSPARC or Pentium Pro processor.

Table 15. Practical Web server capability by platform, assuming no other load (e.g., no search engines or other server-side processing). Operating system is Solaris 2.5.1 with the Solaris Internet Server Supplement.

Platform	Hits/day	Sustained connections/sec
SPARCstation 5, 110 MHz, Netra *i5* or 133 MHz Pentium	8.2 million	95
SPARCstation 20, 75 MHz SuperSPARC or Netra *i20*	9.5 million	110
SPARCserver 1000E, 1x 85 MHz	7.7 million	90
Ultra–1/170 or Pentium Pro	26.8 million	310
Ultra–2/2200	54.0 million	626
UE3000, 167 MHz/1 MB cache	28.0 million	325

Multiprocessor scalability of Solaris 2.5.1 Web performance is substantially lower than for most other operations—scaling well to only two processors, compared to 24 processors for NFS and as far as 50-60 processors for typical DBMS applications. The lack of scalability is primarily due to the basic conflict between typical `http` usage and fundamental TCP/IP design. Over the course of several releases, the Solaris TCP/IP implementation has been optimized considerably for traditional TCP applications such as `ftp`, `telnet` and other applications using persistent connections such as DBMS clients. Because `http` is relatively new, the Solaris TCP subsystem has not yet been highly tuned for multiprocessor scalability.

Substantial improvements are anticipated in the next two releases, but for releases that are available at this writing, the very busiest Web sites must resort to server farms and techniques such as round-robin DNS, rather than large multiprocessors.

4.1.7.3 Round-Robin DNS

The most common way to apply a group of servers to providing service for a large Web site is the use of *round-robin Domain Name Service* (RRDNS, a variant of the DNS used nearly universally for IP address resolution). The principle is simple: clone the site content on several machines, and have the local domain name service map requests from each client to one of the identical servers on a rotating basis. This arrangement works well precisely because of the characteristics of `http` traffic. Connections to the server are short-lived and frequent, giving the firewall many opportunities to look up the server's address; each lookup returns a different member of the cluster.

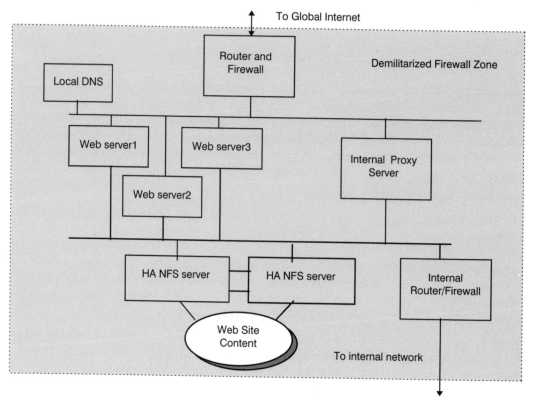

Figure 17. Round-robin DNS configuration for very large Web sites

Ensuring the same content on all systems is not as difficult as it might seem. One simple solution is to place all the content on an NFS server and have each of the servers obtain the content via NFS. Even the largest server farms are not so busy as to overwhelm a large NFS server: a raw `http` request rate of 3,000 `http` connections per second is well within the capability of a dual-processor NFS server, even if every `http` connection results in an NFS read. Of course, with UFS caching on the clients (the Web servers), the NFS traffic is often less than half this rate. An even more effective configuration uses CacheFS to further reduce the load on the NFS server.

Any Web site busy enough to warrant a RRDNS is important enough to ensure full-time availability. The Web servers themselves are replicated, and both the DNS server and the NFS server can be easily replicated. The NFS server requires a high-availability configuration such as Solstice:HA-NFS. The presence of a second NFS server ensures that sufficient NFS capability is available in even the largest site. A large RRDNS configuration using Solstice:HA-NFS is shown in Figure 17.

The RRDNS approach (which also works for `ftp` servers, but not for email hubs) is effective for sites that are maintained within a single physical domain. Perceived response changes very little as the load is transferred between the various Web servers. When the members of the logical cluster are geographically distributed, several problems appear. The first problem is the matter of replicating content between the cluster members. NFS over wide-area networks may or may not be able to solve the problem, depending upon internal infrastructure and the distance between nodes. The biggest issue is that clients will perceive wide variances in response time as their service comes from different parts of the globe. The clients send requests to a single, well-known address, and that address is responsible for providing the data, in whatever way is reasonable. This approach leads to providing service on a round-robin basis, rather than clients requesting that service on a geographic basis. In some ways, RRDNS is the right solution to the wrong problem.

4.1.7.4 Operating Many Addresses

When several machines operate together in a cluster to provide a common set of services, users can take advantage of a feature in Solaris originally implemented for Solstice:HA products, logical interfaces. Each physical interface in the system can be assigned multiple IP addresses, permitting the interfaces to respond to all of them. For example:

```
# ifconfig hme0 plumb
# ifconfig hme0 myhost netmask + broadcast + -trailers up
# ifconfig hme0:1 plumb
# ifconfig hme0:1 anotherhost netmask + broadcast + -trailers up
# ifconfig hme0:2 plumb
# ifconfig hme0:2 yetanother netmask + broadcast + -trailers up
```

Solaris permits up to 255 logical interfaces on each physical address. This number is sufficient to handle most situations. A few systems operate many logical servers on a single physical machine, and occasionally even adding additional interfaces does not provide enough addresses. Adding even more interfaces is a possible solution; with 20 quad-port Ethernet interfaces a system can support over 5,000 addresses. The disadvantage of this approach is that it requires considerable network infrastructure, and the associated cabling is unnecessarily complex. In these circumstances, the most appropriate solution is the use of IP address translation by a router or firewall. This solution has the advantage of permitting a system to serve an arbitrary number of addresses and also allows the logical servers to relocate to a different physical system by changing the firewall's address translation table.

4.1.7.5 Storage Subsystem

Pure Web servers make light demands on storage subsystems, since they are usually restricted by either operating system scalability or by network bandwidth—or by the low demand characteristic of the workload. Maximum attainable hit rates are around 350 per second. Even disregarding caching, these represent only 350-700 I/O operations per second, a rate easily handled by 4-7 current 7,200 rpm disks. Since Web service is virtually read-only and is heavily multithreaded—from a disk subsystem's perspective—mirrored or RAID -5 configurations are excellent solutions. Typical intranet servers (10,000 hits/day) can easily manage with a single disk.

A conservative rule of thumb is to multiply the peak hit rate by two to get the peak I/O operation rate. Provide one 7,200 rpm disk for every 75 hits/sec or one 5,400 rpm disk for every 60 hits/sec (see section 7.1.1, *Components of Disk Access Time*) .

4.2 Electronic Mail Servers

Electronic mail is the most commonly provided Internet service. Email processing differs substantially from WWW and other Internet services in that it is nearly always practiced as a background activity with limited latency requirements. Additionally, direct delivery of a message is rare; some sort of aliasing and redirection is applied to virtually every message, especially messages that cross the bounds of the workgroup.

Two distinctly different components make up email processing: the user agent (UA) and one or more message transfer agents (MTAs). User agents are responsible for interacting with users and arranging for their requests to be handled by a network of MTAs. Once a message has been created and queued for delivery, the MTA network is responsible for delivering the mail to its recipients. Email servers usually have primary responsibility for running MTAs, although some also run UAs.

Email usage is relatively low-intensity; most mail messages are small, averaging less than 10 KB each. Overall processing of an individual message tends to be hierarchical, especially for mail that is addressed to aliased canonical addresses (e.g., John.Q.Public@provider.net, as opposed to the eventual delivery address, for example, jqp@mailsys13). Each message is processed several times, especially when routing across multiple domains in large corporate networks. For example, a message addressed to John.Public@Company.com may be delivered to jpq@company.com, which sends it to jpq@boston.company.com, where it is forwarded to jpq@boston_finance.company.com, from which the user's PC retrieves the message. Only one logical message was handled, but the various systems had to handle the equivalent of three messages, rather than one. Although the alias processing is not expensive on any given node, the fact that many systems must handle the message means that the actual number of messages processed may be substantially greater than the number of inbound or outbound messages.

4.2.1 Mail Transfer Protocols

Three mail transfer protocols are in common use on Solaris systems: *Simple Message Transfer Protocol* (SMTP), *Post Office Protocol* (POP) and Interactive Mail Access Protocol version 4 (IMAP4).

4.2.1.1 SMTP

SMTP is the most commonly used mail protocol in Solaris environments, partly because it is bundled with Solaris and partly because it is often a lowest common denominator between heterogeneous systems. The SMTP protocol is implemented by the sendmail(8) daemon. The store-and-forward characteristics of SMTP, combined with the implementation peculiarities of the sendmail daemon itself drive the sizing requirements.

The sendmail(8) daemon delivers the overwhelming majority of email messages in Solaris environments. From a sizing and configuration perspective, the most significant characteristic of this process is that it makes use of three temporary files for every delivered message. Busy SMTP hubs create and destroy an enormous number of files during normal processing. File creation and deletion each require synchronous disk writes, because they involve modification of the file system structure. These files are placed in /var/spool/mqueue, and these characteristics mean that this directory should always reside in a logging file system. Without UFS + logging, the scratch files make unacceptable demands on the underlying storage subsystems of busy mail hubs.

Mail is delivered by appending the formatted message to the recipient's mail file. This operation is simple, but it represents a small faction of the effort required to deliver the message. Since the average mail message is about 6 KB, the task requires only one I/O operation.

From a networking perspective, handling and receiving email is similar to serving Web pages—each entity is small—but there are two major distinctions. Mail traffic tends to come from relatively few sources, and since the SMTP protocol permits transferring many messages on a single TCP connection, this drastically reduces the overhead of creating and tearing down TCP connections. An exception to this rule is the primary gateway for a large corporation or service provider, since it is the nexus point for all traffic going into or out of the corporate intranet.

Additionally, email delivery is less frequent than requests for Web pages. For example, Sun uses email extensively, resulting in about a million messages per day. Only a small proportion of that traffic passes through the firewall to the global Internet. Individual hubs handle far fewer messages.

4.2.1.2 POP

The POP protocol is used almost universally by PCs, especially to collect mail from Internet service providers. Unlike SMTP, which is most often used to transfer messages between MTAs, POP is used primarily to move data from a mail hub to the system that runs the destination user agent. Because POP is used as a batch protocol, POP servers typically do not use a large number of intermediate files, instead copying data directly onto the destination mail file. This method represents much lower overhead on the server than inbound SMTP. In Solaris environments, POP is generally used to transfer mail to end-user clients, and SMTP is used to transfer mail between hubs.

4.2.1.3 IMAP4

The IMAP4 protocol is a client-to-server mail protocol that permits email clients to operate in disconnected mode over relatively thin wires. Its use is increasing rapidly due to the rapid implementation of portable computing and telecommuting. SMTP and POP handle messages in their entirety, either transferring them or not transferring them. Standard user agents read the entire spool file for processing, usually transferring the file from the hub to the client system in the process.

Transferring the entire spool file to the client system for processing may be an expensive operation, especially if the client is connected via a very slow network. This expense is particularly acute if the client connects via a dialup modem. To avoid this problem, the IMAP protocol transfers only the header information to the client, along with whatever message bodies and attachments are explicitly requested.

Overall, clients using the IMAP protocol impose approximately the same load on the hub as typical SMTP clients. IMAP requires that the hub retain data on the server for longer periods of time, increasing storage requirements slightly. In addition, the spool file must be read and processed more than once. In exchange, the server often does not have to transfer the complete body and attachments of many messages. The IMAP protocol is relatively new, as is the Solstice Internet Mail Server implementation, so its usage may change.

4.2.2 Configuring Email Hubs

The most important part of sizing an email hub is the temporary spool space. It is the only configuration dimension that most users might realistically expect to under-configure. Although other facets such as processor power, memory size, network connectivity, and disk capacity are always considerations, only the largest email hubs will encounter these issues.

4.2.2.1 Temporary and Spool Storage

The most important configuration dimension for email servers is the storage subsystem. Two completely different types of storage are required for intermediate files and for semi-permanent message storage. As noted previously, the SMTP MTAs make extensive use of temporary files to ensure that messages in transit can be processed in the event of a system failure. Writing each temporary file involves three synchronous I/O operations, or nine per message. A 7,200 rpm disk drive can deliver about seventy 8 KB synchronous writes per second; dedicating a disk to this purpose permits handling about eight messages per second—about 700,000 per day. When the spool file system resides on a logging file system with a mirrored log, the file system can absorb about 100 writes per second, or about a million messages per day. Reads are not significant since they are cached in memory by the file system.

Departmental servers with fewer than a thousand mailboxes do not handle enough traffic to warrant extreme measures, but for large mail gateways that must handle millions of messages per day, probably the most appropriate choice for the spool file system is a solid-state disk. The disk does not need very much capacity; the temporary files only exist for a few hundred milliseconds. Typical solid-state disks can deliver 1,000 writes per second, sufficient capacity to handle over 100 messages/sec.

The storage file system has very different demands, with few synchronous writes and many reads. And of course, the storage requirements are much greater. The most conservative approach to configuring the storage file system is to configure sufficient random access I/O capability to saturate the outbound network. For example, an email hub with four 10baseT interfaces to clients has about 4 MB/sec of outbound capacity. A disk drive can deliver 75 random access I/Os (8 KB each), about 600 KB/sec. Seven drives are required to saturate the networks—this might be configured as seven drives in a single stripe, or as two four-wide stripes mirroring each other. An Internet server with two T1 lines has about 3 Mbits/sec or almost 400 KB/sec available. This much lighter load requires only one disk drive.

This method is conservative, since it assumes that all networks will be fully busy at the same time. The estimate can be scaled back depending on the characteristics of the user community. For hubs equipped with very fast networks (e.g., 100baseT), configuring storage in this fashion is overly conservative. Although fast clients have the capability to demand a large amount of bandwidth, such demand will happen only occasionally, since the spool files are of relatively limited size. An Ultra–1 client connected to the server via FastEthernet can consume up to 8 MB/sec from the mail storage file system, but it will do so for only a short time. An 8 MB spool file will contain well over 1,000 messages, an unlikely occurrence. Even when it happens, the entire spool file will be completely transferred to the client within a second.

4.2.2.2 Networking

As with Web servers, the output network can often constrain the overall throughput of an email hub. A 110 MHz SPARCstation 5 can deliver nearly 590 messages per second (see Table 16), a sustained data rate of approximately 3.5 MB/sec from disk onto the network. But if the users are receiving mail from the hub via 28.8 Kbit dialup modems, they are restricted to about a 2 KB/sec effective transfer rate—so the server can handle the data transfer requirements of nearly 1,800 simultaneous users! Even when the outbound network is a 10baseT Ethernet (about 1 MB/sec), the server spends all its time waiting for the output network to drain. The output network remains the system bottleneck until the clients are connected by a T3 line.

The inbound network is much less important, since the storage system and then the processor limit the incoming message transfer rate. Even an eight-processor Ultra Enterprise 4000 system equipped with a non-volatile disk for temporary spool space handles only 100 inbound messages per second, a data rate easily handled by a 10baseT network.

4.2.2.3 Processor and Memory

Mail hubs have two distinctly different demands on their processors, namely, accepting messages for delivery to users and transmitting the contents of user mailboxes to their destination, either directly to the UA or indirectly via another MTA.

A 167 MHz UltraSPARC processor can deliver 15 messages/sec when not bottlenecked by temporary spool storage, and an 85 MHz SuperSPARC can deliver five to six messages/sec. Although these numbers are not impressive, they represent far more capacity than most systems demand. Not only is usage typically far below these rates, but since mail delivery is typically handled off-line in batches, small variations in processing time are not important.

Outbound messages are processed at a significantly different speed. These messages are typically transferred in large batches, most often via POP or NFS. Even messages being forwarded by SMTP are handled in batches, since SMTP attempts to minimize the number of connections it makes to external systems—a legacy of earlier extensive use of UUCP as the most common inter-system transfer mechanism. The enormous disparity between processing of inbound and outbound messages is due to implementation of the various MTAs: a process is forked for most messages, several intermediate files are created and destroyed, and alias processing often includes extensive name service lookup activity.

Outbound mail requires only that the server open a connection and transmit the data, avoiding nearly all of the overhead processing.

Table 16. Unencumbered message processing rates, by processor. In practice these rates are nearly always constrained by network or storage bottlenecks.

Task	110 MHz MicroSPARC-II	85 MHz SuperSPARC-II	167 MHz UltraSPARC-I
Inbound delivery	3	5-6	15
Outbound batch delivery	590	1,250	2,480

4.3 ftp Servers

Another common Internet service is the ftp server, whose purpose is to provide access to archives of files. Today, the most common use for ftp service is as an adjunct to a Web server, with the older protocol used to provide more efficient access to large files. The ftp protocol is defined by the RFCs that define the TCP/IP protocol suite. For capacity planning purposes, ftp offers two transfer modes, ASCII and binary. On Solaris systems, binary mode is considerably faster, attaining 70-95% of theoretical network bandwidth; ASCII mode transfers involve conversion of every byte to be translated into an ASCII encoded form for translation. The conversion consumes non-trivial CPU power, and also imposes latency delays transmitting packets. ASCII mode transfers usually operate about sixty percent slower than a binary mode transfer on the same network.

The performance of most ftp servers serving external Internet clients is constrained by network bandwidth. UltraSPARC processors are fully capable of saturating 155 Mbit ATM links, and even low-end processors such as the SPARCstation 5 can run a FastEthernet at over 50 Mbits/sec. In contrast, most servers have relatively slow connections to the global Internet—even a T3 line is only capable of 45 Mbits/sec, whereas most systems have fractional T1 or E1 lines (1-2 Mbits/sec), and many have only ISDN (64-128 Kbits/sec). Under these circumstances, the system is usually capable of delivering far more data than the network can absorb.

One important characteristic of the ftp implementation in Solaris is that the default ASCII transfer mode is *much* slower than binary mode, due to latency injected while the transmitting side stops to encode the data into the ASCII format. In most cases, ASCII mode transfers operate at about 30% of the speed of binary transfers. For this reason, binary transfers are always recommended for users who initiate ftp transfers by hand. Transmissions requested by Web browsers on behalf of users always use binary mode, and an increasing proportion of ftp traffic is requested by this mechanism.

Intranet servers often have much higher bandwidth connections to their clients; in fact, many large corporations are installing 100 Mbit/sec networks across entire campuses. In these circumstances, the performance of an `ftp` server is bounded first by the speed of the processor, and then by the speed the disk subsystem can provide the data to the system (or, for incoming connections, how fast the disk subsystem can absorb the data). As shown in Table 17, most servers are quite capable of filling a network with a single `ftp` session. Note that the speeds quoted in Table 17 are end-user data and do not include overhead for TCP, IP, or media transfers. Additionally, at these speeds, disk performance becomes an issue on either the client or the server. For example, an Ultra–1/170 server can deliver over 120 Mbits/sec of user data to an ATM network—but not if the data resides on a single disk drive capable of a maximum transfer speed of 6 MB/sec (i.e., 48 Mbits/sec). Likewise, if a client is requesting data from the same server via the same network, the transfer will likely be constrained by the disk on the receiving end; few clients use disk striping, so most clients can absorb data at less than the speed of a single disk, about 4-5 MB/sec. Low-end PC disks with MS-DOS file systems can be even slower: 1-2 MB/sec is common.

Table 17. Maximum throughput of CPU/network combinations, assuming adequate client speed and disk bandwidth. Speeds are end-user data, measured in Mbits/sec, using binary mode transfers.

Processor	Ethernet	Token Ring	FastEthernet	FDDI	ATM-155
110 MHz MicroSPARC-II	8.9	12	52	50	57
85 MHz SuperSPARC-II	9.0	12	65	63	90
167 MHz UltraSPARC	9.0	12	72	70	123

Most `ftp` servers, though, are network-limited. The Ethernet and Token Ring connections commonly used to connect such systems restrict maximum system-wide throughput to 9-12 Mbits/sec, and this bandwidth normally must be shared among many clients. Internet servers often supply data to T1 or ISDN lines; at about 197 KB/sec or 16 KB/sec respectively, either of these will be saturated by any Solaris server.

The number of simultaneous users on an `ftp` server is primarily dependent on the network bandwidth available, rather than on the processor, as might be expected. Since a uniprocessor SuperSPARC can easily drive more than 60 Mbits/sec, the system is far from saturated when connected to a slower network. Slower networks, such as an Ethernet , tend to cause the transfers to queue up and therefore operate simultaneously. Memory configuration is not especially important in these situations, because the disk subsystem is not busy supplying slower networks.

⇒ When the aggregate network speed is less than shown in Table 17, configure one processor. The number of users is essentially unlimited in this case.

⇒ When aggregate available network bandwidth *is* in excess of those in Table 17, the clients will not be bounded by network throughput. Configure one 167 MHz UltraSPARC processor for each expected 120 users, or one 85 MHz SuperSPARC for each 45 users.

⇒ Memory configuration is not critical; configure 48 MB on MicroSPARC -based systems, or 64 MB per SuperSPARC or 128 MB per UltraSPARC processor.

4.4 Usenet News Servers

Another service often provided by Internet servers is a news server hub. Usenet news is similar to a mail hub, in that the data being handled is a series of small files. Historically Usenet news was transmitted throughout the cooperating sites using the uucp(1) mechanism, but this protocol has been superseded by the Network News Transport Protocol (NNTP). NNTP is an application level protocol that can be carried on a variety of transport protocols such as PPP and TCP/IP.

The primary difference between the mail systems and NNTP systems is that each news hub retains only one copy of each article. Most mail systems (and all currently popular mail implementations on Solaris) place a copy of each mail message in each recipient's mailbox. From a capacity planning standpoint, a single set of files is served to all clients, rather than sending a unique file to each client as is the practice with mail. For small sites (those that only subscribe to a relatively small proportion of the 6000+ news groups), caching all of the most recent articles may be possible, but the sheer volume of traffic means that most sites will not be able to cache a large enough proportion of the data to be worthwhile.

Typical daily activity for a large site (one that receives most of the newsgroups) is about 120,000 articles per day. Most newsgroups carry articles that are strongly text-based, resulting in an average article size approximately 3-4 KB (incredibly, nearly half of a typical 3 KB article is routing and control information!). A few newsgroups, notably those in the alt.binary.* group, carry relatively large articles, such as images and compiled executable codes. The total incoming data amounts to nearly 4 GB per day! Handling this incoming data requires at least six hours of dedicated connection time on a T1 line, or about an hour on a switched 10baseT Ethernet. The volume figures quoted here are for the standard Internet news feed. Some organizations have their own internal newsgroups, and these can sometimes generate significant additional load.

4.4.1 Expiring Old Articles

NNTP processing occurs in three distinct phases: expiring old articles, acquiring new articles, and distributing articles to clients. The news articles are stored in a hierarchy of directories, one article per file. The fact that average articles are so small leads directly to the use of default file system parameters for inode density, one inode (i.e., one potential file) for every 2 KB of data storage. Providing storage capability for this many inodes results in

11 percent disk space overhead. News is nearly the only application in widespread use that stores so many small files (for additional discussion, see section 9.2.3, *UFS and UFS+ Parameters*).

Expiring news articles is usually a daily process; most administrators schedule it for off-peak hours. The process is simple: remove all the files that are older than a given date, or that reside in a given directory subtree. Usually opening the files is unnecessary, since the file creation date is sufficient information. The unfortunate thing about removing many files at a time is that file system semantics require that the operations be synchronously completed— that is, safely but slowly.

There are two solutions to this problem: the use of a logging file system, or the use of NVRAM disk acceleration. The logging file system accelerates directory updates (i.e., synchronous writes) by clustering them together and making the time-critical operation a serial access disk I/O rather than a random access disk I/O (see section 9.2.1.2, *Performance of UFS+ File Systems*). Accelerating the synchronous disk I/O via NVRAM is another viable option, one that is often complementary to a logging file system. For systems equipped with caching disk arrays, the NVRAM cache is nearly universally used to accelerate write operations. Since caching disk arrays require no host intervention, they are fully compatible with—and complementary to—logging file systems.

Most mid-range or larger servers are equipped with disk arrays, but workgroup and small departmental servers may not be large enough to warrant the expense of a sophisticated disk controller. Such systems can use host-based NVRAM in the form of an SBus PrestoServe; this serves the same function. Although the PrestoServe has only 1 MB of cache, it is completely adequate to greatly accelerate mass file creation or deletion operations (see section 7.1.4, *Write Acceleration with Non-Volatile Memory*).

⇒ Always configure news spool file systems as logging file systems.
⇒ Configure news spool file systems on caching disk subsystems if possible; if these are not available, use host-based NVRAM or PrestoServe instead.
⇒ Never permit news spool directories to reside on the same disk as the root file system.

4.4.2 Inbound Articles

The same techniques for improving expiration performance apply to inbound articles. Processing of inbound news articles occurs throughout the day, as articles are customarily posted to the newsgroups upon arrival. Administrators occasionally choose to accept incoming articles at specific times, but this choice is not common. Receipt of new articles poses a load similar to that of expiring old articles, a stream of synchronous disk writes. The in.nntp daemon accepts a TCP connection from the upstream news hub, and incoming articles are received in batches. Each article is written on disk in a separate file; since the average article is 3-4 KB, the contents of most files are completely written in a single I/O. When the file is closed, UNIX file semantics require that pending writes be flushed to disk before the close operation is completed. The contents of the article file are written with a standard asynchronous operation, but because the article file is closed immediately after a single block of data, the net effect is that both operations are performed synchronously.

4.4.3 Serving News Articles

Of course, the function of a news server is to deliver articles to client news readers upon demand. While expiration and receipt are primarily single streams of activity, servers supply many readers, often many concurrently. Older news readers, such as rn(1u), imposed relatively light loads on the server, because those readers were both direct user agents and not threaded. Direct readers simply requested an article from the server and displayed it for the user to read. This style of usage places a light load on the server because the user specifically directs the client reader to obtain the next article for display; in particular, a human reads the article before asking for the next one. Most newer news readers are able to operate in an off-line mode, in which the reader obtains an entire batch of articles from a subscribed newsgroup, and the client stores the articles in temporary storage for subsequent viewing by a human. From the server's perspective, this type of load very different, because it is very bursty—the load is much more intense, but is not sustained for as long periods of time.

Additionally, newer readers are nearly always threaded. In this context, "threaded" refers to the way that the articles are presented to the user, rather than to any implementation specifics. Threaded news readers, such as the one embedded in Netscape Navigator, trn and xvnews, present threads of discussion grouped together by either subject line or cross-reference tags (for example, the original posting entitled "contents of davy jones' locker revealed" and all of the related follow-up postings). Earlier-generation readers simply delivered each article in the newsgroup in chronological order, and the human reader had to figure out which article was related to the others.

Threading impacts the server is much more than might be expected at first glance. Rather than obtaining the next message in chronological order, the news server must deliver to the client the headers of all available messages in the current newsgroup, so that the client can discover the interrelationships between the articles. Kill files, which exclude undesirable articles for the user, have the same impact. The impact on the server can be considerable: in practice, every client now receives every article in each subscribed newsgroup, instead of just the ones that would be read.

The CPU cost of reading and supplying articles to clients is low. When a user on a very fast client, such as an Ultra–2/2170, visits a newsgroup for the first time in a week or two, the client may request 2,000 articles from the server. Such an activity generates only five percent CPU utilization on a SPARCstation 20 Model 50 server, and on an UltraSPARC processor the utilization is one to two percent. At the same time, it generates considerable activity on the server's disk farm, since retrieving 2,000 articles means 4,000 disk reads (one each to retrieve the file's attributes and the file's contents). These reads are random access, so the performance of the storage subsystem is limited by the number of disk spindles. This operation proceeds at the rate of about 100 I/Os per second, the speed of a single disk drive. The disk subsystem must be configured to handle this type of bursty load from many clients. As discussed in Chapter 7, *Storage Subsystems*, the *least* appropriate configuration for this type of activity is a single large disk drive.

4.4.4 Sizing News Servers

Since most modern news readers are either threaded or have off-line capabilities (and usually both), servers must be sized to suit. The procedure is straightforward. Determine the average number of messages in typical newsgroups to be retained. This level can be maintained with the help of the expiration daemon.

Given a maximum number of supported concurrent users, the storage subsystem can be configured with sufficient resources by allocating about one I/O operation per message in the typical newsgroup per active user. The news spool file system requires one disk drive for every 100 I/O operations. If the spool file system is to be stored on a RAID -5 volume, configure one disk drive for every 80 I/O operations. The 20 percent margin permits some resources to be consumed by the parity computation process; one additional disk is required, to store the parity information. News service is dominated by reads, and requires writes only occasionally. Moreover, the process that issues the writes is not sensitive to the write performance lost to RAID-5 organization—so RAID-5 is a more suitable means of protecting storage than mirroring. Additionally, the file system must be configured with a file system log, and that function requires one further disk. The disks should normally be configured in a caching disk array, in order to take advantage of their significant ability to accelerate directory updates.

Allocate one 167 MHz UltraSPARC processor for every 200 active users, or one 85 MHz SuperSPARC for every 85 active news users. If the clients are connected via slow networks (dialup or ISDN), these estimates will be conservative. This ratio assumes that about a quarter of the active users are actively engaged in scanning a newsgroup—also a conservative estimate, but not excessively so. A 110 MHz SPARCstation 5 can handle about 45 active users. Solaris multiprocessor scalability is excellent, in excess of 90 percent. Few pure news servers are active enough to warrant multiprocessors. Configure memory at about 200 KB per active reader.

Networking is a relatively minor issue. Most news intranet servers will have connections to their clients dictated by the existing infrastructure, and news usage does not impose special requirements. Ethernet is fully adequate for handling even very large populations. Internet connections to the server are rare, except for systems run by Internet Service Providers (ISPs). This class of system must support very large user populations, but their load is throttled by their client connections, which are primarily dialup modems operating at 28.8-33 Kbits/sec (.0036 MB/sec). The low speed of the connections imposes significant limitations on how quickly clients obtain data and make new requests, limiting their impact on the server. Although more capable, ISDN lines are only about four times faster than standard modems (128 Kbits/sec or 0.015 Mbytes/sec); compared to the capabilities of the other parts of the system, neither is very fast. Fifty to eighty active ISDN connections equal the bandwidth of a *single* 10baseT Ethernet.

⇒ Configure one 167 MHz UltraSPARC for every 200 active news readers or one 85 MHz SuperSPARC for every 85 active readers. A 110 MHz MicroSPARC-II can handle about 45 active readers.

⇒ Configure at least 32 MB memory plus 200 KB per active reader.

⇒ Configure one 7,200 rpm disk drive for every 80 active readers, unless the drives are configured in RAID-5 volumes. When drives are configured in RAID-5 volumes, one drive is required for every 70 users. For slower (5,400 rpm) drives, configure one drive for every 60 users, 50 users if configured in RAID-5.

4.5 Firewalls

The last major category of Internet server is the firewall, a system whose purpose is to inspect packets and apply and implement security policies determining if and how to exchange packets between two security domains. Most commonly this function is found between the global Internet and an internally-maintained intranet, but increasingly firewalls are used to compartmentalize information between separate business functions within a single corporate domain.

4.5.1 Firewall Usage

A firewall inspects each packet and performs a rudimentary analysis on what it contains, and then decides what to do with the packet based on what it finds. Firewall software may permit untrusted hosts to exchange data only with specific systems, possibly restricting the traffic to certain types of protocols or even specific services. For example, a firewall may be configured to permit external hosts to send `http` traffic only to nominated internal proxy servers; any other packet directed to the internal proxy servers might be blocked. At the same time, the firewall may be configured to permit `ftp` requests originating in the trusted domain to complete, while blocking any `ftp` request originating in the untrusted domain unless it is sent to a nominated externally-accessible `ftp` server.

Firewalls are often used in pairs to create a "demilitarized zone" or "DMZ," a network that serves as a buffer zone between an untrusted domain and a trusted domain, as shown in Figure 16 (page 158). This mechanism provides a measure of security in two dimensions. The external firewall limits external hosts to transmitting to the DMZ, where each host can be carefully scrutinized for security problems. Even if an external host manages to compromise a host in the DMZ, the internal firewall confines traffic destined for the internal network to specific types of traffic. This arrangement drastically reduces the options available to an intruding virus: it must compromise one of a few closely-scrutinized systems, and then forward its attack via one of a few relatively innocuous protocols, such as `ftp` or `sendmail`. This is not to say that these protocols cannot be compromised, but attacking via these restricted paths is certainly much more difficult than when arbitrary requests may be generated into the internal network from the compromised system.

4.5.2 Sizing Firewall Servers

Firewall systems are typically dedicated systems that have no other responsibilities. Except for log files, firewalls have no requirements for storage. Almost the only requirement is to have sufficient processor power to run the protocol stacks and the policy rules.

The load imposed on a firewall system comes from two basic requirements: the finite, non-zero amount of effort required to transmit or receive a packet through the network interface drivers and protocol stacks, and the larger and more general activity of applying the security policies to each packet.

A surprising amount of CPU attention is required to receive a packet on a network interface, put it into host memory, and process (at least) the IP protocol stack. Maximum packet rates for FastEthernet are shown in Table 18, and additional maxima are shown in

Figure 18. Firewall systems are by definition interposing systems that must read and write every packet, so this overhead is doubled.

Table 18. Maximum transmit or receive packet rates by packet size and CPU. Routing rates are half of these rates. These rates are achieved on 100baseT; comparable media have comparable rates.

	512 bytes	1 KB	2 KB	4 KB	8 KB	16 KB	32 KB	64 KB
SS1000E, 60 MHz	7,878	4,107	1,723	1,181	319	220	140	95
UE 4000, 167 MHz	17,332	8,770	4,741	2,320	1,194	541	291	148

WAN interfaces often consume proportionately higher overhead than LAN interfaces, but their overhead cost is mitigated by their much lower packet rates. For example, running X.25 at E1 speed over an SBus synchronous serial line interface (HSI/S) consumes about 11 percent of a single 75 MHz SuperSPARC processor or about three percent of a 167 MHz

UltraSPARC. This is far higher overhead than the corresponding level of traffic on a LAN (such as 100baseT), but even so, it is hardly significant.

Running the firewall software itself obviously also consumes processor time, and of course the amount of overhead depends on the number and complexity of the policy rules that are applied to each packet. SunSoft's Firewall-1 product imposes about nine percent overhead per packet to apply the first rule. Firewall-1 interposes the policy rule interpreter in the kernel, in order to avoid the overhead of context switching into and out of user mode. A system using standard Solaris on a 167 MHz UltraSPARC processor can route about 7,900 packets/sec, whereas the same system acting as a trivial firewall (i.e., pass all packets in the protocol class) can manage only about 7,200 packets/sec. The surprising amount of basic overhead is due to a relatively complex infrastructure used to expediently locate and determine the applicability of a potentially large set of policy rules. Adding additional policy rules imposes much less overhead—essentially none.

Basic overhead is expended on a per-packet basis; some forms of overhead are consumed on a per-byte basis, if the policy applies to the entire contents of the packet. One of the more extreme examples of such a policy is one that requests encryption of the contents of the packet contents—the encryption must be applied to every bit of the packet. Firewall-1 consumes a total of about 60-65 percent overhead for encrypted traffic when packets are relatively large. For example, ftp throughput is reduced by about 65 percent in a 100baseT environment (i.e., using fairly typical 1,500 byte packets). Degradation is somewhat higher in environments using larger packets, although it is not as significant as might first be expected, since the larger MTU permits fewer packets to be transmitted for a given amount of data.

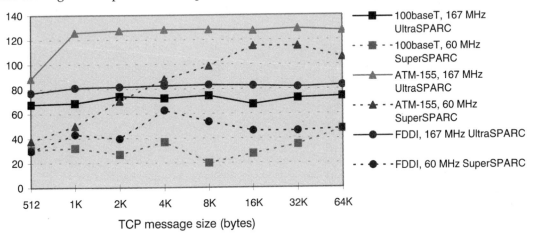

Figure 18. Maximum single-threaded TCP/IP transfer speed by processor and network media. Rates are for user data only (i.e., excluding TCP/IP and media overhead).

Configuring Timeshare Systems 5▤

Timesharing systems represent one of the largest and certainly the least-defined class of server systems. Because servers are now sufficiently powerful that even the smallest systems can easily handle many pure DBMS and especially NFS loads, servers commonly handle many tasks simultaneously. In addition, a certain amount of NFS or timesharing "infrastructure" work is often associated with today's primary generator of server load, the database management system. One common configuration is a DBMS server surrounded by a variety of front-end workstations, which obtain their DBMS binaries and working files via NFS from the same server that handles the DBMS back-end duties. Another common situation is the DBMS back-end server that must also offer front-end services, possibly to a substantial part of the user population.

5.1 Caution: Many Pitfalls to Estimation

In a very real sense, this category is a "catch-all". Any system not otherwise defined is lumped under this classification. Making an accurate configuration estimate is exceptionally difficult, since defining the workload that will be imposed on the target system can be very imprecise. For example, even a rule of thumb such as "provide one processor for every n users" is impractical, because applications such as circuit simulation and some kinds of simulation can easily consume two to four processors *per user* (assuming a multithreaded application), whereas one SuperSPARC or Pentium processor can easily handle 20-50 users in some other applications such as Oracle Financials. Other applications are even less demanding. Additionally, as with the DBMS systems described in the previous chapter, even if the workload is accurately described, it is usually possible only to decide what configurations will *not* be able to handle the given load; it is normally impossible to say with confidence that a given configuration *will* be able to handle a specific load without some specific prior experience with the application.

Fortunately, some factors do facilitate sizing timesharing systems to some degree. First, the laws of averages tend to smooth out overall load, especially for large user populations—although some predictable load peaks nearly always occur. For example, virtually every site reports strong usage peaks at approximately 10:30 AM and 2:30 PM, and idle troughs at approximately 12:00-1:00. End-of-period rushes, for example, end-of-tax-year processing, are also quite predictable. Second, the generalized nature of many timesharing systems means a wide diversity of applications, which tends to spread resource usage across many parts of the system. Not all applications are CPU intensive, and not all are I/O intensive; mixing them on a single system often has a tendency to make more use of the varied resources provided by the system. Of course, the wrong application mix can have the opposite effect!

5.2 Configuration Guidelines for Timesharing Servers

The following questions outline the information required to arrive at accurate sizing information for timesharing systems. The discussion that follows describes how to arrive at an actual configuration using the answers to these questions.

5.2.1 Checklist

- How many processes will be active?

- How many of the active processes use X11 as their user interface?

- Are the applications single-threaded or multithreaded?

- How many users will be active? What proportion of them will be connected via network connections as opposed to direct connections?

- Do the applications use X-Windows for simple user interfaces or for sustained graphically intensive drawing?

- What proportion of the workload will be batch, and how important is batch throughput compared to interactive response time?

- Will the server be a name service provider for a large client community?

- Are the backup and recovery policies consistent with proposed NVRAM and storage configurations?

- How many printers will be active on a sustained basis, and how are they connected?

- How many printers, if any, will require PostScript rasterization via NeWSprint ?

5.2.2 Main Memory

For timesharing systems, the most important single configuration criterion is the provision of sufficient main memory. Although this statement is also true of other types of servers, lack of memory is perceived immediately by timesharing users as greatly increased response time. Essentially no penalty is imposed for configuring too much memory, other than the initial cost, but the consequences of insufficient memory can be fairly described as catastrophic. Shortages of memory result in paging to disk, and since even the fastest disk subsystems are more than 30,000 times slower than main memory, this situation must be avoided. In the SPARCserver 1000E and especially the SPARCserver 2000E and Ultra Enterprise x000 systems, be sure to allow as many memory banks as possible to avoid multiprocessor contention for individual memory resources (see section 6.4.4, *Memory Interleaving* for a more complete discussion).

Unfortunately, timesharing systems often support a wide variety of applications, and memory consumption is very much a function of individual applications. For example, FrameMaker sessions require a minimum of 4 MB memory, an OpenLook mailtool can easily consume 2-4 MB, while a `csh` can require as little as 200 KB. Many applications that require as much as 20-25 MB of memory per user to avoid paging, and some kinds of applications, notably ECAD simulations and some finite element analyses, can easily use 500-1,000 MB of memory per process. In general, the application vendor can provide an estimate of how much memory is required.

In the absence of such information, configure at least 400 KB per active process for dumb terminal applications and 4 MB per process for office-automation X-Windows applications. Especially in an X-Window environment, be sure to take the myriad of "insignificant" utilities such as `xclock` and `xrolotool` into account. Clocks are particularly important because they wake up every second to update the display, causing a large proportion of the processes' memory to remain active.

When in doubt as to actual memory consumption (such as when sizing a system before its application suite has been written), configure memory generously. When the budget is fixed, underestimating processor capability is probably less of a problem than undersizing memory.

⇒ Be generous with memory configurations. Insufficient memory is the most severe form of under-configuration in this class of system.

⇒ Consult application vendors to determine per-process memory requirements. Guessing is strongly discouraged: applications vary widely!

⇒ In the absence of actual data from vendors or developers, configure at least 400 KB per process for dumb terminal applications and at least 4 MB per process for office-automation X-Windows applications.

⇒ Pay special attention to memory requirements for utility programs in X-Windows environments.

5.2.3 Processor Modules

The first question most users ask is how many CPUs they will need to support a given number of users, and this is valid; however, studies at Sun have repeatedly shown that the number of processors is nearly always much less significant than having enough memory to avoid paging. Moreover, in a traditional timesharing system providing accurate estimates of processor usage is impossible without some detailed understanding of the applications and their usage patterns. Table 19 below is provided as a starting point for discussion, rather than as an ironclad rule. In the table, applications are considered lightweight if they are primarily user-interface drivers; they do little computation and generally little I/O. A text editor or word processor is normally a lightweight application. An application such as Oracle Financials, which performs considerable computation as well as I/O, is c onsidered heavyweight. Keep in mind that DBMS applications configured to operate in client/server mode run as much as 30 percent faster than equivalent timesharing configurations.

Table 19. Approximate number of active users per 85 MHz SuperSPARC CPU

Application Weight	1	2	4	8	16
Lightweight (generally ASCII)	75-100	150-200	300-400	600-750	1,200-1,500
Heavyweight (generally X11)	20-50	50-100	100-200	150-375	300-700

In situations where a choice of processor modules is available, larger cache sizes are almost always recommended. When many tasks are competing for processor attention, the system experiences many context switches at a relatively rapid pace. As a result, the cache contents turn over much more quickly than more static single–user workstation use. The larger caches increase the chances that a significant part of the cache's context remains when a process returns to execute on the processor.

The exception to this rule is the gap between the SuperSPARC and UltraSPARC processor families. Because of the UltraSPARC's substantially improved handling of context switching and interrupt processing, UltraSPARC processors with 512 KB of cache are just as effective as SuperSPARC processors with much larger caches—before taking clock rate into account. For example, the 167 MHz UltraSPARC with 512 KB cache is capable of at least twice the processing of an 85 MHz SuperSPARC with 2 MB cache. UltraSPARC processors with 1 MB caches are about 20 percent more capable than equivalent versions with 512 KB (see section 6.2.5.1, *Register Sets and System Interface* for further discussion).

One commor form of "timesharing" server is a standalone server whose CPUs continuously process batch jobs. This is often called a "compute server." This sort of system is easier to estimate, because it can normally consume all of the available processor cycles. Especially now that multithreaded applications are able to consume more than one processor at a time, compute servers are typically configured with as many CPUs as possible. Quad-processor SPARCstation 10 systems have little backplane bandwidth available to satisfy I/O requests; compute servers with significant I/O requirements should opt for the SPARCserver 1000E if four processors are required (refer to section 6.4.3, *SuperSPARC Backplane Consumption* for a more complete discussion).

⇒ Use client/server configurations where possible.

⇒ Use the largest available caches.

⇒ In the absence of other information, configure processors according to Table 19.

⇒ Due to backplane considerations, quad-processor compute servers should be configured in the SPARCserver 1000E rather than the SPARCstation 10 or SPARCstation 20. This is not an issue when comparing between a two-processor Ultra Enterprise 3000 and an Ultra–2, as both systems have far more bandwidth than can be consumed by two processors.

5.2.4 User Connectivity Schemes

Most timesharing systems still utilize an essentially "dumb" terminal mode of operation for many or all of the users. These dumb terminals may be actual terminals (VT100, etc.) connected directly or via a terminal server, or by network `telnet` or `rlogin` sessions from workstations, PCs, or other systems. For the most part, X11 windows started on a server and viewed on a remote display can be considered approximately the weight of two dumb terminals (of course, an `xterm` or `shelltool` that runs on a remote system, but which simply "houses" an `rlogin` or `telnet` session to the timesharing server is the same weight as a similar network login task).

5.2.5 Direct Connection vs. Network Connection

When discussing modern timesharing systems, the question comes up as to how to connect the requisite number of users. In general, with Sun systems, more than 8-16 users should be connected via network terminal servers rather than connected directly. Part of the reason is the lack of onboard character processing capability on the SBus serial/parallel controller (SPC/S). Solaris x86 and PowerPC systems have access to much more intelligent boards that do not suffer from these implementation problems. Additionally, some inherent advantages are gained by concentration of serial lines onto a single remote controller as is done in the case of the terminal server.

Sun's SPC/S is a low-cost implementation that utilizes no onboard buffering or line discipline processing. When characters arrive from the terminal, they must be processed immediately to avoid dropping characters; this processing necessitates an interrupt to the operating system. Moreover, the lack of line discipline processing means that the host system must handle even simple actions such as the processing of the character or line delete keys. For output, the lack of buffering means that at most one character per line can be transmitted to the board's SBus interface in each SBus operation. The small transmission size also implies the use of programmed I/O (see section 6.5.1.4, *SBus Transfer Modes*).By comparison, the Network Terminal Server connects to the host system via the Ethernet port. Especially when configured via the DVMA-based SQEC/S quad Ethernet interface (Sun's most efficient 10baseT Ethernet interface), terminal servers can substantially reduce the number of I/O operations serviced by the host system. The terminal server is sometimes able to handle rudimentary line discipline processing, freeing the host system from these duties. Extensive buffering in the terminal server means that the host can be interrupted only when complete packets arrive from the terminal server, or when a terminal requires immediate host attention (for example, on receipt of a carriage return). On output, the terminal server is able to accept a full Ethernet packet (1,500 bytes) rather than single characters, drastically reducing overhead on the host (compared to the SPC/S). Most serial line applications are dominated by output operations: the most typical scenarios print a prompt, receive a relatively small amount of input (usually less than 80 bytes), and then return a larger response. This scenario is even more pronounced in the case of the forms processing typical of DBMS applications. Printers, of course, are nearly write-only, and benefit more than most other applications from Ethernet packetization when connected via terminal servers.

Terminal servers and the SPC/S board are of roughly comparable efficiency in one application environment, namely when applications operate in the mode known as `cbreak`. In this mode, the system must react immediately to each typed character. The most common application of `cbreak` mode is `emacs` or `vi`, but a number of forms-based applications also use this mode. This is the least efficient operating mode, specifically because it mandates immediate host response for each input character. Fortunately, `cbreak` mode does not apply to output.

For these reasons, network terminal servers are always recommended for large numbers of terminals or serial lines. In this context, "large" means more than 8-16 ports.

If the application for some reason requires direct connections (possibly to satisfy strict latency requirements that might not be achievable with a heavily used network), a large number of aftermarket vendors offer SBus serial interface boards. When choosing among such offerings, look for ones with both significant onboard buffering and more importantly, onboard line discipline processing. If possible, try to find one that utilizes DVMA for transfers rather than programmed I/O. This quality is particularly important on the SPARCserver 1000 and SPARCcenter 2000, which are designed to handle very high throughput for large transfers (see section 6.5.1.4, *SBus Transfer Modes*).

5.2.6 "Active" vs. "Idle" Users

There is considerable confusion in the industry over the simple (but extremely important) definition of a user. Most vendors, including Sun, quote a "maximum number of users" for each of their systems. Beware! These numbers are almost always the maximum number of terminals or terminal sessions that can be physically or logically connected. In particular, they do not have much to do with how much work can actually be accomplished on the system in question.

For the purposes of capacity planning, the term "idle user" refers to a session that is connected but *not* consuming any processor time. Such a user may or may not consume very much memory—this consideration is entirely different. In particular, every process consumes some amount of memory in the kernel, generally on the order of 40 KB-50 KB per process. In addition, each process also consumes some amount of memory on its own behalf. For the most part, it can be swapped out if the user is idle for a long enough time.

Idle users do not count in scalability considerations, nor do they carry any significant overhead other than memory consumption. Sun specifies the SPARCcenter 2000E at up to 3,000 idle users, and the SPARCserver 1000E at 1,000 idle users. All members of the Ultra Enterprise family can handle 3,000 idle users.

Active users are just that: users who are actively doing something. They consume processor time, memory, and virtually every other kind of resource. Most of what follows is concerned with active users.

5.2.7 Maximum Number of Active Users

Solaris 2.5 is the first release to introduce a new implementation of the Berkeley network utilities. Previous editions of Solaris, including Solaris 2.4, used essentially unmodified Berkeley network utilities such as telnet and rlogin. In particular, the basic structure of these daemons is unchanged from the original designs of the early 1980s. Unfortunately, these designs scale poorly to very large numbers of users. In these earlier versions of Solaris, both rlogin and telnet are implemented as user-mode daemon processes interposed between the application process and the network. The daemon handles all incoming and outgoing characters. This arrangement works well for small to moderate numbers of users, but does not scale well because every character must pass into and out of the kernel twice. As a result, each incoming character requires three context switches, as shown in Figure 19.

As a result of this problem, Solaris 2.3 systems can handle approximately 120-200 normally active timesharing users, regardless of the number of CPUs configured. The wide variation is cited because the terminal traffic associated with applications varies widely. For example, conversational mode programs such as typical consultative expert systems usually do not transmit large character streams. Software developers often spend most of their active time in shells or debuggers where character transmission is quite lightweight.

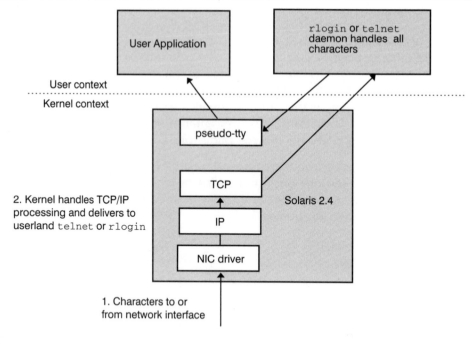

Figure 19. Traditional Berkeley network login processing used in Solaris 2.4 and earlier. Note the three context switches required to handle each and every character.

Subject to other constraints (such as disk I/O bandwidth, main memory availability, and processor consumption), Solaris 2.3 timesharing servers can normally handle these kinds of applications in the upper end of the active user range. Applications that result in substantial terminal I/O—applications that make extensive use of fill-in-the-blanks forms are probably the most common examples—are usually only capable of the lower end of the range. Larger communities still using the older Solaris 2.3 release must be serviced through the use of client/server configurations, with multiple front-end systems connected to single large back ends. This arrangement is most practical in DBMS systems where client/server systems are the norm, but other applications are sometimes susceptible to this approach as well.

5.2.7.1 In-Kernel `telnet` and `rlogin`

SunSoft offered a completely new implementation for `telnet` and `rlogin` in Solaris 2.5[36]. The vast majority of processing associated with terminal processing is now handled strictly within the kernel, avoiding two context switches. The modified organization is referred to as

---

[36] In-kernel `telnet`/`rlogin` were made available in Solaris 2.4 Hardware 11/94 in the form of a patch; they were not a standard part of the Solaris 2.4 product.

in-kernel `telnet`, although both `telnet` and `rlogin` are handled in the kernel. Specifically, the matter of multiplexing characters from the TCP/IP input and output queues, as well as `tty` special characters (such as backspace) are handled by a streams module that operates in the kernel context. The resulting control flow is much simpler, as in Figure 20:

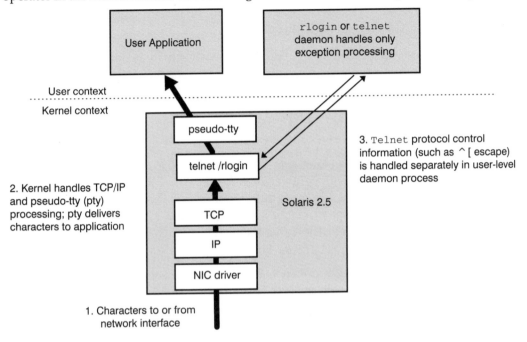

Figure 20. Revised terminal processing using the in-kernel `telnet`/`rlogin` scheme provided in Solaris 2.5. For most traffic, context switching is reduced by 67 percent compared to traditional implementations (Figure 19).

The Berkeley network daemons (`in.telnetd` and `in.rlogind`) are still used, but they handle only exception processing under the in-kernel scheme. For example, they handle the `~.` disconnection escape for `rlogin` and the `^[` command input escape for `telnet`. Handling escape characters is no more efficient than under the original organization, but they are so rare that they pose no configuration issues.

5.2.7.2 Use of `telnet` vs. `rlogin`

Users can choose from a variety of protocols when connecting terminals or other dumb terminal sessions via network connections. Most common are `telnet` and `rlogin`. Research at Sun indicates that `telnet` is the more efficient of the two protocols, although the two scale approximately equivalently. Due to its greater efficiency (`telnet` is inherently simpler than `rlogin`), `telnet` is preferred when the extended features of `rlogin` (e.g.,

8-bit characters or unverified login via `.rhosts`) are not required. The remote shell, `rsh(1)`, falls into the same category as `rlogin`. Beginning with Solaris 2.5, the overhead associated with either protocol ceases to be a consideration, but users of previous releases may find the distinction significant.

5.2.7.3 Low-Duty-Cycle Applications

Even within the timesharing category, a peculiar subclass of activity has been the source of considerable problems with earlier versions of Solaris 2. This subclass is the set of applications characterized by a very high work-to-overhead ratio, most especially those with very high process creation and deletion rates. Creating a process is one of the most expensive operations under Solaris 2 (and UNIX in general), and in Solaris editions before Solaris 2.5, this operation was not especially scalable.

The profile of the applications that scaled most poorly under Solaris 2.3 and Solaris 2.4 included large numbers of users with lightweight tasks, such as editing files, reading occasional email, and other file-management tasks involving small files. Such activities often consumed five or ten times as much processor time to create and reclaim the process as was involved in running the actual application. Many universities with large student populations fit this profile.

Because of the scalability issues with those releases of Solaris, systems running these applications were limited to 200 active users or fewer, even with 12-16 processors. Paradoxically, other improvements in Solaris 2.4 allowed the same system to handle 600-800 Oracle Financial users, even though that application suite consumes *far* more CPU time per user than `emacs`! The difference between Solaris 2.4 and Solaris 2.5.1 is seen in Figure 21.

Fortunately, this issue has been resolved in Solaris 2.5, as reflected in the AIM–III benchmark results. Beginning with Solaris 2.5, the scalability of the terminal connection process ceases to be a configuration issue. As many as 1,500-1,800 terminals can be active on very large systems, such as a 16-processor SPARCcenter 2000E with 85 MHz/2 MB modules. Ultra Enterprise systems equipped with large memory can handle even larger workloads. The configuration issues are then similar to other systems where processor speed, memory consumption, and disk I/O bandwidth are the primary considerations. Timesharing configurations running Solaris 2.3 are ineffective past about a hundred users, and the only real solution to increasing these systems' capabilities is to upgrade them to Solaris 2.4 with in–kernel `telnet`, or preferably to Solaris 2.5.

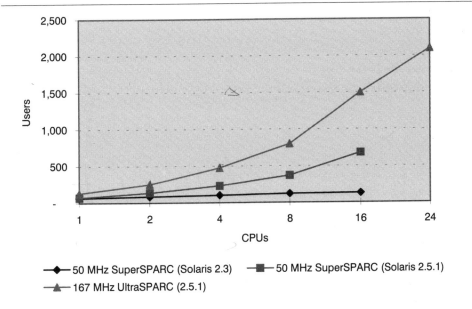

Figure 21. Relative timesharing ability of Solaris 2.3 and Solaris 2.5.1. Solaris 2.3 did not scale well, to say the least.

5.2.7.4 Platform-Specific Considerations

Because timesharing deals fundamentally with very small units of data (in particular, a single keystroke), it exaggerates the strengths and weaknesses of some system architectures. In particular, the extremely "long and wide" architecture of the SPARCcenter 2000E and SPARCserver 1000E handles large amounts of programmed I/O (PIO) very inefficiently. Because of the interaction of the design of the typical PIO SBus boards and the sun4d architecture, it usually takes four to seven 16-byte XDBus packets to transmit each character! These systems are designed to move large blocks of data efficiently, resulting in inefficient handling of very small blocks of data. Unfortunately, the nature of terminal handling is primarily character-at-a-time, and the most obvious way to handle this is PIO. Most SBus serial-interface boards transfer single characters to the host, and thus operate in PIO. Avoid such boards when configuring systems like the SPARCcenter 2000E and SPARCserver 1000E. Note that Sun's SPC/S falls squarely into this category, as it was designed for use with the SPARCstation 1/1+/2 family, which is very different architecturally. Members of the sun4c family feature a very short path from SBus to the processor, as do MicroSPARC -based systems. The much shorter path is possible because sun4c systems are uniprocessors implemented in a much smaller environment than the large multiprocessor servers.

Terminals are best connected to Solaris systems via terminal server. If the application demands physically direct connections to a `sun4d` system (perhaps for security purposes), try to find a serial port interface that has onboard canonicalization and echoplex processing, and that does transfers with the host via direct virtual memory access (DVMA —see section 6.5.1.4, *SBus Transfer Modes*) instead of PIO. Magma and Central Data, among others, offer such products.

Like the SPC/S, the SPARCserver 1000 and SPARCcenter 2000's onboard serial ports have minimal buffering and require considerable processor intervention during use. However, because they are not connected via the SBus, two additional considerations apply. Instead of being connected to the local SBus, the serial port controllers are connected to a separate 8-bit bus that is local to each system board. This bus is known as the *boot bus*. As the name implies, it displays local (to the system board) diagnostic messages during Automatic System Reconfiguration (ASR) and during boot if a processor attached to the boot bus is selected as the master CPU during ASR. Because the boot bus is tightly coupled to the local processors, the onboard serial ports are somewhat more efficient than equivalent ports on the SPC/S. Nonetheless, they are not heavily buffered and they still require the main processor to perform line discipline processing. Furthermore, because the boot bus is connected to the rest of the system by the processors, the serial ports on a system board are not accessible *at all* if no processors are configured on that system board. Use of the onboard serial ports is not recommended for any purpose other than as a system console or diagnostic port.

5.2.7.5 User Connectivity Configuration Summary

The guidelines and recommendations for configuring timeshared users onto a system can be summarized as follows:

⇒ No more than approximately 120-200 *active* terminals should be connected to any system running Solaris 2.3. Larger installations, particularly DBMS installations, should use client/server configurations with multiple front-end systems, each with 120-200 active users. Large systems can easily accommodate many more *inactive* users. Solaris 2.3–based systems running Amdahl's Solaris A+ Edition 1.0 can handle somewhat larger timesharing user communities.

⇒ Solaris 2.4 can handle most commercial timesharing workloads, but should be avoided for lightweight applications.

⇒ Solaris 2.5 can handle most timesharing workloads (Table 20).

⇒ Systems using 167 MHz UltraSPARC/512 KB caches can handle approximately twice as many users as the same number of 85 MHz/2 MB processors.

⇒ 167 MHz/1 MB modules are preferred to 167 MHz/512 KB for obvious reasons; they deliver 15-20 percent more processing than modules with the smaller cache.

Table 20. Typical maximum timesharing user communities in 16–CPU 85 MHz configurations

Workload	Solaris 2.3	A+ 1.0 Edition	Solaris 2.4	Solaris 2.5
Standard commercial	120-200	200-400	200-600	400-1,000
Lightweight	120-200	200-300	200-300	500-1,200
Very lightweight	60-150	200-300	200-300	500-1,500

⇒ Configuration of more than approximately eight terminals or serial lines should be connected via a Network Terminal Server.

⇒ Terminals connected via network connections, either from a Network Terminal Server or another system, should connect using `rlogin` rather than `telnet` if feasible, due to the slightly lower inherent overhead of the former protocol.

⇒ The Sun SPC/S board is recommended only in single units, due to its high operational overhead.

⇒ Do not configure terminals or serial lines onto SPARCserver 1000 or SPARCcenter 2000 systems via the SPC/S board, due to very high resultant programmed I/O rates. The SPC/S is especially well suited for use on low–end systems with tightly integrated SBus , such as the SPARCclassic and SPARCstation LX or the SPARCstation 4 and SPARCstation 5.

⇒ Configure only lightly used serial lines onto SPARCserver 1000E or SPARCcenter 2000E systems via the onboard serial ports.

⇒ The serial ports on each system board of a SPARCserver 1000E or SPARCcenter 2000E system are only functional if at least one processor is configured on that system board.

5.2.8 Network Utilization

Because timesharing systems are usually organized as independent units, network utilization does not affect them to the same degree as other systems operated in client/server configurations. However, because all modern systems exist in a networked context, attention must be paid to the utilization of networks.

5.2.8.1 Remote Dependencies

Timesharing systems often rely upon external name service servers, for as little as Domain Name Service (DNS) or as much as NIS+. Although relatively few requests are made of name services, significant delays associated with excessive network utilization can result in the perception that the timesharing system itself is very slow. Likewise, most timesharing systems today rely on remote file system support such as NFS or NetWare; as with naming services, sluggish response when paging in binaries can result in the false impression that the server itself is not keeping pace with demand.

5.2.8.2 X11 Clients

For most office-automation applications or applications that use the X-Windows system primarily for user interface rather than for graphics, network utilization is not normally an issue. Applications are considered graphically intensive if they do continuous or long-term drawing. For example, AutoCAD is considered graphically intensive if screen regeneration is frequent. Regeneration of some moderately complex drawings can take as long as a minute, with graphical primitives being transmitted continuously. Common Desktop Environment (CDE) and Sun DeskSet applications such as email user agents (i.e., `mailtool` or `dtmail`) and calendar managers (`cm` or `dtcm`), or common office automation packages such as *Interleaf* or *WingZ* are good examples of applications that use X11 essentially for user-interface only. Recent research at Sun indicates that about 30 active X-terminals per network running applications such as *FrameMaker* or *Wabi* can drive the network utilization to 20-25 percent.

> Warning: The one situation in which network utilization can play a very significant role concerns X-terminals or remote X-Window. Graphically intensive X11 programs operated over the network can cause very intense network activity. While this may or may not affect the performance of the users or client systems involved, it can certainly impact other users of the network. For example, a single instance of the `xlock` program used to secure X11 displays can account for 25-30 percent network utilization if operated in one of its graphic modes such as "flame" or "rotor." [37]

5.2.8.3 Network Terminal Servers

Network terminal servers are often singled out for placement on dedicated Ethernets because they are perceived to generate a great deal of traffic. This impression is incorrect; in fact, even a 64-port terminal server operating all ports at full 38,400 baud generates only 245 KB/sec, approximately 20 percent network utilization. However, this figure is rarely approached in practice, where (human) input delays dominate traffic speed. More typically, each port generates many fewer than 90 characters/sec after allowing for think time. At this level a full terminal server generates about 6 KB/sec. Clearly this traffic level is not sufficient to disturb other traffic on the network. However, if the network is busy with other traffic, providing the terminal server with a dedicated network may be worthwhile, in order to maintain good response time for the interactive keystrokes.

---

[37] Deducing how the author came upon this particular tidbit is left as an exercise for the reader…

5.2.8.4 Network Utilization Summary

⇒ Timesharing systems are relatively unaffected by network utilization, except when some subsystem (for example, a DBMS provider) is connected via a network. The notable exception is with X-terminals (or remote X-Window) performing graphic-intensive work.

⇒ Configure up to 30 X-terminals per network (fewer—perhaps many fewer—if the application is graphically intensive, or if the network has other responsibilities).

⇒ Do not configure graphically intensive displays to operate remotely (i.e., by sending the X11 protocol) without careful analysis.

⇒ Network Terminal Servers do not require dedicated networks unless they would otherwise share an Ethernet already burdened with high utilization.

5.2.9 Wide-Area Networking

One task often added onto a typical server's workload is support for one or more wide-area network interfaces. For example, a server might act as a gateway to a dedicated leased-line network such as is commonly found between adjacent buildings. Normally this networking is done via synchronous communication, and connects to the system with an HSI /S board. Maintaining a T1 or E1 line at full speed can consume nearly 20 percent of an older SuperSPARC processor (running a 2,048 Kbit/sec X.25 line at full utilization via SunLink X.25 8.0.2 on Solaris 2.4 consumes slightly less than 10 percent of an 85 MHz SuperSPARC processor). The effect is especially pronounced on the SPARCserver 1000E and SPARCserver 2000E because the HSI/S uses a considerable number of programmed I/Os to accomplish its work. Because of the relatively low throughput of such networks, this load is easily sustainable, but configuration of such networks through dedicated router systems (especially SPARCclassic servers where programmed I/Os are very inexpensive) is recommended when the server is expected to be fully loaded (refer to section 6.4.2.4, *XDBus Design Implications*, and 6.5.1.4, *SBus Transfer Modes*).

⇒ Configure high-throughput wide-area network interfaces (*for example,* multiple T1 or E1 lines at high utilization, or T3 lines) on dedicated systems unless the server is expected to have substantial processor reserve. Moderate- or low-throughput interfaces (single T1 lines or multiple 9.6 KB-64 KB lines) may be configured directly on a server.

5.2.10 Scheduler Tuning

In heavy load circumstances, the scheduler should sometimes be reconfigured with longer time slices (called *quanta*) to provide better performance, as discussed in section 9.7, *Scheduler Features*. This is primarily of use to sites that are already heavily CPU–bound. Except as noted in that section, the use of the real-time scheduling class is not of general use in timesharing environments.

⇒ If the installed system is CPU–bound, consider reconfiguring the scheduler with increased quanta.

5.2.11 Name Service Considerations

DBMS and NFS systems are often called upon to provide naming services to a client community. The most common arrangement is to have an NIS or NIS+ master server residing on a standalone system or on a large system with spare capacity, while other servers in the organization provide slave (NIS) or replica (NIS+) service, primarily to their own clients (NIS was previously known as the Yellow Pages). Alternatively, a fair number of sites use standard Domain Name Service (DNS).

5.2.11.1 NIS and DNS

Both DNS and NIS are quite lightweight operations, and should pose very little overhead on any significantly–sized server. For example, a SPARCstation 1+ with 16 MB memory is quite sufficient as an NIS master server for the author's lab, which includes about 60 systems. The only time it has needed a faster slave server is when testing multi-user applications—the problems occur when the processor is fully committed while the network is attempting to log more than 1,000 users into a large server at subsecond intervals. Other than relatively exceptional circumstances such as this one, the peak load period on an NIS server is when new, very long NIS maps are updated from the master. These occur whenever an administrator runs `ypxfr(1m)` (this program is also run by `cron(1m)`). Unless the maps are exceptionally large (say, with more than 15,000 entries), the peak load period is quite short. Given the approximately 7:1 differential in processor power between the SPARCstation 1+ and a current bottom-of-the-line SPARCstation 4, few circumstances call for a large dedicated DNS or NIS server. Any SuperSPARC–based server should be able to handle virtually any NIS or DNS load literally in its spare time.

5.2.11.2 NIS+ Name Services

While NIS and DNS do not pose a configuration problem, NIS+ can be problematic. For most lookups, the NIS+ load is double to triple that of NIS—in other words, not very heavy. However, especially with large NIS+ maps, some operations can consume large amounts of memory (64 MB) as well as significant processor time. Without attempting to characterize NIS+ demand in detail, configuring much larger servers as dedicated NIS+ service providers is reasonable. For example, a SPARCstation 10 Model 402 with 64 MB of memory is easily capable of handling a community of 200–250 systems. Peak load on large NIS+ servers is intermittent. Even very large communities do not need larger servers than this, since the hierarchical nature of NIS+ domains ordinarily results in division of large–scale NIS+ domains into smaller subdomains that can be handled by desktop–class servers.

⇒ Configure additional processor resources for the specific purpose of handling NIS or DNS name services only when the server is otherwise fully occupied.

⇒ Very large NIS+ domains may require servers as large as a low–end dual–processor system such as a SPARCstation 10 Model 402.

5.2.12 PrestoServe/NVSIMM

Because timesharing systems encompass such a wide range of applications, making a specific recommendation on the use of NVRAM (NVSIMM or PrestoServe) options is difficult. The best guideline is to use NVRAM when the system is expected to be an NFS server, or when the system will create and delete many files on a regular basis. NVRAM is useful when files are created or deleted, because these operations are defined by UNIX as requiring synchronous disk writes: the system may not return control to an application until any operation that modifies the directory structure is safely committed to stable storage. This approach is the only way to guarantee that the directory structure stays consistent in the face of a system outage. As discussed in section 7.1.4, *Write Acceleration with Non–Volatile Memory*, NVRAM options greatly accelerate these operations while simultaneously reducing disk utilization.

The most common (but far from the only) situations that cause files to be created and/or deleted frequently are UseNet news services (for example, NNTP), uucp services, and central mail hubs (especially store-and-forward agent systems such as those implementing X.400 Message Transfer Agents). Some heavily used printer servers with many printers servicing primarily small print jobs also benefit from NVRAM installations. Timeshare systems often run applications that create and delete many scratch files. For example, compilers often create many temporary work files to pass information between compiler phases, and often university timesharing systems that support computer science or research communities have found that creating and deleting scratch files is a substantial proportion of their disk utilization.

Finally, NVRAM is recommended for servers that have large file systems with many small files when speedy recovery from failure is crucial. Although most users are careful to optimize their backup strategy, many do not appreciate that recovery of a backed-up file system is often governed by the speed that the file system can recreate the files coming back off the tape. Because these files do not exist, creating them (and closing them, if they are small) involves a synchronous write operation that stalls the recovery process until physically completed. Recovery of file systems dominated by small files is up to four times faster when accelerated by NVRAM, an important consideration for many organizations. NVRAM can be combined with mirrored disks to significantly reduce the probability of losing a file system, while simultaneously reducing recovery time to the absolute minimum[38].

⇒ Configure NVRAM for timesharing systems that also offer NFS service.

⇒ Configure NVRAM in a timesharing system that must create and/or delete files on a frequent basis.

⇒ Configure NVRAM in systems that must have maximum file system recovery speed.

⇒ Systems configured with caching disk arrays need not configure host-based NVRAM , regardless of application.

5.2.13 Provision for Backup and Recovery

The considerations for backup and recovery in timesharing systems are similar to those for NFS servers. The details of backup and recovery are discussed extensively in Chapter 8. These points are summarized as follows:

⇒ Simple, relatively small backups can be handled with one or two tape drives; their location on SCSI busses is not particularly important if they are not active during the system's working hours.

⇒ Fully consistent backups require the locking of the file system against modifications. This requires unbundled products such as Networker. Again, configuration of the backup devices on the SCSI busses is not especially important if backups are normally run during off hours.

⇒ Mirrored file systems provide the ability to survive complete disk failures, and additionally provide the opportunity to provide continuous access even during fully consistent backups. Mirroring imposes a very small penalty in disk write throughput (a maximum of about seven to eight percent in random access, 15-20 percent in serial access; in multiple-user environments such as those seen by most servers about half of this penalty is to be expected). The default mirroring configuration improves read throughput.

⇒ Mirrored file systems should be configured with each submirror on a separate SCSI bus.

⇒ If backups are to be performed during normal system operation, the backup media should either be configured on their own SCSI bus or on the same SCSI bus as an *off-line* (detached and inactive) mirror, to avoid severe response time problems.

⇒ Configure NVRAM when rapid file system recovery is required in a small-file environment.

---

[38] The combination of mirroring and NVRAM requires at least Solstice:DiskSuite 2.0 and NVSIMM/PrestoServe 2.4.1. This configuration is *not* supported under Solaris 1.x.

5.2.14 Printing Considerations

One task that virtually all systems must deal with is printing. Fortunately, managing a printer is a task that is relatively low-throughput and also much more tolerant of latency than many other tasks. A line printer that delivers 3,000 lines per minute is considered quite fast, yet even the worst case (full 133 character lines) represents only 6.5 KB/sec, and serial printers cannot usually exceed 4 KB/sec (38,400 baud). Even a 20-page-per-minute laser printer such as the NeWSprinter 20 operating at 400 dpi demands a throughput rate of only 620 KB/sec.

Printers are best categorized into those that require host-based rasterization and those that do not. The practical difference is the amount of load placed upon the CPU. Printers not requiring rasterization, for example the Apple LaserWriter II, are lightweight printers; printers such as the NeWSprinter CL+ that make extensive use of host-based processing are considered heavyweight for configuration purposes. Note that some printers, most notably the HP LaserJets, can themselves be configured in quite a number of ways, and depending upon the mode of operation may be a lightweight or heavyweight printer.

5.2.14.1 Remote or Standalone Printers

The least intrusive printers are those that connect directly to the network; they maintain their own spool queues, typically using the Berkeley BSD `lpd` spooling protocol. The most notable members of this class are high-speed, high-capacity printers such as the HP LaserJet 4M when equipped with Ethernet or Token Ring options. Standalone printers usually require only spool space, and are thus considered lightweight, but sometimes they are used in heavyweight ways, for example when a LaserJet 4M is not equipped with its own PostScript cartridge. In this case rasterization may be done in the host, and the resulting output is spooled to the remote printer.

5.2.14.2 Lightweight Printers

Lightweight printers are usually those that have their own PostScript interpreters. The primary configuration consideration for lightweight printers is simply ensuring that the device is supplied with data without interfering with the operation of the rest of the system. For most systems, there is nothing to worry about. For most desktop systems, simply connect the printer via the onboard serial or parallel ports, or via the SPC/S board. The exceptions are the SPARCserver 1000E and SPARCserver 2000E. Lightweight printers are nearly always connected via serial or parallel ports, and the same considerations apply here, as discussed in section 5.2.7.4 above: elimination of programmed I/O operations. For serial connections, this means connecting the printer via a Network Terminal Server (or another system). Avoid directly connecting serial printers to SPARCserver 1000E and SPARCserver 2000E systems when possible, unless printer usage is expected to be light.

Parallel printers are easier to accommodate due to the availability of the low-overhead SPARCprinter SBus interface. Virtually any lightweight printer with a parallel interface can be configured on any Sun server with this board. The 2 MB/sec maximum throughput is well in excess of most printers' ability to absorb data, while the DVMA design permits full operation without interfering with any other system tasks (in fact, most personal printers are designed to handle a data rate of only about 40-50 KB/sec, an order of magnitude faster than the otherwise equivalent serial interface model). The onboard parallel ports found on the SPARCclassic, SPARCstation LX, SPARCstation 10, and SPARCstation 20 incorporate the same design as the SPARCprinter board with the same low-overhead results. A newer design used on Ultra–1 and Ultra–2 uses even less overhead, despite transferring at twice the data rate (4 MB/sec).

5.2.14.3 Heavyweight Printers

Some printers, either by design or by configuration, require considerable preprocessing by the host. In the Sun world, this preprocessing is nearly universally the translation of PostScript output into the printer's native format, and is accomplished with NeWSprint software package. NeWSprint configurations require all of the considerations applied to lightweight printers, as well as some attention paid to the PostScript processing itself.

Because the output of the rasterization process is literally a pixel-by-pixel image of the page, considerably more data is transferred from host to printer than when the printer performs the interpretation. PostScript code varies widely in size, but fairly typical non-textual PostScript output usually amounts to about 50-100 KB per page; before optimization, the 300 dpi rasterized image for a monochrome 8.5″ x 11″ page is over 1 MB. Color output is often three to five times larger. Fortunately, even fast printers (e.g., NeWSprinter 20) only require such images to be moved once every three seconds or so, making the sustained data rate quite low: around 300 KB/sec for monochrome output. Color printers image so slowly (typically 0.33 to 1.0 pages per minute) that even though their images are large (commonly 4-8 MB), data is transmitted only intermittently.

For Sun printers (SPARCprinter, NeWSprinter 20, NeWSprinter CL+) this issue is normally not a concern because the interfaces used to connect these printers have adequate bandwidth (the SPARCprinter and NeWSprinter use a custom video-like scanline interface resident on an SBus board, and the NeWSprinter CL+ is a parallel printer). The large size of rasterized output can be an issue when operating some kinds of printers. The issues are particularly severe for serial printers, which are limited to a data rate of less than 4 KB/sec (38,400 baud provides transfer speeds of about 3,600 cps). The 1 MB raster image requires nearly five minutes to transfer, although most NeWSprinter drivers have sufficient optimization to substantially reduce the size of the transferred image data. Printers configured on parallel ports are often not as fast as anticipated; many "personal" printers have parallel port implementations that cannot transfer faster than 20KB-30KB/sec.

The rasterization process itself is the other large consideration when configuring printing services. Rasterization of a single PostScript image consumes 1-40 seconds of CPU time, depending upon the type and complexity of the PostScript image. Pages containing simple text are generated very quickly, whereas full-color images requiring dithering, zooming, and other complex manipulations take considerably longer. Fortunately, NeWSprint starts rasterization processes at low priority, so interactive performance is not seriously affected by rasterization jobs[39]. The primary configuration issue is provision of sufficient memory to avoid paging when rasterization jobs are operating. Usually it requires about 2 MB for black-and-white printers and 5-6 MB for color printers.

5.2.14.4 Printer Configuration Summary

Configuration rules for connecting and operating printers can be summarized as follows:

⇒ The parallel port on the SPARCprinter SBus board is recommended for high-throughput parallel printers due to its much lower overhead. For those systems with built-in parallel ports, the built-in port is as efficient as the SPARCprinter board.

⇒ Printers that require host-based PostScript rasterization (SPARCprinter, NeWSprinter CL+, and NeWSprinter 20) no longer require a dedicated processor, since NeWSprint 2.5 now launches rasterization processes at priorities lower than interactive users.

⇒ Configure 2 MB of memory per heavyweight monochrome printer, 5-6 MB per heavyweight color printer.

⇒ Configure extensively used serial printers on Network Terminal Servers if feasible.

⇒ Avoid configuring printers (serial or parallel) via the SPC/S board unless the system is expected to have excess processor capacity.

5.3 Case Study 9—University Computing Services

The Geology and Oceanic Studies department at Whatsa Mada University is about to replace its aging computing facilities. Presently, the 18 faculty, three secretaries, and 55 graduate students use a variety of facilities assembled in an ad-hoc fashion. Because the Geology department is physically located several miles from the main campus, the department would like to have an essentially complete, independent computing facility capable of handling virtually all of its computing needs. The list of requirements includes support for a large volume of disk storage containing seismic data, general-purpose timesharing facilities for office-automation activities such as word processing with FrameMaker, electronic mail, UseNet News, and general research support. Most student records are stored on the IBM mainframe at Whatsa Mada U's on-campus computing center, but the department also

---

[39] This feature was introduced in NeWSprint 2.5.

maintains some independent student information. Each of the faculty members has a workstation or PC; the secretaries have PCs; and the graduate students use a small lab with 6 new Ultra–1s, along with 12 X-terminals.

The seismic data will be processed by a dedicated Ultra–2/2200; because the department has no full-time research or administrative staff able to perform system administration, this is the only standalone computing that will be accepted. The seismic data amounts to nearly 700 GB now and will grow to five or six times this volume over the next several years. It presently resides on many reels of 1/2″ tape, but the department intends to invest in an optical jukebox to make all the data available on a near-line basis. Meanwhile, approximately 40 GB of disk space on the new system is to be devoted to staging the seismic data to and from the tapes.

The general purpose timesharing activity must be able to handle at least 30 users running X11 automation applications, including the electronic mail, word-processing, and full-text retrieval software. The timesharing users require about 4 GB of data storage; some of the timesharing users will access the data via NFS some of the time. At least two printers are to be connected to the system, an old line printer and a new color dye-sublimation printer. In addition, a color film recorder will be attached via a SCSI port if available.

The first task, and the one that seems likely to consume the most computing resources on a consistent basis, is the provision of NFS service for the seismic server (practically full time) and the faculty/graduate workstations. The seismic server is a data-intensive NFS task. Sustaining high processing speeds on this server requires a high-bandwidth FDDI network; in this case, only two nodes need to be on the network, so a concentrator is not required: the two systems can be connected via a simple cable in the minimum FDDI network. The seismic server will impose the load of one or two fully active clients if only one or two jobs are expected to run on the compute server; this workload is capable of generating full network capacity. From Table 4 (page 50), the 100 Mbit/sec bandwidth consumes two 85 MHz processors (see *Processor Consumption*, section 2.5.4).

Twelve X-terminals are on the network, in addition to some probable X-Windows applications displayed from the server back to the various workstations. The relatively small number of X–terminals does not require any special networking treatment, but the cautious user would plan for the workstations to be doing some seismic or image processing, resulting in considerable if relatively infrequent NFS traffic on the network. In addition, many if not most geologic applications are graphics-intensive, leading to relatively high network bandwidth consumption if invoked from an X-terminal. To avoid network contention problems, the 24 workstations and 12 X-terminals should be divided onto four or five networks: preferably three nets for the workstations (eight per network) and two for the X-terminals.

The disk requirement for 40 GB of storage for the seismic data means that a minimum of 18 disk drives are required: 40 GB of file system user storage means that the disk drives must have a formatted capacity of 51 GB after accounting for UNIX file system overhead (see section 9.2.3, *UFS and UFS+ Parameters*). Because the usage is not expected to saturate the system (only one or two users are likely to be reading from the seismic data sets at once), configuring these with five 9 GB disks is reasonable. Because the load is not expected to be heavy, one fast/wide SCSI host adapter is adequate. Alternatively, a disk array is quite sufficient. Even with a five–way stripe, the system will not run out of SCSI or FibreChannel bandwidth: the 100 Mbit/sec network is capable of less than 12.5 Mbytes/sec, less than the speed of the five disks and much less than the speed of a SCSI–2 or FibreChannel bus. The "regular" user files require 4 GB of storage space; this requires slightly over 5 GB of formatted disk storage, and can be accommodated with five 1 GB disks or three 2 GB disks. From a packaging standpoint, the best overall configuration is a disk array that combines all of the disk drives. Because the 9 GB disks are physically much larger than most other disks, the smaller disk drives are more suitable. Requirements for 56 GB of disk drives mean configuring twenty eight 2 GB or fourteen 4.3 GB drives for user data. In addition, a boot disk and a UFS+ log disk are required. Either configuration fits in a single SPARCstorage Array. Because 40 users are unlikely to produce more than 15–20 fully active processes (probably less), there is little need for large disk configurations in this application. The SPARCstorage Array requires an SBus slot for the FibreChannel interface.

Two heavyweight printers must be supported (most film recorders do not accept PostScript output, requiring the host processor to rasterize the PostScript), along with one lightweight printer. Both the line printer and the color printer require a parallel port; as noted, the film recorder is to be connected via SCSI. If the host platform is a SPARCstation 20 or Ultra–1, its built-in port can be used; two SBus SPARCprinter boards are required to obtain parallel ports otherwise. Because both heavyweight printers are low-throughput (and high cost-per-page) devices, the demand on them should be low, and little if any additional processing power is required to manage them. Because the line printer is a lightweight printer, it also requires no additional processor.

The SCSI subsystem must also be able to handle at least a 1/2" tape drive, the film recorder, and backup media. The backup and recovery criteria were not supplied. Assuming a relatively typical scheme of dumping the complete system once each week with incremental dumps every night, the backup mechanism must be able to deal with at least 50 GB unattended each weekend. At least three 4 mm stackers (8–20 GB each) or an 8 mm SPARCstorage Library (70–140 GB) must be configured to meet this requirement. The five devices that must be configured strongly suggest the use of two SCSI host adapters: the cabling requirements are considerable, especially for the 1/2" tape—recall that each connector pair is the equivalent of a half-meter of cable (see *Single–Ended* vs. *Differential SCSI Implementations* in section 7.2.4.1). A further host adapter will be required in the near future to accommodate the optical jukebox system—these are normally physically large and require several meters of cabling. Three SBus slots are required to configure the various SCSI host adapters.

Table 20 tells us that with a maximum of approximately 40 timesharing users, one 85 MHz processor is required to support the timesharing activity. The memory configuration should be about 192 MB, or 32 MB + 4 MB per user. This agrees with the approximate requirement for 64 MB memory per processor. Because of the data-intensive NFS configuring 256 MB may be useful. The presence of a heavyweight 24-bit printer also suggests that additional memory may be required.

With at least five required SBus boards, along with at least three processors, the minimum platform is a SPARCserver 1000E. This system provides three SBus slots, plus a fast narrow SCSI–2, and 10baseT interface for every two processors, so six SBus slots are available in the appropriate configuration.

5.4 Case Study 10—Corporate Electronic Mail Server

Intergalactic Transport is a growing Internet Service Provider. IT has a current subscriber population of 24,000 with projections to 85,000–90,000 within the next year. The current issue is email services. Presently email is handled by a server that also handles many other tasks, and the email load is causing serious degradation to other work. IT is searching for a dedicated email processing system able to handle the projected load for the next year.

The email system is responsible for receiving inbound mail from the Internet and storing it for retrieval by customers. Except mail for internal staff, the only retrieval mechanism offered is the use of Post Office Protocol (POP-3). Customers use dialup PPP to connect to IT's central complex and run POP clients to retrieve their mail and transmit queued messages from their PCs. Although a survey shows that current email messages are about 3.5 KB in size today, management asks that the new system be sized assuming a considerable increase in average message size, about 15 KB. Accounting data shows that of the 24,000 current subscribers, more than 90 percent of them connect at least once per day to collect email, 40 percent connect twice per day, and 25 percent connect at least four times per day. Their connection times are surprisingly even, with a slight usage peak—about 15 percent—between 7 am and noon Central Time. (This corresponds to the period from 8 am Eastern time to 10 am Pacific time.) Mail deliveries average about 35 incoming messages per user per day; on average, users are transmitting about a third of that, or 10 emails per day.

The raw storage requirements amount to 15 KB x 90,000 users = 1.3 GB per day. Because POP clients immediately delete mail upon receipt, the active system only requires enough disk storage for about one full week, about 9 GB. Archival storage on slow but inexpensive writable magneto–optical disks will be provided for overflow space and stale files. Each user's mail is stored in a single file; this file averages 15 KB x 35 emails/day = 525 KB per user. In addition, each user uploads about ten emails per day, totaling an additional 150 KB. Total data transfer per user per day is 675 KB.

On average, the daily connection rate will be 90,000 x 90 percent + 90,000 x 45 percent + 2 x 25% x 90,000 = 166,500 connections. Over a day, this number averages out to about 7,000 connections per hour, or slightly less than two per second. With a 15 percent usage peak, the maximum connection rate is still about two per second.

POP clients are never idle, because they are automatic daemons not requiring user input for operation. Accordingly, it is possible to determine the average connection duration. Most of IT's customers have 28,800 baud dialup modems, although a sizable minority (about a quarter) have dual–channel ISDN connections running at 128 Kbits/sec. Typical modems run PPP at about 4–5 KB/sec after allowing for IP overhead and typical compression patterns, so each user connection lasts approximately 675 ÷ 4.5 KB/sec = 150 seconds; an ISDN connection lasts 675 ÷ 15 KB/sec = 45 secs. Between the dialup and ISDN connections, the typical connection will last about 125 seconds; because the arrival rate is about two per second, about 250 sessions will be connected simultaneously.

Each session will open one mail file and read 525 KB from it; since file system I/O blocks are 8 KB, each session represents about 65 disk I/Os, spread across 125 seconds. The overall I/O rate for reads is 65 ÷ 125 = 0.52 I/Os/sec per session × 250 sessions = 130 disk I/Os/sec for the entire system. The system–wide data transfer rate is about 4 KB/sec. Several additional I/Os are required to open the file, remove the file upon completion, and update the parent directory, but these are insignificant (3 ÷ 68 = 5 percent) compared to moving the data.

Inbound mail is somewhat more complex, because `sendmail(8)` creates three files for every incoming message. Two hundred fifty sessions × 10 messages are arriving, taking 150 KB ÷ 7.2 KB/sec (the average transfer rate) = 21 seconds per session. The incoming message rate per session is 10 messages ÷ 21 seconds = 0.48 messages/sec, a system–wide rate of 26 messages/sec after accounting for the fact that incoming messages are only 29 percent of the overall data. Each incoming message creates a file containing the message data, requiring a directory update on creation, two data writes (8 KB each), and another directory update on close. Additionally, a control file is created with a very small amount of control information. All told this requires three disk writes. The `sendmail` daemon deletes both files after delivery, involving two more writes. All told, the inbound mail requires 26 x 7 = 182 disk I/Os per second.

The overall disk I/O rate is about 130 + 182 = 312 I/Os per second. A 7,200 rpm disk delivers about 110 disk I/Os/sec, so this application requires at least three disk drives. Given the requirement for 9 GB of disk storage, three 4.3 GB disks have too much storage with the right access capacity, whereas three 2.1 GB disks have sufficient access capacity but insufficient storage space. Five 2.1 GB disks yield adequate storage capacity if `minfree` and inode density are reduced to reasonable levels. This configuration is much safer because it has reserve I/O access capacity. With only 312 disk I/Os per second (about 2.5 MB/sec), a single SCSI bus is easily able to handle all of the disk activity.

Memory size must be substantial in order to handle the 250 concurrent POP server processes—each process consumes about 1 MB, plus 32 MB for the system itself, yielding a 288 MB requirement.

Although the 250 simultaneous connections ("users") statistic is impressive, processor power is probably not in question. The 250 processes do virtually nothing besides read and write data at an aggregate rate of about 5 MB/sec (2.5 MB/sec to and from disk and an equivalent amount to or from the networks). Less than ten processes are launched per second (mostly sendmail daemons). A single processor is easily sufficient for these loads.

The final configuration consists of a desktop system, ideally an Ultra–1 , with 320 MB of memory (288 MB are required, but Ultra–1 memory must be configured in pairs of SIMMs, so 320 MB is the nearest configuration). An external disk pack with five 2.1 GB disks is required; all five disks can be configured on the built–in fast/wide SCSI -2 bus.

System Architecture 6 ≡

This chapter addresses various technical subjects that bear directly upon system configurations. The topics are general in nature, applying generally to most if not all kinds of servers and systems. Although this chapter specifically addresses Sun products, the concepts are generally applicable to products available throughout the industry.

6.1 A Comparison of System Architectures

The basic architecture of server systems has evolved considerably in the era of open systems. The earliest servers, such as the Sun–3/280, Sun–4/280, and SPARCserver 390, were workstation system cores physically configured in larger enclosures, enabling much richer configurations. As technology costs decreased, UNIX–based servers pushed into departmental and then enterprise environments, greatly increasing server performance requirements. To meet these needs, vendors created purpose–designed servers, and system architects have continuously expanded the size and architectural scope of these systems. Meanwhile, workgroup and small departmental servers have continued to leverage the rapidly increasing technology derived from the desktop workstation. The following discussion points out the architectural differences between generations of Sun's SPARC–based servers; most vendors have followed a similar technology path, although the details vary from vendor to vendor and between high-end and low-end implementations. For the most part, most of the designs are driven by contemporary technology and pricing, although some parts of the architecture are notably better developed in some implementations than in others. This fact is particularly true in the area of I/O bus interfaces.

6.1.1 Workstation–Derived Servers

Early microprocessor-based servers, even relatively large departmental systems, were simple in an architectural sense. The SPARCserver 390 (announced in 1989) used an architecture derived from then-current technical workstations (see Figure 22). The system is architecturally identical to the concurrent SPARCstation 330, a high-end technical workstation. A fast microprocessor connects to memory via a cache; a single VME bus provides peripheral connectivity. For simplicity, I/O also passes through the cache. The cache operates in write-through mode to simplify memory consistency during I/O operations. The processor and I/O subsystem share the memory management unit, ensuring consistency of memory addresses between the two primary operating units in the system. This architecture, with slight modifications, was essentially that of the typical personal computer or PC LAN server in 1995. The most salient characteristics of the workstation–derived server architecture are simplicity and ease of implementation. Although effective in its day, this implementation suffers from contention between the processor and the I/O bus for the virtually addressed cache, and has relatively little I/O bandwidth.

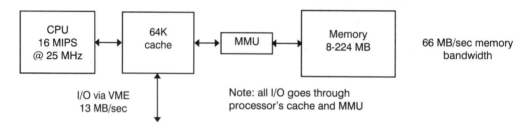

Figure 22. The architecture of the SPARCserver 390 (1989). Most PCs use this architecture with few changes, even in 1996, and PC servers are only slightly more sophisticated.

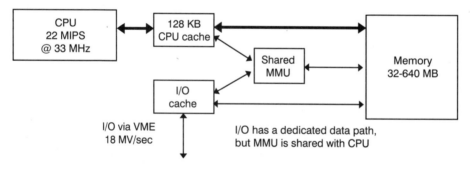

Figure 23. The architecture of the SPARCserver 490, introduced in 1990. I/O functions have a dedicated path to memory, substantially improving the system as a server.

6.1.2 Purpose–Designed Servers

Beginning with the SPARCserver 490 of 1990 (Figure 23), designers created a completely separate path for I/O access to main memory. In order to maintain a consistent memory image and to provide maximum performance with a VME peripheral bus, an I/O cache was placed between the I/O bus and main memory. The processor's cache operates in write-back mode, connected directly to main memory by a dedicated high speed memory bus. The dedicated path from the VME bus to memory through the I/O cache eliminated contention for the processor's cache resources and bus bandwidth. Deliverable I/O capability improved over the predecessor SPARCserver 390 by a dramatic 250 percent, even though the main processor improved by only a modest 38 percent and burst speed on the VME bus remained constant.

In 1991, the SPARCsystem 600MP (Figure 24) extended the architecture in several notable ways: it added symmetric multiprocessing, a completely independent peripheral bus for I/O[40], and the use of user-replaceable processor modules. In addition, the SBus delivers approximately twice the I/O bandwidth as previous VME bus implementations. With some exceptions (such as the I/O cache and the speed of the current PCI I/O bus), this is essentially the architecture of a typical Pentium–based system in 1995 (Figure 25).

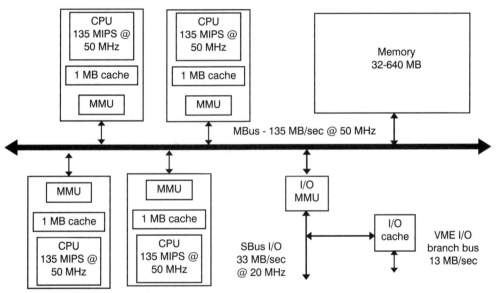

Figure 24. The architecture of the SPARCserver 600MP (1991). This system introduced symmetric multiprocessing, SBus I/O, and denser packaging.

---

[40] In the SPARCserver 490, the VME bus shared the MMU with the main processor; the SPARCserver 690MP provides an independent I/O MMU to completely separate I/O and memory traffic.

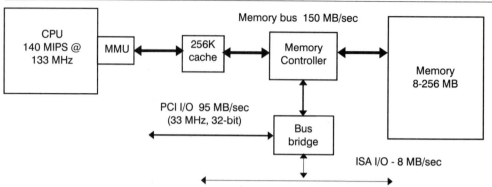

Figure 25. The architecture of a typical 1996 PC or PC server, such as with 200 MHz Pentium Pro systems with PCI and ISA I/O busses. Multiprocessor systems substitute a faster memory bus.

6.1.3 Ultra Servers

The latest desktop SPARC systems from Sun are the Ultra–1 and Ultra–2 workstations. These systems use the new UltraSPARC–I processor, which delivers higher basic processor performance as well as *much* higher performance access to memory. The internal bandwidth of the system is much faster than its predecessor, the SPARCstation 20, leading to very different internal organization. Instead of using a shared backplane, the Ultra–1 and Ultra–2 use a crossbar switch called the Ultra Port Architecture (UPA)to connect processors, memory, and I/O. Between the UltraSPARC–I and the UPA crossbar, real memory transfers—crucial to server applications—are improved by almost an order of magnitude. The crossbar interconnect (Figure 26) runs at a substantially higher clock rate (83.5 MHz) and is twice as wide as either MBus or XDBus. Its architecture also permits much lower memory latency than either MBus or XDBus.

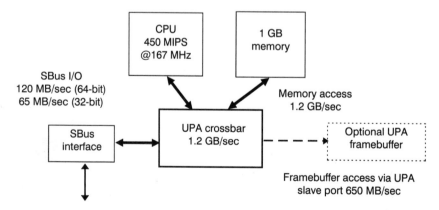

Figure 26. Block diagram of the Ultra Port Architecture (UPA) used in the Ultra–1 workstation.

6.1.4 Enterprise–Class Servers

The SPARCcenter 2000 (introduced in 1992) uses a much more extensive architecture, as diagrammed in Figure 27. It uses many of the same concepts as the SPARCsystem 600MP: user-replaceable processor modules, symmetric multiprocessing, and separate facilities for I/O. This organization is considerably richer than previous systems, but this architecture is also sufficiently complex that direct expansion to a system similar in size to the SPARCcenter 2000 would be difficult to implement. The most obvious differences are many additional processors, a backplane bus with much higher deliverable bandwidth, and a multitude of separate I/O busses. Less apparent but potentially as important are heuristically driven automatic reconfiguration in case of hardware failure, a highly pipelined bus architecture, a programmable address space, multiple memory models, a more advanced SBus implementation, non-volatile memory, and alternate cache coherency protocols.

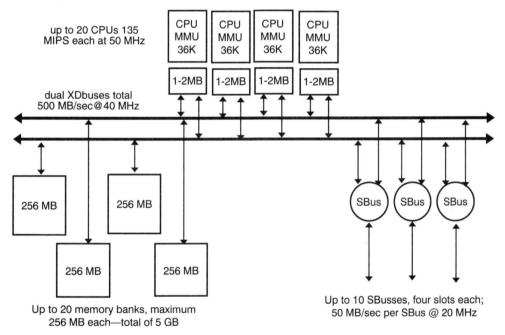

Figure 27. The architecture of the SPARCcenter 2000, offering 20 processors, 5 GB memory, and ten SBusses. The Cray SuperServer 6400 is structurally identical—except larger: 64 processors, 16 GB memory, 16 SBusses, and four XDBusses.

Although expansion capability and overall system balance are much greater than previous generations, the architecture is actually *simpler* than its predecessor. As with any large-scale engineering effort, this architecture (known to the operating system as " sun4d") has to make compromises. It does an excellent job of handling large amounts of data, but in so doing it sacrifices the optimal handling of small pieces of data, as the hierarchical nature of data transfers results in substantially higher latency on most operations. Higher latency has a minimal impact on large transfers, but can dominate processing of small transfers.

The SPARCserver 1000 is essentially a SPARCcenter 2000 with only one XDBus, residing in a much smaller physical package. The smaller system implements the same architecture, using identical chips. The Cray[41] CS6400 is a 64-processor implementation of the SPARCcenter 2000, using four XDBusses. More rigid environmental controls permit the operation of the same chips used in the SPARCcenter 2000 and SPARCserver 1000, albeit at higher clock rates. Sun upgraded both members of the sun4d family in 1994, improving the XDBus clock to 50 MHz and the SBus to 25 MHz. Called the "-E" series, these models differ from their predecessors only by these clock rate differences and the ability to configure the SPARCcenter 2000E with redundant power supplies.

6.1.5 The Ultra Enterprise Server Family

Sun's latest enterprise-class servers are the Ultra Enterprise x000 family. Architecturally, they are an interesting blend between the workstation architecture of the Ultra–1 workstation and the server architecture of the SPARCcenter 2000E. The Ultra Enterprise x000 server family combines the UltraSPARC-I processor with a very fast central bus and physical packaging designed to accommodate either very high processing capacity or extensive I/O capability. The overall design extends that of the SPARCcenter 2000E, sharing many architectural components with the Ultra–1 desktop, all combined with careful attention to packaging details.

Like the SPARCcenters, the Ultra Enterprise systems share processors with their desktop cousins, but the new systems also share the use of the UPA crossbar switch. In the servers, the crossbar serves only as a local connection and as an interface definition, rather than as the system backbone. This detail is small, but is very useful: it permits the workstations and servers to share kernel implementations, rather than requiring two different sets of code as in the previous-generation systems. The Gigaplane system backbone bus connects the many crossbar switches. Like the SPARCcenter 2000E and SPARCserver 1000E, the Ultra Enterprise family offers multiple packaging options within the family. The new systems go beyond their predecessors, permitting members of the family to share most physical components in addition to software. Rather than placing processors, memory, and I/O on a single board, the Enterprise family utilizes processor/memory boards and separate I/O boards. The architecture is shown in Figure 28.

---

[41] The Cray Business Systems Division was purchased by Sun in early 1996; these systems are now sold and supported by Sun.

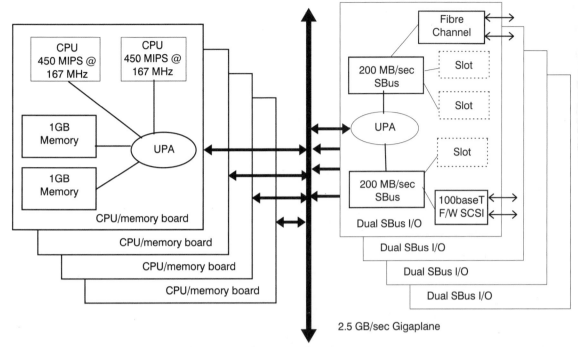

Figure 28. Architecture of the Ultra Enterprise x000 family.

Processor/memory boards carry up to two UltraSPARC processors and two banks of memory totaling 2 GB per board. Local connection between the processors and memory is through a UPA crossbar very much like the Ultra–2 workstation. The UPA connects CPUs and memory to the Gigaplane for system-wide connectivity.

The Ultra Enterprise family has two types of I/O board. One is a pure SBus implementation offering three SBus slots on two completely independent SBusses; the other is a graphics I/O board that provides a UPA slave port as well as a two-slot SBus implementation. The I/O boards are similar in architecture to the processor/memory boards: a UPA crossbar interfaces the Gigaplane to the onboard components, which are binary-compatible with their desktop relatives. The SBusses are full 64-bit implementations, each capable of sustained transfer speeds of approximately 120 MB/sec.

The Gigaplane connects the various boards together and implements a cache coherency domain across all processors and memory spaces. Its design overcomes the limitations found in the XDBus—namely relatively low throughput combined with relatively high latency— while being simpler in implementation. In order to provide adequate bus bandwidth, the Gigaplane is very wide, using 256 data lines and additional dedicated control and address lines. This arrangement permits a sustained data transfer capability of approximately

2.5 GB/sec, sufficient for the maximum configuration of 30 processors. The ability to overlap bus arbitration, address selection, and data transfer reduces memory latency to about 50 cycles. Compared to the XDBus, the Gigaplane is capable of eight times the sustained throughput, while memory latency is about four times better.

With 16 Gigaplane slots, physical packaging restricts the Enterprise 6000 to 30 processors and 30 GB of memory with two SBusses. More typical configurations use fewer processors (say, about 24) and more SBusses (eight are possible with 24 processors). The smaller Enterprise 4000 and Enterprise 5000 have eight slots, while the deskside Enterprise 3000 has four slots.

6.2 SPARC Processor Designs

Many different SPARC processor designs are available now, each designed to meet different goals. The following discussion highlights the most significant features of each from a configuration perspective.

6.2.1 SuperSPARC Family

By far the most common processor in SPARC systems today is the SuperSPARC and its derivatives. There are three slightly different SuperSPARC implementations, all designed by Sun engineers and fabricated in Texas Instrument's BiCMOS process. The original chip was first delivered in 1992 in 33–, 36–, and 40 MHz versions, followed by the SuperSPARC+, which arrived in 1993 at 50– and 60 MHz. The final member of the family is the SuperSPARC–II, offered in 75– and 85 MHz models.

A member of the first generation of superscalar RISC processors, the SuperSPARC was designed to attain relatively low clock rate, but also to accomplish a great deal of work in each clock cycle. Accordingly, it can dispatch up to four separate instructions in each clock cycle: two integer instructions, one floating point instruction, and a branch. When executing out of cache, the processor is able to sustain an execution rate of about 1.3 instructions per clock, although memory delays mean that realistic execution is on the order of 0.85 instructions per clock. Although floating point performance is anemic, integer performance is good, and the chip is among the most efficient on a SPECint92 per clock basis.

Designed to operate in both desktops and servers, the SuperSPARC design actually has two discrete external interfaces, one for MBus and one for an external cache controller. In MBus mode, the processor can be used without other logic to implement multiprocessor systems, and this situation applies in the SPARCstation 10 Model 402 and SPARCstation 20 Model 502. In this configuration, the processor adapts to the MBus clock; if a SPARCstation 20's Model 50 module were plugged into a SPARCstation 10, it would operate at the latter's 40 MHz clock speed.

The processor can also be mated with a SuperCache external cache controller and an SRAM cache array; this arrangement is used in all other SuperSPARC–based systems. The SuperCache also has two different interfaces, one for MBus found in desktop systems and one for XBus for servers. The SuperCache senses the bus type and acts accordingly, permitting most modules to operate correctly in either type of system.

6.2.1.1 SuperSPARC and MBus Interaction

SuperSPARC/SuperCache modules have their own clocks, permitting the module to run asynchronously to the MBus. In other words, the on–board clock runs the module independently of the bus clock. Worth noting is the fact that the module must run at a *higher* clock rate than an MBus. Ordinarily, this is not an issue, but it is significant in the SPARCstation 20 Model 514. The SPARCstation 20 normally runs the MBus at 50 MHz, but the Model 514 modules have an onboard clock set at 50.0 MHz—and the modules must run faster than the bus clock. In this case, the system senses the speed of the modules and adjusts the MBus to 40 MHz (since the SBus clock is derived from the MBus, it is adjusted down to 20 MHz). Applications that are memory–intensive may run noticeably slower on this model of the SPARCstation 20 than on other seemingly similar configurations (although the SPARCstation 10 Model 41 is advertised as a 40 MHz part, it avoids this problem by running the processor at 40.3 MHz, permitting the bus to run at 40.0 MHz).

6.2.1.2 SuperCache Latency Considerations

The SuperCache is always configured with either a 1 MB or 2 MB SRAM cache array (the 2 MB model can only be configured in the SPARCcenter 2000, since the additional address bit and cache tags required to support the larger cache are only present in that system). The 1 MB external cache was quite large for its day, and the designers opted to rely on the large cache and settled for a relatively long path to main memory. When the processor requests data, the large cache is able to satisfy most references quickly—6 clock cycles (5 cycles on 85 MHz modules). The relatively few references that go all the way to memory are quite slow, taking 40–70 clock cycles on MBus systems and 90-190 cycles on XDBus systems. This arrangement works well in practice, although it results in poor performance on the relatively small proportion of applications that do not make effective use of the caches. Applications that fall into this category are those that make extensive use of linked lists; numerically intensive applications that make use of very large *sparse* matrices are particularly sensitive to this design. LISP interpreters and some types of ECAD simulation applications are the two categories that are particularly infamous for this behavior.

The 85 MHz SuperSPARC-II uses a slightly different version of the SuperCache that implements two new memory interface modes, called *prefetch* and *multicommand* (MC) mode. Prefetching requests that the SuperCache obtain additional data from memory in some cases, saving bus transactions. Multicommand mode is especially important for improving performance on XDBus–based systems. Without MC, the SuperCache permits only one transaction at a time to be pending against memory, blocking subsequent references until the first one completes. The system as a whole permits many outstanding transactions, even without multicommand mode.

Consider the situation when the processor stores to memory, then loads from a different memory bank. Without MC, the SuperCache issues the store and blocks; it issues the read 90–150 cycles later, after the store completes. The read also takes 90–190 cycles, so the two instructions take 180–380 cycles. When multicommand mode is enabled, the SuperCache issues the read immediately after the store, so the two instructions take only 100–160 cycles, a significant savings. Even in multicommand mode, the SuperCache permits only two outstanding memory accesses, and the compilers attempt to separate memory references specifically so this situation does not arise frequently. Multicommand is not useful on MBus systems because the MBus and memory system do not accommodate multiple pending transactions. However, the magnitude of the saving means that MC delivers significant performance improvement—about eight percent overall on XDBus systems compared to the same processor with MC disabled.

6.2.2 hyperSPARC™

Similar in some respects to the Sun/TI SuperSPARC, the hyperSPARC processor was designed independently by engineers at Ross Technologies at approximately the same time that the SuperSPARC was being designed by Sun. This chip is also a first-generation superscalar design. Sun did not participate in the design; instead, the Ross team chose to build a fully compatible competing chip to the SuperSPARC using the open and published MBus and SPARC V8 interfaces. The resulting processor makes very different design tradeoffs while pursuing the same overall goal. The same MBus interface is supported, and the two processors implement the same SPARC V8 instruction set with the same semantics, but many implementation details are different. Unlike SuperSPARC, the hyperSPARC design does not include an XDBus interface, configuring these processors in XDBus systems is impossible.

Most fundamentally, the hyperSPARC is a much more conservative architectural design than SuperSPARC, resulting in a processor that accomplishes much less each clock cycle, but which can attain far higher clock rates. Whereas the SuperSPARC can dispatch up to four instructions per clock, hyperSPARC can dispatch only one integer and one floating point instruction each clock. This design simplifies the internal organization and is one of the primary reasons hyperSPARC clock rates approach twice those of the SuperSPARC. Current hyperSPARC processors operate at 150 MHz, while the fastest SuperSPARC runs at just 85 MHz. In order to more easily achieve the higher clock rates, Ross opted for a full custom CMOS process technology. CMOS is a much better–understood technology than BiCMOS for design houses without the resources available to Intel. The parts are fabricated by Fujitsu Microelectronics, Ross's parent company.

6.2.2.1 hyperSPARC Cache Considerations

Another important characteristic is that the hyperSPARC has a much smaller, less complex cache structure. Whereas the SuperSPARC has a large, highly associative on–chip cache (36 KB) backed by a large but relatively slow 1 MB external cache, the hyperSPARC opts for a small, on–chip, instruction–only cache combined with a smaller external data cache. The first 66 MHz hyperSPARC was delivered about the same time as the 36 MHz SuperSPARC, and was equipped with 8 KB instruction and 128 KB data caches. Because the caches are relatively small, the design devotes considerable attention to minimizing the path to memory (newer 100-125 MHz parts have 256 KB caches, and 150 MHz parts have 512 KB). As a result, the hyperSPARC performs far better on precisely those applications SuperSPARC runs very slowly. At the other end of the spectrum, the SuperSPARC's larger cache yields better performance for some applications.

Applications that make good use of cache are a different story. For most workstation applications, the code and data fit comfortably in cache, and the processor is able to run at design speed. The higher clock rate but less sophisticated architectural design delivers approximately the same performance as SuperSPARC processors of the same generation. For single user work, the 60 MHz SuperSPARC is roughly equivalent to the 100 MHz hyperSPARC, and the 75 MHz SuperSPARC is approximately equivalent to the 125 MHz part from Ross. In these comparisons, SuperSPARC usually is slightly faster on integer code, and hyperSPARC is usually somewhat faster for floating–point code.

6.2.2.2 hyperSPARC in Server Configurations

The biggest difference between the two processors becomes apparent when comparing the two for *server* performance. Because servers normally run processes on behalf of many users, the size of the cache is usually a constraining factor. Unlike workstation applications, where the (one) application has a fairly good chance of keeping its cache working set actually in the cache, server systems have to fit many different applications into cache. The larger cache retains more context in fast memory, and resultant performance is noticeably higher. In particular, this result is true of the hyperSPARC -SuperSPARC comparison. The larger caches, combined with a more efficient `bcopy(9f)` accelerator, deliver about 20 percent better performance from SuperSPARC than from otherwise equivalent hyperSPARC (for example, 85 MHz SuperSPARC and 150 MHz hyperSPARC).

The Ross design holds a distinct edge over SuperSPARC for SPARCstation 10 and SPARCstation 20 servers in one category. Because it is fabricated with multichip module (MCM) technology, two complete hyperSPARC processors and their caches can be squeezed onto a single MBus module. The more compact design permits construction of a quad–processor system without physically interfering with SBus slots (SuperSPARC–II modules consume enough power that even if their form factor permitted a full 4-slot SBus configuration, the SPARCstation 20 power supply would not be able to support such a configuration). For some applications, a quad–processor hyperSPARC provides useful expansion headroom, but most such server applications will benefit from moving to a larger platform.

Although Sun has discontinued further development of SuperSPARC follow–ons, Ross and Fujitsu have announced at least one additional hyperSPARC design. The new part, expected to ship in 1996, boosts the clock rate to 200 MHz and use a 1 MB external cache. This processor should have no trouble outperforming the 85 MHz SuperSPARC by a substantial margin, even on server applications.

Although SuperSPARC has improved over time—the SuperSPARC–II has dual TLBs and an improved SuperCache—the simpler pure–CMOS hyperSPARC design has been far easier to scale and improve. Sun had considerable trouble improving SuperSPARC–II's clock rate from 75 MHz to 85 MHz, while hyperSPARC is heading for 200 MHz (and possibly higher). Ross has also added additional integer processing units, substantially increased its external cache, and improved the on–chip caches to 16 KB for data and 16 KB for instructions. (This processor still only dispatches one integer instruction per clock. The additional processing unit permits two integer instructions to be executing simultaneously only if the first issued instruction takes longer than a single cycle to complete. Overall integer performance improves by only a few percent, rather than the more intuitive doubling.)

6.2.3 Summary Comparison: SuperSPARC and hyperSPARC

To summarize the differences between the two primary SPARCstation 10 and SPARCstation 20 processor classes:

- hyperSPARC and SuperSPARC deliver approximately equivalent performance for single threaded applications when SuperSPARC's clock rate is about 60 percent of hyperSPARC's (for example 75 MHz SuperSPARC vs. 125 MHz hyperSPARC).

- SuperSPARC outperforms "equivalent" hyperSPARC by about 20 percent on server applications, due to cache size and `bcopy` accelerator considerations.

- hyperSPARC is considerably faster than "equivalent" SuperSPARC on applications that make heavy use of linked lists.

6.2.4 MicroSPARC and MicroSPARC–II

The lowest–cost parts in the SPARC family, the MicroSPARC architecture is designed almost exclusively to accommodate workstation requirements. Instead of a multiprocessor implementation consisting of several chips, MicroSPARC and MicroSPARC–II systems consist essentially of one main chip. Desktop SuperSPARC and hyperSPARC systems have several large ASICs implementing MBus, SBus, and memory control. The MicroSPARC chip itself contains all of the CPU functions (CPU, cache, and memory management unit), plus SBus and a memory controller.

The MicroSPARC design has, by quite a margin, the lowest (best) memory latency of its generation of SPARC processors. This is a necessity: MicroSPARC–1 has only 6 KB of cache, and MicroSPARC–II has 24 KB. Because the caches are very small, latency to memory is at a premium, and the architecture makes allowances for these realities. In addition, the MicroSPARC is made vastly simpler by not having to make allowances for multiprocessing. Finally, the fact that MicroSPARC is a single integrated chip, with few high–performance off–chip interconnects means that it simply takes less time to get from one functional unit to another. This contributes both to excellent memory latency and to very tight control of the SBus. Boards that are extremely intolerant of SBus or SBus interrupt latencies work very well in the MicroSPARC architecture.

Unfortunately, except for workgroup servers, the MicroSPARC–II does not have the horsepower to run most server applications, and the original MicroSPARC is completely inadequate. Even with low–latency memory, the processor quickly saturates under the heavy memory traffic generated by these applications. Suitable for attribute–intensive NFS servers and current levels of World Wide Web (WWW) traffic, MicroSPARC–based systems should otherwise be used for workstation applications.

6.2.5 UltraSPARC

Using the experience gained from the first generation of superscalar processors, Sun designed the UltraSPARC to deliver leading–edge performance in many dimensions. Although the SuperSPARC family succeeded in delivering adequate performance for most applications, it suffered from a complex design, relatively slow access to memory, contention for a TLB shared between user and system contexts, and moderate ability to copy memory. UltraSPARC uses a relatively conservative full-custom CMOS design (for a second–generation RISC processor), to implement a 64–bit, four–way superscalar design. The new design features a much cleaner system interface, a limited but highly optimized implementation–specific instruction set extension designed to accelerate graphics and server applications, a much faster memory interface—and clock rates ranging from 143 MHz to 250 MHz. The UltraSPARC–1 implements a proper superset of the SPARC Version 9 software architecture.

6.2.5.1 Register Sets and System Interface

One of the primary improvements in the UltraSPARC architecture is a substantially extended register set. The floating point register file is twice as large as on the SuperSPARC . Obviously it improves floating point performance, but more important for server applications, the floating point register file is used by the block memory instructions (see *VIS Instruction Sets* below).

In addition, the 64–bit SPARC Version 9 definition eliminates one key bottleneck found in all previous implementations: a single trap context. Whenever the system is interrupted for unusual processing (such as an interrupt, a floating point exception, a system defined trap, etc.), the operating system must quickly provide scratch register space for the trap handler to process the event. In SPARC V8, a single trap context had to suffice for all system traps, resulting in very complicated code in trap handlers. SPARC V9 defines five discrete trap contexts, dramatically simplifying the code path in a part of the operating system that is very performance–sensitive.

One other feature first implemented in the SuperSPARC –II and carried forward into the UltraSPARC family is the use of separate *translation lookaside buffers* (TLBs) for user and system space. The TLB accelerates the mapping of virtual addresses to physical pages of memory. When the processor spends a considerable amount of time executing in the operating system, a TLB dedicated to mapping system addresses pays disproportionate dividends by privately caching translations for the operating system and protecting that cache from being overflowed by user activity.

6.2.5.2 VIS Instruction Set

UltraSPARC addresses the (different) requirements of both workstation and server applications. The Visualization Instruction Set (VIS) is an extension to SPARC V9 designed to accelerate specific types of graphics operations, such as motion estimation for video decompression and specific pixel–oriented operations used in applications such as MPEG display. The VIS uses opcodes in the range set aside by the V9 definition for custom instruction set extensions.

The VIS instruction set is of little interest to server users, with one major exception: the block load/store instructions. Previous processors were able to manipulate small amounts of data in a single instruction, namely a maximum of eight bytes, the size of a double–precision floating point number. For applications that copy data, this limitation is significant—almost all server applications spend a significant fraction of their time copying data either directly or indirectly via the operating system. The UltraSPARC block data instructions manipulate blocks of 64 bytes, a significant improvement.

Although most direct device I/O is done via DVMA requiring little processor intervention, there are many places in the operating system, its libraries, and applications that copy data in processor loops. For example, Ethernet packets are small enough that they are transferred with programmed I/O. The UltraSPARC is able to copy a full 1,500 byte packet in 48 block load/store instructions, while SuperSPARC requires 378 double–word load/store instructions to complete the same task. A 200 MHz UltraSPARC–1 can copy memory at 270 MB/sec, compared to about 51 MB/sec for an 85 MHz SuperSPARC–II.

Although most SuperSPARC-based systems have `bcopy(9f)` accelerator hardware, the block load/store instructions of the VIS instruction set offer major improvements over the earlier implementations. The primary difference is that because the VIS instructions are simply instructions—instead of supplemental hardware—the copy accelerator is able to accelerate user-mode copies as well as kernel-mode copies. Additionally, because the older hardware is not integrated with the memory management unit (MMU), it requires considerable overhead for setup and teardown. Because the VIS instructions are fully supported by the MMU, they require no special setup. The significantly lower overhead allows the use of the accelerator for all copies, not just larger ones where the savings outweigh the setup time. Finally, since `bcopy(9f)` and `bzero(9f)` are implemented in dynamically loaded libraries, regular applications can make full use of the new capabilities.

6.2.5.3 Memory Interface

Designed with SuperSPARC's memory latency issues clearly in mind, UltraSPARC's memory interface is much more streamlined. The access to the external cache is non–blocking, meaning that the processor can issue a memory access to the cache and remain free to execute other instructions that do not require the requested data. The external cache interface is fully buffered, permitting multiple memory accesses to be outstanding from the processor. Combined with the non-blocking nature of the cache, the buffering is able to hide the six–cycle cache latency in most cases.

The fully synchronous external cache runs at the full speed of the processor, and can provide a full cache line every clock cycle on a sustained basis. This capability is terrific for performance, especially when combined with the high clock rates associated with UltraSPARC, but it makes the cache SRAMs quite expensive.

6.3 Memory Subsystems: Cache and Main Memory

Many Sun systems are now offered with a variety of interchangeable processor modules, often with varying sizes and types of caches. For example, the SPARCstation 10 and SPARCstation 20 were offered in uniprocessor and multiprocessor configurations with or without a 1 MB external cache, while the SPARCcenter 2000 was for a time offered with either the 1 MB external cache or a larger 2 MB version. The cache is the layer of the virtual storage hierarchy closest to the processor; among the layers of the virtual memory hierarchy, it usually has the largest effect on performance.

6.3.1 Cache Organizations

Although all caches have the same fundamental purpose—matching the speed of memory to the speed of the processor—designers use a large number of parameters to trade off complexity, silicon area, and performance. Comparing cache sizes is now very much like comparing clock speeds on dissimilar processors: gross differences (4 MB vs. 4 KB) are indicative, but little else can be determined without considerable additional information.

6.3.1.1 Contextual Division: Unified vs. Harvard

Processors use memory for two separate kinds of storage: instructions to be executed and data to be manipulated. It turns out that these two kinds of data have different locality, and for caches of limited size (certainly those less than 128 KB, and possibly as large as 256 KB) dividing a cache is beneficial, dedicating part to instructions and part to data. Caches that split into dedicated instruction and data caches are said to have a *Harvard* architecture. Caches that do not divide the cache are called *unified*.

Naturally, having two separate caches is more complex to implement and more expensive than having one unified cache of combined size, but splitting the caches permits each to be optimized for its specific task. Dividing the cache also provides each cache some immunity from turbulence in the other. This immunity is especially useful with very small caches, such as the one located in the MicroSPARC–I processor. In the MicroSPARC, the instruction cache (often abbreviated I$) is 4 KB in size, and the data cache (D$) is 2 KB. If the cache were a 6 KB unified cache, a loop that steps through data would quickly replace all of the cache lines, whether used for data or instructions. With a Harvard architecture, only the D$ lines are replaced, preserving the I$ state. This allowance is much less important when caches are large (256 KB or more). As a result, most large external caches (E$) are unified. For small caches (less than 128 KB), a Harvard cache is about as effective as a unified cache of about *twice* the size.

6.3.1.2 Line Replacement: Direct-Mapped vs. Associative

Caches are divided into blocks or *lines*, and sometimes blocks are divided into *sub-blocks*. The caches in most Sun systems are divided into 32-byte lines. However, the external caches managed by SuperCache controllers have two operating modes. When caches are 1 MB in size, the cache lines are 128 bytes; 2MB caches use 256 byte lines; and when operating in

XBus mode, 64 byte sub-blocks are used. The cache sub-block is 64 bytes on XBus-based machines because memory can only transfer units of 64 bytes due to the Xbus organization [42].

Table 21. Operating modes and unit sizes for SuperSPARC external cache modules

Cache Mode	1 MB Cache		2 MB Cache	
	Line Size	Sub-Block Size	Line Size	Sub-Block Size
MBus	128 bytes	32 bytes	N/A	N/A
XBus	128 bytes	64 bytes	256 bytes	64 bytes

Lines or sub-blocks are the units of replacement: when more data must be stored in the cache while the cache is full, a line is displaced and a line-sized chunk of main memory containing the new data is stored in the space vacated by the displaced line. The choice of which line to displace can have a direct bearing on how well the cache performs. A *direct-mapped* cache maps each main memory address to exactly one possible location in the cache. This simple approach works well under most circumstances, especially for larger caches.

One problem with direct-mapped caches is a *line conflict*. Since the cache is smaller than main memory, a given cache line must serve more than one main memory location. Usually the cache line is selected by computing the number of lines in the cache and using the line number within memory, modulo the number of lines in the cache. For example, if the cache is 2 KB bytes in size with 32 byte lines, it has 64 lines; memory is divided into 32-byte lines also, and the first 32 bytes are mapped into the first cache line, etc. This scheme runs into problems when the two frequently used memory locations are separated by exactly a multiple of the cache size. In this case, both memory lines are mapped into the same cache line, and this requires flushing and writing the old line at every single reference to the alternate memory lines! This effectively eliminates the cache from the system, since alternate accesses to the lines require direct manipulation of main memory. Line conflict is much more likely with small caches than with large caches.

For smaller caches, a more complex implementation avoids this problem by permitting a memory location to map into one of several different cache lines. When a processor refers to memory, the cache hardware searches all of the possible locations in parallel to determine which one actually caches the referenced address, if any. The cache is therefore equipped to resolve line conflicts. Caches that permit a memory location to map to multiple cache lines are called *associative*, because the hardware used to search the cache in parallel (actually by content) is called associative memory.

---

[42] SMCC, *SPARCcenter 2000 Design and Implementation*, Sun Microsystems internal publication, November 1992.

The on-chip cache of the SuperSPARC processor is highly associative. The instruction cache is 20 KB in size, and is five-way associative; the data cache is 16 KB in size, and is four-way associative. A memory location referenced by the instruction fetch unit may map into any one of five different cache lines, and the target of a load or store can map into four different cache lines (the cache is actually divided into nine 4 KB regions[43]). Because many cache misses in small caches are attributable to line conflicts, a highly associative cache often performs as well as a much larger direct-mapped cache in actual use. Patterson and Hennesey report that a 32 KB four-way associative cache can have a lower miss rate than a 64 KB direct-mapped cache[44].

6.3.1.3 Addressing: Virtual vs. Physical

Another cache variant involves the type of addresses mapped into the cache, depending upon the logical location of the memory management unit (MMU). Some processors such as those used in the SPARCstation 2 and SPARCserver 600MP Models 120 and 140 (the Cypress/Ross CY605 modules) place the MMU logically after the cache. These caches store virtual addresses in the cache, and for obvious reasons are called virtually addressed caches. This method has the advantage of not having to spend time in the CPU's pipeline translating the address before looking in the cache for the data, making possible a higher clock rate at a given level of complexity. It works well for single-user workstations, or servers that manage relatively few processes. The primary problem with this arrangement is that a context switch makes the addresses invalid because addresses are peculiar to individual processes.

Some caches translate virtual addresses to physical addresses before the cache. Although this approach requires considerable extra complexity to minimize the time required to translate the address before searching the cache, it has the considerable advantage of permitting the cache to be shared between contexts when those contexts refer to the same physical addresses. This occurs frequently in multiprocessors, especially in servers with many active processes. Such systems sustain context switch rates that are much higher than are typically found in single-user workstations. SuperSPARC processors use physically addressed caches.

---

[43] The overall size of the cache was dictated by on-chip real estate considerations. Each bit of static RAM used to make the cache takes six transistors. The 36 KB of cache thus consumes nearly 60 percent of the 3.1 million transistors on the chip—only 1.25 million transistors go to implementing the two integer units (IU), the floating point unit (FPU), the memory management unit (MMU), the cache controller, and the MBus and XBus interfaces.

[44] Patterson and Hennesey, *Computer Architecture: a Quantitative Approach*, p. 421.

6.3.1.4 Write Policies: Write-Through vs. Write-Back

Yet another difference between caches arises out of their policies when faced with a write from the processor into the cache. Because caches contain information that is logically duplicated in main memory, arrangements must be made to ensure that the cache and main memory remain consistent when one or the other updated. One approach is to have the writes into the cache copied immediately to the underlying memory. This method is called *write-through*, and is used in most low-cost systems. Write-through is easy to understand and implement. However, write-through caches have two serious drawbacks: the delay associated with the write to memory, and increased cache-to-memory bus traffic.

Memory delays can be alleviated to some degree by placing a high-speed write buffer between the cache and memory. Writes from the cache are copied into the buffer so the cache can proceed immediately upon issuing the write to memory; the buffer arranges to transfer the write to memory in the meantime. If the buffer receives more writes than the buffer can store, the cache (and the processor) stall until the output queue drains, and buffer space becomes available. This arrangement keeps cache and processor operating at full speed as long as there are not more pending writes than the buffer can store. Fortunately, few enough writes occur in bursts that write buffers are able to eliminate most stalls due to write-throughs.

Increased cache-to-memory traffic is more problematic. In uniprocessor systems, this can be dealt with simply by providing a slightly faster memory controller, or by simply permitting delays—this is the solution chosen by most PC designers. In multiprocessor systems, however, the increased bus bandwidth consumption becomes a problem. Normally the processors all share a single path to memory. In the case of the SPARCstation 10 and SPARCsystem 600, the shared path is the MBus and the memory controller; in the SPARCcenter 2000 and SPARCserver 1000, the shared path is the XDBus. When each processor must commit every write directly to memory, the shared traffic places greatly increased demands on the memory bus.

In order to solve both the write delays and bus contention issues, the cache can be organized to issue a write to memory only when the line is being replaced, rather than at every write. This kind of cache is called a *write-back* cache. It is used almost universally in shared-memory multiprocessors because it substantially reduces cache-to-memory traffic. Write-back caches, sometimes referred to as "copyback" caches, generate problems of their own: now two copies of the data (one in the cache and one in memory) must be kept coherent. This problem is normally solved by requiring that any entity writing directly into memory must flush and invalidate the corresponding cache lines. Usually this problem is confined to authors of device drivers responsible for managing devices that do DMA or DVMA.

The on-chip cache in the SuperSPARC processor is unusual in that it can be normally operated in either of two modes. If the processor does not have an external second-level cache, the caches are operated in write-back mode. This is the case in the SPARCstation 10 Models 40 and 402 and the SPARCstation 20 Models 50 and 502. However, if a second-level cache is present, as in any system utilizing a SuperCache, the on-chip cache is operated in write-through mode, while the second-level cache is operated in write-back mode. This arrangement (Figure 29) is workable even in a shared-memory multiprocessor because the second-level (external) cache is placed between the on-chip cache and the memory bus. Writes from the processor into the on-chip cache are written through to the external cache but *not* directly to memory.

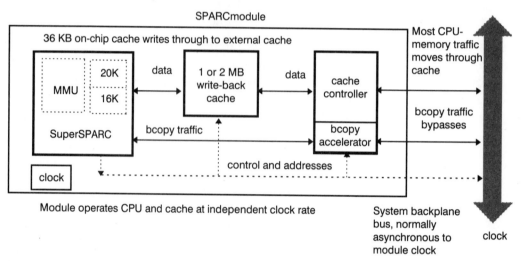

Figure 29. SPARCmodule organization used on MBus and XDBus systems. A few modules, used only on the SPARCstation 10 and SPARCstation 20, do not have a SuperCache.

Table 22. Cache parameters

Product	Organization	Size (Instr/Data)	Line Size	Write Policy
SPARCstation 1, 1+, SLC, IPC	Direct-mapped	64 KB	16 bytes	Write-through
SPARCstation 2, IPX, ELC	Direct-mapped	64 KB	32 bytes	Write-through
SPARCsystem 300	Direct-mapped	128 KB	32 bytes	Write-through
SPARCsystem 400	Direct-mapped	128 KB	32 bytes	Write-back
SPARCserver 600MP	Direct-mapped	64 KB	32 bytes	Write-back

Table 22. Cache parameters

Product	Organization	Size (Instr/Data)	Line Size	Write Policy
Model 1xx				
Classic, LX	Direct-mapped	4 KB (I$) 2 KB (D$)	16 bytes 32 bytes	Write-through
SPARCstation-5	Direct-mapped	16 KB (I$) 8 KB (D$)		Write-through
SuperSPARC on-chip caches	5-way (instr) 4-way (data)	20 KB / 16 KB	64 bytes 32 bytes	Write-back
SuperSPARC with SuperCache	Direct-mapped	1 MB-2 MB	128 bytes or 256 bytes	Write-back (see text)
hyperSPARC 66 MHz	Direct–map	8 KB / 128 KB	64 bytes	Write–back
hyperSPARC 100 MHz	Direct–map	8 KB / 256 KB	64 bytes	Write–back
hyperSPARC 125 MHz	Direct–map	8 KB / 512 KB	64 bytes	Write–back
hyperSPARC 150 MHz	Direct–map	8 KB / 512 KB	64 bytes	Write–back
hyperSPARC 200 MHz	Direct–map	16 KB / 16 KB 1 MB (external)	64 bytes	Write–through Write–back (E$)
UltraSPARC on–chip	2-way (I$) Direct–map (D$)	16 KB (I$) 16 KB (D$)	32 bytes 32 bytes	Write–through
UltraSPARC external	Direct–mapped	512 KB-1 MB	32 bytes	Write–back

6.3.2 Cache Configuration Guidelines

Systems with larger caches deliver higher performance than those with smaller caches, because larger caches yield higher hit rates and less waiting for memory. This differential is particularly noticeable for server applications that spend much of their time copying data, because the external cache controller (the SuperCache) has a hardware accelerator for the kernel's bcopy(9f) and bzero(9f) routines, which are used to copy data and create empty zero-filled pages. Possibly the most common applications dominated by data copies are database management systems. SPARCstation 10s used as DBMS servers should always be configured with SuperCache for this reason. This recommendation also applies to SPARCstation 10s and SPARCstation 20s used in data-intensive NFS environments.

When many users are simultaneously using a system either directly or indirectly, the more cache the better, since the large number of tasks active in a relatively short period of time tends to use up cache quickly (although locality of reference holds while a single task is executing in the processor, it does *not* usually hold when the processor exchanges context to a completely different task). The notable exception to this rule is the NFS server used in an attribute-intensive environment. In this case, the data moved through the cache is not likely to be used again soon. Additionally, the data copying that must be done (typically, very short blocks of memory containing file attributes) is more efficiently done without the SuperCache since the `bcopy` accelerator is designed to efficiently copy much larger blocks of data. The SPARCstation 10 Model 40 and SPARCstation 10 Model 402 and their SPARCstation 20 cousins, the Model 50 and Model 502, make good attribute-intensive NFS servers.

When configuring workstations *for single-user use*, investigate the type of application that will dominate the processing. General-purpose user interface code benefits very little from large caches; the same usually applies to software development environments such as compilers and debuggers. On the other hand, most mathematically-oriented applications benefit enormously from large caches, especially those that make extensive use of array manipulation or large meshes of points. Most array manipulation has very strong locality of reference, making caches especially effective. Finite element analysis, aerodynamics, statistical analysis, image processing (especially those involving fast Fourier transforms), and most geologic applications are all application classes that should be run on systems configured with large external caches.

6.3.3 UltraSPARC Cache Guidelines

The UltraSPARC family has fewer configuration rules, because it is available in fewer configurations. The design requires an external cache, so it is always present. Furthermore, because the memory copy accelerator is now part of the instruction set, it is implemented in the processor core itself, rather than in the external cache controller, and it is also always available. Finally, because the UltraSPARC-1 has far lower memory latency than its SuperSPARC predecessors, configuration flexibility is less necessary. Obviously, with otherwise identical properties, 1 MB caches are always preferred to 512 KB ones. The larger cache typically delivers 20-25 percent additional performance on server applications.

6.4 Backplane Configuration Issues

Most of Sun's systems are shared-memory multiprocessors. In such systems, the bandwidth available between processors and memory is a precious resource. The backplane must be designed for maximum performance while also accommodating physical packaging, expansion capability, and cost constraints.

6.4.1 MBus

The MBus is used explicitly in the SPARCstation 10, SPARCstation 20, and SPARCserver 600MP families, and implicitly in MicroSPARC–based systems such as the SPARCclassic, SPARCstation LX, SPARCstation 4, and SPARCstation 5. In MicroSPARC and MicroSPARC–II systems, the MBus is implemented entirely within the processor, which includes the usual processor elements as well as the memory controller and the SBus interface. In the other systems, the MBus is implemented in a two-slot configuration. The physical MBus is approximately ten inches long, kept as short as possible to permit noise-free operation at the highest possible clock speeds without resorting to expensive measures.

The current MBus implementation used in the SPARCstation 20 uses 64 bit wide synchronous busses operating at 50 MHz; previous systems operated at lower clock rates [45]. At the maximum 50 MHz, the peak theoretical bandwidth is 400 MB/sec. This is the speed that bits are transmitted across the bus, and does not account for bus protocol overhead. However, because the MBus is a circuit switched bus, it is subject to considerable contention issues. The key characteristic of circuit switched busses is that transactions must be atomic. Once a transaction is initiated, it must be rejected or completed before any other transaction may be started, even if considerable delay occurs servicing the request. The net available throughput is considerably less than the peak: approximately 130 MB/sec. Nonetheless, this is fully adequate for virtually the entire range of SPARCstation 10 and SPARCstation 20 configurations (see section 6.4.3, *SuperSPARC Backplane Consumption* for details).

6.4.2 XDBus

The MBus is designed for a physically small environment. For example, at most two MBus slots are in any MBus–based system; the traces making up the bus are less than ten inches long. For a system designed to accommodate 20 processors such as the SPARCcenter 2000, or the Cray SuperServer 6400 (with 64 SuperSPARC processors), such restrictions are clearly unrealistic. The designers of the XDBus required a bus delivering scalable high performance that was also capable of carrying signals the long distances (meters rather than inches) associated with highly expandable systems.

6.4.2.1 Packet-Switched Design

One of the key design characteristics is that systems with many subsystems communicating over a central backplane are dominated by contention issues. Minimizing backplane contention was one of the primary design goals. Accordingly, the XDBus uses a *packet-*

---

[45] The SPARCstation 10 Model 20 operates the MBus at 33 MHz; the SPARCstation 10 Model 30 operates the bus at 36 MHz. All other implementations, including the SPARCsystem 600MP, operate at 40 MHz.

switched design. Requests are transmitted on the bus; the requester then disconnects from the bus while the request is serviced. Eventually the client responsible for servicing the request reconnects to the initiator and returns the data and status. Because the bus is not held while a transaction is being serviced, packet-switched busses deliver considerably more effective throughput than comparable circuit-switched busses. This technology is known as *split transaction*.

The XDBus implemented in the SPARCserver 2000E operates at 50 MHz, the same speed as the MBus in the SPARCstation 20. Implementation of a packet-switched design is considerably more expensive than circuit-switched busses of similar specifications. However, the much higher effective utilization possible with packet-switched busses far outweighs the increased cost of implementation. For example, each XDBus in the SPARCcenter 2000E delivers in excess of 312 MB/sec of usable bandwidth (the paired busses deliver 625 MB/sec), compared to the 130 MB/sec on the MBus. The Cray CS6400 uses four XDBusses at 55 MHz and delivers about 1.3 GB/sec.

6.4.2.2 Pipelined Bus

A fully configured SPARCcenter 2000E includes 50 independent logical units—20 processors, 20 memory banks, and ten SBusses—all connected to the system backplane. Connecting all of these devices within the physical constraints of the MBus is obviously not possible. In order to provide connectivity to many devices, the XDBus is organized in a pipelined fashion. A number of independent XDBus segments, each operating at a relatively high clock speed, are connected end-to-end. This organization permits a physically long bus combined with clock rates of 50 MHz[46]. In the case of the SPARCserver 1000E and SPARCcenter 2000E, one XDBus segment resides on each system board. They are connected by segments carried directly on the physical backplane. The system control board provides a central clock. The XDBus definition is quite flexible and permits a number of different organizations to be implemented at varying cost and performance levels. The design found in the SPARCserver 1000E and SPARCcenter 2000E has moderate implementation cost yet provides some higher performance features.

6.4.2.3 Interleaved Multiple Bus Backplane

The use of a packet-switched design means that the XDBus delivers nearly two and a half times the bandwidth of the MBus. But with nearly five times the expansion capability, the SPARCcenter 2000E requires even more bandwidth than is available from a 50 MHz XDBus. To solve this problem, two XDBusses are used in parallel. Addresses are interleaved across the busses on 64-byte boundaries. The effective bandwidth of the combined bus is in excess

---

[46] The Cray SuperServer 6400 operates the XDBus at 55 MHz in tightly controlled environmental conditions.

of 625 MB/sec. The XDBus definition permits the use of up to four interleaved busses, and the Cray SuperServer 6400 backplane makes use of this capability. The SPARCserver 1000E uses only a single XDBus.

6.4.2.4 XDBus Design Implications

The XDBus is specifically designed to address the problems associated with a high-order shared memory multiprocessor. Specifically, it provides for very high throughput, extensive interleaving, physical length, and sufficient device addressability to accommodate the many subsystems in large servers. However, these attributes are implemented at a cost, specifically in terms of operation latency. This cost is normally not apparent in bulk transfers due to the high available bandwidth and consequent low utilization. However, when many small transfers must be made, the XDBus is much less efficient than other designs. Probably the most common class of application that uses large number of small transfers is programmed I/O that controls peripheral devices. Because requests must cross many independent busses and bus segments when traversing the system, the latency associated with small requests is considerably higher than on systems with simpler architecture. DVMA transfers are much larger and are not significantly affected by these considerations.

For this the reason, two-processor SPARCstation 10 configurations are sometimes slightly faster (two to five percent) than otherwise identical two-processor SPARCserver 1000 systems. The SPARCserver 1000 is always faster than a similar equipped SPARCstation 10 in quad-processor configurations, and of course configuring the smaller systems with more than four processors is impossible. For these purposes, the SPARCstation 20 is essentially a SPARCstation 10 with a 25 percent faster bus clock, and the SPARCserver 1000E is almost exactly a SPARCserver 1000 with a 25 percent faster bus clock. Since the architectures are not structurally different, two-CPU SPARCstation 20s are slightly faster than two–CPU SPARCserver 1000Es.

The same basic relationship holds between the Ultra–2 and two-processor Enterprise x000 configurations. Memory latency on the former is slightly lower, resulting in slightly higher performance. However, the memory latency difference between the platforms is much smaller, as is the overall performance differential.

In general, XDBus–based systems are designed for use in configurations involving four or more processors, where their much higher capacity busses overcome their inherent latency disadvantage.

6.4.3 SuperSPARC Backplane Consumption

The amount of bus bandwidth consumed is extremely variable; however, the following rule of thumb provides a starting point. Measurements have shown that a 50 MHz SuperSPARC with a 1 MB external cache requires 20-25 MB/sec of backplane bandwidth when running typical server applications on Solaris 2.2. Each subsequent version of the compilers and operating system uses slightly less bandwidth. Under Solaris 2.5, the backplane consumption is 18–20 MB/sec for the same configuration. Backplane traffic is reduced by optimizing the instruction schedules and improvements in internal operating system locking tactics. At worst, an 85 MHz SuperSPARC-II processor with 1 MB cache will consume about 50 MB/sec. Under best-case circumstances, the processor consumes essentially no bandwidth: if it is executing entirely from the cache, there is no need to access memory.

The SPARCstation 10 has about 105 MB/sec of backplane bandwidth; when four processors are configured, this leaves little bandwidth available for I/O, and this even at 100 percent utilization. Quad-processor SPARCstation 10 and SPARCstation 20 configurations are appropriate only in circumstances that do not require substantial I/O, for example, in compute servers or in single-user power workstations. Three-CPU server configurations can be fully utilized in any environment. The same guidelines apply to the SPARCserver 600MP because it uses literally the same basic chips as the SPARCstation 10 (processor modules, cache, MBus, and SBus; the memory controller is different but very comparable).

The SPARCserver 1000E has about 312 MB/sec of backplane bandwidth. When the full eight 85 MHz processors are configured, relatively little bandwidth (40-72 MB/sec) remains for I/O when all processors are engaged in non-I/O activities. If extremely heavy computation loads are anticipated in conjunction with heavy I/O activity, a fully configured SPARCserver 1000E *may* run out of backplane.

The SPARCcenter 2000E is designed to offer 16 CPUs *in a balanced configuration*. When sixteen 85 MHz processors are operating, they consume approximately 480–540 MB/sec, leaving 80-140 MB/sec for I/O. Many configurations will not require 100 MB/sec of I/O—compute servers, for example—and so can productively dedicate the backplane bandwidth to support the full 20 processors. The 30-35 MB/sec bandwidth estimate is conservative for the SPARCcenter 2000E because it is configured with 2 MB caches rather than the 1 MB caches in the SPARCserver 1000E; the larger caches have the effect of reducing back plane consumption.

Although 40–72 MB/sec of I/O bandwidth may sound inadequate, consider that a modern 7,200 rpm disk drive is capable of approximately 104 random disk I/O operations per second, 2 KB each, a total of 208 KB/sec per disk. This analysis assumes a DBMS system with 2 KB disk blocks, but the basic facts apply to most applications. At the recommended 65 percent disk utilization level, this rate is about 135 KB/sec per disk. Even 40 MB/sec of bandwidth thus represents over 290 fully active disk drives, and 140 MB/sec represents 1,035 fully active disks. Assuming 100 percent utilization in a fully serial access on each disk (6.5 MB/sec per disk—very unlikely in a server environment), 40 MB/sec represents six fully active disks, requiring at least two disk arrays. The higher 180 MB/sec rate requires over 27 fully active disks on at least nine disk arrays. (Virtually all current disk arrays are limited in one way or another to about 20 MB/sec maximum bandwidth.) Note that these are worst case assumptions. Under normal conditions, Ethernets consume approximately 450 KB/sec of bandwidth, and Token Rings as much as 1 MB/sec. Even in configurations with 10 to 20 networks, this has little impact on bus bandwidth.

By quite a margin, the largest consumers of I/O bandwidth are high-performance graphics framebuffers, which can easily consume 30 MB/sec of bus bandwidth. Fortunately, such devices are not extensively used in server systems. Servers usually have framebuffers for casual use, such as displaying SunNet Manager output or administrative use. The use of a server as a workstation, especially a graphics workstation, is discouraged for these reasons.

6.4.4 Memory Interleaving

The SPARCserver 1000E and SPARCcenter 2000E are offered with two memory densities: 64 MB per bank and 256 MB per bank. Many users prefer to configure the higher density memory in order to achieve the desired memory size with the fewest number of memory banks. Frequently this configuration is chosen to avoid the use of additional system boards. For smaller systems—two to four processors in this context—this strategy is useful. However, for systems that are to be configured with more processors, this approach may result in lower system performance.

The SPARCserver 1000E and SPARCcenter 2000E maximize memory interleave based upon the number of memory banks actually populated. Specifically, the system's boot PROM counts the number of populated memory banks on each XDBus and then configures 1-, 2-, or 4-way interleave on the bus. Memory addresses are interleaved on 64-byte boundaries, the size of requests to memory[47]. In the SPARCcenter 2000E, the two XDBusses should have memory evenly divided across the XDBus. When it is, two-way interleave is additionally configured across the XDBusses, resulting in total interleave up to eight banks of memory (or multiples thereof). If more than eight banks of memory are configured, the remaining banks are independently interleaved as optimally as possible. For example, in a system with 11 banks, the first eight will be interleaved eight ways, the next two will be interleaved two ways, and the last bank is not interleaved at all. In a system with 256 MB of memory, the system provides two configuration alternatives: one bank of 256 MB or four banks of 64 MB. The single bank will be configured with one-way interleave, even on a SPARCcenter 2000E, and the four banks will be configured with four-way interleave.

In larger systems with many processors, more extensive interleave provides more opportunities for traffic to spread memory accesses across as many resources as possible, reducing the potential for congestion and contention. This effect is of little consequence for smaller systems (less than percent), but for memory-intensive applications in eight-processor systems, the difference can be as much as eight to ten percent. When configurations reach 16

---

[47] For details, consult *SPARCcenter 2000 Design and Implementation*.

to 20 processors, the difference can be even greater. In these systems configuring as many banks of memory as possible is clearly beneficial, even at the expense of additional system boards. Furthermore, it is advisable to avoid configuration of an odd number of banks, since it will always result in at least some memory with no (i.e., one-way) interleave and a potential point of contention. NVSIMM memory banks are treated separately and should not be included when configuring memory interleave.

6.4.5 Ultra Port Architecture (UPA)

Although the XDBus offers reasonably high throughput, it is clearly not sufficient for UltraSPARC–based systems. At 50 MHz, the 64–bit XDBus delivers 312 MB/sec, yet a single 200 MHz UltraSPARC can consume as much as 270 MB/sec of backplane bandwidth at peak levels. Even though normal rates are much lower, a new interconnect architecture clearly had to be developed for use with UltraSPARC. Additionally, the performance of some types of workloads provided strong motivation to substantially reduce the high memory latency from the XDBus.

The new design, called Ultra Port Architecture (UPA), retains many of the successful features of XDBus. Like XDBus, UPA is a very wide, packet–switched, high–throughput design suitable for use in multiprocessor systems. The UPA is 128 bits (16 bytes) wide, meaning that it can fill an UltraSPARC cache line in just two bus cycles. One of the ways to reduce memory and I/O latency is to eliminate bus arbitration time. UPA addresses this problem by providing separate busses for addresses and data, permitting data to be transferred while the addresses for the next transfer are being distributed. This solution permits much higher sustained bandwidth for a given burst transfer speed—effective bandwidth is over 1.2 GB/sec, an efficiency greater than 95 percent, compared to 78 percent on XDBus and 33 percent for the circuit–switched MBus.

Partly due to simpler overall design and partly due to separate address and data busses, the UPA architecture reduces memory and I/O latency fairly drastically. In the 83.5 MHz implementation (used with 167 MHz processors), memory is only 28 cycles from the processor, compared to more than 40 cycles in MBus machines and more than 90-190 cycles in XDBus systems. The memory controller accepts commodity SIMMs, although they must be used in pairs (Ultra–1) or in groups of four (Ultra–2) to get the required memory bandwidth.

The UPA design sounds almost too good to be true: it delivers high throughput with low latency, yet can be implemented in just a few ASICs and commodity chips. For a desktop system such as the Ultra–1 or Ultra–2, the design no serious drawbacks, but the crossbar technology used in these systems is difficult to scale up to a much larger system of the size of a SPARCcenter 2000E.

6.4.6 Gigaplane

The Gigaplane bus used in the Enterprise x000 family is a fairly straightforward descendent of the XDBus, although it differs in many details. Like the XDBus, the Gigaplane is a packet-switched bus with pipelining, multiple masters, and a relatively high clock rate. Current implementations operate at 83.5 MHz, half the speed of a 167 MHz processor or one third the speed of a 250 MHz processor. The data width of the bus is 256 bits, so at 83.5 MHz the burst data transfer speed is 2.6 GBytes/sec. This is considerably faster than the 50 MHz XDBus at 312 MB/sec. The Gigaplane implementation uses separate wires for control (arbitration), address transfer, and data transfer, permitting three transactions to be in-flight simultaneously. This extensive pipelining permits the bus to be operated at very nearly 100 percent utilization without significant delays. As a result, the bus is able to sustain 2.5 GB/sec of user data, or 97 percent efficiency. Compared to either the XDBus (about 77 percent) or the MBus (about 37 percent), this is extremely efficient.

Because a single Gigaplane is so much more capable than an XDBus, building very large systems with just a single bus is possible without resorting to the complex interleaving required for the Cray CS6400 or the SPARCcenter 2000.

When combined with the UPA interconnect, the Gigaplane is able to deliver data between memory and the processor in about 50 cycles, twice as fast as the XDBus (90-190 cycles). The impact of lower latency can be dramatic. The impact of programmed I/O latency decreases as message size increases, since the system must manage the interface for each packet that is transmitted or received, and part of that interface management task involves PIO manipulation of the control and status registers. The effect of PIO latency is illustrated in Figure 30, which plots the speed of TCP/IP transfers across at 155 Mbit ATM network for varying transfer sizes. Gigaplane also dramatically reduces processor-to-SBus transfer latency. On the older SS1000E, network throughput increases as the packet rate decreases, but the Ultra Enterprise 4000 is able to run at full wire speed with all but the smallest packets. Both systems easily have enough processor power to run the network at full theoretical speed (about 129 Mbits/sec of user data), but PIO latency significantly delays the older platform for all TCP message sizes smaller than the 9 KB maximum transfer unit on the ATM network.

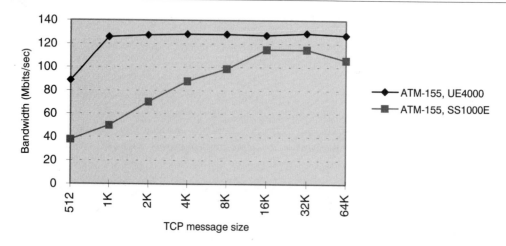

Figure 30. Single-threaded TCP transfer speed over 155 Mbit ATM. Transfers use the Classical IP protocol, rather than LAN emulation, which is about 35 percent slower.

The salient characteristics of recent Sun system backplanes are summarized in Table 23:

Table 23. System backplane characteristics

System	Bus	Speed/Width	Bandwidth Burst (Sustained)
SPARCstation 10 Model 20	MBus	33 MHz, 64 bits	264 MB/sec (86 MB/sec)
SPARCstation 10 Model 30	MBus	36 MHz, 64 bits	288 MB/sec (94 MB/sec)
SPARCstation 10, SPARCsystem 600MP	MBus	40 MHz, 64 bits	320 MB/sec (105 MB/sec)
SPARCstation 20	MBus	50 MHz, 64 bits	400 MB/sec (130 MB/sec)
SPARCstation 20 Model 514	MBus	40 MHz, 64 bits	320 MB/sec (105 MB/sec)
SPARCserver 1000	XDBus	40 MHz, 64 bits	320 MB/sec (250 MB/sec)
SPARCcenter 2000	XDBus	40 MHz, 64 bits (x 2)	640 MB/sec (500 MB/sec)
SPARCserver 1000E	XDBus	50 MHz, 64 bits	400 MB/sec (312 MB/sec)
SPARCcenter 2000E	XDBus	50 MHz, 64 bits (x 2)	800 MB/sec (625 MB/sec)
Cray SuperServer 6400	XDBus	55 MHz, 64 bits (x 4)	1.8 GB/sec (1.4 GB/sec)
Ultra–1/140	UPA	72 MHz, 128 bits	1.15 GB/sec (1.0 GB/sec)
Ultra–1/170	UPA	83.5 MHz, 128 bits	1.3 GB/sec (1.2 GB/sec)
Ultra–2/2200	UPA	100 MHz, 128 bits	1.5 GB/sec (1.44 GB/sec)
Ultra Enterprise x000	Gigaplane/UPA	83.5 MHz, 256 bits	2.6 GB/sec (2.5 GB/sec)

6.4.7 Memory Interleaving on the Ultra Enterprise x000

The Enterprise x000 family systems also offer extensive interleaving capability, primarily because the far higher capabilities of the UltraSPARC processor make them even more necessary. The Enterprise x000 memory controller is capable of interleaving memory across as many as 16 banks of memory (eight fully populated processor/memory boards). The system's power-on diagnostics optimize memory interleave into as many power-of-two increments as possible. For example, six fully populated processor/memory boards have 12 memory banks. The system configures them into one group with eight-way interleave and one group with four-way interleave.

Although interleave is somewhat more flexible than the SPARCcenter 2000E, interleave configuration still requires some careful attention. Consider a system with two banks of 32 MB memory and two banks of 256 MB memory. SuperSPARC-based systems interleave only identical banks, so configure these as a pair of two-way interleave groups. The Enterprise x000 will interleave dissimilar memory, so the system configures it as a single four-way interleave group for the first 32 MB, and as a two-way interleave group for the remaining 224 MB. Although this group is (correctly) reported by the system [48] as being a four-way interleave group, it only delivers four-way performance when accessing the first 64 MB of the 320 MB!

6.4.8 UltraSPARC Backplane Consumption

Individual memory banks have a maximum sustained transfer rate of approximately 350 MB/sec, and a 167 MHz UltraSPARC-1 can copy memory at approximately 220 MB/sec. Since a copy operation at this speed requires 440 MB/sec of bandwidth, this operation must be supported by at least two memory banks. A reasonable rule of thumb is to configure memory on every processor/memory board that has processors (these boards can be configured with either no memory or no processors, as well as the more usual configurations). Because contention delays are proportionately more costly on faster processors, the impact of insufficient memory interleave is more keenly felt on UltraSPARC-based systems than on their predecessors.

> Note: sustained backplane and memory bandwidth consumption are *nowhere near* these peak rates.

Sustained memory bandwidth requirements are approximately 90-110 MB/sec per processor for 167 MHz UltraSPARC processors with 512 KB caches and 85-100 MB with 1 MB caches. Comparable figures are 20-25 MB/sec for 60 MHz SuperSPARC+ processors equipped with 1 MB cache. These are merely ballpark figures and vary with cache size, software version,

---

[48] Interleave configuration is reported by `prtdiag(8m)`.

compiler and operating versions, and a variety of other considerations. For example, a processor that is running typical matrix multiplication routines is able to retain all of its code and nearly all of its data in cache, resulting in very low memory bandwidth consumption. Per-processor backplane consumption is slightly lower when many processors are configured, due to the larger aggregate amount of cache state being retained. During sampled runs of the TPC-C benchmark, a dual-processor system consumed about 105 MB/sec per processor, and an eight-processor system running four times the load consumed about 99 MB/sec per processor[49].

For many types of computationally intensive applications, a 30-processor Enterprise 6000 with 60 memory banks is an excellent configuration. At the other extreme, the same configuration is unlikely to perform nearly as well when asked to execute many simultaneous LISP codes. LISP programs tend to miss caches (and hence use memory) far more heavily than FORTRAN codes. C and COBOL are similar to FORTRAN, whereas C++ and other object-oriented languages tend to be somewhat heavier consumers of backplane (see Figure 31).

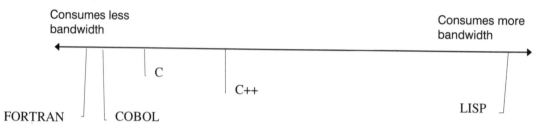

Figure 31. The spectrum of high-level languages from a memory bandwidth consumption perspective

⇒ For optimal performance, especially for multiprocessors with more than six to eight processors, configure as many memory banks as possible to reduce memory contention. Often this means configuring less–dense memory modules.

⇒ Configure SPARCcenter 2000 or SPARCserver 1000 memory in groups of two or four identical banks wherever possible.

⇒ Most Enterprise x000 configurations should have populated memory on every processor/memory card that configures processors.

---

[49] This data was obtained during a run using Solaris 2.5.1, Oracle 7.2.2, and SPARCcompilers 4.0.

6.5 SBus Configuration Issues

Most Sun systems use the SBus for I/O, although the SPARCsystem 600MP uses a VME bus in addition to an SBus. Some SPARCengines designed for embedded system applications also offer a VME bus. Three different versions of the SBus standard are currently in use, namely A.0, A.1, and B.0. The B.0 implementation has been adopted by IEEE as a bus standard, known as IEEE-1496.

SBus is very similar to the PCI bus now popular in the PC world. Both are designed to be I/O busses (as opposed to more general busses such as memory backplanes), have small form factors requiring fairly substantial electronic integration, and have fairly similar performance characteristics. Had PCI been available when the SPARCstation 1 was being designed in 1988, Sun would probably not have developed a whole new bus design, but the PCI standard did not appear until 1993. Like most other vendors, Sun is moving in the PCI direction, but with several million SBus slots already in place, SBus will continue to be significant for some time.

6.5.1 SBus Implementations

Every Sun system implements the SBus in a slightly different manner, accepting various engineering tradeoffs in the categories of ease of implementation, performance, cost of implementation, etc. Although they are, for most practical purposes, completely interchangeable and interoperable, each implementation has its own idiosyncrasies. The various implementations differ in width, burst transfer size, clock rate, transfer modes implemented, and bus integration mechanisms. Uninformed users often opt for the widest and/or fastest clocked implementation based upon paper specifications. Unfortunately, the large number of variables means that obtaining the highest performance I/O bus is a difficult choice. On the other hand, the choice of which SBus to use is rarely significant, since in practice all current SBus implementations can meet almost all requirements.

6.5.1.1 Bus Width

SBus is a parallel–transfer bus, meaning that many bits are transferred simultaneously. All current implementations use 32 data wires and 32 address wires (some older systems, such as the SPARCstation 1, use fewer address bits). Normally, one set of 32 wires carries data on one clock cycle, and the other set carries the I/O address on a subsequent clock cycle. In the default mode, the bus width is 32 bits. However, systems that implement the full Rev B.0 SBus have an additional mode in which the address lines are used during the data cycle to carry an additional 32 bits of data, a total of 64 bits. This arrangement permits 64-bit and 32-bit boards to share a common form factor. The SPARCstation 10 SX, SPARCstation 20, and all UltraSPARC-based systems offer the 64–bit extension. Previous systems use only the base 32–bit implementation.

Note that 64-bit SBus boards *are* compatible with existing 32-bit busses, because the standard requires these boards to support 32-bit mode as well. Forward and backward compatibility in 64-bit mode is achieved by using the address lines to transmit the address on one clock cycle, and then using them again on the next clock cycle along with the data lines to transmit the second 32 bits of data.

Bus width is a well-understood parameter, but its importance is often overestimated in the context of I/O busses. Most modern I/O requirements are met by 32-bit implementations. At this writing, only four types of SBus boards can reasonably exceed the capacity of a 32–bit SBus: very high–performance graphics framebuffers (such as the Evans & Sutherland Freedom 3000), 155 Mbit/sec and 622 Mbit/sec ATM interfaces, and HIPPI network connections. For most common uses, other SBus parameters are much more important.

6.5.1.2 Burst Transfer Size

The SBus hardware accepts data to be transferred in bursts. This is the amount of data the bus can accept each time a unit arbitrates for the bus. The burst size is roughly analogous to packet size on a network, and the bus width can be compared to the rated transfer speed of a network. The size of these bursts, like the size of network packets, governs the efficiency and hence the overall throughput of transfers on the bus. The bus hardware accepts one burst at a time; it then arbitrates for control of the bus and then transmits as much data per clock cycle as the bus width permits. On a platform that implements a 4–word (16–byte) burst size, a 2 KB transfer on the bus requires 128 bus arbitration/address/data transfer cycles, compared to just 32 overhead cycles when using a 16 -word system. The number of arbitration cycles is important because arbitration, address, and data transfer all consume time on the bus (some busses can overlap arbitration and sometimes address transfer with data transfer, usually by using more wires, at some implementation cost). For some reason, bus width and burst transfer size are commonly confused.

SBus bursts are defined by the standard to be 1-, 2-, 4-, 8-, 16-, and 64-bytes in length; platforms supporting the 64-bit extension also support a 128-byte burst size. The maximum burst size supported varies with hardware platform. In particular, only the SPARCserver 1000 and SPARCcenter 2000 implement the 64-byte (sometimes referred to as "16-word") burst size. The SPARCsystem 600MP, SPARCstation 10, SPARCstation 20, and SPARCstation 2 families implement 8-word bursts; all other 32–bit platforms use 4-word bursts. Platforms that support the 64–bit extension implement all burst sizes. SBus burst size is negotiated individually for each slot at boot time. The burst size used is the smaller of the maximum size supported by the host SBus and the target. Burst size, along with a number of other parameters, is negotiated on a per-slot basis during system boot.

The available burst size affects the speed of transfers across the SBus , but usually not by a significant margin. Its primary effect is on bus utilization, since the same amount of data requires more bus overhead for smaller bursts. The most common situation in which the burst size has consequential impact is when SBus traffic must cross an SBus bridge, as in the SBus expansion products. In these cases, small burst sizes severely limit the effectiveness of the SBus bridge.

6.5.1.3 SBus Clock Speed

The most obvious SBus implementation parameter is its clock speed. In most older Sun systems, the SBus clock is taken from the system clock, either directly or through a divider, subject to the maximum defined clock speed of 25 MHz. In the SPARCsystem 600MP, for example, the system clock is 40 MHz; this is well above the maximum clock speed for the SBus, so the SBus is operated on a divide–by–two basis, or 20 MHz. The same is true of the SPARCstation 10. Most SPARCstation 10s operate the system clock at 40 MHz, and the SBus clock is 20 MHz, but early models such as the Model 20 and Model 30 clocked the MBus at 33 MHz or 36 MHz; these systems operated the SBus at 16.5 MHz or 18 MHz[50]. SPARCstation 20s operate the system clock at 50 MHz and the SBus at 25 MHz. The SPARCserver 1000 and SPARCcenter 2000 operate their SBusses at 20 MHz, independent of the system clock or processor clocks. MicroSPARC and MicroSPARC–II systems operate their SBus by divider off the processor clock; 50 MHz systems use divide–by-two to run at 25 MHz, and110 MHz systems use divide–by–five to run at 22 MHz. Interestingly, the 70 MHz versions of these systems use a divide–by–three to run the SBus at 23.3 MHz, and 85 MHz systems use divide–by–four, resulting in a 21.25 MHz SBus.

Fortunately, most newer systems, including the SPARCserver 1000E, SPARCcenter 2000E, and all UltraSPARC–based systems, dispense with clock dividers and simply run the SBus at the full 25 MHz, regardless of system bus or processor clock speed.

6.5.1.4 SBus Transfer Modes

Every SBus offers at least programmed I/O (PIO) and consistent mode direct virtual memory access (DVMA). The DVMA transfer mode is similar to the more common direct memory access (DMA), except that the addresses presented are *virtual* addresses, rather than physical addresses. The I/O bus is responsible for arranging for virtual–to–physical address translation. Most SBus platforms have a memory management unit dedicated to each SBus for this purpose (usually known as the I/O MMU).

Under PIO, the processor uses load and store instructions to "manually" transfer data on the bus. Programmed I/O is used primarily for managing control and status registers on SBus

---

[50] Because most of these systems have been upgraded to faster Model 41, -51, or -61 systems using asynchronously clocked modules, the SBus can be run at these lower clock speeds while the CPU(s) run at much higher frequencies. This configuration is *not* supported, nor is it in accordance with the upgrade instructions (which upgrade the SBus clock to 20 MHz), but it has been known to happen.

boards, although some boards also use PIO for transferring user data. Because it requires the processor's intervention, and because it necessarily operates with smaller burst sizes, PIO is usually more costly than DVMA. (SPARC processors define loads and stores only on quantities up to 64 bits, precluding the use of larger burst sizes. The UltraSPARC –1 has an implementation–specific block load/store mechanism that handles 64 bytes in a single instruction; this is much more efficient—see section 6.2.5.2, VIS Instruction Set). DVMA requires a relatively complex setup and teardown process for each I/O operation, so short transfers are most efficiently handled with PIO. For large transfers such as disk blocks (which are nearly always at least 2 KB, typically 8 KB, and sometimes much larger), DVMA is the preferred transfer mode. Consistent mode DVMA automatically ensures that the memory image is consistent without device driver intervention. This consistency is important in shared-memory multiprocessors because it permits device drivers to be used without modification.

In some implementations, the SBus provides an additional transfer mode, called Stream Mode DVMA. Stream mode uses hardware that is not part of the shared memory. Users of stream mode must make explicit arrangements to keep the transfer hardware consistent with shared memory (for example, by flushing buffers after writes and invalidating buffers before starting reads). The advantage of stream mode DVMA is that it permits considerably faster transfers, especially for reads. Table 24 summarizes the various SBus implementations and their characteristics. The Solaris 2 drivers for the SCSI host adapters, the FibreChannel host adapter, the quad Ethernet interface, ATM, FastEthernets, FDDI interfaces, and NVSIMM/PrestoServe all support stream mode DVMA. Since stream mode DVMA was introduced some time ago (1992), most third–party device drivers have integrated stream mode support on platforms that offer it.

Table 24. SBus implementations and capabilities

Platform	Burst Size	Bus Width	Clock	Speed (Read/Write)	Stream Mode
SS1	16 bytes	32 bits	20 MHz	12/20 MB/sec	No
SS1+, IPC	16 bytes	32 bits	25 MHz	15/25 MB/sec	No
SS2, IPX	32 bytes	32 bits	20 MHz	15/32 MB/sec	No
SS10, SS600	32 bytes	32 bits	20 MHz	32/52 MB/sec	No
LX, Classic	16 bytes	32 bits	25 MHz	17/27 MB/sec	No
SS4, SS5	16 bytes	32 bits	21.25 MHz-23.3 MHz	36/55 MB/sec	No
SS1000, SC2000	64 bytes	32 bits	20 MHz	45/50 MB/sec	Yes

Table 24. SBus implementations and capabilities

Platform	Burst Size	Bus Width	Clock	Speed (Read/Write)	Stream Mode
SS1000E, SC2000E	64 bytes	32 bits	25 MHz	56/62 MB/sec	Yes
SS10 SX	128 bytes	32/64 bits	20 MHz	40/95 MB/sec	No
SS20	128 bytes	32/64 bits	25 MHz	62/100 MB/sec	No
UltraSPARC	128 bytes	32/64 bits	25 MHz	90/120 MB/sec	Yes

6.5.2 Interfacing the SBus to the Host

Peripheral busses are often compared on their raw specifications, such as bus width, bus clock, and maximum theoretical throughput. However, the I/O bus is only useful in the context of a complete system. Often the measures taken to integrate a high-performance I/O bus into the overall system architecture are more important to maintaining high performance I/O than the design of the bus itself. Sun server architectures are carefully designed to minimize the impact of I/O upon the other resources in the system, as well as to maintain high throughput levels. In particular, the high-end server implementations are specifically designed to attain high I/O throughput and minimize the impact of other I/O on the system backplane and on the processor complexes.

6.5.3 Virtual Address Translation—the I/O MMU

The SBus operates in virtual address space in order to simplify some common kinds of I/O operations (for example, disk scatter/gather operations). Virtual address translation must be provided for the SBus to properly interface with physical memory. In older Sun systems (desktops before the SPARCstation 10 and servers before the SPARCserver 490), the SBus shared a single memory management unit with the main processor. Contention for the MMU occasionally caused I/O bottlenecks or surprisingly low computational performance during heavy load situations.

Beginning with the SPARCserver 690 and SPARCstation 10, a separate memory management unit was dedicated to the SBus, eliminating contention for a key hardware resource. The SPARCserver 1000, SPARCcenter 2000, and Ultra Enterprise x000 provide an I/O MMU for every SBus in the system.

6.5.4 SBus I/O Cache Interface

One of the problems posed by the XDBus backplane is that it is much wider than the SBusses for I/O. In the SPARCcenter 2000, each backplane bus is 64 bits wide and runs at 40 MHz, whereas the SBus is only 32 bits wide and operates at 20 MHz (the situation is the same in the SPARCcenter 2000E, with the clocks running 25 percent faster). Without other arrangements, the XDBus would waste 75 percent of the backplane bandwidth during transfers, since an XDBus write operation is four times as fast as the SBus it targets. For read operations, the XDBus would waste a similar amount of bandwidth as the SBus transfers 32 bits per cycle into the dual XDBusses.

This problem is addressed by connecting the SBus to the XDBus via an I/O cache. Each I/O cache (IOC) contains four 64-bit cache lines and connects an SBus to a single 64-bit XDBus (each SBus on a SPARCcenter 2000 thus has two separate IOCs operating together). Each of the four SBus slots has a dedicated cache line in each IOC. The IOC performs bus width-matching services in both directions, eliminating wasted cycles.

The organization of the IOC also helps maintain concurrency of I/O operations on the SBus . By accepting responsibility for transfers between the SBus and the XDBus , the IOC is able to permit each SBus slot to have a pending I/O operation without blocking operation of other slots.

6.5.5 Maintaining SBus Concurrency

In addition to the organization of the I/O cache, the SBus implementation in the SPARCserver 1000 and SPARCcenter 2000 is designed to maintain concurrency of operations. Because the SBus is a circuit-switched bus, each one can have only one pending I/O operation. The problem is that the bus is held busy while a request is pending, even if the SBus target is waiting for service from either the host XDBus or from a peripheral located on the remote side of the SBus target. Normally, the target must perform some sort of service on behalf of the requester that is completely independent of the actual bus transfer time. For example, during a transfer from a SCSI host adapter to main memory, the SBus operation includes both the time necessary to physically transfer the data from the host adapter to memory and the time required to obtain the attention of the memory controller. Either the host adapter or the memory controller may be busy with other activities, resulting in even more latency.

In the SPARCserver 1000 and SPARCcenter 2000, the SBus attempts to complete the operation as soon as it is requested. If it succeeds (in the example, if the memory controller is not busy), the operation proceeds directly. If the operation cannot be immediately satisfied, the SBus arbiter rejects the operation with an error acknowledgment. Because the requester has received a reply, it disconnects from the SBus, freeing it for use by other clients. In the strictest sense, an error has not occurred, but the SBus specification *requires* that operations that receive error acknowledgment be retried at least once. The SBus then arranges to grant the bus to the pending requester only when the request can be immediately satisfied. In the intervening time, the bus is free to service other clients.

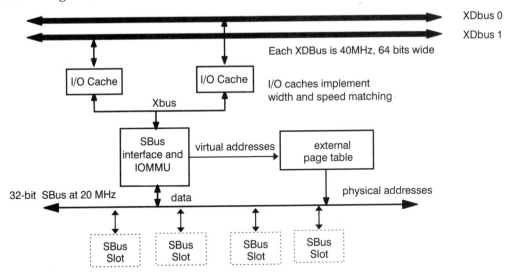

Figure 32. The I/O unit of the SPARCcenter 2000. Each I/O unit implements an independent SBus, permitting very high aggregate system throughput.

In essence, the SPARCcenter 2000 implementation treats any request that cannot be serviced without delay to be an error. When the client obtains the bus and issues a retry, the request is actually serviced. This arrangement provides the effect of split transactions on a simple circuit-switched electrical implementation. Combined with the non-blocking design of the I/O cache, the SPARCcenter 2000 implementation dramatically minimizes bus contention, especially in large configurations or when using slow peripherals.

6.5.6 Ultra Enterprise I/O Boards

The Ultra Enterprise x000 family uses an I/O board separate from the processor/memory board as was found on the SPARCcenter 2000E. The SBus I/O board (Figure 33) uses two 64-bit SBusses, with three available physical SBus slots. In addition to the physical SBus slots, the I/O boards have a FibreChannel interface with two ports, a 10/100Mbit FastEthernet interface, and a single-ended fast/wide SCSI-2 port. The FastEthernet and SCSI-2 are implemented using the same chip as on the SunSwift SBus board, and are located together on one SBus along with one of the SBus slots. The other SBus serves the FibreChannel and two SBus slots. On this board the SBusses are completely independent and can transfer simultaneously to the UPA crossbar, although of course only one of the busses may be transmitting through to the Gigaplane at any given moment. Because the Gigaplane is a packet-switched bus, both SBusses can and often do have transactions pending on the centerplane, but they cannot initiate or complete those transactions at the same time. The internal architecture is shown in Figure 33. The UPA performs speed- and width-matching between SBus and Gigaplane, much as the I/O cache did in previous systems.

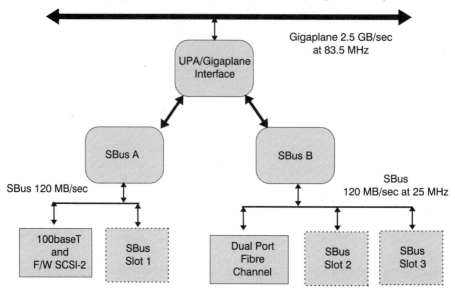

Figure 33. Block diagram of the SBus I/O board used in the Ultra Enterprise x000 family.

The graphics I/O board implementation (Figure 34) is visually almost identical, but differs internally in quite a number of particulars. The primary difference is that only a single SBus is on the graphics I/O board, so all of the built-in devices are configured together with the two physical SBus slots. The third (center) slot is actually a UPA slave port that connects directly to the UPA crossbar switch. This slot is used to configure a Creator or Creator3D high-performance framebuffer.

6.5.7 Peripheral Bus Usage Issues

Bus protocol overhead and especially device control overhead decrease the attainable bus throughput appreciably. Bus arbitration, handshaking, and related activities all consume time on the bus; this time cannot be used for transferring user data. Device control can—and often does—consume a significant amount of peripheral bus time. User data constitutes the majority of bytes transferred on a peripheral bus such as SBus , but a surprising proportion of bus operations are *not* used for moving user data, but rather for carrying control signals from the processors to the peripherals and status messages in response.

Most SBus devices are managed through the use of control/status registers. When the processor wants to issue a command to a peripheral, it stores the appropriate bit pattern into the target's control registers. To check the completion status of an operation, the processor reads the status registers. For example, issuing an I/O request to the Sun DWIS/S fast/wide SCSI host adapter takes 10-15 programmed I/Os to or from the device's control/status registers. Some low-cost or low-speed devices require as many as 150-200 programmed I/Os to accomplish a single user I/O request! Most control registers are very small—generally 32 bits—and hence control/status operations usually use the smallest and least efficient burst transfer sizes, reducing the overall efficiency of the bus. In addition, contention for the components of the bus among various clients can also reduce the net throughput observed by users.

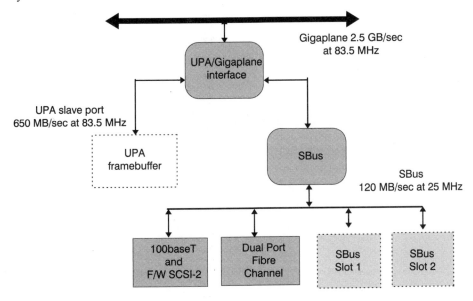

Figure 34. Graphics I/O board architecture. This board is an alternative to the dual-SBus implementation in Figure 33.

One consequence of the use of control registers is that their small size (nearly always 32 bits or smaller) means that these programmed I/Os utilize the smallest SBus burst sizes. These are the least efficient transfer modes available on an SBus, and when abused can noticeably reduce overall throughput. Small block I/O is the most sensitive to bus latency. This consideration does not apply on systems with moderate latency such as SPARCstation 10 and SPARCstation 20 platforms (except in rare real-time situations), but it can be a significant issue on sun4d systems, which have long processor–to-Sbus latencies. Typical I/O activity such as managing disk I/O via a SCSI or FibreChannel host adapter requires relatively few control actions, so bus latency is not at issue. However, activity such as driving a GX framebuffer—which is entirely driven by PIO—can be drastically slower (as much as 40-70 percent slower) on SPARCserver 1000E than on otherwise comparable SPARCstation 20 systems.

UltraSPARC-based (`sun4u`) systems have much lower memory and programmed I/O latency than SuperSPARC-based systems. As a result, the newer systems are able to handle small units of I/O *much* more effectively than their predecessors. This is difficult to measure with most familiar benchmarks, but real-time applications may be much more comfortable on `sun4u` systems for this reason.

These comments apply generally to all of the commodity I/O busses used in the industry. For all of these reasons, the maximum attainable bandwidth is considerably lower than the peak speed normally cited by vendors. As a result, the throughput figures in Table 25 are the maximum attainable in practice. For highly contended SBusses, especially those configured with both high-performance framebuffers and high speed network or SCSI busses, the net throughput may be as much as ten percent lower due to contention issues.

6.5.8 Minimizing SBus Latency

Circuit-switched busses cannot deliver 100 percent of their rated bandwidth without encountering severe increases in latency due to contention for the bus. To avoid contention problems, I/O bus utilization should not exceed 75-80 percent. Consider alternatives if the SBus bandwidth required by the application exceeds about 20 MB/sec on a SPARCsystem 600MP or SPARCstation 10. At 30 MB/sec of active I/O per SBus on the SPARCserver 1000 or SPARCcenter 2000, consider additional system boards for the purpose of obtaining additional SBus bandwidth (about 40 MB/sec on -E series systems). Nearly all "built-in" devices found on Sun system boards are actually connected to the system via SBus. For example, onboard SCSI and Ethernet interfaces are always connected via SBus. The only exceptions are serial ports and the time-of-day clock. Recall that framebuffers are by far the largest consumers of SBus bandwidth.

⇒ Configure an additional SBus (i.e., system board) into a SPARCserver 1000 or SPARCcenter 2000 when throughput demands on a single SBus exceed 30 MB/sec (40 MB/sec on the 25 MHz/sec of SPARCserver 1000E or SPARCcenter 2000E).

Table 25. Typical and peak bandwidth demands of various SBus devices. See Appendix A for descriptions of these boards.

Board	Description	Typical Bandwidth	Transfer Type	Width (Bits)
FSBE/S, DSBE/S	Fast SCSI-2 + Ethernet	4 MB/sec	DVMA/PIO	32

Table 25. Typical and peak bandwidth demands of various SBus devices. See Appendix A for descriptions of these boards.

Board	Description	Typical Bandwidth	Transfer Type	Width (Bits)
SunSwift	Fast/wide SCSI–2 + FastEthernet	12 MB/sec	DVMA	64
SOC	Dual 25 MB/sec FibreChannel	16 MB/sec	DVMA	64
ATM 1.0	155 Mbit ATM (full-duplex)	10 MB/sec	DVMA	32
ATM 2.0, 155 Mbit	155 Mbit ATM (full-duplex)	10 MB/sec	DVMA	64
ATM 2.0, 622 Mbit	622 Mbit ATM (full-duplex)	50-100 MB/sec	DVMA	64
DWIS/S, SWIS/S	20 MB/sec fast/wide SCSI-2	8-10 MB/sec	DVMA	32
SBE/S	10 MB/sec SCSI-2 + Ethernet	4 MB/sec	DVMA/PIO	32
SCSI	5 MB/sec SCSI-2	3 MB/sec	DVMA	32
Thick Ethernet	10 Mbit/sec Ethernet	500 KB/sec	PIO	32
SQEC/S	Quad 10BaseT Ethernet	3 MB/sec	DVMA	32
FastEthernet 1.0	100 Mbit/sec FastEthernet	4 MB/sec	DVMA	32
FastEthernet 2.0	MII 100 Mbit/sec FastEthernet	4 MB/sec	DVMA	64
FDDI/S	100 MB/sec FDDI	6-8 MB/sec	DVMA	32
TRI/S	16 MB/sec Token Ring	800 KB-1.2MB	PIO	32
HSI/S	2x T1 synchronous serial lines	200 KB/sec	PIO	32
SPC/S	8-serial, 1-parallel port	5 KB/sec	PIO	32
ISDN	Basic rate ISDN	40 KB/sec	PIO	32
SPRN-400	12-ppm + 2 MB/sec parallel	2 MB/sec	DVMA	32
NP20	20-ppm printer interface	3 MB/sec	DVMA	32
VideoPix	10 fps, 8-bit Video interface	6.5 MB/sec	PIO	32
SunVideo	30 fps, 24-bit video interface	5-20 MB/sec	DVMA	32
MG1, MG2	Monochrome framebuffers	250 KB/sec	PIO	32
GX, GX+	8-bit color framebuffers	4-12 MB/sec	PIO	32
Turbo GX, TGX+	8-bit color framebuffers	8-20 MB/sec	PIO	32
GS	Low-cost 24-bit color	15 MB/sec	PIO	32
GT	24-bit color framebuffer	20 MB/sec	PIO/DVMA	32
ZX	Midrange 24-bit color	20-30 MB/sec	DVMA	32
SunPC 486	SunPC accelerator	5-20 MB/sec	DVMA	32
E&S Freedom 3000	High-performance 24-bit color	40+ MB/sec	DVMA	32

6.5.9 Configuring Additional SBus Slots

Inevitably, some configurations require more SBus slots than those available in the host platform. Regardless of how many expansion slots designers manage to squeeze into each platform, some users want to use just one or two more boards. SBus expansion products are designed to fill this requirement. Unfortunately, SBus expansion is an attractive idea that nearly always falls short of expectations.

Each SBus Expansion Box and SBus Expansion Subsystem provides two or three additional SBus slots when configured into these systems (these products are also supported on the SPARCstation 1, 1+, 2, IPC, and IPX). Both products consist of an SBus adapter that is configured into the SBus of the host system. A cable connects the adapter to a pizzabox containing three slots (SBus Expansion Box) or to an expansion board containing four slots (SBus Expansion Subsystem). The expansion board uses the 9U VME form factor to match the VME chassis in the SPARCserver 600MP family. The expansion adapter is a single-wide SBus card. The SBus Expansion Box contains its own power supply and also provides power and mounting space for two 3.5" x 1.6" disk drives. The SBus Expansion Subsystem draws power from the host's VME cardcage. A maximum of two SBus Expansion adapters are permitted in a configuration; expansion subsystems may *not* be daisy-chained. The internal architecture of SBus expansion subsystems is shown in Figure 35.

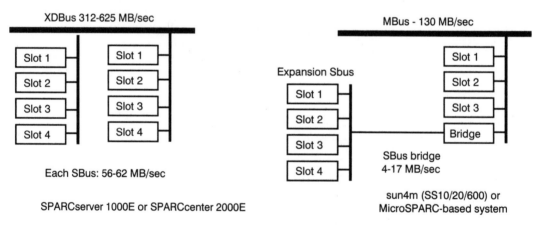

Figure 35. Comparison between sun4d system with multiple SBusses and sun4m system with SBus expansion

Each system board in the SPARCserver 1000E and SPARCcenter 2000E contains a complete, independent SBus. Configuring additional system boards thus significantly increases the overall SBus capacity of the system: each SBus is capable of sustaining about 56 MB/sec for reads (from the SBus to the XDBus) and about 62 MB/sec for writes. Adding another SBus permits the system to handle an *additional* 56–62 MB/sec of I/O traffic. Even disregarding the bandwidth and latency issues, configuration of most SBus expansion systems to these systems is moot, since their systems' peculiar interpretation of the SBus standard's error–retry handling means that SBus expansion products do not work (see section 6.5.5, *Maintaining SBus Concurrency*).

Since the desktop systems and the SPARCsystem 600MP systems have only a single SBus, no advantage comes from configuring options in particular slots. However, these systems can use the SBus Expansion Box or SBus Expansion Subsystem to obtain additional SBus slots with limited functionality.

In these products, the expansion SBus is daisy-chained through the host SBus. Instead of connecting directly to the MBus, the expansion SBus connects to the original SBus by an SBus–to–SBus bridge.

The function of the bridge is to accept packets coming from or destined for SBus targets residing in the expansion SBus and "route" them onto the appropriate SBus for delivery. One of the restrictions of the SBus expansion subsystems is that each SBus slot has a slot configuration register (SCR), which governs a number of characteristics. Although most SBus boards use the default slot configuration, some boards do set the SCR to non-default settings when negotiating setup during system boot (the GT, ZX, and TurboZX advanced graphics adapters use this feature). If such a board is located in the expansion SBus, this operation will set the SCR of the slot where the SBus expansion adapter resides *in the host SBus*, and all slots in the expansion SBus would have to be prepared to deal with these settings. For these reasons, use of such boards is not supported in an SBus expansion unit.

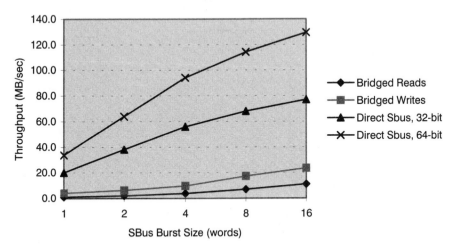

Figure 36. End-user throughput of an SBus, compared to an SBus bridge

The design of the SBus bridge imposes some throughput limitations worthy of note. Because each "logical" SBus operation expands into three separate transfers (across the host SBus, across the bridge, and across the remote SBus), each with its own latency, SBus expansion systems impose a non–trivial overhead. For practical purposes, this overhead translates into reduced throughput. Table 26 shows the maximum sustainable performance for various types of usage, and Figure 36 compares host SBus performance with that of an SBus bridge. Especially relevant is the fact that most graphics framebuffers depend heavily on programmed I/O, which becomes a 1– or 2–word burst when transferred on the SBus.

Table 26. SBus bridge throughput as a function of burst size

Burst Size	Sustained Reads	Sustained Writes
1-word	1.04 MB/sec	4.0 MB/sec
2-word	2.03 MB/sec	6.25 MB/sec
4-word	3.76 MB/sec	9.68 MB/sec
8-word	6.88 MB/sec	17.26 MB/sec
16-word	10.94 MB/sec	23.42 MB/sec

Because of the significant additional latency associated with the SBus bridge, combined with the fairly severe bandwidth restrictions, the configuration of high-performance peripherals in either of these products is strongly discouraged. This recommendation is particularly applicable to systems whose SBus supports only small (four-word) transfers such as the SPARCstation LX and SPARCclassic. Unfortunately, these are the platforms that would otherwise benefit the most from SBus expansion, because they have relatively few slots, and because their inherent memory and interrupt latencies are low enough that the SBus expansion subsystems would be useful.

In the SPARCsystem 600MP, SPARCstation 10, and SPARCstation 20 families, configuration of disk peripherals via the SBus bridge is marginal. Because these systems and their SCSI host adapters support a relatively large 8-word burst size, the throughput into the system *may* be high enough to satisfy some applications[51] (the SPARCstation 10 SX and SPARCstation 20 implement 32-word (128 byte) bursts, but only in 64-bit mode, which most SBus bridges do not support). For example, for servers where random access dominates I/O time, the 5.2 MB/sec limitation permits approximately 660 8 KB disk I/O operations per second (5.2 MB/sec is used because the bridge should be utilized under 75-80 percent to avoid further latency issues). Since a current 7,200 rpm disk drive is capable of about 78 x

---

[51] The FibreChannel host adapter does not work in an SBus bridge.

8 KB random I/O operations per second, connecting eight or nine active disks through an expansion SBus is reasonable. Of course, serial transfers from these disks will be severely restricted. These drives are capable of 6.5 MB/sec each, and at most, one of them will be able to transfer across the bridge at a time.

⇒ Avoid configuring SBus expansion subsystems if at all possible.

> Note: *The SBus Expansion Subsystems are designed to permit more combinations of options, rather than more of a single option.* For example, the standard SPARCstation 10 supports four GX framebuffers; configuration of an SBus Expansion Box does *not* permit the use of five or six GX framebuffers. The value of the SBus Expansion products is that *other* options such as an FDDI/S or SBus PrestoServe may now be configured in combination with those four GX framebuffers. The *only* exception to this rule is that additional FSBE/S and DSBE/S boards may be configured into the SBus Expansion Subsystems, beginning with Solaris 2.2. Whereas at most, four FSBE/S and DSBE/S boards are supported without SBus Expansion subsystems, a total of seven SCSI busses are supported using SBus Expansion[52].

6.5.10 SBus Interrupt Distribution

The SPARCserver 1000, SPARCcenter 2000, and the Ultra Enterprise x000 family offer many SBus slots for configuring peripheral options. The architecture of these systems is such that SBus slots are all equally accessible to every processor—no "distance penalty" applies for accessing an SBus board that is physically distant from the processor. Nonetheless, configuration of SBus options does require some attention to detail. Specifically, since Solaris 2.3, the operating system uses a static interrupt distribution mechanism. Under this scheme, interrupts from a given SBus are always sent to a processor designated at boot time. In most configurations, each SBus will send interrupts to a different processor. The alternative[53], sending interrupts to the "next" processor in round–robin fashion, turns out to substantially reduce the effectiveness of the processor caches, although it results in faster scheduling of interrupt threads. As a result of static interrupt distribution, interrupts from an SBus are transmitted to a "nominated" CPU for processing.

Static interrupt processing means that SBus boards should be distributed evenly across the SBusses in a system. In particular, high-performance boards that generate many interrupts should be separated onto as many SBusses (and hence as many processors) as possible. FibreChannel host adapters and FastEthernet interfaces tend to generate the most interrupts

---

[52] This is on a per-SBus basis. Many more SCSI busses are supported on platforms with multiple SBusses, such as the SPARCserver 1000 and SPARCcenter 2000.

[53] Used in Solaris 2.2. Later editions can use round–robin interrupt distribution by adding the line `set do_robin=1` in the `/etc/system` file.

and warrant the most attention. Within an SBus, every slot is treated identically. In the process of placing SBus boards on SBusses, placing identical boards on the same SBus sometimes improves system performance , because identical boards share the same interrupt handling code. This arrangement maximizes the chance that the interrupt handling code is "hot" in the nominated processor's cache. For example, given two FibreChannel host adapters, a FastEthernet and an FDDI, and two system boards, the recommended configuration is to put both FibreChannels on one SBus and the two network boards on the other.

The Ultra Enterprise x000 systems operate in precisely the same way as the SPARCcenter 2000E, with the additional proviso that a single SBus I/O board has two distinct SBusses, thus using two different designated interrupt CPUs.

Because of static interrupt distribution, the distribution of the I/O load across SBusses can occasionally have a rather surprising impact on overall performance. When the system is heavily loaded, the interrupt load from one or more SBusses can push one processor to 100 percent utilization, limiting I/O performance on those busses. After installation, monitor CPU utilization and especially distribution in a multiprocessor system with the mpstat(1m) command. If one CPU takes a large number of interrupts (shown in the ithr column), and that CPU regularly stays at or near 100 percent utilization, and some substantial fraction of the CPU time is in the system context relocating one or more SBus boards into another SBus may be worthwhile. A simpler experiment is simply to try round–robin scheduling.

The impact of static interrupt distribution over dynamic interrupt distribution is subtle—worth only one to three percent in most cases—because the processors do not normally run at full utilization.

⇒ Evenly distribute SBus options across as many SBusses as possible in a SPARCserver 1000, SPARCcenter 2000, or Ultra Enterprise x000.

⇒ If configuring multiple boards that share a device driver, placing them in the same SBus will tend to improve the efficiency of the cache of the nominated processor.

⇒ All SBus slots are capable of handling either master or slave SBus boards, with the sole exception of slot 3 in SPARCstation 1 and SPARCstation 1+ systems. Slot 3 is the rightmost slot when viewing the system from the back. This slot accommodates only slave boards, such as PIO framebuffers.

⇒ Except for the above rules, no other criteria restrict placement of SBus boards, either within a system (between SBusses) or within an SBus.

6.6 The VME Bus

By 1991, the standard 32-bit VME bus was becoming obsolete. Its definition limits it to about 40 MB/sec burst throughput, with most actual implementations limited to 25 MB/sec or less in practice. Because of this performance limitation, expensive backplane design (when compared to smaller mezzanine busses), relatively large physical size, and power dissipation, VME lost favor throughout the industry. However, two factors argued for continued VME expansion: the tremendous number of existing peripherals and the design freedom made possible by the much larger form factor (especially the so-called 9U form factor used in Sun's VME servers). At the time, creating designs such as the VX and MVX imaging accelerators or the ISP-80 IPI string controller within the size and power constraints of SBus and other mezzanine busses was beyond the technological limit; so the SPARCserver 600MP included VME expansion.

6.6.1 VME Standards

Motorola and the VME steering committee have defined several versions; the VME Rev C.1 definition has been officially accepted by the IEEE as IEEE-1014. Sun systems from the 3/160 to the 4/260 implement VME rev B.2. The SPARCserver 300, SPARCserver 400 and SPARCserver 600MP implement VME rev C.1. There is some talk in the industry about widely implementing 64-bit versions of VME called VME64 and VME64+, but these are neither standard nor popular at this time. They seem unlikely to attain much popularity with the advent of PCI and its derivatives. All versions of VME are circuit-switched busses.

6.6.2 VME Form Factors

There are three common VME form factors, known as 3U, 6U, and 9U. Most VME boards offered by Sun were in the 9U form factor[54], which is approximately 14" x 17". This form factor was chosen over the 6" x 9" 6U form factor because of the much greater integration possible on the larger board (the 9U/6U decision was made in 1985 with the introduction of the Sun-2/160). The 3U form factor is even smaller, about 3" x 6", and is not especially common. Most VME boards not built specifically for the Sun world are 6U. Sun and many third parties offered 9U-to-6U adapters that permit the use of a 6U board in the standard Sun 9U card cage.

The VME card cage itself provides both physical mounting and signal connections. Timing restrictions built into the VME standard limit the number of slots in a cardcage to 21. Sun offers expansion up to 16 slots; if more slots are required, third parties offer a multitude of

---

[54] Only Sun's Sun-3E and SPARCengine 1E processors, and their attendant peripheral boards, were 6U form factor. Other SPARCengines, such as the SPARCengine 300, were 9U implementations.

expansion cardcages. In these schemes, the last slot in the primary cardcage is used by an expansion board that provides a "jumper" cable to a cardcage with additional slots. Each slot has access to the entire VME address space[55]. Boards residing on the backplane must choose an address space, treating that space as exclusive property. Usually, this address space is selected by jumpers or DIP switches located on the board. Device drivers must be informed of the addressing mode, as well as the physical address space of each board, usually in the kernel configuration file.

6.6.3 VME Backplane Connections

The VME standard provides definitions for three different backplane connections, one of which is optional. These connections are referred to as P1, P2, and P3; the P2 connector is optional. P1 and P3 carry the standard VME signals, including power and ground. The P2 connector is specified by the standard as "implementation defined." Sun often used the P2 area for Sun-specific, high-performance data transfer across the backplane. Most Sun processors with VME use the P2 to connect the main CPU board to offboard memory (the 3/200, 4/200, 4/300, 4/400, and 4/600 models all used this backplane connection for—different—private memory bus implementations). Sun used the implementation defined nature to provide high-speed synchronous private memory busses: transfers across the P2 run at 66 MB/sec on the 3/200, and up to 270 MB/sec on the SPARCsystem 600MP. Sun also used a private memory bus in some of its older VME-based accelerated graphic accelerators, such as the CXP and GXP. These multiboard framebuffers used a *different* bus protocol to communicate between boards. To avoid conflicts between the main memory bus and the graphics bus, the P2 part of the backplane is divided into two or three discrete areas (depending upon the number of slots in the backplane). The VME backplane configurations are shown in Figure 37.

In addition to addressing on each board, two board-level characteristics are configured on the VME frontplane. (The frontplane is the part of the VME backplane physically on the other side of the actual board plug receptacles. These are usually accessible from the *front* of the system.) These are the *bus grant (BG)* and *interrupt acknowledge (IACK)* jumpers as in Figure 38. Presence of the jumper permits the circuit to pass through the slot without requiring the board to take any action. Consequently, slots that are not in use should be jumpered. When the jumper is removed, no circuit is present, and the signal is forced onto the board. This process permits the board to intercept the signal and act accordingly.

---

[55] There are actually a variety of (overlapping) VME addresses: a24d32 (24-bit address, 32-bit data), a32d32 (32/32), a16d32, a24d16, etc. Virtually all Sun boards use the a32d32 space.

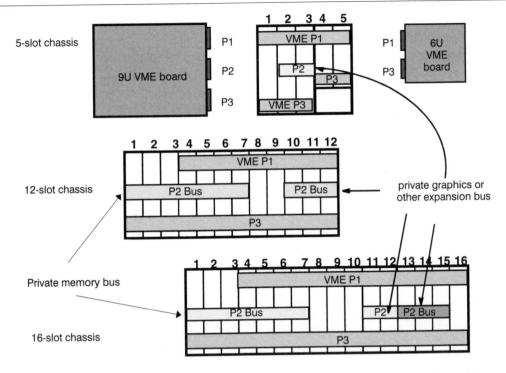

Figure 37. VME backplane configurations. P2 connections were used to implement private high-speed CPU-memory busses and graphics backplanes.

The signals in question (BG and IACK) are both generated from the VME controller, which on Sun systems is always located on the CPU complex. Normally, both the IACK and BG jumpers are pulled (i.e., the signal routed onto the board) for boards that are *bus masters.* Misconfiguration of the jumpers—for example when the jumpers are pulled in an empty slot—causes boards "downstream" (in higher numbered slots) to fail to respond. Sometimes, misconfigured jumpers can cause apparently random VME interrupts to "appear" in the system.

Bus masters are boards that can assume control of the bus and initiate transfers to and from the board and main memory. Boards that are not masters are referred to as slaves. Slave transfers must be initiated and managed by a third party, generally the CPU. Generally speaking, high-performance direct memory access (DMA) boards that transfer a great deal of data such as disk controllers and advanced frame buffers are bus masters. Other, less demanding boards, such as the TAAC-1 visualization accelerator, are VME slaves (all VME masters also permit VME slave operation). All Sun VME-based systems except the Sun-4/100 support both VME masters and VME slaves (the 4/100 did not support VME masters other than the CPU itself).

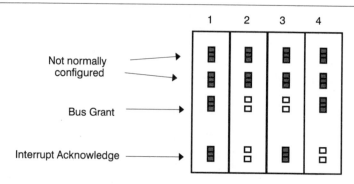

Figure 38. Typically configured VME frontplane jumpers

6.6.4 I/O Cache Interface to VME

As defined by Motorola, the VME devices may interact with memory in quantities of two to 32 bytes; larger transfers are broken down into 32-byte transactions. Each transfer requires setup time as well as transfer time, and more importantly, it drives up bus residency. Obviously, the larger the transfer, the more efficiently the bus is used, since fewer setups are done. Older Sun servers (through the 4/300 series) permitted arbitrary-sized transfers to take place at the discretion of the device and its driver. However, in the 4/400 and 4/600 processors, Sun implemented an I/O cache (IOC) between the VME bus and the memory bus. The cache collects VME transfers and bursts all transfers to and from memory in 32-byte blocks, greatly increasing the efficiency of the bus and bus/memory interface. Suitable arrangements are made for transfers that are not full increments of 32 bytes. The IOC is essentially a write-back cache with a 32-byte line size, placed between the VME and memory busses.

The use of the IOC enables SPARCservers to sustain DMA transfer rates (18-25 MB/sec) very close to the practical limit of 27.9MB/sec[56]. These transfer rates apply *only* to so-called stream I/O transfers performed under DMA or DVMA. Stream I/O supports one transfer mode: sequential, unidirectional, block-sized, and block-aligned to and from memory. Non-stream transfers (such as those typically performed by programmed I/O) defeat the IOC mechanism by spreading transfers out across multiple IOC bursts. The transmitter appears to be a very slow device due to the large amount of overhead involved. In addition, the hardware ensures that non-stream operations are cycle-by-cycle coherent with the system caches, due to the fine-grained nature of the transfer. This approach is considerably less efficient than stream operation. For these reasons, programmed I/O transfers operate at about 4 MB/sec on 4/300 systems and at about 5 MB/sec on 4/400 systems (in addition to consuming considerably more attention from the main processors). Avoid non-stream I/O whenever

---

[56] Patterson and Hennesey, p. 532.

possible, although some VME peripherals have no DMA hardware and must operate in non-stream mode[57]. Common Sun VME boards are listed in Table 27, along with typical bandwidth consumption.

Because private P2 bus operations are not VME transactions, the IOC has no effect on transfers across these busses. These busses are usually synchronous and always oriented toward block transfers, and an IOC would not appreciably accelerate these subsystems.

Table 27. Maximum and typical bandwidth consumption of VME boards

VME Board	Maximum Bandwidth	Typical Bandwidth
ISP-80 IPI-2 String Controller	6.0 MB/sec	6.0 MB/sec
FDDI/DX Dual-attach FDDI	12.5 MB/sec	4.0 MB/sec
Asynchronous SCSI host adapter	1.2 MB/sec	1.0 MB/sec
SNC Network coprocessor (NC400/NC600)	1.2 MB/sec	0.9 MB/sec
ie2 Ethernet	1.0 MB/sec	0.5 MB/sec
ALM-2 Asynchronous Line Multiplexor	350 KB/sec	10 KB/sec
MCP Synchronous Communications Interface	750 KB/sec	250 KB/sec
IBM Channel Attach	3 MB/sec	3 MB/sec

---

[57] In the 4/400 systems, the IOC was shared with the onboard Ethernet interface. This arrangement is not necessary on the 4/600 systems because the Ethernet is provided with its own buffers.

Storage Subsystem Architecture   7

The delivered performance of many applications is governed by the speed at which data can be retrieved from storage, usually from high speed disk. This situation is particularly true of DBMS systems. Because disk access is the slowest "high-performance" part of a system, it usually receives the most careful attention during configuration. However, because disk subsystems are also the most complex parts of a system, a wide variety of misconceptions and false notions promote suboptimal configuration of disk subsystems.

Designing an optimal disk subsystem requires an understanding of how disks operate, how they are used, and what portions of the disk access take time. This information provides insight into how to effectively optimize and use disk subsystems.

Many factors influence the configuration and optimization of a storage system, including reliability, performance, data accessibility, and cost. Since typical disk drives are about 30,000 times slower than typical memory, mistakes made in the configuration of the disk subsystems make a *very* large impact on the overall performance of the system. Similarly, because disks are usually the system component that are found in the greatest numbers, and because they are almost the only moving parts in the entire system, the reliability of the storage subsystem dominates the reliability of the system as a whole.

Disk drives are now typically combined into virtual disks. The following sections address many of the difficult questions associated with the usage, design, and optimization of disk subsystems. Individual disk drives are considered first, followed by disk interconnection strategies, and finally the complex disk structures required to build enterprise–class systems. Finally, the last section applies the architectural information to real–world configuration issues.

7.1 Individual Disks

A disk drive consists of a number of stacked platters that are joined together by a common central spindle. Most current disk drives have between two and nine platters, although some of the newer and smaller drives with have only one platter. Both sides of the platters are used, except that one surface of one platter in the "stack" is usually reserved for the drive's own use. Head alignment and/or rotational position sense tracks are often stored on the reserved surfaces. The platters rotate together at a constant high speed, usually 3,600-7,200 rpm. The data is read or written by tiny read/write heads as the target location flies past. Each head is capable of manipulating only a very small portion of its assigned platter surface at one time, so the heads are mounted on a common multi-pronged assembly known as a disk arm. The arm moves radially across the surfaces in such a way that the entire recording surface can be accessed by appropriately moving the disk arm. Although a few drives are configured with electronics that permit more than one read/write head to transfer data simultaneously, commodity disks activate only one head at a time.

The storage area of the disk is divided into units according to the electromechanical adjustments made to retrieve the data. The address of a piece of data is generally given in three dimensions by the cylinder, platter, and sector. The ring of data swept out on a single platter as the platter rotates is called a track, and tracks are divided into 512–byte blocks of data, called *sectors*. Occasionally disks are formatted with sectors larger than 512 bytes, but SCSI disks always use 512 byte sectors because the size is mandated in the SCSI standard. The number of sectors per track is dependent upon the physical size of the platter and the recording density. Surprisingly, these can vary even on a single platter (see section 7.1.1.3, *Zone Bit Recording*). In order to access the data, the arm must be positioned so that the read/write head is over the correct track. Then the data can be read or written when the correct location flies under (over) the head. Although the disk arm has a head for each side of each platter, usually only one is accessible at a time. When the platters of a disk drive are taken as a group, each radial position of the disk arm sweeps out a track on every platter, and the group of tracks sharing a single disk arm position is called a cylinder (see

Figure 39).

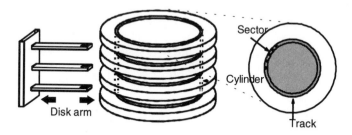

Figure 39. The physical geometry of a disk drive. Each sector is 512 bytes; a track consists of all the sectors in a ring, and a cylinder consists of all tracks that share a common seek position.

7.1.1 Components of Disk Access Time

Hard disks are so well integrated into most operating environments that users think of the disk subsystem as a "black-box": the user requests a block of data, and the disk returns it. At a macroscopic level this view is a valid, yet even in relatively simple systems, many complex activities must be completed even to get the request to the disk drive, let alone complete the operation. Understanding the intermediate steps involved in processing a disk request is essential to understanding the capabilities of a disk subsystem. Storage systems consisting of aggregations of disk arrays are even more complex, but fortunately the same principles apply as the size and complexity scales up.

7.1.1.1 The Path of a Disk I/O Operation

A simple SCSI subsystem consists of four main components: the host computer, the SCSI host adapter, the embedded target controller, and the disk mechanism itself. When the operating system receives an I/O request from the user, it converts the request into a SCSI command packet. The requesting process is blocked pending the completion of the I/O operation, unless the request was issued asynchronously[58]. The command is then transferred across the host's I/O bus (SBus or PCI) to the SCSI host adapter[59]. The host adapter then accepts responsibility for interacting with the target controllers and their devices.

Next the host adapter selects the target by asserting its control line on the SCSI bus when the bus is available; this period is known as the selection phase. When the target responds to the selection, the host adapter transfers the command to the target; this period is called the command phase. If the target is able to satisfy the command immediately, it returns the requested data or status. Normally the command can only be serviced immediately if the command is a status request or if the command requests data that is already resident in the target controller's cache. If the operation is a read, the data is not usually available, so the target disconnects, freeing the SCSI bus for other operations. If the operation is a write (i.e., transfers from host to the target), a data phase immediately follows the command phase on the bus, the data is transferred to the target's cache, and the target disconnects. Writes are

---

[58] The term "asynchronous I/O" is heavily overloaded! In this case, the term "asynchronous" refers to when the calling process is notified that the I/O operation has been completed. Some processes, notably DBMS engines, can productively issue many I/O operations and keep track of the completions themselves. This task is accomplished via the `aioread(2)` and `aiowrite(2)` system calls. This sense of the term "asynchronous" is completely separate from the notion of synchronous and asynchronous SCSI transfers.

[59] In Sun systems, all SCSI host adapters are connected to the system via an SBus, even if they are not physically located on SBus cards. Some other systems have SCSI host adapters built onto EISA or PCI busses.

not acknowledged until the data is actually stored on the disk platter, because the target controller's cache is subject to power failure (if an interruptible power supply is available, the disk's controller can be specially configured to acknowledge writes as soon as they are committed to the cache, substantially improving write performance in many cases).

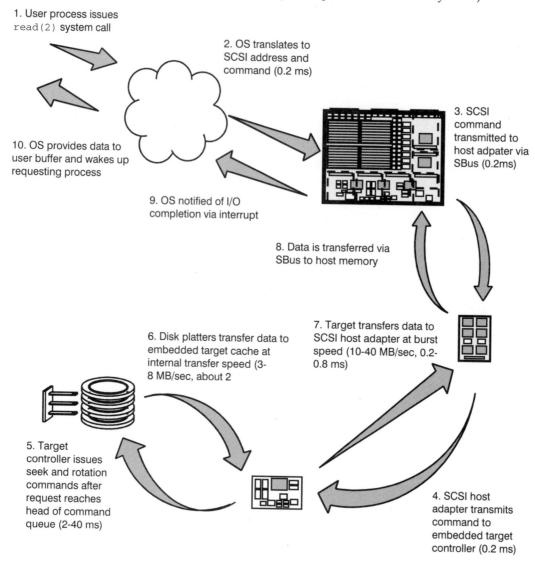

1. User process issues
read(2) **system call**

2. OS translates to SCSI address and command (0.2 ms)

3. SCSI command transmitted to host adpater via SBus (0.2ms)

10. OS provides data to user buffer and wakes up requesting process

9. OS notified of I/O completion via interrupt

8. Data is transferred via SBus to host memory

7. Target transfers data to SCSI host adapter at burst speed (10-40 MB/sec, 0.2-0.8 ms)

6. Disk platters transfer data to embedded target cache at internal transfer speed (3-8 MB/sec, about 2

5. Target controller issues seek and rotation commands after request reaches head of command queue (2-40 ms)

4. SCSI host adapter transmits command to embedded target controller (0.2 ms)

Figure 40. The life history of a SCSI disk I/O operation. Even this diagram omits the considerable complexity of SCSI bus arbitration, device selection and execution details, such as command queuing.

In disk arrays, this process is effected between the disk drive and the array controller and between the array controller and the host bus adapter.

After disconnecting, the target resumes its own processing while the bus is free to service other requests. If the target is not capable of command queuing, it has only the single command to execute. However, if command queuing is enabled, the command is scheduled into the target's work queue, and the highest priority command in the queue is processed. When the request becomes the highest priority, the target controller computes the physical address or addresses necessary to satisfy the I/O operation, and then the disk mechanisms are activated. The disk arm is repositioned, the appropriate read/write head is prepared, and the platter is sensed to compute when the data will fly under the head. Finally, the data is physically read or written to the platters. If the data is being read, it is stored in the target controller's cache. Sometimes the target is able to perform readaheads while the arm is correctly positioned.

After the physical I/O is complete, the target controller reconnects to the host adapter when the bus is free, followed by a data phase (if the data is moving from target to host), and then a status phase to describe the results of the operation. When the host adapter receives the status phase, it verifies the correct completion of the physical operation at the target, and notifies the operating system accordingly. The entire process appears in Figure 40.

One of the characteristics of the SCSI I/O process is that a large number of steps are usually invisible to the user. In particular, usually seven phase changes take place on the SCSI bus (select, command, disconnect, reconnect, data, status, disconnect). Each phase takes time to execute, requiring consumption of SCSI bus utilization. Many targets take a surprising amount of time to select, disconnect, and reconnect. Low-speed devices such as tape drives and CDROMs are particularly culpable.

Although this example shows details peculiar to SCSI subsystems, nearly all modern disk subsystems operate in approximately this fashion. All large–scale disk subsystems have this type of complexity, especially since most larger disk subsystems are constructed out of SCSI components.

7.1.1.2 Mechanical Disk Operations

The various electromechanical actions necessary to address a specific data block have a significant impact on how long reading or writing a block takes. Moving the disk arm radially (seeking) costs between 0.5 and 40 milliseconds, depending on how far the arm must be moved. The other mechanical operation—waiting for the platter to rotate until the block flies under the head—costs 4.2-8.6 milliseconds; this delay is known as rotational latency. Finally, the platter is selected electrically when the mechanical operations have been completed. Because platter selection is an electrical rather than mechanical operation, it takes an insignificant amount of time. Figure 41 and Figure 42 together illustrate the relative proportion of disk I/O times for both random and sequential operations (the figures use the same scale).

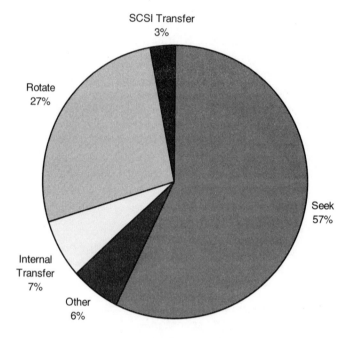

Figure 41. Relative size of disk I/O time components for random-access I/O. SCSI transfer times assume 20 MB/sec bursts.

When the data block flies under the read/write head, the head performs the actual I/O operation. The time to actually transfer the data from the platter to the disk arm is called the *internal transfer time*, and is dependent upon the rotational speed and the density that data is recorded onto the platter. Although rotational speed is constant for any given disk, recording density is usually variable. For typical disk drives, the internal transfer speed varies between about 2 MB/sec and 7 MB/sec. The data is transferred from the disk platter to the intelligent disk controller embedded in all SCSI disks. For the typical I/O request of 8 KB, internal transfer consumes 1-4 milliseconds. In addition, I/O requests spend 0.5-2 milliseconds (depending on host processor speed) being processed in the operating system. Finally, the data must be transferred over the SCSI bus. At the 20 MB/sec speed of a fast/wide SCSI bus, the typical I/O takes an additional 0.39 milliseconds.

7.1.1.3 Zone Bit Recording

The internal transfer speed varies because most disks use a recording format called zone bit recording (ZBR) that makes use of the geometric properties of a spinning disk to pack more data into the parts of the platter farthest from the platter center (the only exceptions are entry–level disks with very low capacities, typically in the 200-300 MB range). Traditional recording formats record data in a constant linear density: data stored on the outermost cylinders of a platter flies by the read/write heads at the same speed as data stored on the innermost cylinders. Originally, this technique permitted the read/write electronics to operate at a single speed—reducing complexity—but the disadvantage was that data is recorded less densely on outside cylinders than on the inside cylinders. Disks using the ZBR format record data at constant density per unit of area; every cylinder is recorded at the same density. Since the outside cylinders hold more data than the inside cylinders (they are physically larger in area), the fact that the platters spin at constant speed means that the radial position of the head determines the speed the data flies under the heads. Because the data flies by the head at different speeds, the internal transfer speed is also variable. Cylinders are grouped into zones, classifying cylinders by performance and capacity. The fastest zones correspond to the lowest-numbered cylinders; density, capacity, and internal transfer speed decrease as the cylinder numbers increase (cylinder zero is the fastest, largest, and densest cylinder, while the highest-numbered cylinder is the slowest, smallest, and least dense).

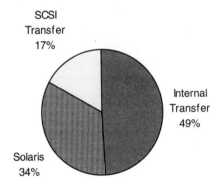

Figure 42. Relative size of disk I/O components for sequential-access I/O. Compare with Figure 41. The relative size of the pie graphs correspond to the magnitude of random-access vs. sequential I/O.

The practical effect is that cylinders on the physical outside of the disk outperform cylinders on the inside of the disk by a wide margin—often 50 percent. For example, the Seagate ST11200N 3.5" 1 GB disk is listed as transferring at 3.5-5.1 MB/sec. This margin is relevant for sequential transfers, but variable density recording format also impacts random access performance. Data on the outside cylinders not only flies by the read/write heads faster—the reason the transfer speed is higher—but these cylinders are also larger, meaning that a given quantity of data will be spread over fewer large cylinders, leading to fewer arm seeks (or further discussion see section 7.6.2.2, *Data Layout Considerations*).

Because the fastest zones are in the lowest-numbered cylinders, the default layout of a single–disk system places the free disk space after operating system installation in the slowest zone of the disk. Very few servers have just one disk, so this is rarely a problem, but single–disk workstations may choose to configure their disks differently.

7.1.1.4 Decoding the Specifications

One of the common problems with "under-performing" systems is the inappropriate expectations set by the way the computer industry describes its products. The problems are especially acute in the peripheral area, where the use of confusing specifications has led to widespread misunderstanding of the performance characteristics of SCSI subsystems. Penetrating the specifications is crucial to understanding how to configure disk subsystems to meet specific requirements.

7.1.1.4.1 Megabytes vs. Millions of Bytes

Perhaps the least obvious but simplest confusion is the disk vendor's use of the term "megabyte." Disk vendors use the term to mean one million bytes, specifically 1,000,000 bytes; the SCSI standard also uses this notation. Most computer users and operating systems, however, interpret disk space in units of 1024 kilobytes, which is 1,048,576 bytes. With disks now 9 GB in size, this five percent differential is often quite noticeable! a "424 MB" disk is actually reported by the operating system to be 404 MB in size. This reporting policy is maintained by the entire industry, despite its confusing nature. Combined with the overhead that UNIX file systems impose by default (see section 9.2.3, *UFS and UFS+ Parameters*), the reported disk size useable by applications is only about 79 percent of the normally quoted formatted capacity.

The matter of units also applies to transfer speed specifications. A disk rated to transfer 5.1 million bytes per second can *never* transfer data faster than 4.9 MB/sec.

7.1.1.4.2 Burst Speed vs. Internal Transfer Speed

Disk vendors usually cite the SCSI burst speed of a disk's embedded controller. For example, the Seagate ST42400N 5.25" 2.1 GB disk is rated at 10 MB/sec. This specification indicates how fast the disk's embedded controller transfers data on the SCSI bus. It does *not* account for SCSI command or state changes; rather it is the speed that bits are transmitted on the SCSI bus. In particular, this speed can be sustained only when both the source can supply data that quickly and when the destination can consume data at that rate. As a practical matter, this speed is attained only when the controller is operating on data that is being transferred between host memory and the controller cache (step 7 in Figure 40, page 264).

In most cases, however, a host request to the disk cannot be immediately satisfied by the embedded cache, and the data must be read from the disk platters. For random I/O's, this read requires mechanical motion from the disk arm; the time required to perform the seek (2-37 milliseconds) completely overwhelms the bus transfer speed (0.39 milliseconds for 8 KB at 20 MB/sec). Doubling the burst speed to 40 MB/sec or halving it to 10 MB/sec has little effect on the overall time required to service the I/O. Even for sequential I/O, where seek and rotation time are minimal to nil, the burst speed is never observed because the data must be read from or written to the disk platters. Most vendors now also provide a specification called the "internal transfer speed" or the "platter speed."

The internal transfer speed is the speed that bits are read from the disk platters to the read/write head; it does not include other factors. The internal transfer speed is much lower than the burst speed for all current disk drives. For example, the Seagate ST32550N 2.1 GB disk has an internal transfer speed of 3.8-5.1 MB/sec. The transfer speed varies because this disk uses zone bit recording. Even the fastest internal transfer speed is much slower than the burst speed, and the internal speed then governs the speed of sequential transfers. Note that the internal transfer speed applies even to writes to the disk. Because the embedded controllers use volatile memory (i.e., they are subject to data loss if the power fails), they are operated as safe write-through caches, meaning that data must be completely written onto the permanent storage medium before the write operation is considered complete and acknowledged.

Most SCSI disk drives can be configured to commit writes into their embedded caches. But without an uninterruptible power supply, this practice is unsafe. All disks shipped from major vendors (including Sun) have this feature disabled, but always check disks obtained on the open market, especially those sold primarily into the PC space. Note that read operations are not subject to this restriction, and SCSI target controllers now implement fairly aggressive read-ahead algorithms when sequential access patterns are detected. As a result, most SCSI disks can read noticeably faster than they can write.

One of the major implications of this distinction is that a single disk with a 40 MB/sec burst transfer speed is unlikely to be much faster—if any—than a similar disk with a 20 MB/sec (or 10 MB/sec) burst speed. There *are* issues with SCSI bus utilization, and with respect to utilization the higher burst speeds are useful (refer to *Mixing Different–Speed Devices*, section 7.2.5.4).

7.1.1.4.3 Internal Transfer Speed vs. Data Speed

Although the internal transfer speed is much more reflective of the true capability of a disk than the SCSI burst speed, even internal transfer speed does not accurately convey how fast data can be transferred to or from an application. The reason is that the internal transfer speed measures the speed at which *all* data flies by the read/write heads. This measurement includes a considerable amount of formatting information used by the disk itself. Much of this data is error correcting codes (ECC) that prevents most disk errors from resulting in corrupted data. The ECC codes are sufficient to detect the loss of an entire 512–byte sector and to correct most smaller errors. The size of the ECC data is also seen in the large difference between the formatted and unformatted capacity of a disk; for example, the unformatted capacity of a 669 MB disk is actually 760 MB.

All the information necessary to compute a reasonable approximation of the average end-user data transfer speed is provided in the /etc/format.dat file, used in older releases of Solaris to describe the physical characteristics of disks to the format(8) program and to the various disk device drivers. (Beginning with Solaris 2.4, the SCSI disk driver probes the disk to obtain physical characteristics. The file remains part of the system for backward compatibility and to handle the few remaining non-SCSI disks.) Specifically, what is needed is the size of a track, and the rotational speed of the disk. The data speed of a disk is:

$$Speed = \frac{Number\ Of\ Sectors\ Per\ Track\ *\ 512\ *\ rpm}{60\ seconds}$$

For the Sun 1.05 GB disk (usually a Connor CP1080E or a Seagate ST31200W), the format.dat entry is:

```
disk_type = "SUN1.05" \
  : ctlr = SCSI : fmt_time = 4 \
  : ncyl = 2036 : acyl = 2 : pcyl = 2038 \
  : nhead = 14 : nsect = 72 : rpm = 5,400
```

So the data speed of this disk is:

$$\frac{72\ sectors\ Per\ Track\ *\ 512\ bytes\ *\ 5400\ rpm}{60\ seconds} = 3.24\ MB\ /\ sec$$

This is the speed that user data can be transferred, assuming no mechanical seek or rotational time. This computation is approximate because of the variable-speed nature of ZBR disks. In order to simplify higher-level programs, the embedded SCSI controller presents an idealized disk geometry to the outside world (SCSI's primary design goal was simplification of higher-level programs by hiding device specifics—see section 7.2.2, *SCSI Design Principles*). This idealized geometry glosses over differing track sizes and speeds. The idealized geometry presented by the target controller is the reason that vendors can qualify multiple sources for disks and have them all work. For example, Sun has shipped at least four different models of 1.05 GB disks, and all of them work equivalently, despite widely varying physical geometries.

Note: As useful as the /etc/format.dat file is, it can be misleading, and furthermore it is unnecessary. Beginning with Solaris 2.4, the SCSI disk drivers (sd and ssd) probe the disk and determine all necessary parameters directly from the drive. They make adding an arbitrary disk to a Solaris system much easier than on most other operating systems (just plug it in with suitable cabling) but this technique has the disadvantage of making it rather difficult to investigate the disk's operating parameters during operation[60].

7.1.1.4.4 Average Seek vs. Typical Seek

Another disk specification that is often misunderstood is the average seek time. As quoted by disk vendors (and system vendors who OEM the disks), the average seek time is the sum of all possible seeks, divided by the number of possible seeks. This is mathematically truthful, but it is quite misleading.

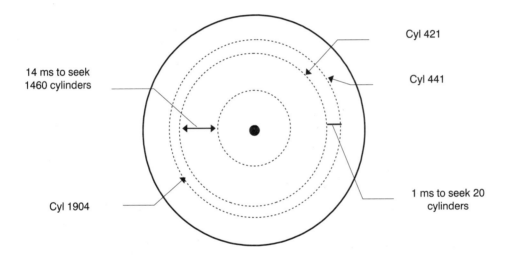

Figure 43. Seek times are proportional to physical location on the disk. Seeks between nearby cylinders such as 421 and 441 are much shorter than seeks to distant cylinders, for example, from 441 to 1904.

The physics involved in moving the disk arm are such that a short seek takes much less time than a long one. For example, a track-to-track seek takes 1.7 milliseconds on the Seagate

---

[60] If necessary, the options can be obtained by decoding the output of "prtconf -pv". If detailed knowledge about particular drives is available, the scsi subcommand can be invoked if format(8) is started with the -e argument. This makes the mode sense select pages available.

ST42400N 2.1 GB 5.25″ disk, whereas a full-stroke seek takes 37 milliseconds, more than 20 times as long. The average seek specification for this disk is 11 ms. In particular, note that a full-stroke seek takes much longer than twice the "average" seek. The average seek is definitely not the same thing as a "typical" seek. Indeed, the operating system goes to great lengths to minimize seek distances. See Figure 43.

The configuration implication here is that storing data together as closely as possible will save considerable access time. In particular, putting two "hot" slices on a single disk is a good way to end up with very poor performance[61]. Consider a disk that is sliced (partitioned) into two halves, with each half equally busy. Every access that hits the "other" slice must seek from the average position in one slice to the average position in the other slice, about half of the maximum possible seek distance. Because half the maximum seek is a *very* long time, a better configuration might be to put the two different slices on two different disks so that each of them have a much more limited seek range. (A maximum-length seek can cost as much as 20 ms on a 3.5″ disk and nearly 40 ms on a 5.25″ drive—sufficient time to execute as many as 100 million instructions on a fast UltraSPARC or Pentium Pro processor!) The impact of excessive seek distance is easy to dismiss—until it bites a real application. It is sometimes possible to make a 10-20 percent change in the overall performance of a disk–bound application entirely through management of seek distances!

7.1.2 Disk Access Patterns

All disk I/O operations fall into one of two categories: sequential access and random access—the distinction being whether or not the disk must perform a seek/rotate operation to locate the information. For example, a process reading the disk sequentially reads block 0, then block 1, and then block N. As long as the blocks are located within the same cylinder of the disk, the disk arm does not move, eliminating the most costly part of servicing an arbitrary disk I/O. Furthermore, since the blocks are normally stored sequentially around each track, waiting for the platter to rotate into position is unnecessary—the data is already available once the first block in the track is located. Eliminating the rotational delay avoids the second most costly part of the I/O process.

The time required to service sequential access is dominated by internal transfer time, whereas random access is dominated by seek and rotation time. In practice, seek specifications do not vary widely within each generation of disk drives; for random-access I/O, the primary determinant of performance is the drive's rotational speed (see Figure 44). Since the seek and rotate times are a large proportion of the time spent in random–access I/O, in fact, it follows directly that sequential I/O is much faster than random I/O. Wherever possible, applications should try to convert random I/Os into sequential ones; unfortunately,

---

[61] This performance usually occurs as a result of dividing a single disk into many logical pieces; it is one reason why Solaris supports only eight slices per disk.

such conversions are much easier prescribed than performed. Disk I/O on multi-user servers is almost *all* random–access. Even when every user is accessing the disk sequentially, the interleaving of all of the various requests results in a jumbled–up queue for the disk, requiring a seek for virtually every access. A subsystem that tests well on a sequential access microbenchmark (such as the public–domain *bonnie*) may or may not perform well for real applications, since the actual work may not resemble the test.

7.1.3 Storage Capacity vs. Access Capacity

For the random access I/O that servers normally generate, disk access times are dominated by the platter rotational speed and the seek time. As a result, drives that spin at the same speed perform about the same, regardless of capacity or physical size. The most effective ways to increase disk access capability are to get faster-spinning drives, and simply to have more drives!

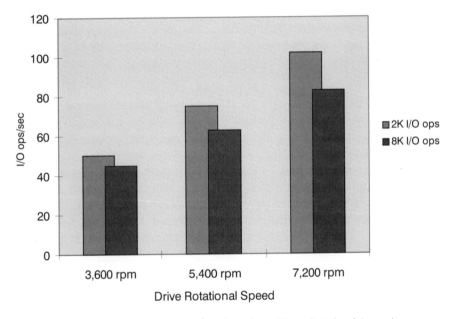

Figure 44. Random access I/O capability is a function of how fast the drive spins

Although the 5,400 rpm Seagate ST43401N 2.1 GB disk has more than five times the storage capacity of the 4,400 rpm Seagate ST1480 424 MB disk, it provides only 24 percent more accessibility. Because of differences in the efficiency of the embedded target controller's firmware, the Seagate ST31200W 1.05 GB disk is actually faster than the 2.1 GB disk, despite identical operating specifications! For these reasons, the greatest I/O access capability is most often achieved by using the *smallest* feasible disk, rather than the largest, even when the larger disk may have superior specifications in every way. For a given amount of storage, the access capacity (potential I/O operations per second) is dramatically greater—more than seven times greater, in fact—when using the 1 GB disk than when using equivalent storage in 9 GB disks—see Table 28.

Table 28. I/O capacity for 190 GB of storage (1995 street pricing)

Disk	# Req'd	Ops/disk	SCSI Busses	Cost	Price/ MB	Price/Op	IOPS	MB/Sec
1.05 GB	186	78	16	$400	$0.47	$6.34	14,508	320
2.1 GB	93	105	8	$1020	$0.53	$10.65	9,765	160
4.3 GB	46	108	4	$1480	$0.37	$14.69	4,968	80
9 GB	22	85	2	$2245	$0.26	$27.81	1,870	40

The additional host adapters required for the smaller disks provide much greater serial throughput capability. Configuring storage subsystems solely on storage capacity is almost always a serious mistake—yet that is precisely what most users do.

Unfortunately, configuring disk subsystems is not as easy as finding the right disk drive. Using the smallest possible disk is not only the most costly, but it also often consumes much more physical space. For most systems, it is possible—and usually appropriate to mix configurations of large– and small–capacity disks to achieve good performance with reasonable cost. Furthermore, without taking special precautions, subsystems consisting of many small drives are more likely to fail than storage systems built up from fewer large drives. RAID disk organizations are the key to extracting maximum performance from all disk configurations, as well as to eliminating or minimizing the impact of the inevitable disk failure. Specifications for many common disk drives are provided in Table 29.

Table 29. Disk drive specification summary

Disk	Size	Bus	Seek	Internal Transfer	Burst Transfer	RPM	Cache
535 MB	3.5" x 1"	SCSI–2	12 ms	2.5-3.0 MB/sec	10 MB/sec	5,400	256 KB
911 MB	8"	IPI–2	15 ms	6.0 MB/sec	6 MB/sec	3,600	N/A
1.05 GB	3.5" x 1.6"	SCSI–2	11.5 ms	2.9-5.0 MB/sec	10 MB/sec	5,400	256 KB
1.05 GB	3.5" x 1"	SCSI–2	10.5 ms	2.9-5.0 MB/sec	20 MB/sec	5,400	256 KB
1.3 GB	5.25"	IPI–2	11 ms	3.0-4.5 MB/sec	6 MB/sec	5,400	N/A
1.3 GB	5.25"	SCSI–2	11 ms	3.0-4.5 MB/sec	5 MB/sec	5,400	256 KB

Table 29. Disk drive specification summary

Disk	Size	Bus	Seek	Internal Transfer	Burst Transfer	RPM	Cache
2.1 GB	5.25″	SCSI–2	11 ms	3.8-5.0 MB/sec	10 MB/sec	5,400	256 KB
2.1 GB	3.5″ x 1″	SCSI–2	8.5 ms	6.2-9.0 MB/sec	20 MB/sec	7,200	512 KB
2.9 GB	5.25″	SCSI–2	10.5 ms	3.6-5.4 MB/sec	20 MB/sec	5,400	512 KB
3.0 GB	8″	IPI–2	15 ms	3.0 MB/sec	6 MB/sec	3,600	N/A
4.3 GB	3.5″ x 1.6″	SCSI–2	10.5 ms	5.5-8.25 MB/sec	20 MB/sec	5,400	512 KB
4.3 GB	3.5″ x 1″	SCSI-2	8.5 ms	6.2-9.4 MB/sec	20 MB/sec	7,200	1024 KB
9.0 GB	5.25″	SCSI–2	10.5 ms	5.5-8.25 MB/sec	20 MB/sec	5,400	1024 KB

7.1.4 Write Acceleration with Non-Volatile Memory

Over the years many designers have observed that writes can be committed to fast electronic non–volatile memory instead of writing to slow mechanical disk drives. Today these functions are implemented in two basic forms: host-based NVRAM and disk–controller–based NVRAM.

The various non-volatile memory (NVRAM) options provide acceleration for synchronous disk writes. These operations are extremely slow because the `write(2)` system call blocks until the data is safely committed to non-volatile storage [62]. Without NVRAM, the data must be physically written onto a disk drive—a *very* slow process. A 5,400 rpm disk drive can sustain only 40–65 synchronous disk writes per second, even at 100 percent utilization.

All of the options operate on the same basic principle: disk write operations are intercepted and committed to non-volatile memory. Committing the data to memory is much faster than the same operation to physical disk—about 20 times faster. The managing software arranges for the data to be transferred to disk (asynchronously) when do so is convenient, either when the data has aged (usually a few hundred milliseconds) or when the cache manager needs the memory for some other purpose.

For environments that have many disk writes, especially synchronous disk writes, NVRAM write acceleration offers three benefits:

---

[62] Normally, writes are cached behind and are not synchronous. Synchronous operation is specified by modifying a directory, by issuing a write remotely over NFS, or by opening the file with the O_SYNC flag.

- Greatly accelerated response on synchronous write operations: synchronous disk operations are committed and acknowledged up to 20 times faster.

- Write cancellation: because the cache management software issues transfers to disk in 8 KB blocks, repeated writes to the same 8 KB blocks are canceled. This often happens when rapidly updating directories, since directory entries are much smaller than 8 KB— only a single 8 KB write is transferred to the disk, rather than a large number of much smaller ones.

- Lower disk utilization: disks that are heavily write-bound often experience much lower utilization. This is partly due to transferring less data to the drive as a result of write cancellation, but also because synchronous writes are converted to asynchronous ones, permitting the standard "elevator" seek algorithms to operate normally (see section 7.2.4.5, *SCSI Command Queuing* for further discussion of the elevator algorithms). Unaccellerated synchronous writes are dispatched to the drive at high priority in order to minimize the latency of the operation. When NVRAM is configured, the operation is acknowledged before the disk is involved, obviating the necessity for heroic measures to reduce latency.

A common misconception is that NVRAM buffers are used to simply absorb data quickly, necessitating very large NVRAM configurations. In practice, the benefits of NVRAM are due primarily to the effects noted above, in which moderate sized buffers are more than adequate. For these purposes, 8-128 MB is plenty (see section 7.5.11.2, *Controller-Based RAID*). These caches are also often mistaken for read caches, where very large buffers sometimes are beneficial, but so much other caching is done in complex server systems that read buffering at the SCSI host adapter or disk array level is nearly always redundant. In particular, extensive buffering is done in the host's I/O buffers—see *Caching File System I/O* in section 9.1.5—and track buffering is accomplished by the embedded target controllers resident in each disk drive.

7.1.4.1 Host–Based NVSIMM and SBus PrestoServe

Originally developed specifically as an NFS write accelerator, the SBus PrestoServe board and its derivative, the non–volatile single inline memory module (SIMM—the non-volatile derivative is an NVSIMM) are in fact general–purpose accelerators for any synchronous file system write. As implemented by Legato (the implementers of the original VME PrestoServe board) and later Sun, the driver arranges to intercept the synchronous file system write operation and uses the information to operate a non–volatile RAM cache.

The SBus PrestoServe is a single–width SBus board containing 1 MB of static RAM and a lithium battery. The various NVSIMM options are SIMM "popsicle sticks" that utilize static, battery-backed SRAMs instead of DRAMs. Different models are designed for the SPARCstation 10 and SPARCstation 20 family, and others are offered for use in the

SPARCserver 1000E and SPARCcenter 2000E, respectively. Like the PrestoServe, NVSIMMs use a lithium battery to preserve the contents of the static memory even when no power is present. The batteries have a life of several years; they are recharged from line current during normal operation.

The NVSIMMs for SPARCstation 10 and SPARCstation 20 have a capacity of 2 MB, and consume one of the two available wide-memory SIMM sockets (in the SPARCstation 10 SX and SPARCstation 20, these two wide-memory sockets must be shared with video SIMMs— refer to Figure 45). The options for the SPARCserver 1000E and SPARCcenter 2000E have a capacity of 4 MB and 8 MB, respectively, and consume one memory bank in each of the host platforms. Although theoretically possible to use quite a number of these options, Sun supports only two NVSIMM options in a single system. Only one SBus PrestoServe is supported in a system (SS10, SS20, SS6x0MP, LX, Classic, SS2, IPX), and the use of SBus PrestoServe is in practice mutually exclusive with NVSIMM. In the SPARCstation 10 and SPARCstation 20, where both SBus PrestoServe and NVSIMM are supported, NVSIMM is preferred unless the system must utilize the memory sockets for maximum main memory configuration.

Each of the eight SIMM locations can hold a 16 MB or 64 MB SIMM. Each extra-function SIMM socket accepts one of:
• 16 Mb or 64 MB SIMM
• 4 MB or 8 MB video SIMM (SX only)
• 2 MB NVSIMM

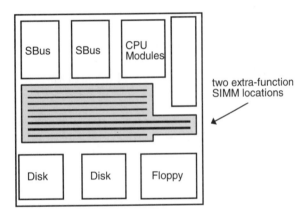

Figure 45. SPARCstation 10 internal layout, showing SIMM locations. The SPARCstation 20 is very similar.

The small SBus option is not functional in large servers, because the driver software does not understand multiple I/O busses, a feature of virtually all large systems. This lack of support is not of practical concern very often, since the same large systems that have multiple I/O busses are also equipped with caching disk arrays on a nearly universal basis.

Caution: The use of host-based NVRAM (either PrestoServe or NVSIMM) is functionally incompatible with the use of disk drives that are shared between independent computer systems. NVRAM is incompatible with shared-disk usage because it implements a system-private data cache; in the event of a system failure, this cache is not accessible to the other system(s) and as a consequence their "view" of the state of the disk is inaccurate. NVRAM may be used in these configurations as long as the NVRAM is not applied to any of the shared disks. The use of caching in the disk's embedded SCSI target controller is fully compatible with multi-initiator SCSI configurations because all systems have access to the cache. Moreover, these caches do not retain state independent of the disk media—they are operated as write-through caches, so that cache and disk are always consistent. This cache coherency problem is not found in the subsystem-level NVRAM products (by design).

7.1.4.2 Controller–Based NVRAM

Once useful for nearly every large server, the importance of host–based NVRAM write acceleration has been reduced in recent years, because most disk arrays have similar acceleration. For example, Sun's SPARCstorage Array has 4 MB-16 MB NVRAM on its controller board, and many disk arrays have even larger NVRAM caches. The effect is usually comparable when the disk array hosts a file system, but the array controllers are also able to accelerate many more types of access. Because the host–based NVSIMM operates by intercepting the file system synchronous write operation, it can only affect performance of that operation. Controller–based NVRAM can improve all types of write operations, and depending upon the precise nature of the firmware, may be responsible for some considerable acceleration in other dimensions.

One notable acceleration performed by the NVRAM in virtually all caching disk arrays is referred to as "raw write clustering." When presented with a stream of small writes to sequentially ordered addresses, most SCSI disks perform the writes directly without optimization, although such writes can often be clustered into larger, much more efficient operations. For example, four sequential 2 KB writes can be issued to the disk as a single 8 KB write, with the same end result but with 75 percent lower overhead and considerably higher throughput. Controller-based NVRAM is discussed further in section 7.5.11.2, *Controller-Based RAID*.

7.2 The SCSI Subsystem

The Small Computer System Interface (SCSI, usually pronounced "scuzzy") peripheral bus is probably the least-understood architecture in the Solaris world, although every Sun system has had SCSI since 1986 and SCSI is clearly the dominant I/O interconnect in server applications in the industry. The term SCSI refers to a particular set of standards defined by ANSI that defines a mechanism for implementing a "data highway" with well-known characteristics between a host memory bus and a wide variety of peripherals.

Two standards have been adopted to date, and a third is in draft form. The initial 1986 standard, now known as SCSI–1, defined workable specifications for the bus protocols, command set, and electrical environment. The standard was revised in 1992 to correct deficiencies in the original specification (especially regarding synchronous transfers), and to create a "menu" of additional high-performance options, such as fast mode, wide mode, and tagged queuing. The revised standard is the current SCSI–2 standard used by most vendors today, including Sun.

7.2.1 SCSI–2

The SCSI–2 specification has been wildly successful, attaining nearly universal acceptance. It has resolved most of the minor inadequacies of the original SCSI standard and provides new features. However, a number of shortcomings have become apparent in the last few years, primarily because of the very widespread usage of SCSI in ever-larger and more sophisticated computing systems. Limited addressability, loopholes in the electrical definitions for multi-initiator SCSI, and cabling limitations have come under particular criticism. At the same time, performance expectations have also increased over the years.

7.2.2 SCSI Design Principles

Because it was originally intended to address the needs of small, inexpensive systems, SCSI is oriented toward achieving excellent results at low cost. Accordingly, it was designed to be simple, and especially to provide flexibility to configure peripherals without having to radically change arrangements in the host computer.

In previous peripheral standards such as SMD and IPI, a disk controller or string controller contained most or all of the subsystem's intelligence. These controllers are complex and expensive, and must be tightly integrated into the host environment. Placing the intelligence in the peripheral permits relatively easy, system- and device-independent peripheral communication by abstracting the host interface. When peripheral controllers were tightly integrated into the host, changing peripherals typically meant a new release of an operating system, because all of the device management software resided in the host.

7.2.2.1 Peripheral Intelligence

The basic SCSI design premise is that intelligence is distributed throughout the subsystem. Most of the processing is done in the peripheral itself, rather than in some central entity. In almost every case, most device processing is handled by a microprocessor located in each device; this is referred to as an *embedded controller.*

One consequence of this organization is that intimate knowledge about a device is available only to entities at the remote (peripheral) end of the SCSI bus. This information is often used for optimization. The practical result is that most optimizations must be implemented in a device's embedded controller, complicating matters in large high–end configurations. On the other hand, a high degree of device abstraction successfully permits an astonishingly wide variety of devices to be connected via SCSI, ranging from high–performance disks and tape drives to floppies, image scanners, printers, multiport serial interfaces, other computers, and even projection displays. The power of the distributed intelligence architecture permits even serious exception conditions such as bad blocks to be handled without notifying the host system.

In order to achieve the desired high level of device independence from the host operating system, SCSI devices present a very simple architecture. For example, the geometry of a disk drive is presented as a linear sequence of uniform disk blocks, even though in actuality a disk has a much more complex multi-dimensional geometry consisting of surfaces, cylinders, tracks, densities, bad block maps, and a multitude of other details. The device itself is responsible for providing translation services from the simplified SCSI notions to the more complex reality. This arrangement permits the host system to communicate with a wide variety of peripherals in a very high–level, idealized fashion.

The incredible rate of innovation in the open systems market—and especially in the mass storage segment—is made possible by standards like SCSI. Device independence is for the most part taken for granted: SCSI disk drives are almost universally interchangeable, and tape drives as disparate in implementation as DLT–4000, 3490E–compatibles, 1/2″ 9-track, QIC-11, and even SD-3 can all be driven by a single device driver.

7.2.2.2 Disk Failures and Predictive Failure Analysis

One of the places that SCSI has simplified operational procedures for users is in defect management. Disk drives are complex electromechanical devices, and they fail at rates much higher than most other components in a computer system. With older disk interconnect technology such as IPI or SMD, the host (specifically the device driver) was required to recognize disk errors and manage a list of defects for every disk drive. (Defects and bad blocks are *inevitable* with disk drives. The only solution is to make disks with as few defects as possible, find those, and make sure that they are never used.) As a result, Solaris has a generalized facility for managing defect lists, due to the historical support for SMD and IPI drives. For SCSI disks, the embedded target controller manages the defect list directly, with absolutely no host intervention. The defect list is managed on a part of the drive that is not even visible to the host adapter. As a result, bad blocks are never even noted to the host, and the host's defect list is left empty[63].

---

[63] Disks are normally delivered with null defect lists. Unfortunately, it occasionally leads to confusion, because defect lists have traditionally been managed by the host, so an empty host-visible defect list is quite an unusual occurrence. In the SCSI case this is the correct behavior!

One technology that has been developed to lessen the impact of disk failures is *predictive failure analysis (PFA)*. This is most commonly found in embedded SCSI controller firmware. The PFA firmware monitors the intimate movements of the disk arm, noting adjustments that must be made to accommodate normal operation, such as thermal recalibration and bad block remapping. When normal procedures approach their limits—for example, if the thermal recalibration detects that a track is about to migrate into another track, or if the defect management code is running out of spare blocks—the PFA code signals an impending failure through the normal SCSI error reporting mechanism. The failure signal permits replacement (either through hot sparing or manual means) before data loss occurs.

PFA is quite useful for handling some types of failures, but it has limitations that are not often obvious. Most disk failures are due to either electrical failures or firmware bugs. Such failures are not predictable, let alone detectable or reportable. No trouble is found on more than half of all failed disk drives returned to the vendors--they test perfectly, implying that the failures were either transient hardware problems or firmware bugs. Additionally, some failures that are detectable by the target controller, such as a shorted SCSI selection line, are also not reportable because they affect the reporting mechanism itself. Although these types of errors significantly limit the general usefulness of current PFA implementations, PFA is a useful feature that can help avoid data loss in the minority of failures that are predictable.

The fact that such an advanced feature can be implemented in a peripheral with virtually no host involvement is a tribute to the original SCSI design principles.

7.2.3 SCSI Organization

SCSI fundamentally defines a peripheral bus; in its most basic form, the bus is parity-protected, 8 bits wide, and transfers data in parallel. Data may be transferred either asynchronously or synchronously. When operated in synchronous modes, the bus clock runs at 5 MHz. All devices connect to the bus and communicate with the host over that channel. It is completely distinct from the system's peripheral bus, except for an intersection point where the two join. This point is called the SCSI *host adapter*. The host adapter is best thought of as a bus intersection through which data passes from one bus to the another. The overall SCSI organization is shown in Figure 46.

7.2.3.1 SCSI Host Adapters

In Sun systems, SCSI host adapters are usually built into the system boards, and are also offered as SBus expansion boards. Within the industry people commonly refer to the host adapter as "the SCSI controller," but this term properly refers to targets on the bus; controllers are almost always part of the devices.

System components that reside on the peripheral bus (SBus or VME in Sun systems, ISA, ESIA, MCA, or PCI in most Solaris x86 or PowerPC systems) transfer data to peripherals residing on the SCSI bus by sending the data to the host adapter, along with a command and a destination address. The host adapter is then responsible for completing the transfer to the device and notifying the host system of the completion status of the actual device's transfer. In the other direction, a peripheral responding to a host request transfers the data to the host adapter, which in turn is responsible for transferring the data across the peripheral bus to the final destination.

Some PC SCSI host adapters provide buffers in order to enable transfers to occur without requiring control of both the system peripheral bus and the SCSI bus. This provision is not necessary on Sun's SPARC systems, which have SBus (and on Solaris x86 or PowerPC systems with PCI), because the peripheral busses are fast enough to permit rapid transfers and are rarely congested enough to cause delays. Moreover, even on Solaris x86 systems using the older and slower EISA or ISA busses, the data is already cached at both higher (the Solaris virtual memory cache) and lower levels (the target's embedded controller cache). Adding another layer of caching would increase the complexity of keeping all of the caches consistent. However, older systems running Solaris x86 benefit much more from SCSI host adapter caching, because these systems often use the much slower ISA, ESIA, or MicroChannel peripheral busses.

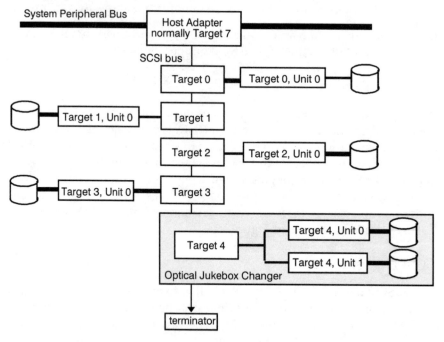

Figure 46. SCSI organization as typically found in Solaris systems

Like almost every other part of modern servers, SCSI host adapters are increasing rapidly in complexity. For example, the host adapter chip used in most older Sun SCSI host adapters, the Emulex FAS101/236, is a simple implementation that merely handles transfers between the SBus and SCSI busses. (This chip is used on all `sun4c`, `sun4m`, and `sun4d` built–in host adapters, as well as Sun's SBus SCSI host adapters that implement fast but not wide SCSI. It is controlled by the `esp` device driver.) Unfortunately, this simplicity results in the host adapter interrupting the host processor for every phase state change on the SCSI bus. Four to seven interrupts per I/O represents considerable overhead to the host. In addition, the simple nature of the device means that each I/O requires a relatively large number of programmed I/O operations for device control.

The much newer Qlogic ISP–1000 chip is used for Sun's SBus–based fast/wide SCSI host adapters such as the DWIS/S and SWIS/S. The design incorporates a small RISC processor inside the host adapter, used for interrupt management and command interpretation. Although the use of an embedded processor in the host adapter results in considerable additional complexity, it reduces overhead substantially. Programmed I/O requirements are reduced by about 85 percent, and host interrupts are reduced to less than one per I/O. Less than one interrupt is taken per I/O on average because a single interrupt can serve more than one I/O if they can be transferred together from the host adapter. The FAS366 chip used in the Ultra–1 and Ultra–2 systems is simpler—and less efficient—than the ISP–1000, but more efficient than the FAS101/236.

7.2.3.2 SCSI Addressing

Each device residing on the SCSI bus has a unique address consisting of two parts: a *target id* and a *logical unit number* (LUN). The bus is organized in a hierarchical fashion, as shown in Figure 46. The host adapter itself must also have an address. SCSI target ids are sensed on the bus by asserting the data line corresponding to the device's target id. Consequently, 8-bit implementations permit eight target ids; wide implementations permit 16 or 32 target ids. Since it is impractical to copackage other devices with the host adapter, the maximum theoretical configuration of an 8-bit SCSI bus is 56 devices (seven independent targets with eight logical units each). Usually the target id resolves to an embedded controller.

Some peripherals use more elaborate addressing schemes. The most common implementation is a SCSI disk array. These devices present a single target on the bus, and the various RAID constructs implemented by the controller are addressed by the host as LUNs of the controller. Of some importance is that Solaris 2 supports only eight LUNs per target, although most vendors can now handle many more through the use of alternate mechanisms (each device must declare that it can support alternate LUN specification during its initial negotiation with the host adapter). In other implementations, the target controller may be responsible for multiple devices as in a robotic tape library with several transports and a stacking mechanism; each device might be assigned a LUN. These devices usually are the sort that is logically a single entity with several subunits, such as an optical jukebox with multiple read/write transports. Such a product is normally configured as a single target, with each of its internal components configured as a unit.

One way to think about the entire addressing scheme is to think of targets as street addresses. In such a scheme, each building (target) has an address on the street (the SCSI bus). Most devices are like single–family homes, while more complex devices are more like small apartment buildings in which each dwelling has both a (common) street address and its own apartment number (see Figure 46).

Arbitration on the SCSI bus is done by the simple mechanism of granting the bus to the highest-numbered target that requests the bus. For this reason, host adapters are nearly always target 7. Normally, the best approach is to assign high-bandwidth peripherals to lower-number targets in order to ensure that slower devices such as tapes are not "starved" for access to the bus. This virtually never arises in commercial applications, but real-time applications may encounter subtle delays due to SCSI arbitration in casually configured systems.

Wide SCSI uses a 16–bit wide bus, permitting 16 target ids. As with "narrow" SCSI, the host adapter takes one of those targets, leaving a practical limit of 15 targets. Because narrow SCSI addresses are a proper subset of the addresses for wide SCSI, configuring both wide and narrow devices on a single bus is possible. For obvious reasons the narrow devices must be at the remote end of the bus. The host adapter is customarily configured as target 7 even on wide SCSI busses, in order to accommodate narrow devices, although the priority scheme remains the same. In practice this configuration has little relevance on wide SCSI, since wide busses rarely have many devices on them unless they are all disk devices.

7.2.3.3 Multi–Initiator SCSI

As noted above, most systems normally configure the host adapter of each bus as target 7, LUN 0, but this assignment is not fixed. If some peripheral insists upon being configured as target 7, reconfigure all of the host adapters in a system to another target address by setting the `scsi-initiator-id` variable to a suitable address in the system's PROM. One particularly interesting variant of this scheme is to configure a single SCSI bus with *two* host adapters, each on a different system (see Figure 47).

This arrangement, known as multi-initiator SCSI, is commonly used to provide two systems with access to the same disk drives. To be effective, this requires that the device drivers support the SCSI *reserve* and *release* commands, which permit hosts to allocate devices amongst themselves. Support for reserve and release was introduced in Solaris 2.4. Multi–initiator SCSI is usually used to create what is intended to be a highly–available pair of systems.

Unfortunately, this arrangement has some serious drawbacks. In particular, there is little isolation of system faults, so if one system panics or creates some sort of abnormal electrical circumstance on the bus, the result on the other system is undefined. In particular, no semantic provision is made for handling I/Os that are pending on the bus when one or more of the initiators reset the bus. Without transactional I/O semantics at the application level, the state of a multi-initiator disk set is undefined and could become inconsistent during such circumstances. (This ambiguity is in the SCSI–2 standard itself. It is expected to be addressed in the forthcoming SCSI–3 specification.) Another loophole in the SCSI–2 standard that makes multi–initiator unsuitable for high–availability configurations is that although the SCSI–2 standard defines reserve and release mechanisms to indicate ownership of devices, it does *not* define a standard way to break the reservation, should the owning system crash or otherwise become available. A less dignified but possibly more alarming issue is that few devices are tested in multi-initiator environments. Since each disk drive and SCSI host adapter now contains a computer real-time operating system, the interactions between components of a multi-initiator configuration are extremely complex.

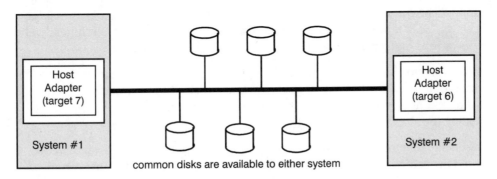

Figure 47. The most common use for multi-initiator SCSI configurations (but see text)

Multi–initiator SCSI can also be used to provide relatively high–speed system–to–system communications over short distances, and some peripheral computer vendors offer products such as vector processing accelerators connected to systems via SCSI. This type of master/slave relationship is much safer than the peer–to–peer relationship found in most multi–initiator configurations. This functionality normally requires that the host adapter be capable of operating in peer-to-peer mode; as of Solaris 2.5.1, only the esp host adapter driver supports this functionality.

> Caution: Multi-initiator SCSI configurations are *architecturally incompatible* with the use of host–based buffering products such as PrestoServe and NVSIMM. Multi–initiator SCSI is also incompatible with SCSI host adapters that cache data on–board. Any host-based cache stores data in a location that is inaccessible to a failover host. This statement is not true of NVRAM caches that are resident in shared disk resources, because they are accessible even in the event of a host failure.

7.2.3.4 SCSI Command Sets

In addition to defining new varieties of interconnection strategies and protocols, the SCSI–2 standard defined an extension to the original SCSI command set. Sun began implementing SCSI–2 commands in SunOS 4.1.1, and all Sun systems beginning with the SPARCstation 2— and in particular all current systems—meet or exceed SCSI–2 specifications.

The commands used by host systems to request specific actions of devices are defined in the SCSI standard. The commands defined in the standard are quite diverse and surprisingly high-level (e.g., "seek tape file 12" and "format disk"). No major system or peripheral vendor implements or uses much more than the most basic subset of commands.

One of the factors precluding more extensive implementation of SCSI commands is the consequent requirement for even more powerful embedded SCSI controllers: present embedded disk controllers usually consist of fairly dense circuitry that is already approximately the size of the host disk drive itself.

The sophistication of embedded disk controllers is already quite high. For example, the relatively old Seagate ST42400N 2.1 GB disk uses an embedded controller that contains 640 KB of RAM, 384 KB of ROM, and an Intel 80186 processor running at 16 MHz with hardware support for disk-specific operations. The 384 KB of ROM contains a complete real-time operating system of considerable sophistication. This complexity is especially relevant in multi–initiator SCSI configurations, where misunderstandings between different editions and models of firmware are the rule rather than the exception. To put this in perspective, this amount of code is similar to MS-DOS 5.0 combined with Lotus 1-2-3 Release 2. It's not possible to boot MS-DOS on the controller, but the familiarity of the specifications should convey how complex these devices have become—this configuration is almost exactly the same as the original IBM PC, less a video controller!

7.2.3.5 SCSI Bus Transactions

SCSI subsystems are so good at hiding complexity and implementation details that most users have no idea what actually happens on the SCSI bus. Although system configuration does not require an intimate understanding of SCSI bus transactions, an understanding of what transpires in a SCSI I/O provides insight on how SCSI busses should be configured.

Typical SCSI I/O transactions are actually accomplished with quite a number of operations on the bus. All of these operations consume SCSI bandwidth and residency time. When a target or host adapter wants to initiate a transfer on the bus [64], it must *arbitrate* for access. If multiple devices request control of the bus at the same time, control is granted to the unit (initiator or target) with the highest numbered address. Once control is granted, the initiator *selects* the target, followed by the transmission of the *command*. The target must now decide if it can service the request immediately. If it can, for example, if the command is a read and the requested data is found in the target's onboard cache, the data is transmitted with a *message-in* or *message-out*. More likely, the request cannot be immediately serviced (if a read misses the cache, or if the request is a write) and so the target *disconnects*. At some later time, the request can be serviced, and so the target *arbitrates* for the bus and *reselects* (reselection is usually known as reconnect). If data is to be transmitted, it is sent via message-in or message-out, and then the I/O completion status is transmitted with a *status*. Finally, the command is completed with a *disconnect*.

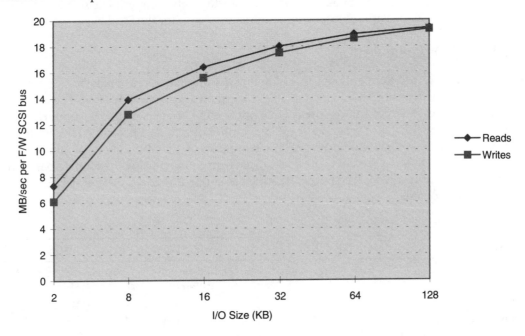

Figure 48. The impact of I/O size on SCSI bus throughput. The efficiency of the SCSI bus is low for 2 KB and 8 KB I/O sizes that are common in DBMS and file system I/O. This curve was generated using an ISP-1000 fast/wide host adapter and Seagate ST32550W disks, but is generally representative of SCSI configurations.

---

[64] In normal operation under Solaris the host adapter is involved in all transfers, but SCSI makes no such requirement and many real-time operating systems offer intra-SCSI transfers as an option.

All told, six to eight state changes occur on the bus, and the initiator and target are often processing during the various phases. The bus is busy except between a disconnect and arbitration for reselect. It takes 460 microseconds to transfer 8 KB of data on a fast/wide (20 MB/sec) bus, or 160 microseconds for the 2 KB blocks typically used by DBMS systems. These figures represent only the data phase, including about 50 microseconds of overhead. The other phases consume 120–170 microseconds per I/O, amounts that do not vary with I/O size. One reason that overhead is relatively high is that only user data is transmitted at the full SCSI burst speed; commands and status are always communicated using the async transfer mode. This arrangement results in the graph seen in Figure 48.

If the target controller were to hold the bus for an extra 10 microseconds per state change— about 50 instructions for typical 16 MHz target processors—the transaction time is lengthened by 60-80 microseconds. This is nine percent of the transfer time for 8 KB blocks and 35 percent of the transfer time for 2 KB! The efficiency of the target controller can have a very substantial impact on SCSI bus utilization. Unfortunately, no mechanism exists to measure this efficiency without extensive equipment to monitor the SCSI bus.

7.2.4 SCSI Optional Features

Many of SCSI's features are optional, meaning that the implementers of a device may choose to implement them or not to, or may implement them on a case–by–case basis. The host adapter probes each target and discovers what options the target is willing to support. Every target on a bus negotiates independently of every other device, so a host adapter with five targets can and often does end up with five different sets of communications parameters. The basic parameters required of all devices are asynchronous transfers, 8–bit data path, and no parity. Obviously, physical characteristics such as single–ended vs. differential signaling cannot be negotiated.

Table 30. SCSI optional features (see 7.2.6, *SCSI-3*)

Feature	SCSI–1	SCSI-2	SCSI–3
signaling	single–ended	single-ended or differential	single–ended, differential or low-voltage differential
command queuing	N/A	optional	optional
transfer clocking	async or sync	async or sync	async or sync
fast transfers	5 MHz	5 MHz or 10 MHz	5 MHz, 10 MHz or 20 MHz
transfer width	8–bit only	8-, 16- or 32-bit	8–, 16– or 32–bit
parity	N/A	optional	optional

7.2.4.1 Single–Ended vs. Differential Implementations

Two electrical signaling conventions are defined for SCSI. In one form, the host adapter transmits ground and data signals, and the "one" state is measured determined by the difference between the data and ground signals. This is known as *single–ended* SCSI and is the lowest-cost and by far the most common implementation. The alternative signal definition is called *differential* SCSI, in which the data signal is transmitted along with its inverse. The "one" or "zero" state is determined by comparing the signal with its inverse (see Figure 49).

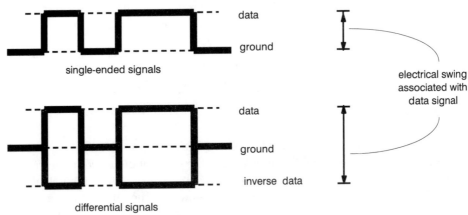

Figure 49. Single-ended vs. differential signaling. Differential signals swing farther, making it much easier to distinguish "0" from "1", especially in electrically noisy environments.

Although single–ended is less expensive to implement, it physically cannot carry signals as far. Synchronous single–ended implementations limit the physical length of the SCSI bus to six meters—three meters while operating in fast/narrow (10 MB/sec)mode. Single-ended implementations running at 20 MB/sec are limited to just 1.5 meters. Many low–cost implementations fail in this area, leading to unreliable configurations.

Differential implementations can carry SCSI-2 signals up to 25 meters. These distances include all of the signal path inside of each peripheral unit, most of the traces on the embedded SCSI controllers, and all the way from the host adapter to the terminator, along with all of the cabling that connects the peripherals. In addition, each pair of connectors that the signal must cross amounts to another foot or so of cable length, due to impedance and other electrical considerations. The impedance associated with most connector pairs also accounts for the equivalent of about half a meter. Most peripheral boxes have a surprising amount of cable inside. For all of these reasons and a variety of other arcane electrical trivia, three and even six meters often does not go as far as one would expect.

> Note: Exceeding these limitations results in a bus that performs unreliably or sporadically, especially when operated at or near the defined limits [65]. When the limitation is exceeded, the symptom is usually a stream of messages from the SCSI host adapter driver. The messages usually refer to an incomplete SCSI command, a data overrun, or a parity error.

Sometimes this manifests itself when probing the SCSI chain upon bootup or from the PROM (from the `probe-scsi` verb in a machine with Open Boot PROM). Usually when this happens, disk labels are listed as either corrupted or missing. The label probably is not missing from the disk; rather the SCSI subsystem cannot get the label data transferred to the host. Devices operating in synchronous mode are substantially more sensitive to bus length and impedance.

> Note: Single–ended and differential signals have *exactly* the same performance characteristics if other parts of the SCSI subsystem are the same.

7.2.4.2 Termination

Several kinds of terminators are available: passive, active, and regulated. Older Sun terminators (such as the very old DB50, as well as the original metal–casing micro–SCSI model) were passive or active, but not regulated. In these terminators, the voltage on each signal line was not controlled. The regulated terminators (which have the word "Regulated" embossed on them) are required for SCSI bus operation at 10 MB/sec. Regulated terminators use a small circuit in the terminator to control the electrical environment on the bus, minimizing noise. Failure to use regulated terminators in a fast SCSI environment leads to SCSI time-outs, data overruns, and retries. High performance requests become unreliable in noisy environments, especially as cable lengths increase. Regulated terminators are not necessary when differential signaling is in use, since noise is much less of a problem.

7.2.4.3 Synchronous and Asynchronous Data Transfer

Another difference between SCSI implementations is in the timing of data transfers. The standard defines two basic types of transfer: synchronous and asynchronous. These terms

---

[65] Solaris systems encounter impedance and termination limits somewhat more frequently than other operating systems because the SCSI subsystem normally requests maximum capabilities from the device. If the device negotiates for synchronous transfers, fast/wide mode, command queuing, and SCSI parity at maximum defined speed, they are precisely what Solaris uses for operating parameters. Some other operating systems (notably AIX and many DOS SCSI device drivers) request less than maximum capabilities in deference to the marginal nature of some SCSI devices. This limit should not be an issue with Sun-supplied devices, which are qualified to operate reliably at full capability.

refer to the mechanism by which the SCSI host adapter and its targets coordinate data transfers. Under the asynchronous discipline, data can be transmitted at an arbitrary time; the sender need not wait for a specific clock cycle to begin its transfer; the sender and receiver need not be in clock synchronization. Synchronous transfers may occur only at specific clock phases. The clock is either transmitted as part of the bus or is agreed upon by the host adapter and target when the target is first initialized. In the SCSI world, asynchronous transfers require that each byte transferred between the host adapter and the target be explicitly requested and acknowledged. This requirement imposes a practical limit on the maximum transfer speed to and from the host adapter.

While this approach is adequate for low-speed devices such as some tapes, WORM devices, and CD–ROMs (even for 12X drives that transfer at about 1.4 MB/sec), it is not very useful for high performance disks or many of the faster tape drives. Accordingly, most high speed devices resort to synchronous transfers. The host adapter negotiates transfer speeds with each target when the targets are set up. If for some reason a synchronous speed cannot be negotiated with a target (e.g., the target does not support synchronous transfers), the host adapter will fall back to asynchronous transfers[66].

7.2.4.4 Fast SCSI, Wide SCSI, and Fast/Wide SCSI

Vendors now implement most of the options defined by the SCSI–2 standard. In particular, the SCSI–2 standard includes the notions of *wide SCSI, fast SCSI, and fast/wide SCSI*. The SCSI–1 standard defines a peripheral bus with the addressing and transfer characteristics noted above, along with an 8-bit data bus, all carried on a 50-pin shielded cable. SCSI–1 limits transfer speeds to 5 MB/sec. Fast SCSI retains the 8-bit nature of the bus and so can use the same physical cabling as SCSI–1; it differs by permitting 10 MB/sec synchronous transfers. Wide SCSI doubles or quadruples the width of the data bus to 16- or 32 bits, permitting 10- or 20 MB/sec synchronous transfers. When combined with the fast option, 20 and 40 MB/sec transfers are possible.

However, since too few wires were in the now-traditional 50–pin cable, the SCSI committee chose to add a second cable (with 66 pins) to the configuration, known as the B-cable . The B-cable carries the additional data lines, as well as enough other signals to permit the use 32-bit wide SCSI transfers. Fortunately, fast/wide 16-bit SCSI is overwhelmingly implemented with a single 68–pin cable, rather than with a dual-cable arrangement.

Wide SCSI implementations also offer extended addressing, permitting up to 16 targets on a bus (including a host adapter). They permit many additional targets to be configured, increasing the flexibility of the SCSI subsystem. However, with 16 targets contending for the

---

[66] The current negotiated transfer speed between host adapter and devices can be obtained from "prtconf -v".

bus, utilization problems can be as bad on 20 MB/sec fast-and-wide SCSI as with eight targets on 10 MB/sec fast SCSI (see section 7.2.5, *SCSI Bus Utilization*).

Wide SCSI and fast/wide implementations are now common, and fast SCSI has become the minimum typical offering, even in PCs and workstations. Most of Sun's current Ultra–1 and all Ultra–2 workstations offer built–in fast/wide SCSI–2, although previous generation systems such as the SPARCstation 10 and SPARCstation 20 had built–in host adapters that implemented only fast SCSI.

7.2.4.5 SCSI Command Queuing

In the context of the original 1986 SCSI definition, performance and optimization were very much secondary issues. The target controllers required microprocessors that were quite expensive at the time, and the intended hosts were small and not mission–critical in nature. However, by the time the SCSI–2 specification was being drafted, performance and optimization had become far more important. Accordingly, SCSI–2 defined the fast and fast/wide transfer modes to improve raw performance. Optimization was addressed by the addition of *command queuing*, often called *tag queuing*. Sun first implemented command queuing in Solaris 2.1.

One of the obstacles to optimization in SCSI is the high degree of autonomy granted to devices in the SCSI environment and the resulting lack of optimization information. The only entity that has the device–specific information necessary to perform optimization is the target controller. Moreover, target controllers only have access to directly–attached devices. Performing global optimization across the entire subsystem is not possible, as was customary in earlier peripheral subsystems designed for high performance (e.g., IPI). The SCSI–1 standard aggravated this already difficult situation by permitting only a single command to be pending to each target. This eliminated any possibility of optimization, which is performed by acting upon the most advantageous outstanding request—but if only one request can be outstanding, no optimization can occur!

Under SCSI–2 command queuing, the target controller is able to accept multiple outstanding commands. The target may process and complete outstanding commands in any order, returning status and possibly data associated with each operation when it is available. A *tag* is added to each command (hence the term "tag queuing"), permitting each entity to associate the request and subsequent replies. In addition to giving the target controller the flexibility to choose the order of operation execution (for example, to minimize seek distance), command queuing also permits a target to begin execution of the next physical operation before acknowledging one that has completed.

To see how command queuing improves performance, consider a sequence of writes issued to a disk. This operation benefits from command queuing even when only a single command is queued. The target obtains one block from the host and issues the writes to the heads. While the mechanism is performing the write, a second write arrives and is placed in the queue (it is not acknowledged to the host since it is still resident in volatile memory). When the first write is completed, the heads begin work on the second write—before the status of the first one is transmitted. If command queuing were not in effect, the host would not even transmit the second write to the target until the first one is completed and acknowledged. Command queuing permits the two bus transactions to be overlapped with physical disk activity, in effect saving the time for both. For applications that require many small disk writes, command queuing provides a significant improvement—for example, about 15 percent on Sybase bulk loads.

The more traditional method of optimization is the selection of the optimal request from all requests in the queue. For example, if the queue contains requests for cylinders 540, 32, 212, and 1720, the controller might choose to service these in the order 1720, 540, 212, 32 if the disk arm is already positioned near cylinder 1720. This tactic, known as the "elevator" algorithm, is not successful in practice because command queuing requires a relatively full queue of pending requests to each target before it has very much impact. If only one or two requests are in the queue, extensive reordering is impossible, so this method benefits systems that are under heavy I/O load. Unfortunately, command queuing is most effective when the disk is heavily loaded, but long queues normally result in very long response times (see section 7.6.2.1, *Reducing Disk Utilization)*, and the configuration is best improved by reducing the utilization rather than by optimizing within the longer queue Command queuing provides only minor improvements in I/O throughput for the single–threaded tasks commonly found in workstations.

Although it does not solve the entire optimization problem, SCSI command queuing does make devices somewhat more tolerant of excessive SCSI bus utilization than devices that do not offer this support. Non–queuing devices permit only a single outstanding command, so they must transmit the results of the current command before obtaining the next command and beginning to execute it. When the target supports queuing, it maintains a list of pending commands in its internal memory. When a command is completed, the next command is known and can be initiated, even before the bus is available to obtain new commands or transmit results from completed commands.

7.2.5 SCSI Bus Utilization

Traditional recommendations for optimum performance suggest that no disk string should be utilized more than about 40 percent of the time. Such recommendations are based on extensive experience with mainframe disk structures, which have very different architecture. In particular, most older mainframe disk subsystems have no caching at the disk, therefore the read/write head must have access to the string or disk controller to perform *any* transfer at all. If the string is busy when the data flies under the head, the system must wait for the next opportunity to do the I/O—necessarily at least 8.3 milliseconds later (on a 7,200 rpm disk), an eternity as far as computers are concerned. This timing disaster is infamous in the mainframe world as an "RPS miss"—a rotational position sense miss. Because SCSI targets always have local caches, internal transfer is decoupled from SCSI bus transfer, permitting *much* higher bus utilization on SCSI than on other I/O busses, such as typical unbuffered IPI (see *IPI* later in this chapter, and Figure 57 and Figure 58 on page 309 in particular).

A crucial configuration question involves the capacity of a SCSI bus to carry commands and data. There is no fixed answer to this question, but several categories can be identified. For some of these categories, the answers are quite clear. Since a disk drive is capable of delivering in excess of 6 MB/sec, attempting to drive five or more such devices on a single fast/wide SCSI bus clearly will not permit all of the devices to deliver full performance.

7.2.5.1 SCSI Bus Throughput—Sequential Disk Access

SCSI is a protocol that has relatively high overhead—recall that a typical I/O requires eight state changes on the SCSI bus. Although frequently overlooked, each of the states consumes some bus time, and in some cases can be a significant issue. For small I/O sizes, SCSI overhead approaches 60 percent! Consider Figure 50, which depicts how performance of the bus increases as more and more disk drives are activated on the bus. The bus in use is a fast/wide SCSI-2 with twelve 7,200 rpm disks; all targets negotiate for the full 20 MB/sec burst transfer speed.

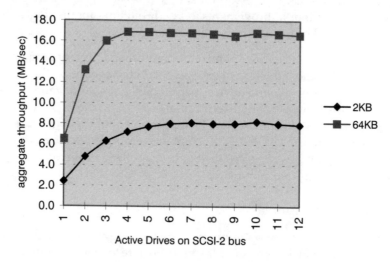

Figure 50. Sequential throughput as drives are added to a fast/wide SCSI bus

The graphs clearly show that for sequential I/O, seek and rotation times are not significant, and bus utilization (and contention) considerations are at issue. Of special interest is the graph for 2 KB I/Os, indicated by the dashed line. Bus throughput rises linearly until the data rate reaches about 8 MB/sec, and no additional performance results beyond five or six disks. This fact is surprising to most users, because the capacity of a fast/wide SCSI–2 bus is 20 MB/sec. The difference is accounted for by SCSI command overhead. The 8 MB/sec rate represents about 4,100 I/O operations/sec on the bus, about the maximum available on a 20 MB/sec bus when using such small and relatively inefficient commands (see section 7.2.3.5, *SCSI Bus Transactions*).

Nonetheless, the bus is fully capable of delivering more data, as the solid line shows. These curves reach almost 18 MB/sec by making much more efficient use of the bus—this is achieved by transferring 64 KB per I/O, resulting in 95 percent fewer commands issued on the bus. Somewhat higher utilization can be attained by using even larger I/O sizes, but most disk drives presently can handle no more than 64 KB–128 KB in a single I/O request.

SCSI command overhead limits the throughput of a SCSI bus under sequential I/O conditions, but the graphs also show what is *not* a problem. Although performance does not increase as additional drives are activated on the bus, neither does performance suffer from activating more than the optimal number of drives.

⇒ Plan data layout so that only 4-8 disks per fast/wide or fast-20 SCSI bus are fully active in sequential access mode, depending on average I/O size. Large (64 KB) I/O sizes saturate the bus with as few as four drives, whereas eight drives can be handled if I/O sizes are only 2 KB. Fast-40 busses can handle 8-16 drives.

⇒ Expect throughput of a bus to be substantially lower than the rated burst speed for most applications.

⇒ For sizing and configuration purposes, a disk array connecting a number of disk drives is equivalent to having the disk drives directly connected to the host-connected bus.

7.2.5.2 SCSI Bus Throughput—Random Disk Access

As is usual when disk I/O is concerned, random access conditions are completely different from sequential access conditions. Consider Figure 51, which is similar to Figure 50, except that the I/O is completely randomized, meaning that the disks must seek before every I/O. Under these circumstances, the throughput of a single disk drops from over 6 MB/sec to 210 KB/sec (105 x 2 KB I/Os per second per drive). Because the target controllers are able to manipulate the disk arms and platters while disconnected from the bus, throughput scales *very* linearly—99 percent—all the way to the addressing limit of the fast/wide bus, 15 targets. Under fully random conditions, the throughput of the SCSI bus is not an issue. Of course, 1,800 I/O ops/sec 2 KB each moves only 3.6 MB/sec, so the fact that the bus does not limit throughput is to be expected.

In this situation, the disks themselves are the limiting factor—all 15 disks are running at full utilization, and the 20 MB/sec bus is only about 45 percent utilized. The fast/wide bus can handle 30-35 disks under these conditions, even if *all* of the drives are fully busy. This situation occurs only rarely, and as a practical matter, a single fast/wide bus is usually capable of handling two or three disk arrays and 70-90 drives. Fast-40 busses can handle even more (see 7.2.6, *SCSI-3*, later in this chapter).

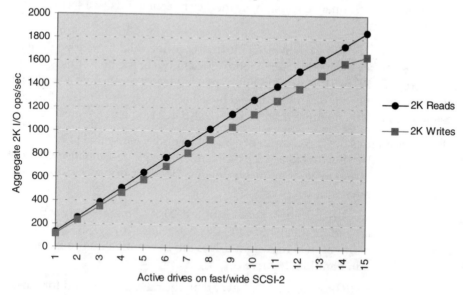

Figure 51. Scalability of random access I/O, as disks are added to the SCSI bus. The I/Os are 2 KB and fully random. Disks are Seagate ST32550W 7,200 rpm 2 GB models on a Sun SWIS/S host adapter.

⇒ If data access is fully random, performance does not limit the number of fully active drives that can be configured on a SCSI bus. As many as 70-90 drives can be configured via multiple disk arrays on a single SCSI bus.

⇒ Under random access conditions, configure one or two disk arrays on a single fast/wide or fast-20 bus. Up to four disk arrays can be configured on a fast-40 bus.

7.2.5.3 SCSI Bus Throughput—Tape Drives

Disk drives represent one type of SCSI bus configuration issue. Tape drives present a different type of problem, although the basic issues are the same as with disks. Tapes are much slower than disks, yet are normally configured on the same SCSI busses. With typical tapes offering data transfer rates of 0.5–1.5 MB/sec, they are much slower devices than disks, so expecting to configure one bus with far more 1 MB/sec tapes than 6 MB/sec disks is reasonable. Unfortunately, this is not the case. The primary issue is that because most tape drives are not considered "high–performance" devices, they do not select the highest available burst transfer speeds, resulting in much higher bus utilization than one might expect.

The Exabyte EXB–8505XL is representative of this class of devices. It transfers to tape at about 550 KB/sec; it selects standard synchronous SCSI transfers, meaning burst transfer speeds of 5 MB/sec. Figure 52 shows a graph similar to that seen for sequential disk access. Because the drive uses 5 MB/sec burst transfers, the total capacity of the bus is 5 MB/sec, even if the host adapter is capable of more throughput (in this case, the host adapter is fast/wide SCSI–2, capable of 20 MB/sec).

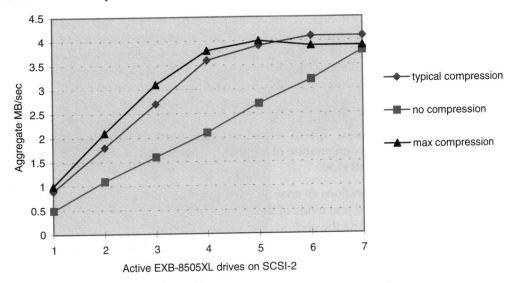

Figure 52. SCSI bus throughput as a function of active tape drives. Tapes are Exabyte EXB-8505XL, 8 mm drives with burst speed of 5 MB/sec.

The three curves correspond to different compression modes available on this drive. The filled–circle graph shows bus throughput resulting from transferring data to the drive without compression. The low data rate permits the bus to handle as many drives as can be configured (the drives do not support wide addressing). However, with maximum realistic compression enabled, throughput rises much more rapidly, and the 5 MB/sec bus becomes a limit with just four active drives (refer to *Compression* in section 8.1.3 for further discussion). Despite the ability of the host adapter and bus to operate at 20 MB/sec, the fact that the devices choose to operate in a different mode results in considerably higher bus utilization than might otherwise be expected—four or five drives moving a total of 4 MB/sec completely saturates a "20 MB/sec" bus!

7.2.5.4 Mixing Different Speed SCSI Devices

One very common misunderstanding about SCSI devices is how faster devices are—and are not—affected by slower devices configured on the same SCSI bus. Usually this question arises when a new fast SCSI disk is to be configured on the same SCSI bus as an older (probably not as fast) disk. The question is equally applicable to all SCSI configurations, such as mixing disks and tapes or mixing disks and CDROMs. This is most commonly expressed as a question such as "If I have a fast disk and a slow disk, do transfers happen at fast speeds or slow speeds?" The answer, of course, is a definitive "Yes!"

The SCSI standard is carefully defined so that management of an individual device is as independent as possible of its environment. In particular, it includes as much immunity from other devices residing on the SCSI bus as possible. The host adapter negotiates an appropriate burst transfer speed and transfer mode individually with each device on its bus. The bus is driven at the limits of the capability of each device. Given a bus with a 10 MB/sec fast synchronous disk, a 3.2 MB/sec synchronous disk, and a 250 KB/sec asynchronous tape drive, transfers between host adapter and target controller are done at each of these

"____" ___fers to the SCSI burst speed, rather than actual

arbitrary combinations of devices on a SCSI bus

In particular, the utilization of the bus varies

he transfer, and slow devices may monopolize

ance of other devices. The preceding discussion

pabilities of various targets can affect overall

tion of slower active devices *does* have an

figured on the same bus. In the example above,

the tape drive. Given the asynchronous transfer

ta to the tape will take a full quarter of a second.

n, even ignoring the SCSI overhead associated

ives transfer at approximately 400 KB/sec using

specially those which are "not performance—

bus utilization. In the final analysis, slower

o not select high enough burst transfer speeds to

, though, have no effect on other peripherals

wishing to use the bus.

Bus utilization considerations are not severe on workstations, where nearly all I/O is directly associated with a single user. However, on servers, bus utilization can play a large role, especially when designing backup strategies. Most tape drives are much slower than disks, and many of them use the less efficient asynchronous SCSI protocol, resulting in very high bus utilization. This shortcoming is compounded by the fact that the firmware in many of the lower-speed devices is not highly optimized, resulting in substantial "invisible" SCSI utilization overhead. When many devices are present in the system, segregate low-speed devices onto a private SCSI bus in order to maintain system-wide throughput.

7.2.6 SCSI-3

A new SCSI–3 standard is now being drafted, with prospects for adoption and commercial implementation in 1996 or later. SCSI–3 will address most of the shortcomings in SCSI–2, and add many new options, including serial transfer modes to improve transfer speed by eliminating skew, optical media to permit much longer cable runs, and packetized communication for processor–to–processor exchange. Although SCSI–2 is nearly 100 percent upward compatible with SCSI–1, full SCSI–3 is not completely compatible with existing SCSI–2 implementations due to the aggressive and hardware-oriented nature of many of the proposed extensions. Fortunately, software—especially at a user- or DBMS level—will not be affected.

Some of the less aggressive and more compatible of the proposed SCSI–3 features are already being implemented by vendors. For example, Sun's SPARCstorage Array uses SCSI–3 commands transmitted on FibreChannel media. The FibreChannel media itself is now part of the SCSI-3 standard group.

Probably the most common SCSI-3 feature being implemented today is faster burst transfers. SCSI-3 provides for doubling the synchronous transfer speed, to 20 MB/sec on an 8-bit bus, known as *fast-20*. When combined with 16-bit or 32-bit data widths, copper SCSI-3 is capable of 40 MB/sec and 80 MB/sec transfers. A number of vendors are now offering fast-20 and fast-20/wide host adapters and disk array controllers, and a few fast-20 disks are coming onto the market. SCSI-3 also defines a new electrical standard called *low-voltage differential* signaling, which enables higher data transfer rates in a low-cost implementation. Doubling the transfer rate from 20 MB/sec to 40 MB/sec imposes a further distance restriction on cabling. Differential fast-40 implementations can be cabled up to 12.5 meters, compared with 25 meters for fast/wide. Single-ended fast-20 implementations are limited to 1.5 meters.

SCSI-3 is a *very* large standards effort, encompassing more than 20 different technologies and command sets. The major components are shown in Figure 53.

7.3 FibreChannel

SCSI is by far the most common peripheral interconnect today, although others are in common use. The primary disk interconnect used by Sun today is FibreChannel (FC), an ANSI standard (ANSI X3T9.3) that defines a SCSI-like command set but which is carried via a fiber optic connection instead of copper wires. Sun's SPARCstorage Array uses a FibreChannel connection to carry standard SCSI-2 commands and data. Although FibreChannel is an ANSI standard, it has been brought under the SCSI-3 umbrella. Future

FC standards will be generated as a subset of the SCSI-3 specification, which includes a bewildering variety of options, for command sets, interconnect media, and interoperability.

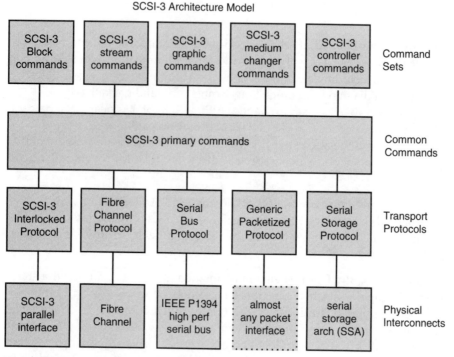

Figure 53. The ambitious SCSI-3 road map published by ANSI

7.3.1 FibreChannel Topologies

The familiar SCSI-2 really has only one or two ways to connect: a tree of peripherals is connected to a host. Alternatively, the peripheral tree is connected to two hosts via some sort of multi-initiator arrangement. FibreChannel has *three* very different topology options:

- point-to-point, in which a device connects to exactly one other device;

- arbitrated loop (normally abbreviated FC-AL), in which the peripherals and one or more hosts are connected together in a ring topology using many point-to-point links; FC-AL is architecturally similar to a full-duplex FDDI;

- fabric, in which switches and hubs are used to create an arbitrarily complex network, possibly including multiple paths from a host to a peripheral.

These topologies are shown in Figure 54.

FibreChannel devices use a flat, universal addressing structure in which every device is assigned a unique address, known as the *world wide name (WWN)*. The WWN must be unique in the FC topology; because FibreChannel domains can potentially be connected into arbitrary fabrics, the usual practice is to assign completely unique WWNs to devices, in much the same way that Ethernet addresses are assigned uniquely.

The SPARCstorage Array uses the simplest of these options, a point-to-point link that connects a disk array controller to one or two hosts. The controller connects to a host via a point-to-point link using a two-strand fiber cable. FibreChannel is a full-duplex medium, requiring a strand for each direction. The SPARCstorage Array can be connected to two hosts through the simple expedient of having two (independent) FC interfaces. Expanding the point-to-point mechanism into a more complex network is impossible without resorting to hubs and switches and the use of a fabric.

7.3.2 FibreChannel Transfer Specifications

The FC standard defines several classes of signal, corresponding to different capabilities when combined with actual fiber connectors. Each signal type uses a different type of laser, so the varieties are *not* interchangeable. The classes are normally described in terms of their data speed, or 25 MB/sec, 50 MB/sec, and 100 MB/sec. Because FC is a full-duplex standard, transferring between two devices at double these speeds is theoretically possible, although in practice few devices are capable of handling this much data. Although Sun has fielded over 20,000 SPARCstorage Arrays using FC-25, the industry as a whole deferred acceptance of FibreChannel until the arrival of FC-100 parts. The market seems to have bypassed FC-50 completely. A few vendors are now delivering products capable of FC-100 interoperability, but little volume has been achieved to date (mid 1996). However, every major storage vendor is planning FC-100 products in late 1996 or early 1997, and a safe bet is that high-end storage will be dominated by FC-100 products by 1998.

7.3.3 FibreChannel Distance Capability

One of the most useful capabilities of the FC medium is that its lasers are capable of transmitting signals reliably over distances that are far in excess of those attainable using standard copper SCSI technology. Whereas SCSI-2 is limited to six meters in single-ended implementations and 25 meters using differential transceivers, FibreChannel uses 50 micron multimode fiber capable of 2 km transmission distance, although Sun itself offers cable lengths only up to 15 meters. The FC standard permits distances up to 10 km.

One of the most useful capabilities made possible by FibreChannel is the ability to geographically disburse storage across much wider distances than with other technologies. With a practical cabling distance of several kilometers, it is possible to mirror data onto two different disk arrays located on opposite ends of a campus, or even nearby in a metropolitan area. Because the FC connection operates at full disk subsystem speed, disaster recovery can be simplified without loss of performance. This capability is similar to the those offered by a few mainframe disk vendors, with one major exception: the FC operates at full FC speeds with negligible transmission latency, whereas the wide-area disk mirroring available on some mainframe storage units is subject to significant delays due to wide-area networking latency. For bandwidth-sensitive applications, FC offers full 25 MB/sec or 100 MB/sec transfer rates, compared to a maximum of 5 MB/sec for T3-based WAN mirroring.

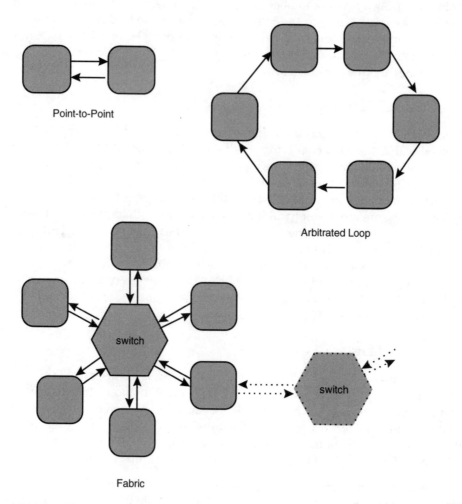

Figure 54. FibreChannel topologies. The SPARCstorage Array currently uses the point-to-point topology.

7.3.4 The Sun FC-25 Implementation

The SPARCstorage Array uses a standard FC-25 link to connect its array controller to the host. Host systems connect to the FC via a FC host adapter, similar in purpose to a SCSI host adapter. The adapter is a logical intersection between the system's I/O bus (SBus) and the FC peripheral bus. Each host adapter has two *optical link modules*, permitting the host adapter to interface to two independent FC busses. When configured with two busses, both are managed by a single interface chip (the serial optical coupler, or SOC).

7.3.4.1 I/O Latency and Queuing Considerations

Although the burst transfer speed of the FC is 25 MB/sec, the existing implementation is in practice not capable of sustaining user data transfers at this speed. The obstacle is not so much the capability of the interface chip to move data, but rather a limit to the number of pending commands that can be managed by the SOC. Each SOC can handle at most 255 pending I/O commands, which can occasionally become a limitation for single FC interfaces and which normally limits throughput on FC host adapters using two ports. Forecasting how much I/O this represents is difficult, because throughput is dependent upon both the number *and latency* of the pending commands.

Consider an I/O load consisting of 2 KB sequential transfers (a load typical of tablescans on a Sybase System 10 DBMS). If the average latency of the I/O request is 2 ms—normal for this workload with a 7,200 rpm disk drive—queuing theory tells us that the SOC is capable of handling approximately 3,600 I/Os per second. However, when the I/O size is 8 KB and the workload consists of random access I/Os heavily concentrated on relatively few disk drives, so that the average I/O latency is 240 ms, the SOC is only capable of about 1,900 I/Os per second. In neither case is the fiber itself limiting the transfer capability. Neither figure represents an impressive throughput level: 3,600 I/Os 2 KB each is about 7 MB/sec, while 1,900 I/Os per second represents about double that throughput.

7.3.4.2 Host Adapter Capabilities

These cases do not show the full capability of the FC host adapter, though. In the first case, the throughput is restricted by the I/O size; 2 KB means that relatively little data is moved per request. The second case shows what happens when the I/O service time is driven into borderline conditions. Both are relatively extreme conditions, although both do occur in normal usage. More typically, the service time is much lower—10 ms-25 ms—while the I/O size is normally larger, typically 8 KB and as large as 128 KB. In these circumstances, the FC is capable of far higher transfer rates. Using either 8 KB or 64 KB I/O sizes, sequential transfers can be driven across the FC at maximum rates in excess of 22 MB/sec, primarily limited by the ability of the SPARCstorage Array controller, rather than the FC implementation. Attaining 2,600 I/Os per second in random access mode is easily possible with either 2 KB or 8 KB I/Os. In light of these realities, the second port on each FC host adapter is *primarily* useful for archival storage connectivity.

Table 31. I/O capability of FC-25 ASIC implementation

	Random Access, I/O Operations/sec	Sequential Throughput, MB/sec
single FC interface, one SOC	3,330 I/O ops/sec	19.7 MB/sec
dual FC interface, one SOC	3,900 I/O ops/sec	26.5 MB/sec

⇒ Configure the second FibreChannel port on any FC host adapter primarily for low-use applications, such as archival storage.

7.4 Intelligent Peripheral Interface (IPI–2 and IPI–3)

In addition to SCSI, the committees defined a mass storage organization known as the Intelligent Peripheral Interface (IPI, ISO 8318-3). IPI and SCSI were regarded as complementary standards, with IPI being the high–performance (and higher-cost) system designed for minicomputers and mainframes, and SCSI intended for PCs and small systems. It is now clear that IPI has no future, as SCSI and FibreChannel have usurped the high–end market. The IPI discussion that follows is intended as background material for users who have an installed base of IPI systems.

Both IPI and SCSI define physical standards for connectors, cabling and the like, as well as electrical protocols and both device-level and subsystem-level command sets. Whereas SCSI is intended to provide an inexpensive, flexible mechanism for interconnecting a relatively small number of devices of quite diverse type, IPI is explicitly intended to address the needs of high-performance, high-capacity disk subsystems such as those found in current mainframes and high-end minicomputers. Other devices may be accommodated—but only if they essentially appear to be disk devices, such as "solid-state" semiconductor disks.

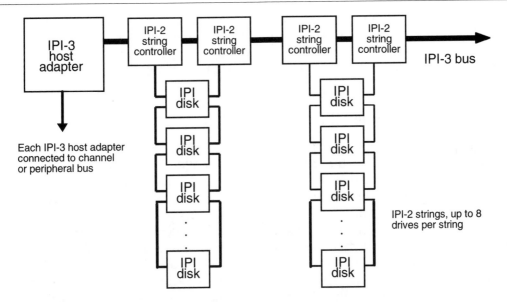

Figure 55. The idealized IPI storage hierarchy

7.4.1 IPI Design Goals

As its name indicates, the IPI standard is designed to permit the application of processing power to take advantage of as much optimization as possible, resulting in the highest possible performance. Toward that end, global optimization information is made available to the highest levels of processing. The idealized IPI model is defined in four levels:

- Level 3: I/O Channel Protocols, which define logical-level commands, command queuing and stacking rules, buffering mechanisms, timing-independent transfer characteristics, and logical volumes and addressing.

- Level 2: Disk String Protocols, defining device-specific commands, timing, physical device, and volume addressing;

- Level 1: Primitive transfer details, including the bus protocols;

- Level 0: Mechanical and electrical, which define the cables, connectors, and low–level electrical details.

Like SCSI commands, IPI commands defined in the channel protocol are quite high-level; they are intended to provide a mechanism for widely distributing I/O processing in a very complex, extensive computer system. On the other hand, the commands defined in the string protocol are quite low-level, as they are intended to control a completely unintelligent disk device.

7.4.1.1 Fully Implemented IPI

In a fully implemented IPI system, a number of IPI–3 host adapters connect to the main system busses (in a Sun system, they are connected to the VME backplane bus). Unlike the SCSI host adapter, which is essentially a buffered data portal, an IPI–3 host adapter is normally a complete I/O computer (the IPI standard refers to these as *facilities*). Each facility is responsible for the management of a number of logical disk strings. Each disk string consists of one to eight disk drives, interfaced to the host adapter by an IPI–2 string controller. The string controllers are connected to the host adapter via a high-speed IPI–3 bus, with a maximum of sixteen strings per bus. Like the IPI host adapter, the string controller is an intelligent device, responsible for optimizing access along its string. Both the IPI–3 bus and the IPI–2 string reflect the massive facilities envisioned for IPI installations: both permit cable runs of up to 50 meters.

Sophisticated IPI implementations permit a disk drive to be connected to multiple strings, via additional ports. Multiported disks may be used either for connection to multiple string controllers in a single system[67], for connection to string controllers in another system, or both. When two ports on each drive are connected to a single system, maximum (16) string controllers are placed on each IPI–3 bus, and four IPI–3 host adapters can connect 256 drives. The idealized IPI storage hierarchy is shown in Figure 55.

7.4.1.2 Intelligence in the IPI Subsystem

All of the intelligence in an IPI subsystem is vested in the host adapter and in the string controller. Even relatively primitive operations such as bad-block mapping must be performed by the string controller. The disk drives themselves have no intelligence, nor for the most part do they possess local caches. As a result, an IPI disk must have a variety of conditions satisfied in order to perform a data transfer:

- the read/write head must be positioned over the correct cylinder,
- the data must be about to rotate under the head,
- the requesting string must be free, and

---

[67] Some vendors offer four or even eight ports on various models of disk drive. Some implementations even bind several platter/head assemblies together into a logical "disk pack," addressed as a single entity. These options are, of course, quite expensive.

- the string controller must have a free buffer.

Because the bus is a shared resource that is required for virtually any operation to be initiated or completed, contention for the bus is a *much* greater problem under IPI than for SCSI. For this reason, no more than three disks should be configured onto a single IPI–2 bus. Contention becomes a severe problem when the full eight disks are configured on one bus (see section 7.4.2.1, *Disk Configuration with the ISP–80*).

7.4.1.3 Optimization

In order to provide sufficient information for the string controller to sensibly organize a queue of requests, IPI disks normally provide the rotational position of their platters and the radial position of the read/write head(s) to the string controllers. Each string controller then has enough information to sort a series of disk requests. Because so many conditions must be satisfied for a transfer to occur, effective use of this information is vital to high performance.

Sometimes a string controller may be faced with a choice of obtaining data from one of two drives on its string that are about to become ready to transfer. In these circumstances, an IPI–3 channel may be able to route new requests to an alternate string if the drive in question is connected to multiple strings. A channel can even transfer an existing request from one string to another (even if the request is the next one the queue, satisfying all of the transfer criteria could take as long as 8-25 ms, even with very fast disk drives). By maintaining state information about each string, and by possibly executing parts of the host system's operating system, the IPI channel can substantially offload the main processors and simultaneously optimize access to the disks.

7.4.2 The Sun IPI Implementation

Sun's IPI implementation is considerably less extensive than the fully–implemented standard. The IPI–3 facility is not physically implemented. Instead, each string controller is treated as being paired to exactly one host adapter, and the facility is emulated (trivially) by a device driver without associated hardware. The IPI–2 strings are directly connected to the main system backbone bus (VME). Because each string is connected to only one host adapter, and because Solaris has no facilities for managing or optimizing access to a single drive by multiple strings, the second port on present IPI disks is useful only for connection to a second system. The simplified Sun IPI implementation appears in Figure 56.

IPI subsystems, especially the full-blown implementations, are designed to perform best in situations where massive loads cause fairly long queues to form for each I/O device. If requests form queues that are short or non-existent, the intelligence of the various devices in the IPI hierarchy is largely wasted. IPI excels in heavily loaded servers where I/O requests are the primary work. IPI is generally not appropriate in a workstation, where a single user is unlikely to generate sufficient load for the IPI processors to perform much optimization. In a workstation, the usual case is to have one or two active processes, only one of which generates substantial disk activity. Furthermore, most processes that generate disk activity do so one at a time, waiting for the current request to complete before issuing another. In such a circumstance, creating long queues is difficult.

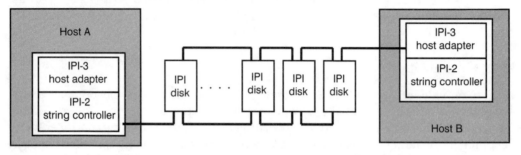

Figure 56. The (drastically simplified) Sun IPI implementation. Each host permits only single-ported access; the second port on each drive is available for attachment to a second host.

7.4.2.1 Disk Configuration Using the ISP-80

The Sun ISP-80 string controller implements a 6 MB/sec IPI–2 bus (comparable to a 5 MB/sec SCSI-2 bus). In serial transfer mode, the 911 MB disk transfers at 6 MB/sec, while the 1.3 GB IPI disk transfers at up to 4.5 MB/sec. Consequently only one fully active disk sho uld be configured no more than one per string when the disk access pattern is sequential! In practice, the performance is even more restricted, as shown in Figure 58. The older 1.0 GB disk transfers at only 3.0 MB/sec; at most two active 1.0 GB disks should be configured on a string. Under random access, these drives are approximately equivalent. Up to four fully active disks can be accommodated on a single bus, although scalability does not approach linearity. Although the ISP–80 implements rotational position sensing, the lack of buffering on the drives results in substantial lost performance as the bus nears saturation (Figure 58).

7.4.2.2 Genroco S224 SBus IPI–2 String Controller

The Genroco S224 is a single–wide SBus IPI–2 string controller implementing approximately the same organization as the Sun ISP-80 VME controller. The advantage of this board is that it is in the much smaller and less expensive SBus form factor, permitting SBus–only systems such as the SPARCcenter 2000 to operate with the IPI disks. For customers who have a significant installed base of IPI drives, for example, connected to SPARCserver 470s, SPARCserver 490s, and SPARCserver 690s, the S224 offers the opportunity to upgrade to a much more capable platform without requiring replacement of often-significant banks of IPI mass storage. In addition, the disk drive manufacturers are still producing the highest performance disk drives with IPI interfaces. For example, the 2.9 GB Seagate ST43200K offers 5.25″ disk drives with dual read/write heads. Unlike typical commodity disks, these drives can activate two read/write heads simultaneously, permitting the arm to read from two disk surfaces. The result is internal transfer rates approximately double the speed of commodity SCSI drives. The Seagate drives offer serial transfer speeds of 9 MB/sec. These are of little or no value in a random access environment, but for data-intensive NFS servers and DBMS servers that are dominated by long serial operations, the much higher serial transfer rates can be useful.

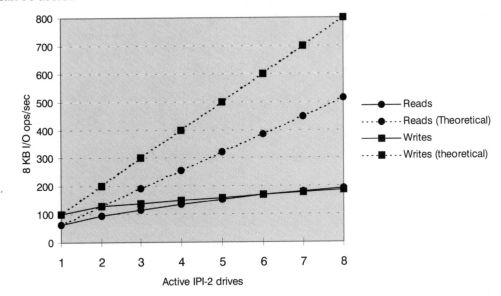

Figure 57. Throughput of an IPI-2 string under random access conditions. The unbuffered IPI-2 drives do not scale nearly as well as SCSI-2, seen in Figure 50 (page 294).

The burst transfer speed of the IPI–2 bus is 24 MB/sec, permitting throughput comparable to that of a fast SCSI–2 bus when using typical disks such as the Seagate 1.3 GB Elite-1 and 2.1 GB Elite-2. The S224 is considerably more efficient with CPU usage than the DSBE/S and FSBE/S interfaces, because it requires only one interrupt per I/O operation, compared to one per SCSI phase state change. The S224 is comparable in efficiency to the DWI/S interface, which requires slightly less than one interrupt per I/O operation (the average is less than one because more than one I/O completion message can be piggybacked on a single interrupt).

Unlike previous generations of IPI disks, the Seagate Elite-3 drives have onboard buffers, permitting significantly higher IPI bus utilization than the Sun 1.3 GB IPI disks. In serial access environments, at most four fully active drives are recommended because the very high throughput offered by the drives is close to the throughput available on the shared IPI–2 bus. In random-access environments, the full eight disks can be configured per string if buffered drives are used.

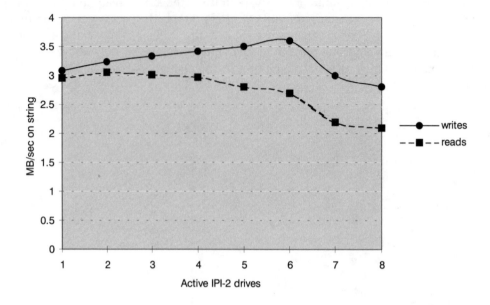

Figure 58. Throughput of an IPI-2 string under sequential access conditions. Individual drives transfer at 4.5 MB/sec. Compare with Figure 50 (page 294).

7.5 Berkeley RAID Concepts

Since the mid-1980s, disk drive manufacturers have concentrated primarily on dramatically decreasing the cost of storage. The result has been a remarkable improvement in storage density and especially in cost per unit of storage. A current disk array such as the SPARCstorage Array contains 63 GB of storage space, packed into about half the volume of a single 575 MB "SuperEagle" disk drive of 1987, and cost of storage has dropped from over $39/MB to considerably less than $1/MB.

Although this decrease certainly has made storage much more affordable and practical, the emphasis on storage density has resulted in two consequent configuration problems. First, because a single disk mechanism now controls as much as 9 GB, the reliability of disk mechanisms becomes much more important. The failure of a disk results in the inaccessibility of 25 times as much data, but disk drive reliability has increased only about ten times in the same time period (from about 75K hours to more than 800K hours).

In addition, the performance of disk drives has increased by a factor of only about three in most dimensions, as shown in Table 32. By comparison, processors have improved by approximately two orders of magnitude in the same period of time. As a result, the performance of disk subsystems has been placed at an even greater premium than before, and this trend will likely continue for the foreseeable future.

Table 32. Historical comparison of disk drives

Dimension	Fujitsu "SuperEagle" 575 MB (1987)	Seagate "Barracuda–2" 2.1 GB (1995)	Improvement
Burst transfer speed	2.4 MB/sec	7.1 MB/sec	2.9x
Average seek time	24 ms	8.5 ms	2.8x
Rotational latency	8.3 ms (3,600 rpm)	4.2 ms (7,200 rpm)	2.0x
MTBF	75,000 hrs	500,000 hrs	6.6x
Volume	~8,000 cubic inches	~17 cubic inches	~450x (!)
Storage capacity	575 MB	2,100 MB	3.6x
Price	~$23,000	$1,020	22.5x

To combat both of these problems, researchers at Berkeley began experimenting with ways of combining commodity disk drives in organizations designed to enhance both reliability and performance. The resulting research has come to be known as "RAID," an acronym for *Redundant Array of Independent Disks*.

The original Berkeley papers defined six types of RAID organizations, numbered 0 through 5. The basic strategy of RAID organization is simply "divide and conquer": use lots of little disks in place of one very big one. These organizations have become the basis for most modern disk subsystems, although some enhancements have been advanced over the years. The basic characteristics of the various Berkeley RAID organizations are shown in Table 33.

One thing to keep in mind about RAID: there are no free lunches. Some RAID organizations are fast, some are inexpensive, and some are safe. None deliver more than two of the three.

Table 33. Quick summary of RAID levels

RAID Level	Strengths	Weaknesses
RAID–0 (striping)	Fast, simple	Subject to member failure
RAID–1 (mirroring)	Fast, simple	Doubles storage cost, not as manageable as RAID–10
RAID–10 (0+1 or 1+0)	Fastest RAID, most resilient against member failure, esp. RAID–1+0	Requires many member disks; most expensive RAID in terms of disk drives
RAID–2	Protects storage using Hamming codes instead of XOR functions	Not very flexible in practice
RAID–3	Protects storage using parity scheme, fast	Slow random access, hard to implement

Table 33. Quick summary of RAID levels

RAID Level	Strengths	Weaknesses
	sequential access	with SCSI member disks, bottlenecks on parity disk
RAID–4	Sequential access OK, random reads OK	Writes bottleneck on parity disk
RAID–5	Good random access, sequential access good only if heavily cached; least expensive protected storage	Writes can be *very* slow
RAID–6	Safer than RAID-5	Twice the overhead of RAID–5, writes are even slower

7.5.1 Terminology

Three terms specific to reliability are commonly used in the context of disk arrays. They are also easily (and commonly) confused, although they refer to three quite different concepts.

- The first term is the Mean Time Between Failures (MTBF). It refers to the average time between failures of a component or a system. In the context of arrays of disk drives, it usually applies to the hardware components. For example, the MTBF rating of a disk drive may be quoted at 200K hours, meaning that the typical disk of this model will operate for 200K hours before failure. As with any statistical measure, an *individual* disk drive might fail after 200 hours of operation, although that same disk might instead run 400K or even 1,200K hours before failing. Sometimes MTBF is applied to the system as a whole. For example, a system with 1,000 disk drives operating independently would have an estimated MTBF of 200K ÷ 1000 = 200 hours if each of the disks has that same 200K hour MTBF.

- Mean Time To Data Loss (MTTDL) refers to the amount of time that a system or subsystem can operate before it suffers a failure sufficient to lose data. If all of the disks in a system are operated independently, this quantity is the same as the MTBF of the system. However, disk subsystem designers go to elaborate lengths to increase MTTDL in spite of relatively constant MTBF of components. A mirrored pair of disks that store the same information will not lose data unless *both* of the pair fail, an event that is considerably less likely than the failure of *one* of the pair. It is crucial to note that MTTDL does not imply completely continuous system operation. If both disks of a mirrored pair are connected to the host system via the same SCSI host adapter, the failure of the host adapter causes the data resident on both members of the pair to become inaccessible. Yet no data will be lost, because restoration of the host adapter will permit the system to access the data on either or both of the disks. Most of the emphasis on data reliability design goes into maximizing MTTDL.

- The final notion, the Mean Time To Data Inaccessibility (MTTDI), is not formally defined in the literature. However, the notion of providing uninterrupted access to data is gaining substantial importance as disk array technology becomes affordable and moves into increasingly larger and more important application areas. Designing a disk subsystem for improved MTTDI is somewhat more demanding than designing for improved MTTDL, although many techniques can be applied to both problems.

> Caution: A high MTBF, MTTDL, or MTTDI does not imply that any given disk construction will actually run for precisely (or even approximately) that amount of time without a failure. These measures are *only* statistical!

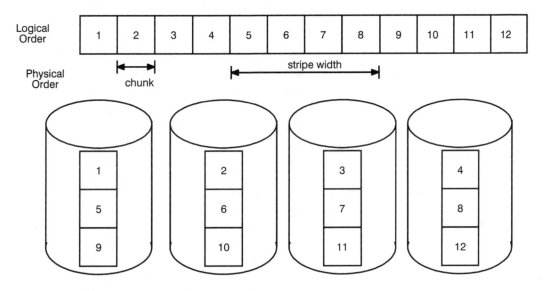

Figure 59. Striping (RAID-0) organization. The chunk is sometimes referred to as the *interlace* or *stripe unit size*.

7.5.2 RAID–0: Striping

The first Berkeley RAID type defined was RAID level zero, most commonly referred to as *striping*. Under striping, a number of physical disk drives are organized in "strips" and addressed as a single logical unit. Each disk drive is divided into units called "chunks," and successive chunk–sized logical data blocks are physically stored on different disk drives. (Solstice:DiskSuite uses the term *interlace* for the chunk size, although the actual entities are identical. The SPARCstorage Volume Manager uses the term *stripe unit size* for the same quantity.)

Consider a RAID–0 volume consisting of four member disks, organized with a chunk size of 32 KB. The first 32 KB chunk of the logical volume is stored on drive 0, the 2nd 32 KB is stored on drive 1, the third on drive 2, and the fourth on drive 3. The fifth data chunk is located on drive 0, after the very first chunk, and so on, as shown in Figure 59:

Striping delivers high performance with relatively low complexity and low cost, albeit at considerable risk to data reliability.

7.5.2.1 Reliability of Striping

The striping organization has three notable features. First, and possibly most important, the reliability of the entire RAID–0 volume depends on *every* member disk drive; the failure of *any* member disk results in a loss of data. Striping is not able to benefit from the hot sparing technique because the entire volume becomes unusable the instant a failure occurs. System operation is thus interrupted immediately. Similarly, striping does not gain very much from hot pluggable disks either. Data is lost when any member fails, and with considerable interruption in service. Being able to repair the disk without rebooting is of little consolation. Hot sparing is not useful because nothing but backups can reconstruct the data. Thus:

$$MTBF_{RAID-0} = MTTDL_{RAID-0} = MTTDI_{RAID-0} = \frac{MTBF_{disk}}{n}$$

For a typical six-wide stripe consisting of disks with 500K MTBF, the volume MTBF and MTTDL are thus 83,000 hours, slightly over nine years. Nine years is a long time, and given the small systems that have been traditional, disk failures are an infrequent occurrence. However, in 1996 a typical Solaris server has in excess of 100 disks, and configurations with 1,000 disks are not unusual. A system with 100 disks configured in stripes is likely to suffer a failure on one stripe or another every 5,000 hours—about once in seven months.

7.5.2.2 Performance of Striping

The second consequence of the striping organization is that for many requests, the logical request causes the activation of two or more member disks. Performance is optimized for a request that is the same size as the stripe width, since all of the disks are active and transferring maximum data per request.

The third consequence of the striping organization is that the responsibility for the transfer has been divided up among more than one member disk, resulting in lower utilization of each disk than if the data were resident on a single disk.

For sequential access, which is dominated by the actual transfer time from the disk platters, striping usually enhances performance considerably. Performance of random access requests can also be enhanced by striping, because of the lower utilization on each member disk. The striping organization is nearly universally able to improve system performance. Its liability is its reliance on the reliability of every member disk. Given a 4-wide stripe with a 32 KB chunk size, consider a request for 128 KB of data starting at block 6. This request is satisfied by reading blocks 6, 7, 8 and 9, all from separate disk drives. If the seek and rotation times are small—as they are for sequential access—the transfer time for the entire 128 KB I/O operation is dominated by internal transfer time of the disk drives. If the internal transfer speed of a single member disk is 4 MB/sec, the aggregate speed of the four-disk stripe is about 15 MB/sec.

The sequential performance of stripped logical volumes approaches the aggregate bandwidth of the member disks times the number of active disks, as long as other system limits are not exceeded (such as operating system configuration, SCSI bus, disk array controller, or host processor limitations). Striping can achieve very high throughput; single-threaded reads up to 55 MB/sec have been observed on large configurations (see section 9.4, *Veritas VxFS File System*). Random-access performance is not improved in single–threaded circumstances, since the governing factor in such cases is the seeks and rotation time of the member disks.

Performance of RAID–0 volumes does not normally increase linearly, since the member disk drives are typically not operated in *spindle sync*. In other words, under RAID–0 the member disks spin and seek independently. As a result, logical I/Os suffer delays due to the randomized nature of the requests compared to the physical positions of the disk arm and platter. Spindle sync is discussed later in more detail in the discussion of RAID–3 performance.

Note: A common misconception is that striping only improves sequential disk access. Random access performance *is* improved—dramatically—in multitasking or multi-threaded environments, because the utilization of each disk is reduced by an average of 1/N (for a stripe width of N disks). The lower utilization results in shorter service queues on each member disk, yielding better I/O performance.

Multiple threads accessing a set of disks sequentially imposes *random* access on the member disks, because the various requests arrive at the member disks in random order. Nearly every request to the member disk requires a seek (and probably a rotate) for servicing.

One situation where striping does *not* improve disk utilization is when hot spots are accessed much more frequently than other parts of the volume. The most common instance of this is a named pipe that is written on a continuous basis. This scenario can result in uneven access to one of the member disks in the stripe.

The surprising thing about this circumstance is that the data is not causing the high disk utilization, but rather continuous updates to the last modified time on the pipe itself (the data is never written to disk because it is transmitted via shared access to kernel memory within the operating system). In cases like this one two solutions can help. One is to employ an NVSIMM to Presto-ize the file system containing the named pipe; this results in the effective cancellation of most of these writes. Since the actual disk writes are deferred, most of the updates never need to be written: they are obsolete by the time the disk would have been updated. Another solution is to set the sticky bit on the named pipe [68]. This approach risks the updates to the last modify date in the event of a system crash, but neither the consistency of the data sent over the pipe nor the integrity of the file system are endangered by this practice.

Worst-case performance for a stripe occurs when the request size is very small and crosses a chunk boundary. For example, performance of a stripe (of virtually any configuration) will be less than that of a single member disk when the request size is 1K bytes and crosses a chunk boundary. Such a request requires both drives to be activated, for request sizes at the minimum efficiency—latency degrades while throughput is not improved.

Because the entire stripe fails at the instant any of its member disks fails considering the performance of a failed stripe is not interesting. Obviously, this is the primary problem with stripes.

7.5.2.3 Choosing Striping Parameters

The choice of chunk size and stripe width can have substantial impact on the performance of stripes. At first glance one might expect that using a minimum size chunk would permit optimum performance; additionally, using a maximum stripe width is a logical conclusion. These do not account for two commonly overlooked details. First, every I/O must be processed through the device driver as well as other operating system functions such as virtual memory mapping. Every disk I/O requires a fixed overhead cost, measured in terms of processor cycles, interrupts, and programmed I/Os. These overheads are expended regardless of what processor performs the RAID computations. Ideally the request size to each disk is kept relatively large—up to the typical 64 KB maximum imposed by the embedded SCSI controllers found in most current disk drives. Some newer drives now permit up to 256 KB per I/O.

The choice of stripe width is governed by administrative and performance considerations. Performance in random access environments is maximized by including as many member disks as possible. Since only one or at most two disks are involved in any given I/O request, disk utilization, disk response latency and disk queues are minimized when the number of member disks is maximized. This optimal result is accomplished with a relatively large chunk size, for example 64 KB-128 KB. Performance in sequential access environments is maximized when the size of the I/O request is equal to the stripe width, *and* the chunk size is

---

[68] Setting the (historically named) sticky bit causes the system to defer updates to the entry's directory entry. Normally this tactic is undesirable, since data could be lost, but in this case there is no data at all, so this consideration does not apply. Setting the sticky bit is accomplished with: "chmod +t named_pipe_file".

large enough to justify the cost of doing an I/O. Under Solaris 2, this size is typically at least 2 KB, and usually larger. When typical I/O requests to the stripe are 8 KB or less, it rarely worthwhile to stripe individual disk accesses across multiple member drives—from a performance standpoint—since this means that the requests to member disks are 4 KB or smaller. In this case, latency and utilization are improved, but throughput does not improve—at best—and overhead is definitely increased.

7.5.2.4 Concatenation

Striping requires that all member disks be the same size. If they are not, the size of the volume is set to the lowest common denominator, and the excess storage capacity on each member disk is lost. Most controller-based RAID implementations do not even permit such unusual configurations.

A special case of the RAID–0 organization is called *concatenation*. Rather than use strips of disks from each member interleaved together, the member disks are merely lined up one after another. This organization is more flexible than striping, because it does not restrict the mix of disk drives: the member disks may be of any size, and none of the storage space is lost. Unfortunately, concatenation does not improve sequential I/O performance because I/O requests virtually never span disk drives. Random I/O is helped by concatenation to the extent that the logical volume is full. When the volume is full, the data is spread across all member disks. When the volume is less than full, the last disks are unused, and do not contribute to lowering disk utilization.

For these reasons, concatenations are recommended only for administrative convenience, such as to construct very large file systems consisting of multiple logical volumes or metadisks, or to grow file systems beyond their originally specified size.

7.5.3 RAID–1: Mirroring

RAID level 1 was developed to combat the reliability problems associated with individual disk drives and particularly with striping. Also occasionally referred to as *disk shadowing*, mirroring makes use of the fact that individual disk drives are actually very reliable: current disks are usually rated at between 150,000-500,000 hours (17-57 years) between failures. For system configurations involving hundreds or even thousands of disks, the reliability of the overall disk farm can drop to only 1,500-5,000 hours—a few months—simply because they have so many disk drives. The largest Solaris-based systems have in excess of 2,000 drives; with a 500K hour MTBF on the drives, such a system has an expected MTBF of only 250 hours, about ten days. Mission-critical systems obviously must take steps to avoid the consequences of a disk failure.

The basic principle behind mirroring is simply to arrange matters so that a disk failure does not lose data—it only incurs overhead to reconstruct the lost data, or perhaps to operate in a reduced mode in which performance may not be at full levels. Data continues to be available in spite of the failure. Under the mirroring scheme, one or more extra disks are reserved for each original data disk. Every member disk is organized identically, and when data is written to the logical volume, it is written separately to every member disk. When a read is directed to the logical volume, the data can be retrieved from any of them, since they are all the same. If a member disk fails, the data is recovered from the surviving submirror or submirrors. Under normal circumstances, the choice of which survivor supplies the data is a matter of administrative policy. Policies are considered in section 7.5.3.3, *Mirroring Performance*.

7.5.3.1 Mirroring Data Reliability

Most commonly a mirror is a two-way mirror, but three-way mirrors are useful in some circumstances, particularly when performing online backups in adverse conditions. (Some implementations, such as VxVM, implement even more extensive mirroring—as much as eight–way mirroring. Such extensive protection seems to be overkill.) Mirroring makes a huge improvement in data reliability: with only a 250K hour MTBF for a member disk, a two–way mirror provides data reliability (MTTDL) in excess of 6.3×10^9 hours. For this reason little requirement arises for three–way (or more) way mirroring, at least not solely for reasons of reliability. Such calculations presume that the failures of disk drives are independent; if both members of a mirror reside in the same cabinet, a fire could well destroy both copies of the data. With mirroring, even configurations with thousands of disk drives can enjoy essentially unlimited data reliability.

The MTTDI is primarily dependent upon other factors (in particular the access paths to the member disk drives), but for the disks alone the MTTDI is the same as the MTTDL.

7.5.3.2 Mirroring, Hot Swapping, and Hot Sparing

Two features that are commonly confused are *hot swapping* and *hot sparing*. Components that can be physically removed and replaced without interrupting system operation are called hot swappable. The most common hot swappable component is a disk drive, although it is becoming more common to have hot swappable power supplies, disk or storage controllers, or even internal system components such as CPUs. Typically the term hot swappable applies to a component that has particular electrical characteristics.

Hot sparing refers to components or subsystems that are continuously available without interruption. Specifically, hot sparing refers to situations in which an extra component is configured into the system and is used to provide an automatic replacement. For some components without internal state, such as power supplies, the distinction between a hot spare and a hot swap is limited to the automatic nature of the replacement. Power supplies are differ from   components such as disk drives whose purpose is to maintain state (specifically to store data): to be useful, a hot spare must be able to retain access to the original's data.

Because a hot spare requires the recreation of the stored data, the technique is not applicable to stripes. Once a stripe suffers a disk failure, the data on that stripe is no longer available and automatically replacing the data is impossible. However, for disk organizations that preserve access to the data—mirroring or forms of parity-based RAID -they can quickly copy the data onto an automatically allocated spare disk. Hot sparing relies upon other redundancy mechanisms to permit the data from the failed disk to be recovered and copied onto the replacement disk.

In the context of disk subsystems, hot swapping is really useful only if hot sparing is also in use. Hot sparing provides substantially improved data reliability and protection from interruption of data access. Hot swapping then provides a further measure of protection against service interruption, since it makes possible the replacement of failed drives. This can be done at leisure since the data remains fully protected. Hot swapping eases the mind of administrators using hot spares who worry about running out of hot spares. This concern is needless, since even one hot spare improves the reliability of a mirrored volume by approximately two orders of magnitude.

Stated in terms of reliability, hot swapping improves the mean time to repair (MTTR), whereas hot sparing also improves MTTDL. In addition, depending on other configuration parameters, a hot spare may also improve the MTTDI and MTBF of its associated volume.

Hot sparing in particular provides greatly improved data reliability. Consider a two-way mirror supported by a hot spare. With the mirror alone, data can be lost if both member disks fail. If the hot spare is activated upon detection of a failure of either member disk, data is copied from the surviving member to the hot spare. The resync process takes about 20 minutes for 1 GB or 2 GB disk drives (see section 7.5.3.5, *Mirror Resynchronization*). With this organization, the only way to lose data is to suffer a failure on the surviving original member while the data is copied to the hot drive, or to suffer a failure on the surviving member *and* the hot spare replacement (three failures in all, or two within a very short time window).

Hot swappable disks permit failed components to be replaced without interrupting system operation. When combined with mirroring, RAID–3, or RAID–5, hot sparing and hot swapping permit essentially continuous system operation in the face of the inevitable disk failures.

7.5.3.3 Mirroring Performance

Performance of a mirror is a mixed bag. Obviously writes must be committed to all members, and since the operation must be atomic to be useful— a write operation must be either complete and successful to all members, or never complete on *any* member. Even best-case write performance is degraded from that of a single disk. Fortunately, the writes need not be issued or performed sequentially, only that they be treated as a logical group.

A common misconception is that writes to mirrors necessarily take twice as long as writes to non-mirrors. Ordinarily, this is far from true. Most mirroring options provide two administrative policy options concerning mirrored writes: parallel member writes or serial member writes. If the default parallel write policy is in effect, the volume management software *dispatches* writes to the member disks serially, but the physical I/Os are *serviced* by the individual disks in parallel. Since the process of dispatching the disk I/O consumes a matter of a few hundred microseconds, compared to the typical 15 ms (i.e., 15,000 microseconds) required to service physical I/Os, subwrites to a mirror happen essentially in parallel. The timeline for this operation is shown in Figure 60.

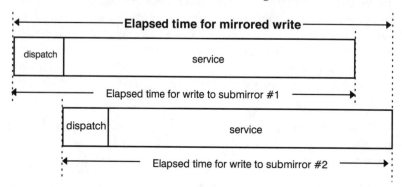

Figure 60. Time sequence for a mirrored write operation

Under most circumstances the write performance of a two-way mirror is about 25 percent less than that of a simple disk for activity that consists solely of disk writes. For more generalized applications, the overlap between I/O and other processing reduces the apparent degradation. The degradation is illustrated in Table 34, which details the amount of time required to build a new 1.85 GB file system for a single disk and various configurations of multi-way mirrors.

Table 34. Time required to build a file system on 1.85 GB mirrors

| | Mirror Write Mode | |
Logical Volume	Parallel (default)	Serial
single disk	0:43	0:43
two-way mirror	0:51 (18 percent degradation)	1:12
three-way mirror	1:02 (44 percent degradation)	1:40
four-way mirror	1:13 (69 percent degradation)	2:08

Given the large overlap in the servicing of the mirror's sub-writes, asking why the write degradation is even 15 percent is reasonable. As with striping, the culprit is seek and rotate time for disk spindles that are not maintained in sync. The writes consequently take varying amounts of time, and since the write to the mirror is not considered complete until the writes to all submirrors are complete, the performance of the mirror is effectively the speed of the slowest member disk.

Read performance of mirrors differs substantially from write performance. In the sequential read case, the performance is normally the same as that of a single member disk, since that is typically what is being accessed. Only one member must provide data, since all members contain the same bits. An extremely cautious implementation might read all members and compare, but this is rare to the point of extinction outside the domain of completely fault-tolerant systems such as the ftSPARC™. The case of single–threaded random access is the same as for sequential: the performance is essentially the same as that of a single member disk. The best performance case for mirrored disks is random-access reads in a multithreaded or multitasking environment. In this case, the system is able to use the least busy member that holds the requisite data. Since more than one member is available to satisfy such requests, disk utilization is reduced by 1/N (where N is the number of duplicated members).

7.5.3.4 Mirroring in Reduced Mode

When a protected RAID volume suffers the failure of one of its member disks and is forced to rely on backup mechanisms, the volume is said to be operating in *reduced* or *degraded mode*. In typical mirroring implementations, when a disk error is detected on a submirror, the entire submirror is flagged as being in an error state and the submirror is taken off-line. Once the submirror is off-line, the volume reverts to behaving essentially as a mirror of one less submirror. For the common two-way mirror, the volume behaves as if it were a regular disk for all practical intents and purposes. Although this behavior is very simple and is expected, it is quite a different situation from other RAID organizations operating in reduced mode.

7.5.3.5 Mirror Resynchronization

When one of a mirror's disks fails, it must eventually be replaced, either automatically (via the hot sparing mechanism) or manually. The process of bringing a replacement disk to be up-to-date is called a *resync* operation. The most straightforward way of performing a resync is to copy all of the bits from the known good disk to the replacement disk, and this operation is precisely what mirror implementations do when a full disk must be resynced. Normally a full resync is performed at a reduced speed—often at around 1 MB/sec per member disk—in order to reduce the impact of a resync on normal system operation.

Normal operation is both possible and encouraged during mirror resync operations, since data is fully available. At such rates the disk drives are not fully utilized, permitting other activity without long disk access queues and the consequent delays.

Because submirrors are sometimes temporarily taken off-line (for example, to perform online backups), submirrors can sometimes become partially out-of-date, requiring a partial resync. A partial resync can be accelerated by copying only the disk blocks that have changed since the submirror was offlined. The most common technique used for this purpose is called a *dirty region log* (DRL), in which a bitmap is provided for each member disk, with one bit per disk region indicating which regions have been updated since one or more submirrors have been offlined or detached. Typically, regions are 32 KB in size; as a result, the DRL is normally quite small (for an entire 9 GB disk, it need be only 144 KB in size). Because the proportion of the data storage that is actually updated is normally quite small—often only two to five percent of the disk's storage capacity—the use of a dirty region log greatly accelerates the partial resync operation. Dirty region logging is *not* the same as the update log used in RAID–3 and RAID–5 organizations, nor is it related to the file system journal used by logging file systems such as UFS + or Veritas VxFS.

The location of the dirty region log varies with implementation. For Solstice:DiskSuite , the DRL resides on two of the replicas (specifically, the first two replicas configured), whereas VxVM asks the administrator to assign a disk location when the mirror volume is created. Because of the size of DRL (or rather, the lack of size), the DRL does not impose any significant configuration constraints. The only consideration is that writing the DRL does require physical disk access, so a system with mirrors that are written frequently will tend to keep the disk arms hovering near the DRL. If other high-priority activity is on the disk(s) that contain the DRL, the prudent administrator will configure the first two replicas onto low-usage disk drives, saving the system from waiting on long seek times (see section 7.1.1.4.4, *Average* vs. *Typical Seek*).

7.5.4 RAID–1+0: RAID–1 Volumes with RAID–0 Submirrors

Simple mirroring is now rare, primarily because the size of volumes has grown to exceed the size of physical disk drives. In order to reduce administrative complexity to manageable levels, creating mirrors whose submirrors are stripes is now customary, as in Figure 61.

7.5.4.1 RAID-1+0 Parameters

Because all of the data is mirrored, the reliability of RAID–1+0 is comparable to that of simple RAID–1 mirrors. Typically the mirroring software will take an entire mirror off-line when any member disk fails, so the reliability of a RAID–1+0 volume can be expressed as:

$$MTBF_{RAID-1+0} = \left(\frac{MTBF_{disk}}{N} \right) width$$

where *width* is the stripe width of the submirrors. For a typical configuration with disks whose MTBF is 200K hours, the MTBF of a two-way mirror consisting of six-wide stripes works out to about 1.11×10^9 hours, compared to 30,000 hours for a six-wide RAID-0 stripe.

The performance of a RAID–1+0 volume is also a compromise between that of striped volumes and mirrored volumes. Sequential and random reads benefit from both organizations, although random reads only benefit from mirroring in the multithreaded case. As one might expect, writes to RAID–1+0 volumes typically approach the speed of RAID–0 stripes, but due to the overhead of writing two copies for mirroring, RAID–1+0 is somewhat (about 30 percent) slower.

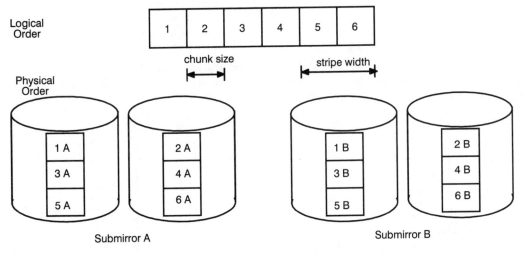

Figure 61. RAID-1+0 organization: mirrors whose submirrors are stripes

7.5.4.2 Mirroring/Striping Order of Operations

Logically speaking, a RAID–1+0 volume consists of a mirror with stripes for submirrors. However, this organization can be implemented two subtly different ways. One way is to construct two stripes, and that are subsequently joined to construct a mirror, as shown in Figure 62. The difference is that RAID–0+1 is one mirror whose submirrors happen to be stripes, whereas a RAID–1+0 is actually four mirrors striped together. The notation indicates the order of operations: RAID–0+1 builds stripes first, then mirrors them together; RAID–1+0 reverses the order of operation. This may seem to be an esoteric difference of interest only to the theoretician, but in practice these two have significantly different resilience to disk failure.

When RAID–0+1 (the single mirror) suffers a disk failure, for example, disk 4 in the figure, an entire submirror is offlined; in the RAID–0+1 case, submirror A, consisting of four members, is offlined. Furthermore, any subsequent failure in submirror B will result in the loss of the entire logical volume. This behavior meets the Raid Advisory Board (RAB) definition for mirroring; the volume is able to survive the failure of any member disk without resorting to parity computations and their associated overhead. In the RAID–1+0 configuration, the failure of disk 4 will degrade only mirror D. Mirrors A, B, and C are still fully protected, and only the failure of disk 8 will disable the entire volume. This organization delivers significantly higher reliability, because it can suffer as many as four member failures before data is lost. It exceeds the RAB definition for mirroring.

Commercial implementations of RAID–10 (used here to refer to both variants) are often unclear as to which is offered. For example, Solstice: DiskSuite 4.0 uses a syntax in the md.tab configuration file that strongly implies that it implements RAID–0+1, but in fact the effect is that of RAID–1+0. On the other hand, SPARCstorage Volume Manager implements only RAID–0+1, and hence behaves differently. Some firmware–based RAID controllers implement RAID–0+1 while others offer RAID–1+0. The Sun RSM Array 2000 implements RAID-1+0. Check with your vendor!

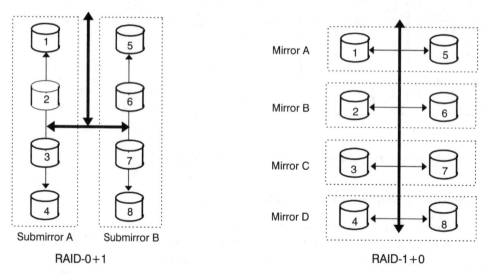

Figure 62. The subtle difference between RAID-0+1 and RAID-1+0. The latter delivers significantly higher data availability, although the former precisely satisfies the definition of mirroring.

7.5.5 RAID–2: Hamming Code Arrays

The RAID–2 organization uses the algebraic notion of *Hamming Codes* to generate a set of redundant information that permits recovery from disk failures. However, Hamming Codes are relatively complex to compute. Perhaps most importantly, the nature of the Hamming algorithms places restrictions on the number and organization of the member disks. Combined with the relative complexity of the Hamming computations, this lack of flexibility means that few (if any) RAID–2 implementations have appeared commercially.

7.5.6 RAID–3: Striping Protected by Parity Computation

RAID–3 is an attempt to avoid the difficulties of both RAID–0 and RAID–1. The problem with RAID–0 is reliability, and the primary problem with mirroring is the expense of duplicated disk drives and their associated disk controllers and other infrastructure.

RAID–3 builds upon the disk organization of striping, but it additionally uses an extra disk column to store a computed parity block. The system computes a parity bit for each bit in the stripe width, and stores the parity data on the corresponding chunk of the extra disk, as Figure 63 shows:

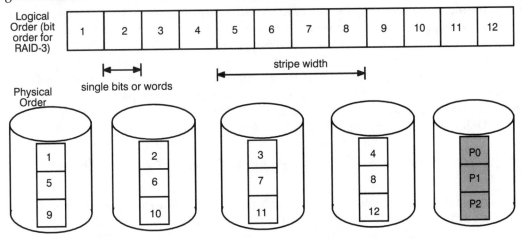

Figure 63. RAID-3 data organization. Parity information is concentrated on a single member disk, creating a bottleneck for multitasking or multithreaded writes.

The keystone of RAID–3, RAID–4 and RAID–5 is a simple, reversible form of parity computation. Under this scheme, the chunks of an entire stripe width are subjected to a bitwise exclusive-or function ($\oplus$ and abbreviated XOR). The XOR has the special property that it is reversible simply by applying it twice to the same data. This is used in RAID parity computations by computing the parity as:

$$P = c_0 \oplus c_1 \ldots \oplus c_{n-2} \oplus c_{n-1}$$

where c_j represents the data from each chunk in the stripe and n is the number of member data disks in the volume. Then, when any member disk—including the parity disk—has failed, its data can be computed from the surviving members:

$$c_{missing} = P \oplus c_0 \oplus c_1 \oplus \cdots \oplus c_{missing-1} \oplus c_{missing+1} \oplus \cdots \oplus c_{n-1} \oplus c_n$$

Virtually every commercial implementation of RAID–3, RAID–4, or RAID–5 uses some form of this mechanism.

7.5.6.1 Performance of RAID–3

RAID–3 uses the same basic data organization as RAID–0 (in that it spreads the data evenly across the member disks), and for that reason it has many of the same strengths: sequential read and write performance is optimized for requests large enough to involve the entire stripe width, and performance is minimized for requests that are very small and whose address spans two member disks. On the other hand, the parity computation does change quite a bit of the performance equation. In particular, the use of a dedicated parity disk means that any write request to the logical volume *must* involve the parity disk. For single–threaded sequential read I/O, the performance of a RAID–3 volume is similar to that of a stripe. Unless a member disk fails, RAID–3 and RAID–0 volumes perform identically. For single–threaded sequential writes, the requirement to compute the parity for each stripe width imposes a slight degradation when compared to simple stripes (typically about five percent).

However, in other environments, RAID–3 does not fare so well. As with single–threaded reads, multithreaded reads do not involve the parity disk or parity computation, so this case does not suffer (or gain) from RAID–3. RAID–3 units that operate in spindle sync, described below, are a different matter. In a multitasking environment, the parity disk quickly becomes a major bottleneck: every write to the logical volume requires a write to the parity disk, no matter where on the member disks the data resides. As a result, the multithreaded write performance of a RAID–3 volume is typically very similar to that of a single member disk, specifically the member disk used for parity. For primarily single–threaded environments, such as those dominated by some types of scientific computing, and possibly some kinds of decision support applications, this tradeoff is acceptable. For most servers, which are called upon to handle primarily multitasking environments, RAID-3 rarely is a suitable solution.

RAID-3 is one of the most controversial forms of RAID today. Strictly by the definition of RAID-3, the chunk size or interlace is 1-bit to 1-word in size, which makes it virtually impossible to implement using inexpensive commodity SCSI disks: the definition of a SCSI disk includes operation in 512-byte blocks! Thus most vendors that offer "RAID-3" have opted to implement RAID-4 or RAID-5 instead[69]. For the single-threaded sequential access patterns that work best with RAID-3, RAID-5 performs at almost exactly the same speed (see section 7.5.8.3, *RAID-5 Performance*).

7.5.6.2 RAID-3 and Spindle Synchronization

Most true hardware RAID-3 implementations make use of an optimization known as *spindle synchronization*. Under normal circumstances, disks in a disk subsystem—even a "hardware" RAID unit—do not operate in lock-step. This approach permits I/O requests to the disk subsystem to proceed independently, assuming that they do not involve the same physical resources. However, since RAID-3 is primarily oriented toward optimizing I/O requests that span all member disks, spindle synchronization optimizes RAID-3 performance. Each request to the logical volume must wait for *all* of its subsidiary physical I/Os to be finished before being considered complete. If the member disks are not in synchronization, they are subject to average rotational latency and seek distances, causing additional delay.

When all member disks are operated in spindle sync, the rotational positions and disk arms are kept synchronized, making all of the member I/O requests very nearly the same duration. Because RAID-3 optimizes single-threaded requests, RAID-3 configurations usually perform best when operated in spindle sync. However, for random access I/O, spindle sync is a disaster: precisely because the disk mechanisms are tied together, a spindle-synchronized RAID-3 volume behaves precisely as if it were a single very large, very safe parallel transfer disk drive. The random request rate for all logical I/O requests is then identical to the request rate for an individual member disk, less a small amount of overhead for RAID. For these reasons, spindle-synched RAID-3 units are essentially never useful in server configurations.

---

[69] Nonetheless, they claim RAID-3 functionality. This claim is only a slight stretch: RAID-3 can be viewed as a RAID-5 volume whose parity is stored on a single member. In all cases, RAID-5 operates at least as fast as RAID-3 without spindle synchronization, and in multithreaded cases the former is much faster. This mild deception is found in virtually every significant "RAID-3" implementation in the Solaris space.

7.5.6.3 RAID–3 Performance in Reduced Mode

RAID-3 is specifically designed to continue providing access to data in the face of the failure of a member disk. However, the RAID-3 definition does not offer any assurance that the performance of such a volume will remain, and in fact, performance is *not* maintained. When the volume suffers a member failure, it is said to be operating in *reduced mode*.

True RAID-3 volumes are normally operated with spindle synchronization, so their performance is not as affected as with some other RAID organizations. Because RAID -3 "stripes" the data with a segment size of 1-bit to 1-word, I/O to or from a RAID -3 nearly always involves an entire stripe width. Writes to a reduced volume are actually slightly faster than to normal volumes, since all of the drives are written anyway—when in reduced mode, one fewer drive is written than normal.

Reads, though, are another story. The read operation normally involves reading each of the data disks (the parity disk is not read; thus N-1 drives are read). The data is then assembled and returned to the host. Reading from a reduced volume requires reading the same number of drives (the failed member is not read, but the parity disk is) and then the computation of the XOR before assembling the data and returning it to the host. Degraded reads—to a *true* RAID-3 volume—are thus slightly slower than to a normal RAID -3 volume.

7.5.6.4 Data Reliability of RAID–3

A RAID–3 volume is able to withstand the failure of exactly one of its member disks—and no more. A RAID–3 volume has reliability of

$$MTBF_{RAID-3} = \frac{MTBF_{disk}^{\;2}}{N-1}$$

where N is the total number of member disks. For a 5-wide volume plus parity (total of six member disks) made up of current 500K MTBF disks, the volume MTBF is approximately 5×10^8 hours. RAID–3 reliability can be enhanced by using hot spares; the effect is similar to that of hot spares on mirrors.

As with other parity-protected forms of RAID, the computed data reliability of RAID -3 depends upon failures being independent. However, not all member disk failures are independent! In particular, a RAID-3 volume whose members reside in a disk array can quite easily be subject to dependent failures. The most common occurrence is the failure of the disk *controller* rather than the member disks themselves. From the host this appears to be the failure of multiple member drives, and most parity-protected RAID volumes are unable to survive this condition. Disk array controllers that can be configured with redundant controllers *are* capable of withstanding this type of failure.

7.5.7 RAID–4: RAID–3 with Independent Disks

Strictly speaking, RAID–3 implementations use a chunk size of one bit or one word. In practice, they rarely do, because I/O requests are rarely so small, especially in the RAID–3 context, which is skewed toward heavy sequential—that is bulk—I/O. Using larger chunk sizes usually amortizes the effort of doing a member I/O over a much larger block of data. RAID–4 is an attempt to address this issue. Instead of bit– or word–sized chunks, RAID–4 uses a chunk size more comparable to that of RAID–0, for example, 2 KB-128 KB. This arrangement is easier to implement using commodity SCSI disks, because SCSI disks present a fixed interface clearly defined by SCSI, in which the minimum addressable unit on a disk is a 512–byte sector. Virtually all commercial RAID devices built out of SCSI disks that are labeled "RAID–3" are actually RAID–4 for this reason (or are RAID -5, for reasons of performance in random-access situations). RAID–4 is also somewhat easier to implement than RAID–3 because it does not require the drives to be in spindle–sync.

As one might expect, RAID–4 has basically the same strengths and weaknesses as RAID–3: it excels at sequential throughput, but writes performance is limited to the speed of the single parity disk. Reads, whether sequential or random, perform about the same as RAID–0 stripes.

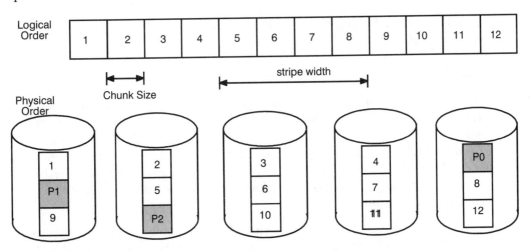

Figure 64. RAID-5 data organization. Parity is distributed across all members, eliminating the primary objection to RAID-3.

7.5.8 RAID–5: RAID Optimized for Random Access

The primary weakness of the RAID–3 structure is that it cannot adequately handle the demands of multitasking environments. To address that requirement, RAID–5 was developed. It also leverages off the basic striping disk organization, but rather than dedicating a single disk to the storage of the parity data, the parity data is mixed into the stripe width. The stripe width is augmented by the "parity" drive, resulting in sufficient storage space.

Under RAID–5, most of the parity chunks are located on the member disks, and some of the data is located on what was the dedicated parity disk under RAID–3, as in Figure 64.

7.5.8.1 RAID–5 Data Reliability

As with RAID–3, the use of the XOR parity generation function combined with a dedicated disk drive's worth of parity storage means that data reliability is very high compared to striping or simple disks. Also as with RAID–3, the use of hot spare disks means even higher MTTDL than a conventional RAID–5 logical volume. Reliability is lower than that of mirroring, though, since only two member disk failures result in a loss of data. As with RAID–3, the MTTDL is:

$$MTTDI_{RAID\text{-}5} = \frac{MTBF_{disk}^{\ 2}}{(n-1)}$$

Clearly the reliability is still dependent upon the number of member disks, a liability that does not afflict mirrors.

7.5.8.2 RAID-5 Write Log Organization

One of the key issues with all parity-based RAID organizations is that they involve the conversion of a logical write into multiple physical writes. The array management software (whether it runs in the host or in a dedicated processor in a disk array controller) must arrange for these multiple writes to be committed atomically. Otherwise the computed parity data and the actual data may get out of sync, resulting in a corrupted volume. Nearly all array management software avoids this problem by using a logging mechanism to implement a two-phase commit process.

Under this scheme, each logical volume is provided with a commit log similar to that used for fast partial resyncing of mirrors, as well as a buffer area for storing actual updated data and parity blocks. When a write request is issued to the logical volume, the new parity block is computed and written in the buffer; next the log is updated, indicating that a write is pending against the data on the member disks. Once the data is safely placed in non-volatile storage, the array management software writes the updated data and parity onto the member disks, and finally the log is updated to reflect a clean status for the affected blocks. If any part of this process is interrupted, for example, by a catastrophic power supply failure or a host crash, the array management software is able to restore the RAID volume to a fully consistent state. This process is illustrated in Figure 65.

The implementation of the logging mechanism varies among RAID implementations. VxVM makes the log explicit during the configuration of a RAID-5 volume by requesting disk resources for the log.

> Caution: Although VxVM permits a RAID-5 volume to be created without a log, but this option should *never* be used. If this option is selected, an untimely crash can cause the parity blocks to become out of sync with the data blocks!

The RAID-5 log is written very frequently, but because pending writes to the volume stay in the log for only a few milliseconds, the log contains only a few entries.

Solstice: DiskSuite uses the same basic strategy. Instead of permitting user specification of the log location, DiskSuite simply uses a reserved part of some of the disks as a *prewrite area*. The prewrite area functions as a commit log and eliminates the possibility that a RAID-5 volume could be created without appropriate integrity guarantees. The prewrite areas reside on some of the member disks, but because they are replicated, a failure cannot compromise both the prewrite area and the members. Unfortunately, the fact that the prewrite areas reside on member disks means that this practice results in some very long disk seeks, with the consequent loss of performance. DiskSuite delivers about 15 percent lower RAID-5 write performance than VxVM on equivalent configurations.

When using RAID-5 on a SPARCstorage Array, the log function is managed in the host, so a SCSI I/O is always issued for commits and clears to the log or prewrite area. These writes have a useful life that is shorter than the aging window of data in the array's NVRAM cache, so at least half of the log activity can be canceled if NVRAM fast writes are enabled. The commit is cached in NVRAM; before the data is actually posted to the physical log disk, the clear operation rewrites the same block, eliminating the necessity to write the original data to the disk. Because RAID-5 writes cannot begin to write either changed data or parity until the log commit completes, accelerating these operations via NVRAM results in a 40-50 percent improvement in RAID-5 write performance.

Firmware-based RAID implementations most often make different arrangements. Instead of writing the log on disk, most allocate a small area in their onboard NVRAM as a log buffer. This provision avoids the necessity to operate the SCSI subsystem, especially since the eventual state of all log blocks will be clear except in failure conditions. Refer to 7.5.11.2, Controller-Based RAID, for additional discussion.

7.5.8.3 RAID–5 Performance

The performance of RAID–5 volumes is widely misunderstood. The read case is much simpler than the write case. For reads, the performance of a RAID–5 volume is almost exactly the same as that of a stripe using comparable resources. "Comparable" in this context means that having the same number of data disks, e.g., a RAID–5 volume with five data disks and one parity disk is comparable to a five disk RAID-0. Maximum performance is achieved for sequential reads when the request is stripe aligned (i.e., the beginning of the request is aligned with the beginning of a data chunk on a member disk) and the request size is an integer multiple of the data width of the stripe (i.e., the chunk size times the number of data disks). Multithreaded reads on RAID-5 are even faster than comparable RAID-0: since the parity is distributed throughout the volume, the volume is distributed over one additional drive, with resulting lower disk utilization.

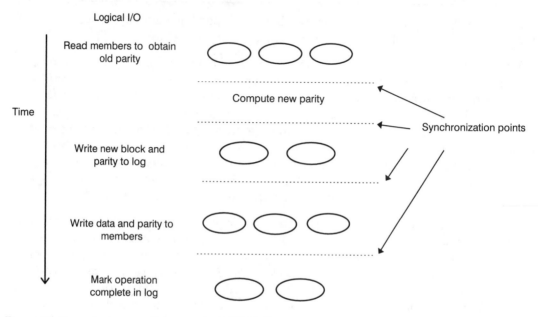

Figure 65. Two-phase commit process for RAID-5. Processing must stop at each synchronization point.

As with RAID-0 and RAID–3, minimum performance occurs when the request size is minimal and the request spans two member disks, it this requires activating at least three member disks to complete one logical I/O (two data members and the parity member, assuming that the information necessary to compute parity is already cached in memory).

For writes, the picture is far more complicated. The first problem is that the logical write typically involves a read-modify-write cycle, because the array management software ordinarily does not have access to the other data in the target stripe to compute the new parity information. This situation forces the reading of the old data for the purpose of recovering the rest of the parity context. Then the new data is inserted into the disk image, and the data and the updated parity are then written back to the disk. There are three cases:

- The write modifies the entire stripe width. In this case, the old parity context need not be recovered because it will be completely replaced. The write requires physical writes to each of the member disks and to the parity disk. In this case, the performance will be approximately 1-((n-1)/n) compared to a comparable stripe, solely due to the parity write. For typical RAID–5 volumes involving three to five data disks, degradation is about 20-30 percent compared to single independent disks.

- The write modifies more than one member data disk, but less than the entire stripe width. In this case, the parity context must be recovered, forcing a read/modify/write cycle; furthermore, at least three physical writes must be performed. Typically two reads, two data writes, and a parity write must be issued, and the speed of the RAID–5 volume in this case is degraded by roughly 80 percent when compared to an independent disk.

- The write modifies exactly one member data disk. In this case, the parity need not be read, since it can be computed as if the disk had failed. The write thus involves one data write and one parity write, so performance is degraded by up to 50 percent, compared to an independent disk. Sometimes the penalty is not so large since the data and parity writes can be issued in parallel. Unfortunately, as we will soon see, this optimization cannot usually be applied.

In practice, a number of other factors come into play. First, because of the necessity for safe (i.e., two-phase) writing to avoid data corruption, a number of additional steps are actually involved. In particular, three additional writes are added to the process: two to update the dirty region logs and one to write the updated data and parity blocks (these are almost universally written together for performance reasons). Even worse is the requirement that the log and data writes must be executed in a precise, sequential order to preserve their semantics!

7.5.8.4 RAID–5 Performance in Reduced Mode

The primary motivation for RAID organizations is to combine high performance with high data reliability. RAID–5 attains good performance in environments dominated by read access, and it can withstand the failure of a single member disk. However, the performance of a RAID–5 volume is the subject of considerable misunderstanding, and the performance of a RAID–5 volume operating in reduced mode is even less well understood.

Under normal circumstances, most reads to a RAID–5 volume do not involve reads to all member disks, and no reads involve the computation of parity. However, when a member disk has failed, the only way to retrieve data from the volume is to read *all* member disks and use the parity mechanism to determine the contribution of the failed member. Consider a RAID–5 volume with six member disks (i.e., five data disks plus parity), and a 16 KB chunk size. In normal mode, an 8 KB read at offset 32 KB activates only the third member disk. Of course, the fourth disk would be used in the event that the parity block for this stripe is on one of the first three disks. This work is the same amount as required for an equivalently configured RAID–0 volume. If some disk other than the third disk has failed, it has no direct effect on this particular request, since the parity need not be computed.

However, if the third disk has failed, the only way to retrieve the data is to read all of the surviving members and compute the data from the missing member. This overhead is large! In this case, it means issuing five physical reads and computing the parity, more than a five-fold increase in the amount of work compared to either a normally operating RAID–5 or RAID–0 (or for a single non-RAID disk, for that matter).

The degradation associated with the failure of a RAID–5 member disk can be expressed in terms of the number of physical I/Os that must be processed to handle a typical I/O stream. We consider only I/O requests smaller than the size of the chunk since larger ones would be treated as multiple smaller ones. For (n-1)/n of the disks, exactly one I/O is required. But for 1/n of the requests, (n - 1)/n I/Os are required, so the total number of I/Os is 2 (n-1)/n. By comparison, a volume operating normally requires just n I/Os. The overhead required to recover from a failure increases with the width of the volume. Also, the cost of storage associated with the RAID–5 decreases in direct proportion to the width of the volume.

Even this comparison underestimates the net impact on performance in multithreaded environments, because it does not account for the dramatically increased disk utilization seen on each of the surviving member disks—the utilization is approximately doubled. If the member disks were already running at utilization in excess of 50 percent, the system may become heavily bottlenecked on the member drives, causing much greater degradation than might be expected. In addition, additional degradation may occur if seek times are increased due to the higher I/O load.

Fortunately, the situation for writes to a degraded RAID–5 volume is much better. More or less, writes to RAID–5 volumes are so much work that writing to a degraded RAID–5 is as fast as or even faster than normal RAID-5 writes! All of the normal parity computations must be performed, whether or not the write involves a failed member. A failed member is simply bypassed, resulting in slightly faster write performance to a degraded volume!

7.5.8.5 Choosing RAID–5 Parameters

RAID-5 is a complex organization, and deciding precisely what configuration to use can be difficult. However, the RAID-5 organization itself provides some insight into its strengths and weaknesses.

From a reliability standpoint, RAID-5 is identical to RAID-3: it is able to withstand the failure of exactly one member disk before losing data accessibility. Consequently, the first decision involves the level of reliability required. If the object is to preserve existing data in the event of a member failure, the requirements are much less strict than if continuous operation is required. In the latter case, the first consideration is how to avoid losing more than one disk in a single event. For practical purposes, this means either configuring one member disk per controller (if the controller and/or its data path is not fully redundant), or choosing a disk array controller that is redundant. The former strategy provides the most security, albeit only for configurations that uses many array controllers. Additionally, if this configuration is constructed with VxVM, a further disk drive is required for the log disk, and is an additional complication (Solstice: DiskSuite does not have this additional issue—see section 7.5.8.2, *RAID-5 Write Log Organization*).

The characteristics of the RAID-5 write operation lead to the most useful RAID-5 configuration choices. The most important strategy is to try to arrange for as many full-stripe writes as possible. If the application is dominated by a particular write transaction, optimize for writes of this size, especially if the RAID implementation does not convert partial stripe writes into full stripe writes (neither Solstice:DiskSuite nor VxVM implement this optimization—see section 7.5.11, *RAID Implementations*). This optimization is accomplished by arranging matters so that the typical I/O size is the same as the data width of the volume. The data width is one less than the number of member disks, multiplied by the chunk size. For example, if the typical I/O size is 60Kbytes on a RAID-5 volume consisting of six member disk, the desired chunk size is 12 KB because the data width is five member disks * 12 KB = 60 KB.

If the typical I/O size is not easily determined, or if writes vary widely in size, the most suitable strategy is to configure the chunk size large enough that reasonably common I/O sizes do not involve multiple member disks. For example, choosing a chunk size of 1 KB is virtually guaranteed to perform poorly in a DBMS environment, because virtually all DBMS systems use logical block sizes of 2 KB or 8 KB (historically biased toward 2 KB). Writing 2 KB onto a five-disk RAID-5 volume with 1 KB chunk size means that three member disks must be involved.

7.5.9 RAID–6: RAID–5 with Additional Protection

RAID–5 volumes are a major improvement over unprotected striped disks in that they can withstand the loss of a member disk without interrupting service. However, this organization only permits the system to withstand a single failure, which is insufficient for a few applications. RAID–6 is defined as an intermediate position between the reliability of RAID–1+0 and the much less costly but much less failure–resistant RAID–5. RAID–6 doubles the number of parity disks from one to two, thus permitting two members to fail while still maintaining service.

In theory, this intermediate position is reasonable, but the practical effect is not especially impressive. RAID–6 provides the practical impact of a RAID–5 volume with instantaneous hot sparing, essentially eliminating only the relatively small resynchronization period. In exchange, the RAID processor must perform an additional write operation for each logical write (and of course it has an additional member disk for read and XOR operations).

Few commercial (if any) RAID systems implement RAID–6, partly because RAID–5 with hot sparing provides sufficient availability for most applications, but also because of the implementation structure of most firmware–based RAID implementations. RAID–5 volumes are very unlikely to encounter two *unrelated and independent* member disk failures within the resynchronization period. If two failures occur in a typical RAID–5 subsystem within the resynchronization time, they have an overwhelming chance of being related in some way (for example, an electrical short on an internal SCSI bus, or perhaps some sort of disk or controller firmware bug).

In these cases, RAID–6 is of questionable value, because typical RAID subsystems are tightly integrated into a relatively small environment. A more plausible solution for the problem is to use host–based RAID-5, spreading the data across more member disks than typical installations. Host–based RAID can configure the six member disks of a 5 data + 1 parity RAID–5 volume across six independent disk arrays with six host connections, six disk controllers, and six cache accelerators. This type of configuration is more able to withstand many types of related failures, although even it is not completely immune to failures.

7.5.10 Common Misconceptions about RAID

Most RAID implementations use some sort of disk array controller, either as a concentration point for I/O, or as an additional processing node that actually implements much or all of the RAID function. Two misconceptions commonly surround these RAID implementations.

First, many users have the mistaken impression that RAID systems use a read-and-compare approach when performing reads. Although this would be useful for detecting some classes of disk media errors, the overhead would be considerable (double for RAID -1 and $O(n)$ for parity-based RAID). It would also result in much higher disk utilization, in addition to lowering throughput and increasing I/O latency. For these reasons, reads from RAID devices are not verified unless a member disk reports some sort of error during the read process. Disk drives store enough error-correcting information on the platters to correct very large errors and to detect even larger ones; the SCSI and FibreChannel interfaces also parity-check data transfers, making a read-and-compare approach unlikely to be productive [70].

Another notable misconception about disk arrays is that they are inherently faster than strings of disks. Although RAID devices can indeed be faster than regular strings of SCSI disks, the performance improvement is due to the RAID organization, rather than to acceleration associated with the array controller. In practice, array controllers permit high

---

[70] Paranoid applications can still impose even tighter requirements. For example, in the fault-tolerant ftSPARC system, the disk device driver transparently implements disk block checksumming. In essence, no matter what physical disk device is provided to the host, the system implements a form of end-to-end checksumming on the storage subsystem.

throughput I/O, but for applications that are extremely sensitive to I/O latency, many array controllers may inject too much latency. Disk arrays are normally connected to hosts via either SCSI or FibreChannel; disks are in turn connected to the array controller with more SCSI busses. Because an I/O must be transferred on two peripheral busses—including two or more bus arbitrations—each I/O requires additional elapsed time required to cross the additional peripheral bus. Random I/O is not affected to the same extent as sequential I/O, because random I/O involves much more seek time. The additional 1.0 ms-1.5 ms is measurable but not significant compared to the 10-20 ms required for the disk to service the request. Sequential I/O does not involve the extensive time associated with seek and rotate, resulting in 1-2 ms service times on standard SCSI disks. In the sequential I/O context, the additional 1.0-1.5 ms represents a significant change in latency. Most applications are not sensitive to disk array latency, but real-time applications may encounter unexpected delays.

7.5.11 RAID Implementations

Two common types of RAID implementation are available: host-based and controller-based. They have far more similarities than differences, but they do differ in some significant ways, notably in terms of flexibility, overhead, and performance. As one might expect, the two designs make rather different tradeoffs. Most of the issues are quite different from their common understanding.

7.5.11.1 Host-Based RAID

Solstice:DiskSuite and SPARCstorage Volume Manager () both implement RAID functions in the host system. The underlying physical disks are visible to the operating system and its administrator, and RAID functions are implemented in a virtual device driver interposed between higher levels of Solaris and the device driver for the physical disk subsystem.

The primary benefit of host-based RAID is flexibility: RAID functions can encompass any available disk drive, regardless of packaging or location (see Figure 66). Arbitrary location of member drives is extremely useful when designing storage subsystems for high data availability (MTTDI), because completely separate data paths are easy to specify. For example, host-based mirroring can specify that one submirror resides in a cabinet in the same room as the host, whereas the other submirror may be located in another building several kilometers away and supported by a separate power grid. In the event of the failure of member disks, the location of hot spares in other enclosures reduces the likelihood of related failures lowering overall volume MTBF.

VxVM can also transparently relocate data between arbitrary disks during operation. Controller-based RAID implementations rarely implement this feature, and they have the fundamental limitation that they have access only to the drives directly under their control, usually a much smaller set of resources than the system as a whole. A few controller-based

RAID implementations have the ability to relocate data during operation, but in practice, this is of limited value. For example, HP's AutoRAID implementation permits automatic conversion of RAID-5 volumes into RAID-1+0 volumes (and vice versa) if data access patterns suggest that it is appropriate. The problem with implementing it in a disk controller is that it can only operate on the disks residing in its own cabinet. In order to convert a RAID-5 volume into a RAID-1+0 volume, the RAID-5 must consume less than a third of the available drives (e.g., a six-disk RAID-5 volume requires that the controller have access to at least those six drives, plus ten more for the equivalent RAID-1+0). This arrangement also is structurally limited to operating on volumes that are less than half of the capacity of the disk array. Although such operation is certainly possible, allocating half of each disk array for scratch purposes is an unlikely proposition. It would be less expensive to simply mirror everything and be done with it. If the relocation function is located in the host, the problem is reduced to reserving a system-wide single pool of conversion space, and operations are possible on volumes up to half of the capacity of the entire system.

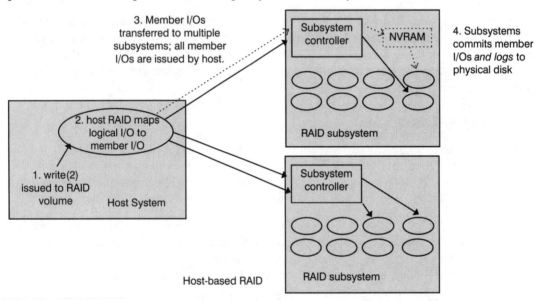

Figure 66. Host-based RAID. Logical-to-physical mapping is performed by the host processor, so members of the RAID volume may reside on any host-attached disk. This capability is useful when configuring for high failure resistance. In exchange, the host must consume bandwidth and I/O management overhead.

One of the criticisms of host-based RAID is that it is thought to be slower than controller-based RAID, especially for the XOR computations involved in RAID-5. Host-based RAID *is* usually slower than controller-based RAID, but not for the commonly accepted reason: the XOR computations are actually handled faster in host processors, for the simple reason that they are faster, more sophisticated processors at any given time. For example, a fairly typical 1996 disk array uses a 486DX2-66 CPU, a scalar processor that can execute about eight XOR operations every 12-15 clock cycles. A typical host processor in a Solaris system is a 167 MHz UltraSPARC, which can execute two XORs every clock cycle—and which runs at a substantially higher clock rate. Another common misconception is that the overhead of running the XOR computation imposes significant load on the host, but computing the XOR for a 64 KB chunk consumes about 30 microseconds on a 167 MHz UltraSPARC—about three percent of the effort required to perform a RAID-5 write.

7.5.11.2 Controller-Based RAID

One of the advantages of running RAID in an external subsystem processor is indeed lower host overhead, but not for XOR computations. The real overhead in controller-based RAID implementations (Figure 67) is the management of the various member I/Os. Host-based RAID-5 forces the host to manage two sets of I/O operations: the logical I/O (to the RAID-5 volume) and the member I/Os that are used to implement the logical operation. These can be quite substantial, since every SCSI I/O requires a finite, non-trivial amount of processor attention (about a millisecond). Since a RAID-5 write operation generally requires five or six member I/Os—including reads to obtain old parity information and writes to the log, data, and parity—the overhead can become sizable. Although this possibility is a concern, most systems do have the necessary processor power to handle this overhead, especially since the performance characteristics of the RAID-5 organization mean that write-bound applications will likely opt for mirroring instead.

A secondary consideration is the use of host connection bandwidth. When the host implements the RAID function, it must issue I/O operations to each of the member drives, consuming bandwidth on the I/O busses connected to the host. This recommendation is not an issue for read operations, since the data must eventually be transferred from the member drives to the host, but writes to any type of RAID-including mirroring—consume additional host bandwidth. Most systems have far more host bandwidth than required (due to small I/O sizes—see section 7.2.5.2, *SCSI Bus Throughput—Random I/O*), so it is not normally a practical concern, but configurations that write heavily to host-based RAID-5 volumes may encounter this problem.

The most significant reason to use controller-based RAID-5 implementations is that they have an architectural advantage for manipulating NVRAM write acceleration. Controller-based RAID implementations are tightly coupled to NVRAM, whereas host-based RAID must either use a host-based NVRAM or manipulate a remote NVRAM via an I/O bus. The *Netra n* NFS server takes the former approach. It uses an uninterruptible power supply to convert a large section of host memory into a very large NVRAM cache (up to 512 MB). This approach is viable for single systems, but is unsuitable for dual-host high availability configurations.

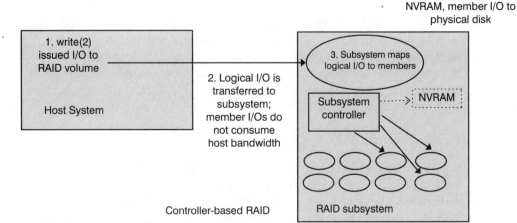

4. Logs committed to NVRAM, member I/O to physical disk

1. write(2) issued I/O to RAID volume

Host System

2. Logical I/O is transferred to subsystem; member I/Os do not consume host bandwidth

3. Subsystem maps logical I/O to members

Subsystem controller

NVRAM

Controller-based RAID

RAID subsystem

Figure 67. Controller-based RAID implementation has no access to drives in other logical locations, but physical I/Os are managed by the subsystem controller, rather than by the host. Log operations can be committed entirely to NVRAM with impunity.

Standard implementations of host-based RAID-5 using the SPARCstorage Array manipulate a remote NVRAM cache. The host converts the logical I/O to member I/Os and issues regular disk writes to a caching disk controller such as the SPARCstorage Array. The host relies on the outboard controller to accelerate writes to the member disks. In particular, the logical I/O cannot be directly accelerated. Log writes are almost always substantially accelerated by an outboard NVRAM, even when the RAID computation is performed in the host. Because the host does not have direct access to an NVRAM cache, the write must be broken into member I/Os before it can be accelerated. Unfortunately, this situation requires that almost the entire RAID-5 operation must be completed before any write acceleration can be applied: no writes can be issued until the entire parity computation process is complete.

Controller-based RAID implementations have complete access to local NVRAM , so they can commit the *logical* write into memory and acknowledge it to the host, providing a substantial latency advantage. The controller can map the logical write into its constituent parts and issue the I/Os to the member disks at its leisure. Several useful optimizations such as write clustering, write cancellation, and inter-stripe coalescing can be implemented under this arrangement. Finally, the commit log can be written to mirrored NVRAM without having to issue a member I/O, saving overhead.

By delaying the writes to member disks for a few milliseconds (usually less than 100 ms), the controller may be able optimize sequential throughput by consolidating logical I/Os that are sequential. Sequential I/O can often be optimized by converting partial stripe writes into full stripe writes. Sequential I/O is usually issued well within the aging window, permitting the controller to perform write clustering on the logical I/Os. For example, five consecutive 2 KB logical I/Os can be issued to the member disks as one 10 KB. If the chunk size is larger than 10 KB, this optimization can avoid substantial overhead—even if the write cannot be converted to a full stripe operation—because five 2 KB I/Os would require five read/modify/write cycles. Finally, when multiple logical I/Os are directed to a single stripe width, the controller may be able to cache data required to compute parity, avoiding either read I/O or additional XOR computation.

Some RAID-5 implementations have clever implementations that are able to short-circuit some of the agonizingly slow parts of RAID-5 writes. For example, NVRAM caches can convert most sequential RAID-5 writes from read/modify/write operations into full-stripe writes. This algorithm is found in many disk array firmware implementations. Sequential writes are improved because the NVRAM cache is able to retain parity information for "recently accessed" stripe widths, permitting the RAID-5 operation to proceed without waiting for parity reads. This optimization permits full-stripe throughput for most types of sequential write operations and has the side benefit of lowering member disk utilization by a significant margin. The algorithm does not affect *random* updates very much (because the parity information would not be cached), but it can provide a remarkable improvement in cases where the system is dominated by sequential RAID-5 writes. One common application that benefits greatly is the loading of a Sybase System 10 DBMS, a process that customarily issues long streams of 2 KB sequential writes.

As can be seen from this discussion, NVRAM caches in disk controllers are used almost exclusively to satisfy write requirements, rather than reads. Furthermore, data resides in the NVRAM for very short periods of time. These characteristics tend to limit requirements for large NVRAM controller caches. In practice, little performance difference separates an 8 MB cache and a 64 MB cache. Many controllers provide the option to divide NVRAM along physical boundaries and mirror between the pairs. Unless the controller is equipped with a *very* small NVRAM (4 MB or less), the added reliability of mirrored cache greatly outweighs the performance benefits of doubling the cache size. For example, any performance gain from upgrading a 32 MB cache to 64 MB is usually less than five percent for writes, and is usually nil for reads.

⇒ Select mirrored NVRAM cache over non-mirrored caches of double the size, when the controller provides this option.

7.5.11.3 Combining RAID Implementations

As usual, most configurations have a place for both host-based RAID and controller-based RAID. Controller-based RAID is strongly preferred for applications that must write RAID-5 volumes, but its advantages do not extend to read operations, which operate at about the same speed and with approximately the same overhead. For mirrored volumes, the flexibility provided by host-based RAID is usually more important than the minor host bandwidth advantage provided by controller-based mirroring. The processor overhead for running host-based RAID-0 or RAID-1 is negligible—less than one percent.

Probably the most compelling use for combined host- and controller-based RAID is the attainment of very high sequential throughput, such as for large decision support systems. These systems are nearly always limited by the bandwidth of the connection between the host and the storage subsystem. A useful configuration in these cases takes suitable volumes implemented with controller-based RAID and stripes them together with host-based RAID-0. For example, a read-mostly system requiring protected storage might implement RAID-5 volumes in each disk array and stripe those logical disks together with host-based RAID-0. Host-based RAID-5 is unnecessary in this case since data protection is already handled at the lower level.

⇒ Use host-based RAID to implement RAID-0 and RAID-1/1+0.

⇒ Use controller-based RAID to implement RAID-5, especially in applications that involve many writes to RAID-5 volumes.

7.5.12 Sun SPARCstorage Array Family

Sun's current disk array products are collectively known as the SPARCstorage Array family. It includes several models, differing mostly in subtle ways. All members use the same basic architecture; the major differences are in packaging and electrical arrangements for the disk drives.

7.5.12.1 Implementation and Packaging

Four controller implementations are available. The original controller, introduced in 1994, used a 40 MHz MicroSPARC-I processor, 4 MB of NVRAM, and six ISP-1000 SCSI host adapters for connecting member disks. All SPARCstorage Arrays use FC-25 to connect to one or two hosts. This controller was made available in two variants, one with single-ended SCSI busses for use in a table-top enclosure, and one with differential SCSI busses for use in a large data center cabinet. The controller was upgraded in 1995 to use a 110 MHz MicroSPARC-II processor, and NVRAM was quadrupled to 16 MB.

There are three packaging variants. The most common one is a desktop enclosure that provides warm-plug capability for three trays, each containing up to ten 3.5" x 1" low-profile drives using industry-standard SCA-2 hot-plug connectors. Each tray carries two SCSI busses connected to the single-ended versions of the controller. Early data center arrays were comprised of a differential controller mounted in a standard storage cabinet with six trays of 5¼" disks. These were primarily intended to upgrade existing disk cabinets; the trays did not have provisions for either multiple power supplies or hot pluggable drives. The latest package uses the same data center cabinet and controller, but uses disk mounting hardware that includes redundant power and fully hot-pluggable 3½" disks.

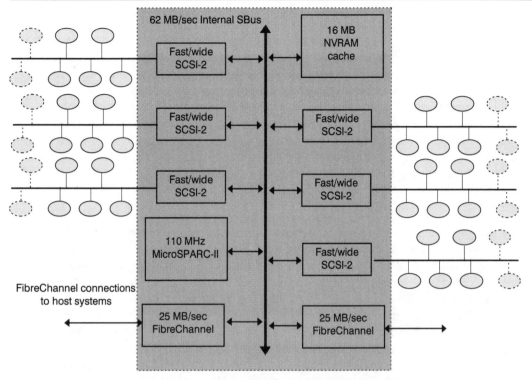

Figure 68. Architecture of the SPARCstorage Array. Desktop/deskside models such as the SPARCstorage Array Model 101, 102, and 112 have only 30 disks due to packaging constraints; these models have only five disks per SCSI bus, whereas data center racks have seven drives per bus.

In Sun's nomenclature, each array's model number consists of three digits. The first digit indicates table-top (1xx) or data center (2xx) enclosure; the second digit indicates which controller model (x0x for the 40 MHz variant, x1x for the 110 MHz); and the last digit indicates the capacity of the member disks in gigabytes. Finally, the indication RSM at the end indicates the use of the fully hot-pluggable disk canisters. For example, the SPARCstorage Array Model 214RSM is a data center rack containing a differential 110 MHz controller and 4 GB disks mounted in hot pluggable canisters. The SPARCstorage Array Model 102 is a table-top unit that differs from the Model 112 in that the former has a single-ended 40 MHz controller instead of the 110 MHz variant.

7.5.12.2 Performance

The real-world performance of a SPARCstorage Array is dependent on a variety of different factors, as is true of all disk arrays. In general, the random access performance of an array is limited by the performance of its member disks, and sequential performance is limited by the controller itself.

The MicroSPARC processor is responsible for managing the SCSI I/Os to member disks, FibreChannel communication with the host, and organizing NVRAM write activity. All RAID computations are handled in the host. All of the major components in the array controller are connected by an SBus. The MicroSPARC processors include an on-chip SBus generator and a memory controller, used to interface the processor to a dedicated control store and the NVRAM cache. Controllers using the 40 MHz processor clock the internal SBus at 20 MHz, resulting in sustainable end-user performance of approximately 18 MB/sec. Newer controllers using the 110 MHz processor run the SBus at 22 MHz, but the more efficient SBus implementation in the MicroSPARC-II permits sustainable end-user performance of about 23 MB/sec.

Inspection of Table 24 (page 242) indicates that these SBus implementations are capable of much higher throughput, and in fact they are. Unfortunately, the use of an NVRAM cache requires that most transfers between the host and the six SCSI subsystems be done in two steps. The data is first transferred to the controller CPU, which places the data in the NVRAM cache; then the data is transferred from the controller to the FibreChannel interfaces. This organization requires each logical transfer to traverse the SBus twice, effectively reducing bandwidth by half. The difference between half of the sustained SBus transfer speed (31 MB/sec) and the actual deliverable data rate (23 MB/sec) is device command overhead. This level of overhead is not unusual on peripheral busses such as SBus and PCI, since device control is normally accomplished through straightforward but relatively inefficient programmed I/O schemes.

This organization ensures that the FibreChannel host connection can never limit the array's performance: in all cases, the full-duplex FC can handle more data than the controller itself can transfer. This also renders moot the notion of utilizing the second FC port to connect an array to the host to obtain additional bandwidth: the controller does not have sufficient bandwidth to feed the additional connection. (Even if did, the administrative issues are difficult to manage. Solaris does not implement multiple parallel data paths to disks, so each physical drive in the array appears to be two disks—one connected via each FC link. Although the software appears to handle the situation correctly in all cases, the possibilities for operator error are legion—and can be catastrophic to data stored on the drives.)

In practice, neither of the controllers is pressed to the limit of its bandwidth very often, for the simple reason that most I/O is random access, and is therefore limited by the ability of the disk drives to deliver the data. The 40 MHz controller can handle about 2,200 I/Os per second, and the 110 MHz version is capable of over 3,300 I/Os per second. Since disk drives are capable of delivering 75-100 I/Os per second (depending on their rotation speed), the older controller can handle thirty 5,400 rpm drives or twenty two 7,200 rpm drives, even at full utilization. The faster controller can handle 44 fully utilized 5,400 rpm drives or thirty three 7,200 rpm drives. Since drives are used equally only on rare occasions, the practical limits are virtually never reached. All of the drives offered in the SPARCstorage Arrays have been 5,400 rpm models except the 2.1 GB 3 ½" model used in the Model 102 and Model 112.

7.5.13 Sun RSM Array 2000

The newest disk array from Sun is the RSM Array 2000. Visually similar to the SPARCstorage Array Model 214, the later model uses the same disk drives and packaging, but built with a completely different implementation strategy.

7.5.13.1 Implementation and Packaging

The RSM Array 2000 consists of a dual-redundant array controller combined with five trays of seven 3.5" x 1.6" disk drives, all housed in a data center cabinet. Density is somewhat lower than on the older model—35 drives are accommodated compared with 42. Whereas the Model 214 uses host-based RAID, the RSM Array 2000 has controller-based RAID. Each controller has a 100 MHz 486DX-4 processor, 8 MB of firmware memory, 64-128 MB of non-volatile cache, and dedicated hardware to assist in RAID-5 parity computation. The controllers connect to the disks via five fast/wide SCSI-2 busses; the host connects to each of the controllers via differential fast-20/wide SCSI-3 busses. Each cabinet therefore has two 40 MB/sec connections to the host.

In addition to fully hot-plug components (controllers, drives, fans, and power supplies), the dual controllers can be configured to in dual-active mode, meaning that both controllers are active and exchanging data with the host. If one controller should fail, a device driver running in the host causes access to the disks to be redirected via the surviving controller. Each tray of disks is connected to both controllers using a multi-initiator configuration. Each controller has either 64 MB or 128 MB of NVRAM cache; to permit the array to survive a controller failure, each NVRAM is split in half and mirrored on the opposite controller. The shared SCSI busses carry the cache mirror traffic between controller; there is an additional connection between the controllers used to receive the status of the opposite counterpart.

7.5.13.2 Performance

From a capacity planning perspective, the most significant features of the RSM Array 2000 are sequential throughput made possible by fast-40 host connections, controller-based RAID-5 performance, and a much larger NVRAM cache.

The fast-40 host connections can each deliver sequential throughput of 34 MB/sec from a suitably configured RAID volume to the host. Given the 5 MB/sec average sequential performance of typical disk drives, 34 MB/sec can only be achieved with RAID volumes that are at least seven disks wide. Suitable examples are a seven-disk RAID-0 or a 6+1 RAID-5 volume. Because individual disks deliver data at variable rates, at least one more disk may be required if the volume resides in the slow zones of one or more member disks.

Like the earlier controller, the NVRAM is used to absorb writes very quickly. When the controller is committing writes into the cache, it can handle about 1,200 writes/sec. Reads may be satisfied from cache, although this is rare due to the small relative size of the cache compared to the disk capacity (256 MB of cache on two fully-configured controllers, compared with 147 GB of disk storage—about 0.1 percent). The controller can deliver reads from the cache at over 6,000 ops/sec. Reads are much faster than writes because writes must be replicated in the opposite controller; even though the writes are cached in NVRAM, delays are incurred as the data must be transferred across the back-end SCSI busses for mirroring purposes.

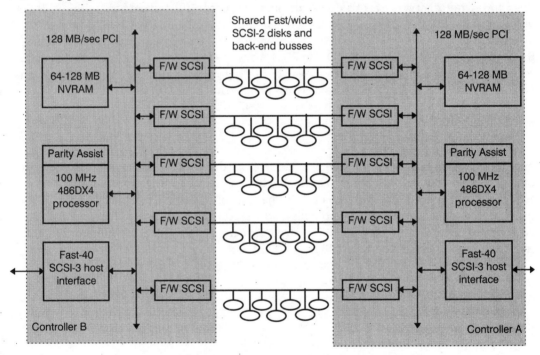

Figure 69. Internal architecture of the RSM Array 2000, including dual active controllers

The controller-based RAID implementation is tightly coupled with the management of the NVRAM cache, permitting much higher RAID-5 write performance than in host-based implementations. The RSM Array 2000 implements all of the optimizations discussed in 7.5.11.2, *Controller-Based RAID. In particular, partial-stripe RAID-5 writes are accomplished at rates much closer to those of individual disk drives than on the SPARCstorage Array.* For example, a 5+1

RAID-5 volume absorbs random 2 KB writes at over 400 ops/sec (about 800 KB/sec), compared to about 60 ops/sec (120 KB/sec)on the SPARCstorage Array Model 214.

7.6 Putting It All Together: Configuring Disk Subsystems

The preceding discussion described many of the architectural facets of disk subsystems and their components. The following section applies this architectural information to the three basic real–world criteria for configuring disk subsystems: performance, reliability, and cost. *When in doubt as to the relative importance of performance or reliability, configure for reliability. The performance of a system that fails is zero.*

7.6.1 Disks in the Real World—Configuring for Reliability

Many users configure systems on the basis of price, and others configure for highest performance. Unfortunately, far too many ignore configuration for reliability. Storage subsystems on Solaris–based systems have grown so fast in the past year or two that the reliability of storage has rapidly become a major unrecognized issue. Disk drives have become almost an order of magnitude more reliable in the past decade, but even this fantastic improvement has been dwarfed by the almost unbelievable improvement in density and price/performance.

7.6.1.1 The Price/Reliability Gap

In 1988, a typical Sun–4/280 had about six disk drives, each with an MTBF of approximately 75,000 hours; the resulting reliability was about 12,500 hours—about 17 months. One failure every year and a half is reasonably easy to manage. In 1992 the typical SPARCserver 690 was configured with about 16 disks, with individual MTBF of about 175,000 hours. The cumulative disk MTBF was about 11,000 hours (15 months). In 1996, a typical SPARCcenter 2000E has more than 250 disk drives with a greatly improved MTBF for individual disks of about 500,000 hours. The reliability of the pool of disks is about 2000 hours—less than three months. Large configurations are becoming increasingly affordable, and systems with a thousand or more drives are becoming commonplace. With 1,000 drives configured, anticipate an average failure rate of one drive every three weeks!

These realities strongly suggest that mission–critical systems *must* configure protected storage. The type and extent of the protection varies with the application and criticality of the data and operation. Disks should *not* be automatically mirrored—at double the storage cost, or more—but *some* storage on virtually every system should be mirrored, or at least protected. *Any storage that is crucial to the system's continued operation must be protected.* Normally this means the root and /usr partitions, as well as swap space and the application binaries. When DBMS systems are involved, the logs and rollback segments usually must be protected, and the log devices of mission–critical UFS + file systems should also be mirrored.

(UFS+ log devices are usually so small that protecting them with RAID–5 turns out to cost more than simply mirroring the relatively small data and being done with it. Moreover, they are virtually write-only, a bad fit for a RAID-5 volume. See *Configuring UFS+ Log Devices*, section 9.2.1.3.)

⇒ Compute MTBF for all crucial volumes. Be aware of the relative reliability of the underlying disk configuration.

⇒ All mission–critical binaries, as well as the operating system, and swap partitions must reside on protected storage. Mirroring is preferred to RAID–5 for this purpose, since a failed system can still be booted from a surviving submirror.

⇒ Every persistent user disk function in a mission–critical system must reside on some sort of protected storage. Crucial DBMS functions usually include data dictionaries, log, and commit buffers.

7.6.1.2 Hot Sparing

Disk functions that are worth protecting should be further protected by some number of hot spares. A multitude of hot spares is not necessary—just a few should suffice. There only need be sufficient hot spares to cover the reasonably anticipated simultaneous failures. For example, if a 5–data+1–parity RAID–5 volume is configured, only one hot spare is required, since multiple simultaneous failures will destroy volume integrity anyway. Hot spares need not be dedicated to single volumes, either. One global hot spare drive can serve many volumes, and a small pool of several drives can be allocated to back a large number of volumes. This method applies when hot pluggable disk subsystems are used, because the hot spare only needs to serve until a physical replacement can be installed, rather than until the next system shutdown.

⇒ *Always* have at least one hot spare available to any protected volume.

⇒ Hot spares are more necessary for RAID-0+1 than for RAID–1+0 configurations, since a single failure can remove all protection in a 0+1 configuration, whereas 1+0 remains mostly protected (see section 7.5.4, *RAID-1+0: RAID-1 Volumes with RAID-0 Submirrors*).

7.6.1.3 Other Reliability Considerations

Configuring storage for maximum reliability typically means eliminating single points of failure, *while minimizing the overall number of components.* For example, given roughly equivalent MTBF, one 4.3 GB disk is considerably less likely to fail than two 2.1 GB disks. On the other hand, the notion that fewer disks are more reliable is *not* universally true. In general, 3.5" disks are much more reliable than contemporary 5.25" drives, and older disks are nearly always less reliable than newer models. For example, the Seagate 3.5" ST15150W 4.3 GB disk is rated at over 500K hours MTBF, whereas the 5.25" Seagate ST41080N 9 GB drive delivers only about 200K hours MTBF. In this case, two of the smaller disks are *more* reliable than one of the larger disks, as well as delivering higher performance. Note that reliability engineers are in the same position as configuration planners: they are predicting the future. Often the achieved MTBF of a disk is very different from the rated MTBF (in some instances field MTBF has achieved only 30 percent of original manufacturer's rating). Check with *your* vendor for field MTBF data. Another vendor selling "the same disk" may or may not have the same product—packaging *can* significantly affect disk reliability, for example, by having different electrical, shock, vibration, or thermal characteristics. Firmware characteristics can also vary widely among suppliers of seemingly the same part.

⇒ Carefully check with the vendor for MTBF of drives *in the proposed packaging.*

⇒ Compare several configurations for overall MTBF. The results can be surprising.

7.6.1.4 Packaging

Minimizing the number of components can mean more than just minimizing the number of disk drives. In particular, look for simple and streamlined packaging. Many disk arrays use an elaborate carrier for each disk drive whose purpose is to interface a commodity disk without hot plug connectors into a fully hot-pluggable subsystem. This solution seems elegant solution and likely to improve system reliability, but careful analysis often reveals otherwise. Literally every component can fail, and most such carriers have a number of wires and connectors in them. Although the failure of the physical carrier is unlikely to have an operational impact, the failure of either a cable or connector is likely to result in an operational disruption.

Multiplying disk enclosures is another common configuration that results in sub–optimal reliability, although it is not as problematic as it once was. A configuration that uses four desktop disk packages is *far* less reliable than a "just a bunch of disks" enclosure with an equivalent number of disks. Consider a system configured with four desktop quad-disk boxes, compared with the same 16 disks in a typical disk array. The disk array will have just one power cord, one SCSI or FibreChannel cable, and probably is self-terminating, whereas the desktop disk enclosures have four SCSI cables, four terminators, and four power cables.

⇒ Minimize packaging and cabling.

7.6.1.5 Environmental Considerations

One final comment on disk reliability is that disks, more than most other computer system components, are sensitive to environmental factors. The MTBF figures quoted by most vendors are for ideal operating conditions—typically in an environment in which temperature and humidity are controlled in the center of the specified operating ranges. When operated at the limits of the approve operating range, reliability falls off substantially. A disk that is rated for operation between 10° and 40°C is about half as reliable at 40°C than at 25°C.

Most large configurations (the ones most at risk from disk reliability concerns) are located in environmentally–controlled data centers, but this generalization is far from universally true, and environmental considerations should be kept in mind when building configurations of this magnitude. Small-scale systems are affected too, but the arithmetic is much more reasonable. For example, an Ultra–1 server with a 30–disk array expects a disk failure about every two years at 25° and about once a year at 35°-40°C. However, the 1,000 drive example above likely will suffer a failure every ten days at 40 °C.

⇒ Operate mission–critical systems in controlled environments to maximize reliability. The systems themselves are not significantly less reliable in high–temperature environments, but disk drives *are*.

7.6.2 Disks in the Real World—Configuring for Performance

Maximizing disk performance amounts to reducing contention for physical resources, and, to some degree, enabling multiple resources to work together on a single problem. The basic strategies are easily derived from the strengths and weaknesses of the various disk organizations.

7.6.2.1 Reducing Disk Utilization

Industry consensus indicates that, for high-performance systems, disk drives should be busy no more than about 60 percent of the time. Disks that are busier than this level should have their access load spread across two or more drives. Device utilization governs how long an *individual* request is pending against the device. Although the device is usually able to sustain its maximum overall throughput rate, individual requests may spend considerably longer time in the service queues, resulting in slower perceived performance for the end user. Figure 70 illustrates this point[71]. This principle applies equally to other resources in the system, particularly busses such as SCSI, MBus, and Gigaplane. Fortunately, most busses have sufficient bandwidth that utilization stays relatively low, even during high activity periods. Disks, have very limited capabilities and are often driven at very high utilization.

> Caution: *The impact of excessive resource utilization cannot be overestimated.* Many systems have a single disk drive that is operated at 99-100 percent utilization. In such cases, the length of the request queue for the disk is also very long—sometimes as many as 80-250 requests may be pending against the drive. Given that most modern disks can service about 100 disk operations per second, a queue length of 80-250 means that requests at the end of queue will experience delays of 800-2,500 milliseconds. *I/O requests*

---

[71] Chen, P. *An Evaluation of Redundant Arrays of Inexpensive Disks Using an Amdahl 5890.* M.S. Thesis, University of California at Berkeley, Computer Science Division, 1989. p. 562.

> *issued against the disk thus suffer delays well in excess of a second, the equivalent of nearly 400 million CPU instructions!*

Even at the 60 percent utilization level the disk can still be a bottleneck. Utilization and the associated latency can be reduced significantly by providing additional disk resources. The time taken to service a specific user I/O request consists of two parts: the time spent waiting for the device to service previously pending requests, and the time spent waiting for the device to service the request. Of these, the device service time is by far the greatest component, since the device is mechanical. Intuitively, a less busy device is able to respond to a given request more quickly. Accordingly, major reductions in utilization usually correspond to improvements in overall perception of performance.

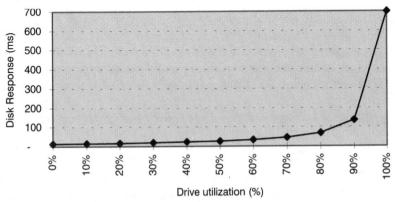

Figure 70. Disk response time as utilization increases. The response time governs the performance of the system as perceived by the user.

By far the most effective way to reduce drive utilization is to spread the access load across as many disks as are economically feasible. This solution can sometimes be accomplished through the simple expedient of logically dividing the data and locating it on multiple disks, for example, by putting one half of the users on one disk and the other half on another disk. Unfortunately, this approach usually falls short of the desired results, because disk access is frequently not coordinated with data volume. In this example, two users out of an entire community may generate 80 percent of the I/O load, and if they happen to land on the same disk, they will cause a severe usage imbalance. The situation is even less clear when the data is of varying usage; for example, the home directories account for more than 90 percent of the disk space on a typical server, yet nearly 50 percent of all disk accesses are made to the root file system, because /var/mail resides there.

Because the division of disk accesses is usually far from clear, especially *within* a specific set of data, disk striping (RAID–0, RAID–3, or RAID–5) provides the easiest, most reliable mechanism to spread data access across multiple disks. A RAID metadisk can be used "as is" in place of a raw disk partition, or with a file system built on top. This flexibility permits metadisks to function for either databases or file systems as appropriate. As with most other facets of disk configuration, the metadisk configuration depends upon the dominant access pattern.

7.6.2.2 Data Layout—Minimizing Seek Time

The magnitude of each of the components of disk access time can be used to optimize the performance of disk I/O subsystems. Fundamentally the idea is to eliminate as many seeks as possible and to minimize the remaining ones. Careful location of data on the physical disks can substantially reduce the amount of time spent waiting for mechanical I/O operations.

The Berkeley Fat Fast File System format used by Solaris divides the disk space occupied by a file system into contiguous segments called cylinder groups. The system goes to considerable effort to keep files entirely within a cylinder group; this minimizes seek distance and seek time. This service is provided transparently by the file system code. Applications that use raw disks must perform similar optimizations, and the most notable consumers of raw disks—database management systems—provide some sort of similar optimization.

Even given these optimizations, administrators can do a considerable amount to minimize seek times. The more data a cylinder can hold, the less often that a seek will be required. The geometry of physical disks is of course fixed, but striping can be used to enlarge the effective size of the cylinder. The effect is to make logical cylinders the sum of the size of the cylinders making up the stripe. Because a given quantity of data now fits in fewer cylinders, the disks must perform fewer physical seeks to access the data.

Reducing seek times is possible even on a single disk. Nearly all disks shipped today use Zone Bit Recording. Because the outside cylinders are physically larger than the inside cylinders, using the these cylinders where possible results in fewer seeks. As with the larger logical cylinders created by striping, the use of a larger cylinder size results in fewer seeks; moreover, the seeks that are still required are shorter.

The fact that long seeks take much longer than short ones leads to a further recommendation: where possible, configure disks with just a single primary purpose. In particular, avoid frequent access to two different partitions of a disk. Database systems are frequently configured with a disk that contains a partition for data tables and a separate partition for logs. The logs are "fitted" onto the end of a disk because they consume relatively little space. However, if configured onto the end of a disk that contains a frequently used table or index, the performance penalty could be significant. It is best to configure frequently used functions onto independent disk arms. If necessary to consolidate multiple functions onto a single disk, configure one "hot" function per drive.

If the number of specialized purposes requires assignment of several functions to a single disk, put the most frequently accessed slices in adjacent slices. The boot disk warrants special attention. For historical reasons, most system disks are configured with at least four partitions (slices): root, swap, /usr, and /export. This organization is far from optimal, since swap will probably be the most frequently accessed slice, and /export is nearly always referenced more than /usr. If a seek outside of the current partition is required, it probably will cross most of the disk, either from swap to /export or vice versa. Configuring the slices in the order root, swap, /export, /usr reduces the length of seeks for absolutely no cost!

The exception to this rule is the configuration of additional swap space. Most systems use dedicated swap partitions for backing store for anonymous virtual memory. However, if a disk must be used for both swap and a heavily used file system, combining these functions in a single partition is possible. The mkfile(8) command can be used to create a swap file, and the swap(8) command is then used to make it active. Creating the swap file *in* a heavily used file system helps reduce disk seek length. The degradation associated with swapping onto a file system rather than a raw partition is less than one percent and can be safely ignored.

⇒ Store frequently–used data in the fastest zones (lowest–numbered cylinders) of a disk.

⇒ Configure only one heavily–used function onto each disk.

⇒ If multiple functions *must* be consolidated onto a disk, configure the most frequently used functions together.

⇒ Striping (RAID–0 or RAID–3/5) can be used to increase the size of cylinders and thus reduce the number and length of seeks.

⇒ If swap space must be configured onto the same disk as another frequently used file system, build a swap file in that file system and swap onto it.

7.6.2.3 Using RAID to Optimize—Random Access

Optimizing disk utilization in the random access case is relatively simple. A stripe of the available disks normally minimizes the utilization. The choice of chunk size is dependent upon the type of usage. If a file system is to be built on the metadisk, choose a chunk optimized for the 56 KB file system blocks as in section 9.2.3.2 *File System Cluster Size*. If the metadisk is to be used as a raw disk for a DBMS tablespace, the default chunk (a disk cylinder) is the most appropriate, since most DBMS systems normally operate with data blocks less than or equal to the size of the minimum chunk. The choice of a large chunk imposes the minimum overhead for splitting I/O transactions yet evenly distributes the data across the drives so that all drives are utilized.

Surprisingly, disk mirroring can also improve disk access performance in some cases. The geometric read mirroring option improves serial reads by using alternate submirrors to supply data—in effect the same as a disk stripe. The other alternative, round-robin, usually improves random reads by permitting load balancing across the submirrors. Writes to a mirror, of course, are not faster than writes to a non-mirror.

⇒ Use any RAID method (0/1/3/5) as appropriate to storage requirements to spread random access workload across as many disks as reasonable.

7.6.2.4 Using RAID to Optimize—Sequential Access

For access that is sequential, the choice of chunk size is important. A stripe of at least four disks on two host adapters with a small chunk size normally yields the highest sequential throughput. If more than four disks are available, the optimal configuration uses four-way stripes and concatenates them together. The small chunk size is used to spread individual accesses across as many drives as possible as often as possible. For very small requests such as the typical 2 KB raw DBMS I/O, breaking up the I/Os into small enough chunks is impossible. Nonetheless, striping normally does improve throughput as it lowers disk utilization, especially in multi-user or multitasking environments. Multithreaded DBMS servers with as few as one active process also benefit from this organization, since most of these DBMS implementations use asynchronous I/O completion notification to generate many simultaneously pending I/O requests. A four-way stripe normally delivers about three times faster serial throughput than a single disk, and a two-way stripe normally delivers about 85 percent more serial throughput than a single disk.

Note that unlike hardware striping, the use of software striping does *not* lock all of the disk arms in the stripe set together. Only the drives that are required to complete an I/O are activated. For example, consider a system that has a four-way stripe with 64 KB chunks. If this system receives a request for 128 KB of data, only two of the four disks will be used; the others will be free to respond to other requests. Even if the request is not aligned on a 64 KB boundary, only three disks will be activated.

⇒ Use RAID–0, RAID–3, or RAID–5 to improve sequential disk performance. Stripe width (or data stripe width) should be chosen to match the typical I/O size.

⇒ Use RAID–0 or RAID–1+0 if the disk I/O load contains a significant proportion of writes (about 25 percent).

7.6.3 Performance in Perspective

After a long discussion about performance, note that users are often more concerned with performance than is warranted. The most common system performance problem *is* a misconfigured disk subsystem, much sleep is lost needlessly over disk subsystem configuration. The disk subsystem may or may not be the limiting factor in a configuration—

and often it is not. For example, many (perhaps most) users are concerned with obtaining as much host-to-disk I/O bandwidth as possible, not recognizing that the typical application does many very small I/Os, rather than moving enormous amounts of data.

At first glance configuring 30-50 disk drives on a single 20 MB/sec SCSI bus seems ridiculous, since a disk is capable of delivering 5+ MB/sec. More in-depth analysis suggests that for the 2 KB random I/O that is normally found in most database applications, 50 disk drives can deliver only about 12 MB/sec, rather than the expected 250 MB/sec. This overall throughput is low even in the extremely unlikely circumstance that *all* of the disks are running at full utilization. Experience shows that 50 disks running at full utilization is often enough to support as many as 300-500 users, if the application is similar to an OLTP workload.

Likewise, the choice between RAID-1 and RAID-5 is often agonizing, since write performance is so drastically different. Yet for most applications that do moderate amounts of I/O, the difference may be small indeed. The TPC-C is reasonably representative of a large class of database applications. When the storage subsystem is configured for RAID-1+0 instead of simple RAID-0, the overall performance decreases by 8-10 percent, rather than the 15-30 percent that one might expect from looking at mirroring performance in isolation. Configuring the same database on RAID-5 storage results in an overall degradation of only 15-20 percent compared to RAID-0. This is particularly surprising given the extreme differential between RAID-0 and RAID-5 write performance (sometimes a factor of four)[72]. TPC-C does *relatively* little I/O, accounting for the higher than expected overall performance.

Of course, for applications that are dominated by I/O activity, such as decision support, online analytical processing (OLAP) and data-intensive NFS, overall performance may be governed directly by I/O performance. For example, configuring a data-intensive NFS server with host-based RAID-5 storage is unlikely to result in acceptable performance—especially if the clients use the NFS V2 protocol, resulting in much smaller I/O sizes to the disk, the particular weakness of the RAID-5 storage organization.

7.6.4 Balancing Performance, Reliability, and Cost

Many different concerns arise when configuring storage subsystems. Performance and cost are hard to avoid, and reliability is always a concern. Balancing these considerations can be difficult, especially in a uniform configuration. For example, a storage system is typically optimized for performance using many small disks, but such a configuration normally costs significantly more than equivalent storage built from much denser disk spindles. Overall

---

[72] In this case, the database log was configured as a mirror, rather than a RAID-5 device, since the small size of the device precluded any savings in disk space. Since this part is the write-bound part of the workload, configuring it with RAID-5 would not have resulted in as good performance.

subsystem reliability may lie with either, depending on specific components. Fortunately, configuring subsystems with many different types of components is nearly always both possible and constructive.

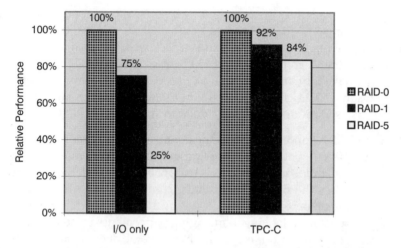

Figure 71. Real-world RAID performance comparison. Despite significant differences in the I/O-only benchmark, an application shows a much less dramatic differential due to varying RAID organizations.

The basic principle for overall configuration is to divide the storage into segments, based upon their performance and reliability concerns. Whether reliable storage should use RAID-1 mirroring or RAID-5 is often difficult. However, dividing the overall data into groups with differing requirements usually results in a configuration that involves both RAID-1 and RAID-5. Deciding between small, fast disks and large, inexpensive ones often results in a system that stores current data on the fast disks but archives most older data on the less expensive storage, possibly protected by RAID-5 instead of the much more expensive mirroring. For example, root and swap should probably always be mirrored (an I/O error in the swap area can cause a system panic). Large historical data sets such as the transaction history for 1986 are unlikely to be updated very often, so they are excellent candidates for storage on large, dense disks and protected by RAID-5. At the same time, current transactions are probably updated frequently. The current transactions, the transaction log, and the rollback segments are mission-critical data. Mirroring is much more appropriate, as is configuration on many small, fast disks.

⇒ Choose RAID levels and storage density on a dataset-by-dataset basis. Dogmatic declarations that one RAID level or one type of disk is "better" than another usually result in configurations with excess cost or performance.

Backup and Recovery 8 ≡

Any system that provides file or data service must also make provisions for backup. The extent to which backup and failure-resistance measures affect configuration varies widely with user requirements. Interestingly, although the performance and configuration of a server's normal operation is primarily governed by the access pattern of the applications, configuration and performance of the backup process is largely independent of application type and is instead much more strongly affected by availability and recovery criteria. The variety of decisions regarding backups can be the most complex part of a configuration!

8.1   The Mechanics of Tape Drives

Tapes are recorded in one of two general formats: parallel or helical scan. Parallel— sometimes called longitudinal—tapes write data in tracks that run parallel to the edge of the tape and to the direction of the tape motion; the tracks are separated by some small distance. A variant of the parallel format is the so–called *serpentine* mode. Serpentine tapes write two sets of parallel tracks (called track groups) in different tape directions. Various schemes for tape reversal are used; some drives use what would otherwise be the rewind time to manipulate the second set of tracks. The effect is very fast rewind time. This is particularly important in media such as the 3490E in which the tape is relatively short compared to the overall volume of data being manipulated.

Helical scan drives write tracks that are oriented about 135° from the tape motion (see Figure 72). If the tape is viewed edge–on in the tape motion direction, the read/write head sweeps out a helix shape. The advantage of this arrangement is that the tracks can be written literally abutting each other, saving considerable storage capacity. Helical recording heads change their orientation slightly from one track to the next, enabling the read heads to detect the difference between adjacent tracks. The major disadvantage of helical formats is that the heads contact the media much more than with parallel formats, causing more tape wear and shorter media life.

The much higher data density of the helical scan drive means that such a drive will deliver two to four times more overall capacity than a longitudinal drive using equivalent media. For some reason, vendors seem to always denote the media sizes in millimeters for helical–scan devices (e.g., 4 mm or 8 mm) while labeling longitudinal media in fractions of an inch (1/2″).

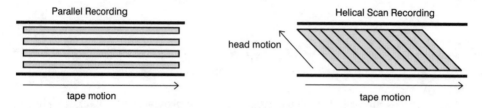

Figure 72. Comparison of parallel (longitudinal) and helical-scan recording formats. Note how much additional data area is available in the helical format, due to the elimination of the inter-track gap.

8.1.1 Blocking Factor

Tapes cannot write an arbitrary amount of data consecutively, primarily because tape mechanisms write ECC information along with the data. This permits the drive to recover from the inevitable data errors. The ECC information must be computed over a fixed–sized block. The size of the block is usually user–selectable, up to some hardware maximum. Some lost space always ends up between blocks; this is known as the *interblock gap*. The size of the blocks, and the consequent proportion of the tape devoted to interblock gaps, can be of considerable importance in planning a backup strategy.

The size of the interblock gap is essentially fixed, so smaller block sizes have a higher proportion of non–user data on the tape, and larger block sizes are more efficient. The difference can be quite remarkable. The `tar(1)` command defaults to very small 512–byte blocks, and a QIC–11 tape drive holds about 24 MB under these conditions. However, when `tar(1)` uses 63 KB blocks, the same tape can store almost 60 MB. The specific margin of data loss between very large and very small blocks is different for each media type, but the basic relationship between large blocks and higher density and throughput holds for all current media.

The useful size of the tape block is usually limited by hardware, since the potential tape block must be transferred in a single operation. The tape controller must be able to buffer the entire block, and this buffer size is commonly limited to something on the order of 64 KB. High–performance drives such as the StorageTEK helical–scan drive have much more buffering (up to 64 MB per transport in the case of the SD-3 Redwood device) and hence can accept much larger blocks. Some older Sun hardware placed a 64 KB maximum on SBus or

VME DVMA transfers[73]. This restriction limited the data transfer size to the eventual device, since the DVMA transfer also had to include the SCSI parameters describing the transfer, limiting the device transfer to about 63 KB. (This limitation is why the traditional maximum useful block size for `tar(1)` and `ufsdump(1m)` is 126 blocks—since blocks are multiples of 512 bytes, this is 63 KB. This limitation essentially does not exist in any current Sun hardware, since DVMA windows are now limited to 64 MB.)

The only drawback to maximizing blocksize is that the blocks consume kernel memory for buffers during transfer. However, this drawback is trivialized by the extremely large memories now available—most servers have hundreds of megabytes or multiple gigabytes of memory, so the difference between 64 KB and 1 MB buffer sizes is minimal in practice.

⇒ Use helical scan devices for maximum density for any given media size.

⇒ Use large block sizes to improve both throughput and tape capacity.

8.1.2 Recording "Inertia"

Some tape drives are able to start and stop the tape media very quickly, whereas others must take elaborate measures when starting and stopping the tape. For example, some models of the old IBM 3420 tape drive were able to accelerate the tape from stopped to 200 inches per second in slightly less than one millisecond. Drives capable of very fast start and stop times are much better able to handle applications that access the tape relatively infrequently. Such drives are often referred to as "start/stop" drives because they can start or stop the media within a single interblock gap. Unfortunately the G–forces implied by this high performance means that these drives can be hard on the media, limiting its life.

The value of these high–acceleration drives is best illustrated by drives that are *not* capable of stopping or starting the media within the interblock gap. Most helical-scan drives (among others) are relatively slow to start and/or stop the media; after the last data access, the media is decelerated slowly, in effect coasting past the last accessed data and well into the next block. In order to access the next block, the drive must then rewind the tape to a point before the last accessed block and then restart the tape (slowly), an action called a *backhitch*. The media must be moving at full data speed before the next accessed block arrives at the read/write heads. This process is very time–intensive. The practical difference can be illustrated by considering how long a typical VCR takes to stop, rewind, and start again— most VCRs take almost two full seconds to effect such an operation, whereas audio tapes can do the same thing in much less than one second (in fact, helical–scan units descend from the original VCRs). Fortunately most backup operations work quite well with either variety of tape drive.

---

[73] All Sun systems introduced before 1992 (*i.e.*, SPARCserver 300's and 400's, and desktops up through and including the SPARCstation 2) had this limitation.

The most common way to work around this problem is to ensure that the next block is ready for the tape before the media completes writing the current block. This task is most easily accomplished by reading or writing in very large blocks, although the nature of some operations is such that this is difficult. The Solaris 2.5 SCSI tape driver, as well as most utilities, handle block sizes of at least 256 KB. These utilities include `dd(1m)`, `ufsdump(8)`, `ufsrestore(8)`, `tar(1)`, and `cpio(1)`.

The configuration impact of highly inertial drives can be significant, especially during recovery procedures. Under most circumstances, recovery from a backup is far slower than the process that created the backup. In particular, high–performance tape drives that are not start/stop units may be forced to stop/rewind/restart for each file that is restored from the backup tape—a process that can mean that the recovery process sometimes can take an order of magnitude longer than the process that created the tape image.

⇒ Use relatively large blocking factors when using drives that have significant start/stop times, such as most helical–scan units.

8.1.3 Compression

Most tape drives now offer some sort of compression or compaction feature. In these systems, a hardware compression engine is placed between the host interface and the read/write buffer. The speed of the compression engine is such that it can always handle the full speed of the media; the net result is that the host interface simply perceives the media/compression unit to be a faster media. The only problem with compression is that it does not apply equally well to all data. For example, a file full of null characters compresses extremely well, whereas a file full of completely random numbers may barely compress at all. Data that is already compressed cannot usually be further compressed. Some understanding of the nature of the data is usually required to obtain an estimate of compressibility. In the absence of any information, a reasonable assumption is that the data will compress by a factor of about 35%(about 1.4:1) For example, a 1 GB file typically occupies about 650 MB on tape.

One problem that arises from the use of compression is the data capacity specification for a given tape drive. When a vendor indicates that a tape drive has a given density, be sure to ask whether that density is achieved with or without compression; furthermore, if the specification is attained with compression, find out what the assumed compression factor is. Most vendors now quote capacities with compression and assume a 2:1 compression ratio, but a few vendors are somewhat more optimistic. Much higher compression ratios are often available, especially in the video playback arena, but these must be clearly distinguished from the compression algorithms used in backup devices. These much higher compression ratios—some as aggressive as 20:1—are the result of algorithms that lose some small amount of data when the compressed data is retrieved and uncompressed. Lossy compression is an excellent tradeoff for video display data, where the eye is fooled relatively easily, but it clearly is not acceptable for data backup.

For most commercial applications such as DBMS systems, anecdotal evidence suggests that the typical compression factor is between 1.3:1 and 1.5:1, rather than the more typically quoted 2:1 ratio. The compression factor varies, because the algorithms used by the tape transports differ slightly.

The compression ratio also figures into the effective data rate of the drive: since the compression is performed after the data leaves the host, throughput normally improves by the compression ratio. Hence a drive that may be able to write a native bit rate of 500 KB/sec on the tape is generally capable of 1 MB/sec effective data rate from the host's perspective—but only if the data is compressible by 2:1. Understanding both the native data rate and the general compressibility of the data is crucial.

8.1.4 Throughput Scalability

One of the key considerations in backup is the size of the data to be backed up. This matter is not one of reducing the overall amount of data, but rather a matter of restricting the size of the individual volumes to be dumped. Often this is reasonably easy in systems that store data in file systems, since the symbolic nature of the addressing (i.e., by file name) means that dividing the file space into smaller, more easily managed sections is fairly easy. For example, in a system with 350 GB of disk managing as ten 35 GB file systems is much easier than managing than two 175 GB file systems. A 35 GB file system can be backed up in about two hours on a DLT–7000 tape, but over ten hours are required to back up the larger file system. Clearly one can be managed within a single eight-hour shift, and the other one cannot. Fortunately, tape drive throughput scales well as the number of drives is increased—several studies at Sun have shown that at least 40 drives can be run at very nearly full speed. For example, an Enterprise 6000 configured with 24 STK Redwoods on 12 fast/wide SCSI-2 busses was able to accept data about 195 MB/sec, a rate within 10% of the theoretical maximum (about 18 MB/sec per bus). Scalability is excellent even on a single SCSI bus, as shown in Figure 52 (page 297). Tape scalability is linear to approximately four drives on a single SCSI bus. When more drives or faster devices are required, additional SCSI busses are required.

The excellent scalability of the tape I/O subsystems means that dividing file systems into smaller sections for management is a useful strategy. This is also a useful tactic even if the data to be backed up is a DBMS, although appropriate division of the name space can be problematic. Most low-end software such as `ufsdump(8)` or older versions of Solstice:Backup generates a single data stream for each file system to be dumped, meaning that throughput is limited to the capability of a single tape. Newer versions of Solstice:Backup and high-end solutions such as Open Vision's NetBackup offer the ability to divide a single file system into multiple data streams, thus permitting vastly faster backup and recovery.

Once the data store is divided into sections, each of the segments can be dumped individually; more important, they can be dumped in parallel, making it much easier to complete dumps in the required time window. This consideration is significant in the context of backups, but it is even more important for recoveries, because they are often much longer in duration than their corresponding backups (see section 8.4, *Data Recovery Considerations* below).

Initial experience with NetBackup suggests that the software is easily capable of backing up large files at rates far in excess of 400 GB/hr (more than 110 MB/sec) when provided with sufficient disk and tape subsystems. File systems with many small files are considerably slower, but generally still faster than 100 GB/hr[74].

8.1.5 Network Backup

Traditional server configurations always include dedicated backup devices, and this is still a viable arrangement in small and some medium-sized systems. In smaller configurations, backup devices are small and inexpensive, and often the data is merely important—rather than mission critical. However, larger installations often have multiple servers and are increasingly found with hundreds of gigabytes or multiple terabytes of data, and backup devices associated with this volume of data are too expensive to replicate. The solution to these problems is the use of one or more network nodes which serve as backup sinks for a number of data sources.

In effect, this is another class of server; and as with other types of servers, provision of sufficient network bandwidth is a crucial matter. It is tempting to provide a backup community with dedicated Ethernets (since most systems have a multitude of Ethernet interfaces, often unused), but this is probably not sufficient. Even the slowest current backup devices (4 mm helical scan drives) are capable of an effective data rate of 1 MB/sec, the maximum speed of an Ethernet. Higher throughput devices demand higher performance networking.

Both FastEthernet and FDDI are viable candidates, with the latter preferred in this application because of its superior handling under high network utilization. The nature of networked backup results in long streams of maximum sized packets—and high network utilization. Using Solstice Networker or virtually any other unbundled backup software, backup of the large volumes of data which normally dictate networked backups easily generates 1.5 MB/sec-4 MB/sec. Single streams of data at this level are easily accommodated

---

[74] Throughput of this configuration is limited by disk access capacity. This project is ongoing as this text goes to print, and the results are not well-optimized.

by FastEthernet, but addition of a second stream, either from a second file system on the same system or from another source-sink pair, would drive network utilization to unacceptable levels.

ATM may be a useful alternative in this application, because its constant-bit-rate (CBR) capability permits allocation of bandwidth to each source-sink pair. Although it may seem expensive to install ATM solely for backup purposes, the bulk of the data in such clusters usually means that the storage overwhelms the cost of relatively restricted networking infrastructure. In limited scale installations, it may be feasible to make use of switchless or hubless point-to-point networks between the source and sink systems (point-to-point networks are part of the standards definitions for all of FDDI, FastEthernet and ATM).

One feasible configuration is to use what amounts to a "tape server." In very backup-intensive installations, the relatively high concentrated use of network bandwidth can consume a full 75 MHz SuperSPARC processor, or half of a 167 MHz UltraSPARC processor. A powerful backup server configuration is a SPARCstation 20 Model 712 with an ATM interface and two or three fast/wide differential SCSI interfaces. This system can sustain 12-15 MB/sec of data being read from the network and dumped to tape. The networking traffic will consume a full processor, and the second CPU in the dual-processor configuration is more than enough to drive several very high-speed backup devices. Minimal memory is required (in fact, the 64 MB minimum for this model is more than enough). Differential interfaces are used because most high-capacity backup devices require the physical space accorded by differential signaling. Not only are these devices usually configured in very large systems, but many of the devices, such as 3480/3490 compatibles, also often found in large stacker or library configurations which also consume considerable space.

The tape server configuration model is most useful in very large installations, which can easily involve millions of dollars of investment in high-end tape drives and robotic libraries. The key issues in configurations such as these are that even very fast networks are relatively slow compared to disk drives and tape drives. For example, 622 Mbit/sec ATM interfaces are capable of approximately 50 MB/sec(about 400 bits/sec) of usable throughput, a rate easily attainable from just one or two disk arrays or several high-end tape drives.

8.2 The Backup Process: Logical vs. Physical

Many implementations of backup software are available, intended for managing a myriad of different data formats, but fundamentally they all boil down to one of two ideas: "copy all of the logical entities in the file store," or "copy the image of the raw media." For the most part, these divide the process into two different configuration problems, in much the same way that NFS applications can be divided into attribute-intensive and data-intensive.

Raw media copies are usually much faster than logical store copies, because the source is read sequentially. Probably the most common example of this strategy is the traditional "dd(1) the disk image to tape" process. In this operation, dd(1) reads the raw disk image (/dev/rdsk/c11t0d1s2, for example), and the raw bits are transferred to the backup media verbatim. The structure of the file system or DBMS that is stored on the device is preserved through the simple expedient of storing the contents of the entire device. Because this process reads the raw device sequentially, the data can be retrieved at full device speed—about 6.5 MB/sec for a single disk drive. This performance is about the same as most mid-range backup devices (DLT–7000 or 3490), and when disks are configured together in RAID units, even the fastest available backup devices can be saturated.

The cost of this high performance is that the entire volume must be backed up as a single entity: because the backup program reads the storage device rather than the logical store, it does not have access to the internal structure of the storage system. For example, when the store is a UFS file system, dd(1) does not have access to the names, permission masks, or last-modified times for individual files. Raw device backups are most useful when the entire device must be backed up.

Most logical backups use a much more sophisticated algorithm than media backups, precisely because they use the logical facilities of the storage system. Instead of reading the underlying device byte by byte, a logical backup program such as ufsdump(1m) reads the superblock to obtain the names of all the directories in the file system, and then reads logical entities such as directory entries one by one, almost always not in device order. For example, ufsdump(1m) dumps a file system from the root of the file system "down" to the individual files. By reading the directory entries, ufsdump(1m) is able to inspect the last-modified date of each file and decide whether or not the file has been updated since the most recent backup.

Of course, incremental backups can comprise much smaller volumes of data than full backups, but this flexibility has a price: because the backup program does not read the media in device order; it must perform costly disk seeks, substantially reducing the throughput available from the disk. This degradation is not severe with large files, but when file systems or DBMS systems store many small files or entities (as most do), the disk seek time dominates the process. In a typical UFS file system containing many files averaging 32 KB in size, most files will consist of data in the directory entry, an inode , and four or five data blocks—all stored in different locations on the disk.

Unfortunately, reading this file is a completely random-access process, since reading each disk block requires a seek; under these conditions, the throughput available from a single disk drops by a factor of about eight: from about 6.5 MB/sec to about 0.8 MB/sec. When the file system contains smaller files, or when large files fragment into smaller pieces, throughput drops to even lower levels. Unfortunately, even combining disks into RAID configurations does not improve matters, since striping does not improve single–threaded random read throughput. This analysis considers a file system that is otherwise quiescent. Under live–load conditions such as an online backup, striping, or other RAID configurations *will* improve disk utilization and hence overall throughput from the file system. However, this difference is probably best described as "less degraded," rather than "improved."

As bad as this situation is, it can be even worse in practice: when dumping to a high-inertia tape drive, delays reading from the disk can cause the tape to overshoot the interblock gap, causing backhitches on the tape, and drastically lowering dump performance. Occasionally a tape drive that has a slower media speed can deliver a higher overall throughput than a tape drive of superior rated media speed, since the slower media avoids overshooting the interblock gap. Fortunately, this situation does not arise very often.

8.3 Backup Strategies

In simple installations, backup often consists of configuring a tape drive and arranging for a cron(1) or at(1) job to invoke ufsdump(8) to perform a backup each night. Simple provisions such as this one have little configuration impact. The user must merely install a tape drive at a free target address on a SCSI bus. However, it requires that the system be quiescent during the backup period. If file systems are in active use during the backup, the results can be inconsistent because the state of the target file system can change while the dump is running. Because the ufsdump(8) program is heavily I/O oriented, it has a tendency to take advantage of the scheduler's bias toward I/O-bound processes, to the detriment of normal user processes. For many installations, the use of ufsdump is sufficient in spite of the drawbacks since no activity occurs outside of normal business hours. If ufsdump(8) must be run during daytime or other busy hours, reconfiguring the scheduler's priority table may be worthwhile, to ensure that heavily I/O bound jobs do not take advantage of the scheduler's default biases (see *Scheduler Tuning* in section 9.7).

8.3.1 Fully-Consistent Dumps

If the consistency of the dump is mandatory, the file system being dumped must be made inaccessible to modifications. One way to do this task is to simply unmount the file system before dumping it. The file system can be remounted read-only if such access is required during the backup. Another option is to lock the file system against the updates while the backup is being performed; most commercial backup software (such as Solstice: Backup or Online: Backup 2.0) also permits larger quantities of data to be dumped in an automated fashion by addressing uniform sets of backup devices distributed throughout the network.

Because these systems prevent the file system from being modified during backup, it is nearly always used off-hours. This method not only permits convenient access to the file systems, it also takes advantage of the fact that most networks are much less busy out of normal business hours. When tape drives are configured in a variety of systems in the network, the backup process dominates most networks. Although slow tape drives are not especially fast in the realm of SCSI devices (500 KB-1 MB/sec for 8 mm and 4 mm helical-scan devices offered by Sun), a single *slow* tape drive is sufficient to load Ethernet and Token Ring networks to the point where users perceive very poor response, and mid-range tapes such as DLT-7000 can load FastEthernet to a corresponding level. Additionally, the volume of data associated with backups—even incremental backups are very often 500 MB to 1 GB, and sometimes much more in environments that include file system-resident databases [75]—is so large that backups can take considerable time. If tape drives are configured in various systems around the network, rather than concentrated on the NFS server systems, the best solution is to configure a private network specifically for keeping backup traffic off of the user networks.

As with simple dumps, this option is normally implemented during non-business hours, and normally has little effect on the configuration of the server itself. In particular, although SCSI bus utilization is often driven far over the recommended maximum, human users are typically not present to perceive the degraded response. However, if batch jobs are run overnight, they can be substantially degraded during the backup. In these circumstances, configuration of the backup devices onto a private SCSI bus becomes mandatory. This measure is usually sufficient to return I/O response time to acceptable levels, because disks are both considerably faster than tapes and because disks normally use the much faster synchronous burst transfer mode. As a result, the backup process normally spends its time waiting for the tape, and disk utilization remains low—and SCSI bus utilization remains high.

8.3.2 Fully–Mirrored Storage

Some sites have much more stringent requirements. Sites that require full-time availability of data can use software or hardware mirroring to replicate crucial data onto two or more separate disks (up to eight–way using VxVM). Whereas a simple ufsdump during the off hours has no real impact on how the system is configured, mirroring clearly requires careful configuration. By itself, mirroring does not solve the real backup problem (nor do other protected storage mechanisms, such as RAID–5). Although individual component failures do not cause loss of data, mirrored data is just as susceptible to application bugs and operator or user error.

The primary considerations when attempting a mirrored storage are write latency and overhead, and sometimes I/O bus utilization. Write latency is minimized by NVRAM caching at the storage subsystem level, although it is not completely eliminated. Overhead can be minimized by running the mirroring function entirely within a disk array (as opposed to use of host–based mirroring via Solstice:DiskSuite or Volume Manager), but this arrangement is susceptible to loss of the array controller and may also not provide access to sufficient storage. Mirroring overhead is relatively minimal, as noted in section 6.4.3.

---

[75] Such as Ingres, Progress, Interbase, and dBase.

I/O bus utilization and disk array utilization can be issues if the system is heavily loaded, particularly when disk storage is configured on SCSI busses connected directly to the host. For typical Solaris–based systems, this configuration is normally found only in desktop systems where the FibreChannel SPARCstorage Array represents too much capacity. Desktop systems are also the ones that typically use relatively low–performance tape drives, precisely the ones that consume surprisingly large amounts of SCSI bus utilization time.

8.3.3 Full-Time Availability

Even mirrored disks must be backed up, because data can be destroy in a fantastic variety of ways, even without disk failure. For example, a legitimate request to remove a directory tree may be accidentally issued by the user. If file systems must be available *all* the time the system is up, mirroring and off-line consistent dump techniques may be combined to achieve full availability.

Such a configuration requires file systems to be mirrored. In order to provide for fully consistent backups, one of the submirrors is detached. The detached submirror contains a complete file system image, and is guaranteed to be consistent at the time it is detached. The detached submirror is dumped using normal techniques. If fully-mirrored functionality is required even during dumps (as might be for installations that are extremely sensitive to data loss), a three-way mirror can be configured. At the end of the dump, the detached submirror is reattached to the online submirror(s), and the mirroring software resyncs the online, updated copy with the reattached submirror. This process typically takes 20-30 minutes for a 2 GB mirror, assuming that the online submirror is not particularly busy. Larger RAID–1+0 mirrors consisting of multiple disks are resynced in parallel (for example, a 20 GB RAID–1+0 volume consisting of ten 2 GB disks takes about 20–30 minutes). The process consumes less than two percent of a 50 MHz SuperSPARC processor, so the overhead is confined to the actual disk I/O itself (obviously if the mirroring is done in firmware by a RAID unit, no host processor overhead at all).

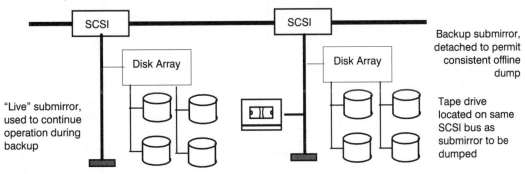

Figure 73. Avoiding SCSI utilization problems when using off-line mirrors

8

This scheme achieves complete availability by providing multiple copies of the file system. By dumping only the detached mirror, the backup process is able to lock the detached copy against modification without interfering with normal system operation. However, this arrangement must be carefully configured to avoid serious degradation of end-user performance.

As with any mirrored configuration, each submirror should be located on a separate SCSI host adapter to provide optimum I/O latency. Likewise, the location of tape drives on SCSI busses should be carefully considered. Because they are relatively slow devices, tape drives have the potential to dominate access to a SCSI bus (the fact that many tape drives use SCSI's asynchronous transfer mode doesn't help matters either). Unfortunately, this potential problem is encountered frequently in actual practice.

The configuration that results in reasonable backup performance and minimal impact on the remainder of the system is to designate a SCSI bus specifically for submirrors that are intended for detached dumps. Then configure the backup devices onto this SCSI bus. Although the utilization of this bus will normally be driven to levels that are considered unacceptable, the only process that are impacted by this utilization is the backup itself, which is typically waiting on the tape drive virtually all of the time anyway.

Configurations that require multiple detached mirrors or that use submirrors which exceed the recommended size of a SCSI bus are even more complex. One possibility is to consider exceeding the recommended maximum SCSI bus size (i.e., by configuring additional disks onto the bus, even if this may cause degradation). Several considerations are important in this scenario. One is that because the submirror is written every time the logical file system is written, delays incurred writing to the backup submirror will delay every write to the file system during normal operation (some would argue that this delay is acceptable, since the fact that the delayed write does not occur during backups helps compensate for the resources consumed by the backup process itself, resulting in more predictable response time for users).

8.4 Data Recovery Considerations

One aspect of what are normally viewed as "backup" considerations is the time (or effort) required to recover lost data. Although systems have become sufficiently reliable that a major recovery is a rare event—ideally it is a complete non–event—the circumstances surrounding a recovery are panic-driven and often involve substantial costly down time. The single most stressful day in the life of a system administrator is the day that he spends watching the tape drives spin slowly back and forth doing backhitches while the entire office waits (the administrator's manager also sweats a lot that day).

The time spent restoring a file system includes both tape motion time and synchronous file system operation time. When data files are large (for example data-intensive NFS or DBMS systems that store tables in the file system), tape media speed dominates recovery time, because of the disk seeks involved.

Servers that operate on large files should configure the fastest possible backup media, in order to retrieve data quickly during a recovery (naturally this helps during backup operations as well). Recovery of this class of data is limited by the speed of tape–to–buffer transfers.

When files are small, as on most NFS servers and timesharing servers, file system operations actually consume far more time than waiting for the recovery media, because file creation involves at least two completely synchronous write operations as the entry is added into the directory (all directory modification operations are issued synchronously) and upon file close. This time is not an issue in large-file environments because file creations are rare compared to data block writes, which are issued asynchronously. However, small-file environments are most often dominated by huge numbers of file creations during file system recovery.

Because small-file environments don't benefit very much from higher tape speed, the most productive option is to increase synchronous write speed by configuring some sort of NVRAM write acceleration (either host–based PrestoServe or NVSIMM or some sort of caching disk array). Because these options accelerate all synchronous writes, file system recovery time is reduced by up to 80 percent in small–file environments. If there is any anticipation at all that rapid recoveries will be required, NVRAM is highly recommended, even if NFS write operations are expected to be rare or even non–existent.

As with their backups, small–file recovery can be greatly degraded by delays writing to the disk, because these delays make high–inertia tapes much more likely o overshoot the interblock gap and have to backhitch. The fastest tapes are the most likely to encounter this problem, often resulting in surprisingly slow restoration times.

Some backup/recovery software (such as hsmrestore(8) from the Online: Backup 2.0 package) will optionally disabled synchronous directory updates. It works around some of the small–file recovery problem, but unfortunately is only a viable option when recovering a file system completely from scratch. Many recovery operations involve only part of a file system, or involve restoring a complete file system into an existing file system. In circumstances such as these, leaving synchronous directory updates enabled is imperative, because a system failure during such a restore runs a high risk of resulting in a corrupted directory structure.

Many sites have requirements for substantial amounts of data that is used intensively for some period of time. Afterwards, the data is required for archival or reference purposes, but need not be instantaneously available. These sites can use file migration techniques, in which data that has not been used for some specified amount of time can be automatically transferred to slower, less expensive storage. Several companies offer such migration products; they are typically found configured with optical jukeboxes for the secondary (backup) media. These devices provide relatively slow, but *very* voluminous storage. Optical jukeboxes making use of 5.25" magneto-optical disks are commonly capable of providing near-line access to 20 GB to 500 GB of data. Jukeboxes utilizing 14" write-once/read-many disks often provide even more storage, currently approaching multiple-terabyte storage capacities.

8.5 Tape Drive Taxonomy

As discussed previously, widely differing backup strategies can impose very different configuration requirements. Some of these go beyond the most obvious storage capacity and sheer tape speed considerations. For example, because nearly all current tape drives are connected via SCSI, configuring backup media on the SCSI bus is tempting—and with virtually disk array except Sun's SPARCstorage Array, this architectural location is the same as the disks. Unfortunately, the high utilization of SCSI busses incurred by most tape drives becomes a critical factor in configuring backup (and recovery!) for large, highly available servers (see *SCSI Bus Utilization,* section 7.2.5). Table 35 (page 376) summarizes the characteristics of the tape drives most commonly found on Solaris systems.

8.5.1 Tape Drives and SCSI Cabling

Tape drives often pose a logistical problem in configurations. Virtually all low–end tape drives utilize single-ended SCSI interfaces, imposing a practical limit on the number of drives configurable on a SCSI bus (since the single-ended cabling permits only a three meter distance if fast signaling is chosen by any device on the bus). In practical terms, four Sun tape drives are all that can be configured on a single bus, because desktop drives come with 0.5 meter SCSI cables. After allowing for the equivalent of 0.5 meters of cabling for each connector pair, the effective length of each cable is 1.5 meters, making four cables (and hence four tapes) the practical maximum.

Generally speaking, physically large drives such as most 1/2" tape drives are the exception to this rule. Due to their much larger form factor, they have far longer cabling, despite commonly using single–ended signaling. Like most others, Sun's tabletop 1/2" drive comes with a three meter cable, and most rack-mount versions come with 4.5 meter cables. In both cases the practical limit is one drive per SCSI bus.

In some cases one possibility is to use a differential–to–single-ended signal converter to connect single–ended tape drives to much longer differential cabling, although this measure is relatively drastic. In this configuration the host is configured with a differential host adapter and standard differential cabling; the convert is connected between the differential cable and the single–ended device.

Most data–center tape drives, such as the StorageTEK Redwood and Timberline, use differential SCSI interfaces, eliminating most of the cabling restrictions. However, most of these drives are so fast that they require dedicated SCSI busses.

8.5.2 Tape Drives and SCSI Utilization

In terms of raw connectivity, Solaris 2 supports the use of up to seven SCSI tape drives on a single 8–bit SCSI bus, subject to the previously mentioned cabling limitations. In theory nothing in the SCSI subsystem prohibits configuring 15 tape drives on a fast/wide SCSI bus, but this many devices is overkill.

The primary issue with configuring many tape drives on SCSI busses is bus utilization. Because tape drives are usually considered "low–performance" devices, they typically do not select the most aggressive transfer speeds. For example, the Sun 4 mm drives select non–fast, narrow, synchronous SCSI transfer mode—5 MB/sec. Older drives selected even slower transfer modes. For example, the Sun 1/2" tape selects 1.0 MB/sec asynchronous transfers, despite a media speed of about 780 KB/sec. The result is SCSI bus utilization in excess of 80 percent, meaning that for all practical intents and purposes, these drives must be configured on private SCSI busses. When SCSI bus utilization exceeds about 40 percent, the ability of SCSI busses to deliver full throughput to multiple tape drives on the bus diminishes substantially. For most purposes, four 8 mm tape drives or two DLT–4000 tape drives are about as many as can be accommodated on a narrow SCSI bus.

8.5.3 4 mm Tape

Descended from consumer Digital Audio Tape (DAT) are two 4 mm standards, known as DDS–1 and DDS–2. Both are helical–scan format drives, with relatively long tape start/stop times. Commercial 4 mm media comes in three sizes: 60 meters, 90 meters, and 120 meters. The 120 meter formulation uses the newer DDS–2 format, and the others are DDS–1. DDS–2 drives are upward compatible with DDS–1 media (virtually all DDS–2 drives automatically sense media type when loaded), although DDS–1 drives cannot read or write DDS–2 media at all. Older Sun 4 mm drives are DDS–1 format, whereas newer drives are DDS–2. DDS–1 drives deliver a capacity of 1.3 GB on 60 meter tapes and 2.0 GB on 90 meter tapes without compression. Newer 120 meter DDS–2 media have a 4.0 GB native capacity.

Both 4 mm formats transfer at about 400 KB/sec without compression and slightly less than 1 MB/sec with typical compression; the only practical difference between the two formats is the physical length of the media and the drive's ability to handle the resultant thinner tape.

One extremely important issue with both 4 mm and 8 mm formats is the choice of physical media. Because both are descended from commonly available consumer technologies obtaining consumer–oriented media is an unfortunate but real possibility. Even worse is that these tapes actually work for a while! This alternative may be a viable for situations that only require storage for a very short period of time (for example, incremental backups between weekly epochal dumps), but in general only data–grade media should be used in these devices, because the less expensive tapes have significantly lower media life.

8.5.4   8 mm Tape

The 8 mm format is the first helical–scan format popularized in the data community. Although the format was developed by Sony, all data–grade 8 mm drives are sold by Exabyte, and various computer vendors OEM them. Therefore 8 mm drives are relatively easy to categorize, since they can be identified by their Exabyte model number. As with disks, tape drive firmware can make a non-trivial difference in performance or reliability; most large system vendors such as Sun offer vendor–specific firmware. In common with 4 mm, avoid using video–grade media.

The two 8 mm media lengths are 112 meters and 160 meters. Exabyte has released four different models of 8 mm drive, the EXB–8200, EXB–8500, EXB–8505C, and EXB–8505XL. Only the EXB–8505XL supports both the older 112 meter tapes and the newest 160 meter format; combined with compression, this drive stores 7 GB in native mode, and about 14 GB with typical compression. The others support only the 112 meter format, with the EXB–8200 delivering 2.3 GB, and the EXB–8500 5.0 GB. The EXB–8505C adds selectable compression, permitting about 10 GB storage in compressed mode.

Because these are standard SCSI devices, data transfers are performed in two steps (see *SCSI Bus Transactions*, section 7.2.3.5). Data is first transferred via the read/write head between the physical media and the embedded target controller. This specification governs the speed of user transfers. Head–to–tape transfers occur at 220 KB/sec on the EXB–8200, and 550 KB/sec on the EXB–8500 models; the EXB–8505C approximately doubles this rate with typical compression.

From the target controller, the data is transferred on the SCSI bus to the host. The transfer mode on the SCSI bus governs SCSI bus utilization, and thus the SCSI configuration. Exabyte has improved selected transfer modes with each model. The EXB–8200 selects asynchronous transfer averaging about 1 MB/sec, whereas the EXB–8500 and EXB–8505C select 3.0 MB/sec synchronous transfers. The latest EXB–8505XL selects 5 MB/sec synchronous transfers, although it transfers to media at the same speed as the other EXB–8500's. For further discussion see section 7.2.5.3, *SCSI Bus Throughput—Tape*.

8.5.5 Sun 4 mm and 8 mm Stackers

Sun offers both a 4 mm desktop stacker and an 8 mm mid–range stacker. The smaller unit has a single DDS–1 drive and holds four tapes, yielding a capacity of 8-20 GB. The larger unit contains two EXB–8505XL 8 mm drives and a magazine capacity of ten tapes; the capacity is 70 GB native and about 140 GB with compression. Like most stackers, they might be best described as high-capacity magazines, rather than full-service library mechanisms that can load arbitrary tapes. Instead, the stackers offer the ability to load the next tape in the magazine upon receipt of the `MT_OFFL ioctl`. This ioctl is issued to the drive from the "`mt offline`" command, permitting the user to cycle through the tapes. The `ufsdump(1m)` command in Solaris 2.3 issues the `MT_OFFL` upon detecting end–of–tape when invoked with the "l" option, permitting automated dumps to the full capacity of the stacker. Full random–access capability is not provided by the basic Solaris environment, but Solstice: Backup 's Jukebox option layers sufficient software over the basic sequential access mechanism to implement random access to tapes in the library. Solstice: Backup also has an unbundled module that can make use of barcode readers to identify physical tapes within the library. The Sun 8 mm library/stacker has an optional barcode reader.

8.5.6 Digital Linear Tape

Presently two forms of what is usually known as "DLT" are available. As the name implies, the format was pioneered and popularized by the storage products division at Digital Equipment. That division has since been sold to disk vendor Quantum, but the DLT formats have become popular in many parts of the industry. DLT drives use a parallel recording format. They come in three different formats, known as DLT–2000, DLT -4000, and DLT-7000. The DLT-4000 format is capable of 1.5 MB/sec in native mode, somewhat less than 3 MB/sec with compression. The similar DLT-7000 format offers much higher performance than the DLT-4000, while avoiding the substantial cost of high-end units. Typical streaming throughput of a DLT-7000 is about 4.5-4.8 MB/sec after accounting for compression.

The media used in DLT devices comes in several varieties, known as CompacTape III (10 GB capacity, used by DLT–2000 drives), CompacTape IIIxt (15 GB, DLT–2000XT format), and CompacTape IV. The DLT–4000 format used by Sun's drives uses CompacTape IV, capable of 20 GB native capacity on a 1,800–foot tape. Sun also offers an autoloading device capable of storing seven tapes, a total of 140 GB native capacity. Many DLT libraries are available with multiple transports and robotic media changers, providing good mid-range solutions capable of 50-100 GB/hr throughput and capacities in the range of 300-1,250 GB. For these reasons, DLT is probably the most appropriate choice for typical medium–scale Solaris server installations. The DLT formats offer capabilities far greater than the low–end 4 mm and 8 mm helical scan devices at much less expense than high–end devices such as 3490E and high–end helical scan drives.

8.5.7 ½" Tape (9-Track)

The 1/2" reel-to-reel tape drive permits exchange of data between Sun systems and older system using the industry-standard 1/2" tape format. The Sun drive supports 6250 bpi, 1600 bpi, and 800 bpi densities. EBCDIC character conversion and byte-swapping are handled with dd(1). The 1/2" tape drive is a relatively fast drive, capable of transferring at about 780 KB/sec. However, because this device selects asynchronous SCSI transfer mode at about 1 MB/sec, SCSI bus utilization is quite high, effectively requiring that this device be configured on its own SCSI bus.

8.5.8 ¼" Cartridge Tape

The 1/4" cartridge tape was once ubiquitous on Sun systems, as it was the primary medium for software distribution, and because it was the only cost–effective tape backup medium. Elderly QIC–11 and QIC–24 tape drives are extremely slow; combined with their use of asynchronous SCSI, they consume SCSI bus bandwidth far out of proportion to their utility. Even the 150 MB QIC–150 drive suffers from this problem. The more modern QIC–2.5G drive still moves at a snail's pace (300 KB/sec), but at least it uses synchronous SCSI to get on and off the SCSI bus quickly, minimizing interference with other devices on the bus. Fortunately none of the QIC devices are used for heavy-duty backup or data exchange purposes. The casual use this device would normally get in a modern server configuration (probably restricted to software loading, etc.) means that configuration location is not very important.

Table 35. Tape drive specification summary

Drive	Transfer Speed		Capacity	
	Native	Compressed	Native	Compressed
4 mm DDS–1	400 KB/sec	~ 920 KB/sec	2 GB	~ 5 GB
4 mm DDS–2	400 KB/sec	~ 920 KB/sec	4.0 GB	~ 8 GB
8 mm (EXB–8200)	220 KB/sec	N/A	2.3 GB	N/A
8 mm (EXB–8500)	220 KB/sec	N/A	5.0 GB	N/A
8 mm (EXB–8505C)	500 KB/sec	~ 1 MB/sec	5.0 GB	~ 10 GB
8 mm (EXB–8505XL)	550 KB/sec	~ 1 MB/sec	7 GB	~ 14 GB
½″ 9-track	780 KB/sec	N/A	120 MB	N/A
¼″ QIC-150	150 KB/sec	N/A	150 MB	N/A
¼″ QIC–2GB	300 KB/sec	N/A	2.5 GB	N/A
3480	3.0 MB/sec	usually N/A	200 MB	usually N/A
3490E	3.0 MB/sec	6 MB/sec	400 MB	~ 800 MB
DLT–4000	1.5 MB/sec	3.0 MB/sec	20 GB	~40 GB
DLT-7000	3.0 MB/sec	~4.8 MB/sec	25 GB	~50 GB
STK SD–3 Redwood	10.5 MB/sec	~14.8 MB/sec	50 GB	~100 GB

8.5.9 3480 and 3490E Compatible Devices

Whereas the venerable 1/2" 9–track tape was once the primary tape interchange medium with mainframe systems, this function has been taken over by the somewhat newer 3480 and 3490 format tapes. The IBM 3480 format is a serpentine tape using relatively low-density media. The original 3480 format writes 18 tracks on a 1/2" tape. The IBM 3480 and 3490 use the same media format, but the "E"–series doubled the tape density, from 200 MB/tape to 400 MB/tape. Later media can store as much as 2 GB—much more than the original format, but much less than most other media. Because of the small amount of data that can be stored per tape, virtually all drives found in the open systems market will be in the denser 3490E format, and most installations will use single drives for data interchange with mainframes. Configuration of multiple drives on discrete SCSI busses is unlikely in most situations, because sites with large 3490E requirements will almost certainly opt for large 3490E libraries.

Compression (usually called "compaction" in the mainframe world) can be optionally applied to improve these densities along with the data transfer rates. The 3490E achieves greater density by writing a second set of data tracks during the "rewind" tape motion. The two track groups consist of 18 tracks each, resulting in 36 total tracks. The elimination of most rewind time is a significant matter when the media is as relatively sparse as the 3490E. This consideration is also relevant to tape change time in a stacker or library. Tape change time is not significant in 8 mm stackers, because even a full minute of rewind time and 30 seconds of robotic search time represent far less than one percent overhead. The same

overhead reduces the effective speed of a 3490E library by 60 percent—to just 1.8 MB/sec over the duration of a long job.

8.5.10 StorageTEK Devices

The "st" (read as SCSI tape) driver in Solaris 2.4 does not support certain features such as 16 bit wide SCSI, reserve/release to prevent multi-initiator sharing, runtime selection of mode select compression, etc. The 16-bit wide SCSI feature is required to support large tape storage products such as the STK Timberline 9490 and the STK Redwood SD-3 SCSI tape storage devices, while the other features such as reserve/release facilitate the usage of these large tape storage products in large mainframe environments where these tape products are shared between several host systems.

These features *are* supported in Solaris 2.5 and later, and Sun now offers explicit support for some high–end StorageTEK devices[76]. In particular, the Timberline and Redwood devices are fully supported. The Timberline is capable of delivering about 5.5 MB/sec sustained throughput, and the Redwood can be operated at a sustained speed of 10.5 MB/sec, and units equipped with the latest SCSI interfaces are capable of about 14.8 MB/sec assuming suitable compression. StorageTEK also offers very large robotic library media changers using these drives as transports. STK Redwood transports and their accompanying libraries seem to be the most appropriate devices for very large data center installations with stringent backup requirements.

---

[76] StorageTEK enjoys a rather unusual position with Sun in this regard. The STK tape drives are presently the only third–party devices not sold directly by Sun that are fully supported by Sun.

Solaris 2

This section describes some of the characteristics of Solaris 2 (and particularly Solaris 2.5.1) that are relevant to configuration and capacity planning. It is by no means an exhaustive attempt to describe the Solaris 2 operating environment, nor is it an attempt to describe all of the features of the operating system implementation.

9.1 Virtual Memory System

The Solaris virtual memory (VM) system is one of the fundamental elements of the operating system. All system activity passes through memory for processing, so efficient memory management is crucial to smooth system operation. The VM system is responsible for providing isolation and protection between processes, organizing data sharing where appropriate between processes, and managing the allocation of physical memory resources. An important part of physical memory management is providing efficient and cost-effective caching on behalf of file systems. The fundamental design of the virtual memory system was first implemented in SunOS 4.0, and the design was contributed to the System V Release 4 (SVR4) effort. Solaris 2.0 was based on the SVR4 reference implementation, and each subsequent release has improved on the basic design without changing the essential characteristics.

Like most modern operating systems, Solaris uses a demand-paging strategy to permit a given set of physical memory resources to serve a much larger set of virtual memory. Solaris processes can address up to 4 GB each. When running many processes, the sum of the virtual memory requirements commonly exceeds even the 30 GB maximum memory on the Ultra Enterprise 6000.

9.1.1 Virtual Memory System Architecture

The VM system uses a form of the classic paged-and-segmented architecture. Logical entities are grouped together into *segments*. For example, all of the code in `libc` is a single segment, as are the stack and data areas of each process. Each segment can be of variable size up to 4 GB. Segments are the unit of protection and sharing between processes. Processes map several segments into a flat 32-bit address space; for example, every process has a data segment, a stack segment, a code segment, and some library segments. Segments are mapped into the address space by address range; a 32 KB shared memory segment (which is simply a memory segment with shared permissions enabled) might be mapped into a process's address space at virtual address 0x00400000 through 0x00408000. Subsequent references to any address in the specified range are mapped into the shared memory area. Because the address space is presently restricted to 32 bits, the sum of the size of all mapped segments must be less than 4 GB. Mapping only part of a segment into an address space is possible. This is important when the size of a single segment can approach the limits of a process's address space, such as when a DBMS process requires access to ten files, each 2 GB in size. The operating system manages file I/O mappings to permit this type of access, and user processes can use the same programming interface to manage their address spaces with very fine granularity (see *Memory Mapped I/O* and *Application Management of Physical Memory* later in this chapter).

For purposes of physical resource allocation, segments and physical memory are broken down into fixed-size *pages*. Although segments could be used as the unit of allocation, pages are used because their fixed size makes reallocation much easier. When a process requires new memory, the system allocates it on a page-by-page basis. The size of a page is hardware-dependent, as Table 36 shows.

Table 36. Page size and maximum MMU mapping capability by hardware platform. Maximum memory is typically limited by packaging constraints rather than lack of address lines or similar hardware support.

System	Page Size	Max. Memory	Max MMU Mapping
4/100, 4/200	8 KB	128 MB	256 MB
4/300	8 KB	224 MB	256 MB
4/400	8 KB	640 MB	1 GB
SS1, SS1+, SLC, IPC	4 KB	64 MB	64 MB
SS2, ELC, IPX	4 KB	128 MB	128 MB
CY601 (SS600MP)	4 KB	640 MB	2 GB
SuperSPARC, SuperSPARC-II	4 KB	16 GB (CS6400)	64 GB

System	Page Size	Max. Memory	Max MMU Mapping
hyperSPARC	4 KB	512 MB (SS20)	64 GB
MicroSPARC, MicroSPARC-II	4 KB	256 MB (SS5)	512 MB
UltraSPARC	8 KB	30 GB (UE6000)	2,048 GB

The use of three separate address types seems excessively complex at first, but each has a specific purpose. The flat address space simplifies memory management code in applications and libraries (recall the extensive memory management problems found in MS-DOS); the segmented address space permits the system to use arbitrarily-sized logical entities; and the paged address space permits easy physical resource allocation. In particular, the use of symbolic segment names is the key to many of the caching and data sharing features provided by the VM system.

The Solaris VM system uses an architecture pioneered by the Honeywell Multics system, in which the entire address space is treated as a single unified virtual storage system. In less technical terms, everything that resides in memory is treated as a single type of object. Shared and unshared executable code, anonymous memory (memory that is allocated during execution, such as via the `brk(2)` and `malloc(3)` calls), and static memory such as FORTRAN common blocks or C global variables, are all mapped into virtual memory and treated equally. Most importantly, the UFS file system is integrated into the virtual memory system: file system objects are managed by the same code that manages any other type of user-accessible memory. File system objects, like all other virtual memory objects, are referenced via a unified addressing scheme that uses physical memory as a simple virtual memory cache.

9.1.2 Data Sharing and Memory Protection

In addition to managing the system's physical memory resources, the VM system allows many processes to run in the same system without fear of interference, deliberate or otherwise. Every process is assigned boundaries and protection keys, permitting processes to specify whether other processes can access their data, and if so, what access is permitted. Access rights are specified by the owning process on a per-segment basis, and may be read, write, or copy-on-write. The latter mode permits processes to share a segment as long as they do not modify its contents; in the event that one of the sharing processes writes on the segment, that process is immediately given its own copy. A single process consists of one or more threads of execution; all of the threads in a process share a single address space.

Another function of the virtual memory system is to organize the sharing of common data between processes. Common information is recognized using common names for data between processes, for example using either file system names or shared memory segments.

For example, virtually every process uses a copy of the `libc` shared library to gain access to basic system call interfaces. Rather than placing a copy of `libc` in memory for every process, the VM system retains a single copy in memory and permits all processes to use a single copy, saving physical memory and operating system resources. This arrangement is conveniently managed by the integrated file system I/O cache.

9.1.3 Memory-Mapped I/O

One of the salient features of the UFS file system is the implementation of file I/O as a component of the Solaris virtual memory system. The key concept is that UNIX files reside directly in the virtual memory system, rather than being separate from the system's memory management. In traditional operating systems, the allocation of physical memory is completely separate from the manipulation of file I/O. For example, as in MS–DOS, file I/O is accomplished by issuing requests directly to devices; data is transferred directly from a device to memory that is explicitly allocated by the application. The operating system is not involved in managing the I/O buffer, except as a consequence of managing the memory allocated to the user process as a whole.

The file system places files directly in the virtual memory system by assigning virtual addresses to file system objects. Specifically, a file is treated as just another virtual memory segment. The `mmap(2)` system call maps a file (that is, the named virtual memory segment) into the address space of the calling process. For example, the code fragment

```
int fd, *floatp, n, offset, fileLength;
char *memory, *proposedAddress;

fd = open ("/tmp/foo", O_RDWR);
memory = mmap (proposedAddress,
            fileLength,
            PROT_READ | PROT_WRITE
            MAP_SHARED,
            fd,
            offset = 0);
```

results in the pointer `memory` referring to the contents of the file `/tmp/foo`. This mapping makes manipulation of the file contents extremely flexible, because the file is made a direct part of the process's address space; any operation that can be applied to in-memory objects can be applied to the mapped contents of the file. For example, the following code fragment treats the first few bytes of the mapped file as a record, reads the contents of the file, and if specific contents are found in the file, takes corresponding action:

```
struct controlRecord {
    int   versionNumber;
    int   daemonProcessId;
    float daemonLoadAverage;
```

```
} *cRecordP;

cRecordP = (struct controlRecord *) memory;
if (daemonProcessId == 0) {
    childProcId = fork ();
    if (childProcId != 0)
      daemonProcessId = childProcId;
}
```

This manipulation is possible because the memory pointer literally points to the first byte of the contents of the file. Because the file can be mapped into any process with suitable permission, this mechanism is convenient for sharing persistent data.

9.1.3.1 Performance and Monitoring Implications

Interestingly, once the file-to-memory mapping has been established, no direct I/O requests are required to accomplish what is traditionally considered I/O activity. Explicit I/O calls are avoided by using the virtual memory system: the file contents are virtual memory objects whose initial location is "not in memory." When the data is referenced, the VM system discovers that the data is not in memory, triggering a page fault. The data is brought into memory by the VM system, and the referring instruction is restarted. When data is written to the VM segment (i.e., to the file), the data is written into the in-memory copy immediately, and arrangements are made to write the data back to the backing store on disk. Most files can tolerate some risk of data loss in the event of a system failure, and modified data is posted to disk by the fsflush(8) daemon at intervals of about 30 seconds. Applications that cannot tolerate this level of risk can specify that writes be issued synchronously to the backing store by specifying the O_SYNC or O_DSYNC flags when the file is opened.

This use of the VM system can considerably simplify the application logic in applications, although provisions must be made for extending files because the extended file would lie outside address range of the original mapping established by mmap(2). Another advantage afforded by the unified VM and file system is that it can considerably improve performance over the traditional UNIX read(2) and write(2) interface. The traditional application programming interface (API) specifies that the data is exchanged between the system's I/O buffers and the user specified I/O buffer. Because the I/O subsystem caches disk data, this semantic implies that data is transferred from the device to a system I/O buffer and then copied to the user buffer. Writes to devices follow the reverse path from user buffers to system buffers to the device. For many applications, the data copying operation is a substantial proportion of the I/O overhead. Use of the memory-mapped I/O model avoids this overhead.

9.1.3.2 Compatibility with Traditional UNIX I/O

Memory-mapped I/O is convenient and elegant, but explicit use of it requires significant source code modifications. For this reason, most applications use the traditional UNIX API, calling read(2) and write(2) directly. One of the most important requirements is therefore to ensure that unmodified applications can coexist efficiently with newer memory-mapped I/O applications. It is accomplished in Solaris by layering the traditional API over the memory-mapped I/O model.

The operating system reserves an internal I/O buffer segment, known as *segkmap*, for use in implementing the UNIX API. All traditional disk I/O passes through this segment. The read(2) and write(2) implementations use mmap(2) functionality to map parts of open files into this reserved area that is accessible only to the kernel. Note that only the logical buffer is unavailable to user processes. The segment is mapped to physical addresses that provide the contents of the files; and since the file system's names are persistent and common to all processes, the same physical addresses are available to each process that is able to map the file.

9.1.4 Physical Memory Management

Physical memory is managed in two sections. At startup time, the kernel allocates some memory for its own use; this memory is used for kernel data structures that are not paged, such as the page tables used to perform virtual-to-physical page mapping and crucial per-process information. Kernel memory is a small proportion of the available memory (generally five to ten percent of main memory, and always at least 6 MB). This can be a considerable amount of memory on richly configured systems. All other memory is placed in a pool called the *page cache*, which is available for any memory use: code, library, anonymous memory, file system, etc.

The page cache can be further divided into allocated memory and the free space list. Memory is placed onto the free space list in two ways: pages are put onto the free space list by the page daemon; alternately, pages that are freed on behalf of the application are placed directly on the free space list. Examples of the latter are static memory or stack segment data that is returned when the application calls exit(2) or munmap(2).

9.1.4.1 Memory Allocation and the Scanner

When an application asks the operating system for a new page, such as when calling malloc(3), the system searches the free page list. If a page is found in the free memory pool, it is allocated to the requesting process. Eventually the system runs out of free pages, and memory must be reclaimed by obtaining it from another page already in use. A system process called the *page daemon* is invoked to implement the system's replacement policy, which is "not recently used" (NRU).

The page daemon scans the page tables for pages that have not been recently used. SPARC MMU hardware provides support for marking access to pages. The page daemon inspects the recently used bit for each page; if the page has been used, the bit is found to be set, and the page daemon turns it off. Otherwise, the page has not been used recently, so it is vacated and placed onto the free page list. Vacating a page means invalidating references to that page in the page tables, although this cannot be done until the page contents are flushed to disk if the page was dirty (i.e., had been modified in memory but the on-disk copy was not up-to-date).

Interrupting the current task to search for free memory is a relatively expensive operation, so the page daemon scans for more than one page at a time. All candidates are vacated and placed on the free space list. The search for free pages always starts after the last page inspected during the previous search, to prevent creation of a "hot spot," in which memory is replaced continuously.

This activity appears in the system statistics as "scan rate," denoted " SR" in the output of vmstat(1), and it provides a measure of how much demand applications are placing on the memory system. The scan rate is the most useful indicator of the relative strength of the memory configuration. Since the scanner runs only when memory is required but not available on the free list, a scan rate near zero clearly indicates that memory is not in high demand. Some scanning is normal, but if the system must reclaim a substantial proportion of the system's memory every second—more than about 10-15 percent—the overhead is probably higher than desired and the time has come to configure more memory into the system. The scan rate is a more accurate initial indication of the health of the memory system than the "pi" and "po" indicators, which represent pagein and pageout operations, because these operations are used to implement file system I/O. As discussed in section 9.1.3, *Memory Mapped I/O*, file system reads are implemented by the system as pagein operations and file system writes are implemented as pageout operations. Thus the pagein and pageout statistics are deceptive in many (and probably most) situations. An application may be reading or writing files and therefore causing VM paging activity even if plenty of memory is available in the system. The pi and po indicators should be investigated only when the scan rate indicates a physical memory shortfall.

9.1.4.2 Paging vs. Swapping

Under normal circumstances, the system replaces only single pages when reclaiming physical memory, but under extreme conditions they may not be sufficient. When the system is critically short of memory, replacing single pages cannot keep pace with the demands being placed on the memory system by many processes running concurrently. To combat these thrashing situations, the page daemon keeps track of the amount of memory being requested, and if the normal NRU mechanism is not able to maintain the free list, more drastic action is taken: entire processes are thrown out of memory. This process, called *swapping*, results in the victimized process having all of its pages reallocated, leaving only an entry in the process table residing in memory. Anonymous memory belonging to the process is copied to the swap area, and any other memory backed by file system storage is flushed to disk. The swapping process continues until the free space list can be maintained. Eventually the process must run again, so anonymous memory is copied back from swap, and the page fault process brings executable code back into memory.

Although this tactic is useful for getting out of critical memory shortages, it is essentially never used in practice. The swapping process is so I/O-intensive that users perceive the system to be unacceptably slow, and systems that must resort to swapping on a regular basis are invariably upgraded with additional memory (processes that are idle for long periods of time, such as the `keyserv(1)` daemon on most systems, *are* normally swapped out).

9.1.5 Caching File System I/O

A physical page is allocated when a process must store more data in memory. Although the virtual page that once was stored in the physical page continues to contain the data until the application no longer wishes to retain the information, the physical page may be reallocated at any time when the system is called upon to allocate memory. However, the physical page is not re-used unless and until some other requirement arises, even though the application may have freed the virtual memory. This arrangement may seem to be a waste of memory, but closer inspection shows the logic behind the design.

Some uses of memory are cyclic. Consider a freshly booted system that does not yet have any virtual memory content. When a user logs on, he necessarily refers to `/bin/sh` and `/usr/lib/libc.so`, and these are brought into memory. When the user logs off, all of his resources are freed, since they are not needed. However, virtual memory that has a persistent name—that is, file system entities such as files or directories—can still be referenced, and if they are, any remaining previous physical mapping would still be valid. In the case of `/bin/sh`, the pages containing the executable code pages are still available in physical memory, meaning that the next reference to them can be satisfied directly from main memory instead of from disk.

The net effect is that the entire page cache is used as a single pool of memory that stores the most recently used data. In systems that are memory-rich, all executable and anonymous memory is kept in memory, along with a large cache of file system data. Most systems are now memory-rich, due partly to the relatively low price of memory and partly to strong motivation to avoid paging and swapping during normal operation.

One of the consequences of this design is a common misunderstanding of the system's operation. Because the page cache is used to cache file system data, memory remains allocated forever—to something—once it has been used. The system loses nothing by retaining old named data. If it is used again before the page is required for another use, this saves getting the data from disk. Otherwise, the page is reassigned when reclaimed by the scanner, and new data simply overwrites the old data (of course, data is first written back to disk if the on-disk copy is not current). In either event, the page remains allocated to valid data. The only problem with this method is that the count of free pages (pages containing no valid data) tends to monotonically decrease, eventually leading to a condition where no pages reside on the free page list. Nothing is technically wrong with this situation—it is the designed behavior—but it continually alarms system administrators, who expect to see free memory. Nearly the only useful information conveyed by the free memory statistic is that the system may have too much memory. Memory is always allocated if the system can find valid data to leave there; having free memory for extended periods of time usually means that more memory is configured than can be used by the application mix.

9.1.5.1 Traditional UNIX Buffer Cache

Disk I/O caching in Solaris is similar to that found in most traditional UNIX implementations, although it differs in subtle but significant ways. Traditional UNIX divides memory into *three* classes: kernel memory, "regular" memory, and a *buffer cache*. The buffer cache is a dedicated I/O cache, used solely as a front end to the file system; it is usually configured at 10 percent of physical memory, although it can range from as little as none to as much as 70-80 percent of physical memory. The key difference between traditional UNIX and single-level VM implementations such as Solaris is that the latter pools together the I/O cache and regular paged memory, and that the I/O cache is dynamically managed by the demand-paging algorithm in the memory management code. For most applications, the single-level store is more flexible and leads to higher performance.

9.1.5.2 Solaris Buffer Cache

The Solaris page cache handles the function of the buffer cache in traditional UNIX systems, and probably it would have been best if references to the term "buffer cache" had been removed from current implementations. However, due to historical accidents in the software development process, an entity called the buffer cache in Solaris. Even more confusingly, it *is* related to the buffer cache in traditional UNIX designs!

In Solaris, the buffer cache is a completely separate entity allocated out of kernel memory that is used to cache file system metadata. UFS metadata is information about files and the file system, such as the superblock and its replicas, directory entries, and access control list entries. The Solaris buffer cache is sized at system startup time based on the size of physical memory and resized dynamically during operation. Because the Solaris buffer cache (as opposed to the page cache) stores only metadata, it can be far smaller than traditional buffer caches. Solaris requires a separate buffer area distinct from the regular page cache because file system metadata does not appear in the address range of the user file that is mapped into memory.

9.1.5.3 Supercaching

Most applications have relatively light I/O requirements, and the use of the page cache as the I/O buffer is a normal situation. However, a few applications are extremely sensitive to I/O performance, and saving any and all I/O time becomes an overriding concern in system configuration. In these cases, a worthwhile effort may be configuring the system so that the memory system is able to cache the entirety of an interesting data set.

If Solaris and the application were both 64-bit ready, this concern would be trivial, but as of Solaris 2.5.1, neither applications nor operating system are capable of handling 64-bit addresses. Thus the most straightforward mechanism for building large in-memory caches—allocation of a giant pool of memory, used to hold a copy of the data as read from the data file or DBMS—is not viable. However, even without fully 64-bit clean code, the UFS buffer cache can be used to circumvent this problem quite easily in most situations. The solution requires no application changes.

The key notion here is that because the operating system manages the MMU translations, it is able to manage very large pools of physical memory. To make any given page of physical memory available to a user process, the system need only change the virtual-to-physical mapping accordingly. The MMU management operation is *far* faster than handling physical I/O (about 25 microseconds compared with 10-20 milliseconds, or 10,000-20,000 microseconds).

When the application data is stored in a UFS file, Solaris uses the page cache to buffer the data in physical memory. After the data has been accessed once in the system, it is retained in memory; further access is accomplished at memory speeds instead of I/O speed. A slight overhead is incurred for the operating system to make the necessary MMU manipulations; this amounts to about five percent overall performance differential compared to having all data directly available in the processes' address space.

The UFS/VM page cache functionality can be used as a strategic cache for some classes of applications. Large systems can sometimes be combined with relatively small data sets to achieve stunning performance. Often it takes the form of caching the entire database or all data files related to a particular application. This technique is known in the literature as *supercaching*, a fancy term for "really, really big caches."

There are several ways to implement supercaches. The MVS mainframe uses a huge external memory called secondary store. This memory is not in the processor's main memory space; rather it is architecturally located between the processor complex and the I/O channels. On 64-bit UNIX systems, it can be implemented using a flat 64-bit address space. On 32-bit Solaris systems the easiest and most effective way to implement a supercache is to use the page cache. Specifically, rather than storing DBMS tables on raw disk or raw metadevices, the tables are stored in UFS files. Oracle, Informix, and DB2 can be conveniently configured in this fashion, and Ingres and Interbase use this method by default. Once the data is stored in UFS files, the page cache is used to buffer their data, eliminating I/Os as long as the data fits in memory. Note that for non-DBMS applications, data is already stored in the file system, so supercaching is a simple matter of configuring enough memory to cache the interesting dataset.

The supercaching technique is spectacularly effective for applications that reuse data, and that are dominated by read activity. In a test at Sun, an inventory management system consisting of a 12 GB Oracle database was run in a supercached configuration and compared with the same database stored on raw disk. On an Ultra Enterprise 6000 with 16 GB of physical memory, the supercached database delivered more than *347 times* the throughput of the standard configuration (654,442 transactions per hour compared to 1,886 transactions per hour). Figure 74 shows these results.

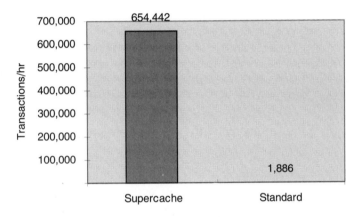

Figure 74. Supercaching performance compared to standard configuration performance. The large differential is due to caching the *entire* database in main memory, rather than reading data from disk.

The incredible performance improvement associated with supercaching seems to be too good to be true, and in many ways, it is. It boils down to the fact that accessing data from memory is far faster than accessing that same data from mechanical disks. Given the performance differential between memory and disk, the supercaching performance is to be expected. Furthermore, supercaching does not improve update-oriented transactions, because the modified data must be logged and pushed back to disk as a part of committing the transaction. The modified data is retained in memory, so further reads to it will be cached, but committing the update itself requires disk I/O.

Supercaching only works when the requisite data can reside entirely in memory on a long-term basis. For applications involving relatively small datasets, configuring large-memory systems and caching the entire dataset are possible. However, large memories are those in the 15-30 GB range, whereas even medium-sized databases are easily 10-20 times this size. A database involving only 15-20 GB is now considered small, rendering the supercaching technique useful only for applications with small datasets whose read performance is of such crucial importance that the price of the very large memory becomes worthwhile.

Memory prices have plummeted recently, but 20 GB of memory still costs far more than a quarter of a million dollars—and more importantly, more than 50 times the price of equivalent disk storage—even neglecting the system infrastructure necessary to configure this much memory. When considering the use of a supercache, recall the five-minute rule (see section 3.5.2.1, *Sizing the DBMS I/O Cache*). Most queries are run *far* less than once very five minutes.

Some applications have specific high-performance requirements on only part of their dataset, possibly only at limited times. In these cases, applying the supercaching technique is possible on a limited basis. For example, a manufacturing system may operate as a transaction processing system during factory hours using a 50 GB database, and the active parts and recent transactions tables may be used for trend analysis each weekend. Supercaching the entire database may not be feasible, but often the performance-sensitive tables may be cacheable. In this case, a reasonable approach may be to load the recent transactions into a supercache at the beginning of weekend operations, releasing the cache during normal factory hours.

9.1.6 Application Management of Physical Memory

The VM system uses a form of the not-recently-used algorithm to decide which pages to replace and which to retain in memory. Overall this technique is an effective—even under heavy memory pressure—because the pages that are most frequently used tend to stay in memory, whereas less frequently used pages tend to be replaced. Occasionally the page replacement algorithm guesses wrong, particularly when multiple large datasets are streamed through the page cache, and changing the VM system's behavior becomes useful.

From the operating system's perspective, the least intrusive way for the application to control physical memory allocation is the use of the mmap(2) system call and the memory-mapped I/O technique. The madvise(2) system call is a facility that permits the application to provide hints to the memory management system, in particular advising the system as to the anticipated access pattern on a range of virtual addresses. Calling madvise(2) with the MADV_SEQUENTIAL indication causes the system to reallocate pages very quickly, rather than attempting to cache the pages for eventual reuse. The MADV_DONTNEED indication releases the physical pages associated with the specified virtual address range. An even stronger hint is transmitted by calling munmap(2), which removes the mapping entirely. Note that the indication applies to the physical pages, so other processes that have the same physical memory mapped will probably soon find that the data is paged out. The MADV_WILLNEED indication is the strongest advisory notice that the virtual address range should be kept in physical memory if possible, to the point of pre-allocating memory and performing physical I/O before the data is actually referenced.

The Solaris versions of most common UNIX utilities, such as `cat(1)` and `cp(1)` use `mmap(2)` directly to minimize their impact on the VM system. This technique has caught some benchmarks unaware: it was once a common practice to `cat(1)` a large file to `/dev/null` for the purpose of flushing the contents of the traditional UNIX buffer cache before running benchmarks. This procedure does not work on Solaris systems, due to the use of `mmap(2)` in these utilities[77].

The use of `madvise(2)` is only possible when the application uses the memory mapped I/O technique. Most applications are ported from environments that do not support this model, and they use the traditional UNIX read/write API instead. Because the `read(2)` and `write(2)` system calls use the page cache indirectly, the application does not have access to the shared virtual addresses associated with the files, and `madvise(2)` cannot be used.

If the application does not use `mmap(2)`, or if advisory mechanisms are insufficient, it is also possible to use a much stronger form of memory management control, namely the `mlock(2)` mechanism. Usable only by the superuser, `mlock(2)` requests that the system make the indicated pages permanently resident in memory and ineligible to be replaced. Most applications cannot be modified to make calls to `mlock(2)` or `madvise(2)`, but the single-level virtual memory design makes it possible to write auxiliary programs that map the interesting regions into another address space and then manipulate the underlying physical memory regions. The following code uses `mlock(2)` to lock the contents of a UFS file into memory:

```
/*
 * lockdown.c--wire a UFS file into memory, preload a UFS buffer cache.
 *
 *      Usage:
 *              lockdown filename &
 *
 */

#include <ltstdio.h>
#include <lterrno.h>
#include <ltsys/types.h>
#include <ltsys/stat.h>
#include <ltsys/mman.h>
#include <ltfcntl.h>

int main (argC, argV)
        int argC;
        char **argV;
{
        int fd, code;
        struct stat statBuf;
        char *address;
```

---

[77] Amazingly, `cat(1)` detects when its output is directed to `/dev/null`, and simply exits!

```
if (argV [1] == NULL) {
        (void) fprintf (stderr, "Usage: lockdown filename\n");
        (void) exit (-1);
} else
        (void) printf ("locking down file %s\n", argV [1]);

/* open the file, enabling access via mmap(2). */
if ((fd = open (argV [1], O_RDONLY)) == -1) {
        (void) fprintf (stderr, "can't open file %s (%d)\n",
                argV [1], errno);
        (void) exit (-1);
}

/* verify permissions to lock down pages */

if (geteuid () != 0) {
        (void) fprintf (stderr,
                "Error: must be root to lock memory.\n");
        (void) exit (-1);
}

/* obtain size of the file */

code = stat (argV [1], &statBuf);

/*      call mmap(2) to map the file into this processes'
 *      address space. once the file is mapped into
 *      our address space we'll ask the VM system to
 *      lock our address space into memory.       */

address = mmap ( (char *) 0, /* system chooses address */
        statBuf.st_size,
        PROT_READ,              /* map it read only */
        MAP_SHARED,             /* share mapping w/other procs */
        fd,
        0);

(void) printf ("mapped %d bytes at offset 0x%x\n",
                statBuf.st_size, address);

if (mlock (address, statBuf.st_size) < 0) {
        (void) fprintf (stderr,
                "unable to lock down: error %d\n", errno);
        (void) exit (-1);
}

(void) printf ("locked.\n");

do {
        sleep (9999);
} while (1 > 0);
```

```
    return (0);

}
```

This code uses mmap(2) to map the entire file into the virtual address space of the auxiliary process; then the process requests that its pages be locked into memory using mlock(2). A successful call to mlock(2) locks all of the memory belonging to the calling process into physical memory, including auxiliary pages such as libraries and the executable itself. All active processes refer to the same physical memory, so the virtual address range for every other process using the file is also locked in memory.

This technique can be used with madvise(2), although coordinating actual application processing (in another process) with the appropriate calls to madvise(2) is much more difficult.

9.1.7 Mapping Virtual Addresses to Physical Addresses

The kernel is responsible for managing virtual-to-physical memory mappings. Applications always operate in virtual address space. The kernel provides each process with virtual addresses, and all requests for further allocation are also granted in virtual space. Mappings to unique names (durable file names, such as data files or executable code files) are brought into physical memory and mapped into virtual addresses for each requesting process. The kernel subsystem that handles these operations is called the *hardware address translation (hat) layer*.

The hat layer does its work by manipulating the memory management unit (MMU) built into the system's functional units. In Sun's systems, a functional unit is either a processor or an I/O bus. One complicating factor is the multiplicity of functional units in larger systems. Each functional unit has its own MMU, and keeping them consistent can be something of an issue. These systems implement a hardware mechanism, called a *hardware demap*, to remove all copies of MMU entries when they are invalidated.

The 32-bit virtual address is now implicit in compiled application code; even when running on 64-bit hardware (such as UltraSPARC), existing applications running in single processes will not *generally* be able to use large virtual address spaces without recompilation. Compiled binaries already use 32-bit arithmetic and 32-bit pointer variables, and running such binaries on a 64-bit clean system is clearly possible, although they will make use of only the first 4 GB of the virtual address space. However, even in a purely 32-bit world, making extensive and productive use of very large memories is possible—without recoding or recompiling applications

One of the significant features of existing MMUs is that, contrary to past designs, the physical address space can be larger than the virtual address space. Earlier systems provided processes with 32-bit virtual address spaces, and mapped these virtual addresses onto the much smaller existing physical memories. For example, the Sun-3/280 offered a 32 -bit virtual address, yet the hardware supported only 17 bits of physical address space—32 MB. As Table 36 (page 380) shows, older systems map 32-bit virtual addresses into smaller physical addresses, but current systems map virtual addresses into much larger physical addresses.

Current systems often require more physical memory than the 4 GB permitted by a 32-bit virtual address, and several SPARC-based systems now support more than 4 GB of physical RAM. These large memories are required by multitasking applications, where the sum of the address spaces can add up to more than 4 GB. These systems are able to accommodate large physical memories by using a MMU that translates 32-bit virtual addresses into larger physical addresses. In the case of the SPARCcenter 2000E and Cray CS6400, the MMU maps 32-bit virtual addresses to 36-bit physical addresses, permitting a maximum of 64 GB. The UltraSPARC MMU maps 32-bit virtual addresses into 41-bit physical addresses, thus restricting these systems to 2,048 GB (2 TB) of physical memory. In both cases, the systems actually support far less memory due to packaging restrictions. There is no reason why Solaris/x86 and Solaris/PowerPC cannot handle large physical address spaces other than that no x86 or PowerPC hardware platform has been offered with MMU capable of managing more than 4 GB of memory—yet.

9.1.8 Intimate Shared Memory

A special case of data sharing between processes occurs when many processes share a single shared memory segment *at the same virtual address in each process*. Ordinarily, each process maps the shared memory segment into its address space at a location determined by the virtual addresses available at the time the segment is attached. Under these (normal) conditions, a shared memory segment is mapped at different virtual addresses in each process that attaches it. However, the shmat(2) system call permits the attaching process to specify the virtual address used to map the shared memory segment into the local virtual address space.

If cooperating processes all map a shared memory segment at the same virtual address, pointers that refer to locations within the shared memory segment are valid for all processes. This approach can simplify processing of complex composite data structures residing in the shared memory segment, and the technique is used by most of the major database vendors, including Oracle, Sybase, Informix, and Ingres. The databases use a central shared memory segment as an interprocess communication mechanism for internal concurrency control and as a centralized shared data cache. The shared data cache is nearly universally more than 64 MB and often approaches 1 GB in size. The maximum segment size is 4 GB in 32-bit versions of Solaris.

This technique works, but without special arrangements, it consumes kernel resources unnecessarily in one specific common circumstance. Using a 4 KB page size, a 64 MB segment uses 16,384 physical pages—and each mapping process uses an equal number of entries in the MMU to map the virtual addresses onto the physical pages. Applications such as typical large 2N DBMS systems may have hundreds or even thousands of active DBMS processes, all mapping a very large shared data cache to the same virtual addresses. For example, a server supporting 5,000 client systems might well be configured with a shared data cache of 2 GB; even using 8 KB pages, each process requires 262,144 entries. If each of the 5,000 shadow processes used unique mappings, a substantial proportion of the system's resources would be used solely for mapping the single shared memory segment.

To avoid this excessive usage, Solaris implements an option that permits such cooperating processes to use the same MMU entries for shared memory, thus saving thousands of MMU entries per process. Saving MMU entries is important because of the limited size of the MMU hardware, combined with the kernel data structures required to manage the operation. Finally, the fact that far less kernel data is used means a dramatic improvement in the efficiency of the processor's data cache. The overall technique improves performance on DBMS systems by about 8-15 percent on an overall basis. The technique of sharing MMU entries between cooperating processes is known as *intimate shared memory (ISM)*, and is available by specifying the SHM_SHAREMMU flag to shmat(2). The primary consumers of ISM—the DBMS vendors—all use the feature when available.

One of the tradeoffs required by the ISM implementation is that the physical pages associated with the intimate shared memory must be locked in physical RAM. Although locking down this much physical memory might theoretically be a problem, in practice it is never an issue.

⇒ If using a 2N DBMS such as Oracle or Informix, be sure to specify that it should use intimate shared memory in the DBMS's configuration files (for example, specify use_ism=1 in Oracle's init.ora file).

9.2 UFS and UFS+ File Systems

The Solaris file system is an implementation of the Berkeley Fat Fast File System (FFFS) originally developed for the BSD 3.x and 4.x releases, but it has a number of enhancements designed to improve performance, to enhance recoverability from a system crash, and to minimize the time-consuming process of checking the integrity of the file system before mounting it. In Solaris 2, file systems are limited to 1,024 GB (1 TB) in size; individual files within the file system are limited to 2 GB. Probably the most significant enhancements to UFS over the original Berkeley implementation is the transaction logging and the integration of memory-mapped I/O. At the same time, finer-grained specifications of access permissions are now made possible by access control lists, and many relatively minor enhancements have been made over the years.

9.2.1 Update Journaling (UFS+ Logging File System)

Solstice:DiskSuite 4.0 provides an enhancement to the standard UFS file system. Known as a *metatrans* device, this feature adds a transaction log mechanism to the existing file system structure. A logging file system is said to be a UFS+ file system.

The purpose of the transaction log mechanism is to improve the reliability of the file system in the face of system interruptions and to improve the speed of recovery during boot by greatly accelerating the operation of `fsck(1m)`. The transaction log operates in a manner very similar to that of DBMS systems. Writes to the file system are first placed in the transaction log along with the block in the file system that is to be changed. Subsequently the write is applied to the file system proper, and the log record is removed (see Figure 75). This arrangement makes possible detecting when a write has been partially committed to the file system, and also to commit the correct data into the file system, even when the write operation has been interrupted.

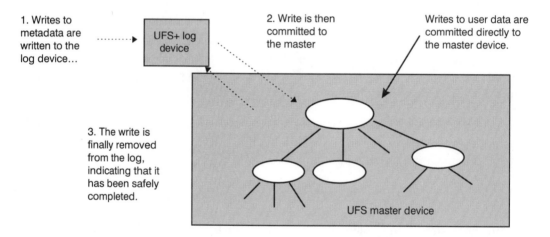

Figure 75. States during writes to a UFS+ logging file system, which logs metadata but not user data. Metadata reads must consult the log device to find possible pending metadata writes. Since user data is not logged, read performance is rarely affected to any significant degree.

The safe–write attributes of the logging file system has two primary advantages. First, the presence of a duplicated copy of the written data ensures that the operation can be completed as requested by the user. The write is either not committed at all (if the system fails before the log is written) or is fully committed, possibly by applying the recorded changes stored in the log to the file system. Although often overlooked, this capability is the primary advantage of a logging file system.

The other reason to use a logging file system is that it greatly accelerates checking the consistency of a file system. One reason that a consistency check is faster is that the file system structure is much less likely to be corrupted, due to the safe-write characteristic. The fsck(1m) process must arrange to have the log rolled forward (i.e., applied) before it inspects the actual file system.

9.2.1.1 Metatrans Implementation Details

A UFS+ file system consists of two components: a master file system and a log. One of the interesting characteristics of the UFS+ implementation is that it is fully upward- and downward–compatible with the on–disk layout of existing UFS file systems. The master file system is exactly a standard UFS file system. It responds to exactly the same programmatic interface and has the same on-disk format as a normal file system, so UFS file systems are converted into UFS+ file systems by simply adding a log device. Removing the log from a UFS+ file system is also possible, although the value of this operation is debatable. Because the programming interface is unmodified, the use of a UFS+ file system is completely transparent to applications.

UFS+ logs metadata changes, but not user data updates. For this reason, log devices can be so much smaller than their master file systems: only metadata is logged, and it is far less bulky than user data. User data is nearly always 8 KB and can be far larger, whereas few individual pieces of metadata are larger than a disk block (512 bytes).

During normal operation, writes to user data are committed directly to the file system in the usual way. Updates to file system metadata, such as directory entries, super blocks, inodes, indirect blocks, or cylinder group headers, are logged to ensure consistency. The log process involves writing the disk address of the changed information and the new information itself onto the log device. The information is also retained in memory, to avoid rereading the data back from the log. Once the metadata is safely committed to the log device, the operation is acknowledged with a success return code and the write system call returns.

Meanwhile, a kernel thread picks up the update and posts it to the correct spot in the master file system. After the post is complete, the log writer thread updates the log record to show that it has been committed. In the unlikely event that the log fills (because updates are being issued by applications more quickly than the log writer thread can post them), further metadata writes will not be accepted and the write(2) calls block until the log becomes available.

The metatrans log device is organized as a circular list of variable-size entries that is placed on a raw disk or metadisk partition. The useful size of the log device is not dependent upon the size of the file system, but rather how often the master file system's directory structure will be modified. The recommended size for logs is 64 MB for most file systems. If the file system will have files created and destroyed much more than usual, a reasonable upper limit is 128 MB.

Typical busy file systems with many pending writes (for example a Usenet news spool) have logs containing 100-200 entries; rolling these entries forward takes 5-10 seconds. Even extremely busy file systems usually have less than 1,000 entries and take less than a minute to roll. Metadevice initialization is performed very early in the boot process; even a busy file system's log is completely rolled forward before the file system integrity checking process is even invoked. Since roll-forward begins when the metadevices are initialized, rather than when the file system is actually checked, the practical effect is that the file system check is virtually instantaneous.

UFS+ file systems suffer file system corruption far less frequently than standard UFS file systems, because of the logging precautions. However, the file system structure to become corrupted by being stored on a device that produces some sort of error. Although this is rare, it does happen when the underlying storage mechanism is damaged or compromised. To handle this problem, `fsck(1m)` will still go through the much longer standard process of checking directory links, free space counts, etc., if applied to a logging file system. The system boot process requests the fast file system check by using the -m argument to `fsck(1m)`; this process checks only the consistency of the log—*and thus the directory structure*—permitting the system boot to safely check and mount file systems within seconds.

9.2.1.2 Performance of UFS+ File Systems

Because UFS+ logs only metadata, the performance of most file system operations is exactly the same as for UFS. In particular, manipulation of user data runs at the same speed as expected from regular UFS file systems. The performance of metainformation access varies. For file systems that are relatively static—that is, most file systems—the log is empty or nearly empty, and metadata reads are affected only marginally. Metadata reads are satisfied from buffer cache, where the data is cached while the log writer thread is in operation.

Metadata writes to the logging file system vary widely. Several considerations arise when comparing performance of the logging file system and the master file system. One of them is the ability of the log device to absorb writes compared to the ability of the master. In the simple (but uncommon) case when the master is on one disk and the log is on another, the logging file system is significantly faster. Writes to the log are performed sequentially, and often the log is small enough to fit in just a few cylinders, where seek distances are short.

In contrast, updates to the master are spread across a large area of the disk, and virtually every write is at a different location and seek distances are moderate to long. In more typical configurations, the master file system is spread across many disks, and the log is usually mirrored. This setup reduces the ability of the log to absorb writes, whereas the multiple disks in the master are able to absorb more. Metadata writes usually are faster to a logging file system when the ratio of log disks to master disks is less than about one to six. When the master device uses more than six disks, the log should be striped across more than one disk.

9.2.1.3 Configuring UFS+ Log Devices

The log is crucial to the functioning of the file system, and precautions must be taken to avoid its becoming a single point of failure. Accordingly, the log device should be mirrored, but not at the cost of excessive resources, since the log is small. Even the largest logs are only 128 MB, so mirroring them is a matter of finding disk spindles. As previously noted, large master file systems may need complex log organizations to meet the combination of performance and reliability requirements. Configure one spindle in the log device for every six spindles in the master. The entire log device should then be mirrored.

For example, consider a 100 GB file system residing on 4.2 GB disk drives. The 4.2 GB disk stores only 4 GB (see section 7.1.1.4.1, *Megabytes* vs. *Millions of Bytes*), so the file system occupies 25 drives. This file system needs about four members in the log disk for performance reasons. Striping four small partitions together achieves the performance goals, but the reliability of the entire file system is compromised by the stripe; the solution is to mirror the stripe. Using a RAID-5 volume for the log would be a sensible idea, since it would reduce the cost of reliability, but the nature of the log accesses (virtually write-only, and almost entirely small blocks) means that the RAID-5 organization's performance characteristics would defeat the purpose of having a complex log.

Fortunately, the use of caching disk subsystems makes reducing the complexity of log devices possible. These disk arrays accelerate synchronous disk writes, precisely the ones directed to log devices, typically improving latency from about 12-13 ms to about 2-3 ms. Storing the log device on a caching disk array reduces the log's spindle requirement to about one log disk for every 30 members in the master device. The log must still be mirrored for reliability, preferably using two separate NVRAM caches.

Ordinarily, host-based NVRAM (NVSIMM or PrestoServe) is functionally equivalent to subsystem-based NVRAM, but this is an exception. The PrestoServe driver and UFS+ do not cooperate, and as a result, applying them to the same file system is impossible. The two features do operate correctly in the same system as long as they do not attempt to combine their effect on one file system.

In summary:

⇒ Always mirror UFS+ logs.
⇒ Configure one log disk (before mirroring) for every six disks in the master device. Stripe multiple log disk members together with a small chunk size.

⇒ Configure log disks in caching disk arrays to dramatically reduce spindle requirements. One log disk is required for every 30 disks in the master device if the log is accelerated by NVRAM.

⇒ Host-based NVRAM is incompatible with UFS+ logs, for implementation rather than architectural reasons.

9.2.2 Access Control Lists (ACLs)

One of the ways that SunSoft has extended the design of the original BSD implementation is the use of access control lists for mandatory access control. Access control lists are ways to describe very precisely who and what may access a file system object. Traditional UNIX implementations use a permission mask on each file system entity. Nine bits are allocated to each of three user classes: the owner, the owner's group, and anyone else (the world). These are adequate for casual use in some environments, but other applications require more precision.

The ACL implementation in Solaris UFS additionally permits the specification of access rights on a per-user and per-group basis, as defined by the POSIX 1003.6 standard. By default, file system entity permissions are governed by the traditional UNIX permissions mask, and default ACL permissions are derived from the permission mask. For example, the UNIX mask 0751 is translated to a default ACL as:

```
user::rwx
group::r-x
other::--x
```

meaning that the owner of the file can read, write, or execute it, but group members can only read and execute, and anyone else has only execute permission. By itself, a single ACL specification is only slightly more precise than traditional UNIX permissions. The difference is that whereas UNIX permissions restrict the meaning of the user and group fields to the creating user and group of the file, an ACL entry can specify arbitrary user and groups:

```
user:dave:-w-,group:lp:-w-
```

which specifies that both the user dave and anyone in the group lp have write-only access to the entity (write-only access might be appropriate for a printer file). The primary value of ACLs is that many can be combined on a single entity, resulting in a very precise permissions specification. A file containing confidential data collected by a daemon might have permissions set this way:

```
setfacl -s user::---,group::---,other::--- file # nobody has access
setfacl -m user:daemon:-w- file # the daemon can write/append
setfacl -m user:bagger:r-- file # 'bagger' can read but not update
setfacl -m user:editor:rw- file # user editor has real control.
```

One significant consideration is that each ACL entry after the default entry consumes an additional inode, effectively reducing the number of files that can reside in the file system.

The example above consumes the equivalent of four files in the file system. Most file systems, particularly those created with default parameters, have far more inodes than necessary (often by a factor of 15 or 20), but inode consumption does warrant some advance consideration, since UFS file systems contain a fixed number of inodes once created (see *inode Density* below).

9.2.3 UFS and UFS+ Parameters

Several parameters should be configured when constructing UFS or UFS+ file systems. These parameters all have defaults, and using them always results in a usable file system, but often these parameters can be tuned for either higher performance or greater usable storage capacity, or both.

9.2.3.1 inode Density

Each file stored in a file system actually consists of several logical entities. These include the directory entry (which includes the name of the file, its permission mask, size, dates of creation, access, and update, and other similar information), the data blocks that contain the actual file data, and zero or more access control list entries. The process of creating a file system involves allocating space for the inodes; the number of potential inodes in a file system is consequently static. Once the file system is created increasing the number of available inodes is impossible, and the number of inodes allocated effectively limits the number of files that can be stored in the file system.

By default, UFS allocates one inode for every 2 KB of usable disk space in the file system. Since each inode consumes a small but finite amount of disk space (about 512 bytes), they consume a considerable amount of space. In fact, inode overhead represents about 11 percent of the total disk space under the default parameters! For modern file systems, this allocation is a substantial over–investment, because file sizes have grown greatly since 1980, when the defaults were originally set. Typical files in 1996 average about 60-100 KB, compared to about 1 KB in 1980.

One inode per 16 KB is a more reasonable default; even this is quite conservative (for existing file systems, the number of inodes in use can be found using "df -e"). For file systems that will be used to store very large files (DBMS tablespaces or data–intensive NFS), much lower inode density is appropriate. One inode per megabyte is as little as might be reasonably required in such file systems; this represents a reduction in overhead of over 99.99 percent.

Although the default is extremely conservative for most file systems, situations that involve many very small files may require even more inodes than the default. The primary application in this category is the file system that contains Usenet news files. The Usenet news format uses one file for every news article. Since articles are typically very short, this application uses a much higher inode density than typical of other applications.

One final consideration is the use of access control lists (ACLs). After the initial entry, each ACL entry is stored in a separate inode. For example, consider the following sequence:

```
% touch file
% setfacl user::rwx,group::---,other:---  file # set default ACL
% setfacl user:dave:r-x file   # gives dave read/execute permission
% setfacl user:noah:--- file   # permits noah no access at all
```

This sequence sets a default ACL, and then two additional, more specific access rights, thus consuming a total of two extra inodes. Such inode use must be factored in when computing the size of file systems. Current usage does not require many inodes for ACLs; traditional UNIX permission modes are stored in the file's directory entry and do not require additional inode storage.

⇒ Configure one inode for every 16-64 KB of data, rather than the default inode per 2 KB.
⇒ Usenet news spool directories should use the default 2 KB.
⇒ File systems that will contain DBMS files (such as for Oracle, Informix, or DB2) should be configured with one inode for every 1 MB.
⇒ Configure additional inodes to accommodate anticipated ACL usage.

9.2.3.2 File System Cluster Size

Since SunOS 4.1.1, the UFS disk block allocator has performed *disk write clustering*. When a file is being extended, the file system clusters blocks (8 KB per logical block) together when it is able. This technique permits the entire cluster to be written to the disk in a single operation. Keeping such clusters together has several important advantages. The most immediate advantage is that only a single write operation is issued to the disk subsystem, rather than several. Writing in a single operation is more efficient from the operating system's perspective since non–zero overhead is incurred performing any disk I/O. The overhead is constant per I/O, rather than proportional to the size of the I/O transfer. In addition, when the file is read later, the entire cluster can be read in a single operation. This saves I/O overhead again, but the more important optimization is that reading the cluster together avoids having to perform a disk seek between the retrieval of each disk block. For files that are sequentially accessed, this is an important optimization. The file system parameter is known as `maxcontig` because it represents the maximum number of contiguous file system blocks that will be stored contiguously on the disk.

Although normal operation to a file system might be fully random access, the process of backing up the data is inherently a sequential process. Configuring a large cluster size solely for the purpose of accelerating the backups may be worthwhile.

By default, the file system clusters up to seven file system blocks together, resulting in a cluster size of 56 KB. This size is historical; older Sun hardware was unable to transfer more than 64 KB in a single DVMA transaction[78]. This limitation has long since been removed, and the advent of disk striping and other forms of RAID has changed the way file system clustering is used.

> Note: Setting `maxcontig` to a non–default value is extremely if the file system will reside on a RAID-5 volume, because the default 56 KB cluster size virtually ensures that writes to the file system will involve expensive read/modify/write operations. See section 7.5.8.3, *RAID-5 Performance,* and 9.2.3.2, *File System Cluster Size.*

Given typical modern practice of spreading file systems across many physical disk drives with striping or RAID-5, combined with the ability of modern SCSI disks to handle relatively large physical I/Os, using much larger file system clusters than the default 56 KB is reasonable. Because random access I/O normally does not read entire clusters, changing this parameter has little effect on file systems that handle primarily random access I/O (positive or negative), but file systems that may be used in a sequential fashion can benefit by using an increased file system cluster size. The file system cluster size should be matched to some integer multiple of the stripe width of the disk metadevice that contains it.

For example, if the file system resides on a five-disk RAID-5 volume whose interlace is 16 KB, the stripe width is 64 KB (one disk is used for parity computation), and the file system `maxcontig` should be set to 8 or 16 blocks. Thus the cluster size is 64 KB or 128 KB.

The file system cluster size is specified when the file system is created via the `-C` argument to the `newfs(1m)` program. It can also be tuned on existing file systems via the `-a` argument to `tunefs(1m)`. One important consideration is that tuning a file system after it has been used does not have precisely the same effect as setting the cluster size when the file system is created. Specifically, tuning the file system after files are written into the file system does *not* reconfigure blocks already written on the file system. When a file system is tuned to change its file system cluster size, consider whether or not to dump and restore the existing data to reallocate the data in clusters.

⇒ Configure `maxcontig` to be an integer multiple of the data width of the stripe or RAID-5 volume that stores the file system.

⇒ File systems that will contain very large, sequentially accessed files should use a `maxcontig`, such as 32 (i.e., 256 KB), that is at least double the data width of its underlying storage device.

---

[78] Specifically, systems using the `sun4` kernel architecture had this limitation: the Sun-4/100, 4/200, 4/300, and 4/400 families had small DVMA windows. All members of the `sun4c`, `sun4m`, `sun4d`, and `sun4u` families have much more capable hardware; most permit 64 MB to be transferred in a single operation.

9.2.3.3 Minimum Free Space Reserve

When a file system is created, a portion of the storage space is reserved against emergency overflow situations. This reserved space is maintained at a threshold called `minfree`, and defaults to ten percent of the file system's size. The ten percent figure is historical, and dates from the time when large data-center disk drives stored 50 MB. The ten percent margin represented a reasonable overflow. It also provided a means of ensuring that the system would not have to search all over the disk looking for a free disk block in the event that a file was being extended when the file system was nearly full.

For many applications, the ten percent `minfree` has become overly conservative. Although files have certainly grown in size, typical file systems have grown much more quickly through the combination of much larger disk drives and the common advent of various RAID organizations. Even a small file system in 1996 resides on a 2 GB disk, and ten- or even fifty-disk RAID volumes have become common, resulting in common file system sizes approaching 500 GB. In such situations the default free space reservation is 200 MB-50 GB! For these reasons, setting `minfree` to one percent is the most reasonable alternative. It still reserves an adequate overflow area, yet makes a large difference in the overhead associated with file systems.

The performance concern is also much less of an issue, since locating free blocks within even a 10-20 MB area is easy. Furthermore, seeks that have to locate free blocks can also have less impact on a RAID volume consisting of many disk drives, than on a single disk drive.

The default values for `minfree` and inode density result in file system overhead of approximately 21 percent of overall storage capacity. With inode density set to 16 KB and `minfree` set to one percent, overhead is reduced sevenfold to 3.5 percent. For most applications, no performance penalty is incurred. (The notable exception would be a small file system with typical file sizes that approach the size of the free space reserve. Even this setup is not an issue unless those files are commonly owned by the superuser, since otherwise the free space reserve cannot be consumed.)

⇒ Configure `minfree` to be one percent on all except root file systems.

9.2.3.4 Rotational Delay

Older disk drives (or more often, their associated disk controllers) were not fast enough to access data at the full speed of the disk platter. In such circumstances a useful optimization was to physically store data blocks out of order, separated by enough radial position that the disk would rotate into position to access the next block while the current block was being processed. For example, consider a disk whose rotational speed is 3,600 rpm (13 ms per revolution), matched with a disk controller whose block processing time is 3 ms. If data blocks are simply written sequentially, reading two requires the disk to miss a revolution:

the first one is read, and by the time the controller has processed it, the second one has already flown under the heads; reading two blocks takes more than 19 ms. If the logically sequential blocks are physically located a quarter of a revolution apart (i.e., 4.25 ms), the platter is still in position to deliver the second block after the 3 ms processing time, and the same operation can be performed in about 11 ms.

Fortunately, resort to this optimization is no longer necessary. Although disk drives now spin more than twice as fast, the processing capability of virtually all disk controllers is easily sufficient to avoid rotational delay problems SCSI disks almost universally have at least a dedicated 16-bit processor for managing disk activities, and these drives *never* need additional rotation delay. For all applications it is best to set rotational delay to zero. This is the default, but users have often been observed using non-default values—with consistently negative results.

⇒ *Always* set `rotdelay` to zero, unless the file system resides on a storage device other than standard disk drives. Even then use a non-zero `rotdelay` *only* on slower devices, such as magneto-optical, floptical, or floppy disk drives.

9.3 Handling Very Large Files

Some applications, notably those that operate on very large data sets that exceed the size of memory, do not fit the UFS/VM model very well, causing considerable overhead. The overhead for manipulating very large files arises primarily from the management of the file as a series of physical memory pages. (This discussion applies primarily to sequential processing of data files, rather than to DBMS tablespaces. The DBMS vendors have either worked around the problem or can fall back on raw disk devices for tablespace storage.) For most files, which average a few hundred kilobytes to a few megabytes, this organization imposes little overhead, and in fact produces significant savings in I/O time for most applications. When file size increases past about 500-700 MB, the sheer size of the I/O operations tends to increase. Instead of an 8 KB I/O (one page) or a 56 KB file system cluster I/O (seven pages), a single I/O might move 8 MB—2,000 pages—in a single operation. This type of I/O size is well outside the consideration of the original Berkeley FFFS design, when even a large multi-user system might not even have 8 MB of physical memory!

The impact of such large I/O sizes is two-fold. Files that exceed the size of physical memory are still moved via the page cache, since this is the mechanism for issuing I/O activity. Unfortunately, caching this data has little value, because it is very unlikely that any process will reference the cached data again before some other data requires the use of the underlying physical memory. In this case, the caching process is wasted effort. To add insult to injury, the kernel is not structured internally to handle large blocks of pages as single entities, so processing of large I/Os is done a page at a time, a method that can be quite inefficient for bulk I/O.

The solution to this problem is to move data directly from the storage device to the user I/O buffer, bypassing any caching mechanism. If possible, the implementation should manipulate large blocks of data in each operation, rather than operating one page at a time. For these reasons, applications that expect to manage bulk file system data, such as large image data, satellite, or other real-time data capture, and high-performance scientific applications should seriously consider the use of alternative file systems. The current UFS implementation is not well suited to this application profile.

9.4 Veritas VxFS File System

One viable alternative is the VxFS file system, available from Veritas Software. VxFS has a number of features that make it well-suited to handling this class of application. Probably the most significant is its (optional) use of a direct I/O path, avoiding VM caching overhead. This permits a VxFS file system to achieve significantly higher single-threaded sequential throughput than UFS.

VxFS also uses a completely different mechanism for allocating on-disk space, permitting more flexible data layout strategies and pre-allocation of space. Data layout policies permit specification of large contiguous extents, cylinder-group boundary alignment, and other performance optimization. Single-threaded sequential I/O performance on VxFS can be excellent: with sufficient resources, data can move at rates in excess of 55 MB/sec. To achieve this performance, multiple disk arrays must be striped together using host-based RAID -0 striping. The application must request direct I/O and operate on very large I/O sizes. The 70 MB/sec rate was achieved using Solstice:DiskSuite striping across multiple fast-40 SCSI host adapters with hardware RAID devices on each bus. The (trivial) application requested 8 MB I/O size on an Ultra Enterprise 4000 system.

Not all of VxFS's data layout features are easy to use correctly. This is not a criticism of the VxFS implementation; rather it is a reflection of the complexity of modern storage subsystems. For example, the complex nature of most large disk devices makes it very difficult to predict the location of cylinder boundaries on the physical device. In fact, the cylinder boundaries are almost certainly inconsistent across the underlying disk devices, because virtually all disk drives use variable-density geometries. Moreover, virtually all large files reside on some form of RAID device or metadevice.

The file system uses a user-data logging strategy, somewhat different than the metadata-only strategy used in UFS +. Each approach has merits. Logging user data increases the integrity of user data at a significant cost in configuration to complexity, since user data is far larger than metadata. When operating on very large files, the log device must have performance characteristics approaching that of the master file system, or the log becomes the bottleneck.

VxFS has other desirable features, such as online snapshot capability, dynamically allocated inodes, and the ability to grow or shrink the file system while mounted. Unfortunately, VxFS is not a complete replacement for UFS or UFS+, since some significant features are not implemented. Although VxFS file systems can accommodate the largest storage devices, very large (> 2 GB) files are not supported, and neither are quotas or access control lists.

⇒ Non-DBMS applications dominated by sequential I/O to files in excess of 500-700 MB should use VxFS instead of UFS.

⇒ Real-time applications that depend on predictable I/O response should use VxFS and pre-allocate disk space if the application cannot be recoded to take I/O response out of the critical real-time path.

9.5 The `tmpfs` File System

Solaris has a special file system type that is used for transitory files, known as `tmpfs`. As the name implies, the contents of the file system are temporary. The unique characteristics of the `tmpfs` are that storage space for the file system is allocated dynamically from virtual memory, and that the file system is initially empty, rather than from persistent storage. From a practical perspective, the `tmpfs` is a useful mechanism for allocating temporary files in high-speed memory. Only temporary files can reside in `tmpfs`, because the contents of the file system are lost during reboot.

Because the file system resides entirely in virtual memory, the memory management system allocates physical memory to back `tmpfs` data, and as a consequence, performance is usually that of a memory-based file, rather than a disk-based file. The performance improvement is not due to caching, as is commonly thought. UFS integration with the VM system results in equivalent caching of reads from regular file systems. Instead, high performance is due to the fact that the data is not written to disk unless physical memory is in short supply.

By default, the Solaris install program configures the /tmp directory as a `tmpfs`. Since /tmp is a `tmpfs`, most transient work files are already placed in memory. For example, compiler intermediate files, editor scratch files, and Web browser files default to this location. For larger servers, this avoids significant I/O.

One less common, but very effective application of the `tmpfs` is as a location for DBMS temporary tables, such as those used to store intermediate results for sort or join operations. Most DBMS systems have provisions for handling these tasks in main memory. For example, Oracle uses part of the System Global Area (SGA) called the Shared Pool as temporary operation storage. This method is effective in most cases, but for applications that infrequently use very large temporary tables, it may not be appropriate to allocate a large shared pool solely for the infrequent use. These applications can be accelerated by placing temporary tables in a temporary file systems, thereby permitting the virtual memory system to dynamically manage the large demands.

This tactic may take some arrangement on the part of the database administrator at system boot time. The database expects that previously created temporary tables are stored on persistent storage; if one or more temporary tables were previously stored in a `tmpfs`, they may not be correctly initialized. If this situation is the case, the temporary tables must be dropped and recreated and reinitialized before normal operation begins.

Some features of UFS and UFS+ file systems, notably quotas and access control lists, are not implemented in the `tmpfs`.

⇒ Use a `tmpfs` file system for storing DBMS temporary tables if the application makes heavy use of sorts or joins, and if other allocation mechanisms are inappropriate.
⇒ Use the temporary file system for ordinary temporary file use.
⇒ A `tmpfs` is only faster than regular file system I/O when write activity is a significant proportion of the I/O mix. Read caching performance is identical for both UFS and `tmpfs`.

9.6 Kernel Asynchronous I/O

The traditional UNIX I/O model uses the `read(2)` and `write(2)` system calls. When an application calls read or write, the caller is blocked until the I/O is completed to the degree required by the application. For writes to physical devices, the caller is blocked until the data is committed to the device, for example until characters are placed on a communications line or the disk block is transferred to the disk subsystem. Writes to a UFS file system are returned more quickly, because UFS normally accepts the write and buffers it into memory, permitting the caller to proceed; the system arranges to have the data transferred to disk independently. Reads must be blocked in any case, because the data is not available.

The asynchronous I/O model modifies the way applications interface with the UNIX I/O system. Sophisticated applications can issue I/O requests and *not* be blocked while the system services the I/O. The application is able to continue with other processing, making possible much greater overall parallelism. Most DBMS systems make use of the async I/O feature. For example, Sybase relies heavily on it.

Two different parts make up the asynchronous I/O implementation, one in the user–level libraries, and the other in the kernel. All Solaris 2 releases have the `aioread(3)`, `aiowrite(3)`, `aiowait(3)`, and related subroutines that implement the user–level asynchronous I/O feature. Solaris 2.3 async I/O is implemented completely in user code.

Beginning with Solaris 2.4[79], the kernel provides direct support for async I/O; this code is usually referred to as "kernel async I/O (KAIO)." KAIO creates a pool of dedicated kernel threads that process async I/O requests submitted by applications. The *kernel* support for async I/O applies to raw disk partitions—in particular, it does not operate on UFS files. This limitation may seem serious, but UFS itself already creates a processing layer capable of improving parallelism in I/O.

The Solaris 2.5.1 implementation of KAIO is the first to permit operation on full 64-bit devices. Previous versions supported device sizes of only 2 GB or less.

9.7 Scheduler Features

Solaris 2 uses the standard System V Release 4 scheduler. It is very flexible, permitting site-specific tuning of priorities, time slices, and interactive/batch bias. As of Solaris 2.3, the default parameters for the timesharing class have been strongly oriented toward timesharing processing at the expense of batch processing. This default provides interactive users with excellent response but can cause batch jobs to take an excessively long time. If the system is expected to handle continuous streams of batch jobs, modifying the default parameters may be necessary. Some kinds of NeWSprint configurations will fall into this category, especially those handling long jobs involving color. Some sites with very heavy batch loads have even created their own scheduling class for batch processing.

9.7.1 Manipulating the Quantum

Even though the scheduler is already biased toward interactive users, some types of very heavy loads can benefit from further tuning of the scheduler. The *quantum* is the period of time that the scheduler permits a process to run before preemption. Phrased another way, it is the amount of processor time that is permitted to a process before the system arbitrarily decides that another process should get processor service.

Research has shown that when Solaris systems run at full or nearly full processor utilization in system–call oriented environments, overall system performance can be improved by changing the scheduler table to provide longer quanta. In the default scheduler table, the quanta range from 40 ms for the top priorities to 200 ms for the lowest priorities. Limited experimentation with heavily loaded 2N DBMS systems suggests that increasing the quanta to 340-400 ms can improve throughput and response time under heavy load (in this context, the term "heavy" means "the load average as reported by w(1) or rup(1) exceeds the number of processors"). Choose the lower end of the range (340 ms) for faster processors

---

[79] Solaris 2.4 includes KAIO, but support for KAIO on layered disk devices such as SPARCstorage Volume Manager or Solstice:DiskSuite is not enabled by default. Support for this functionality on Solaris 2.4 is only available via a patch.

such as UltraSPARC and the higher end of the range for slower processors such as SuperSPARC and hyperSPARC. The performance improvement can be substantial—up to 50-60 percent improvement in response time, combined with 15-20 percent in throughput. System performance increases in these circumstances due to better scheduling of system calls, particularly for semaphore operations. For light loads, when the processors are not saturated, the differential is negligible if present at all.

9.7.2 Real-Time Scheduling

At the other end of the scheduling spectrum, Solaris 2 also offers real-time scheduling, in which processes are scheduled at very high priority with relatively tight response time guarantees. The guarantees are considered "soft" by the scientific community because response latency is normally approximately 150 microseconds (on a SPARCstation 10 Model 41 or 85 MHz SPARCstation 5) with a maximum of approximately 500 microseconds (see Table 37). For the commercial computing normally associated with servers, the real-time scheduler provides an opportunity to segregate key processes into an essentially private scheduling class at high priority. For example, an Oracle server operating in timesharing mode will normally have user processes and shadow processes running on behalf of each user in addition to several back-end processes. Operating the back–end processes in the real-time class permits them to operate without interference from the user or shadow processes.

> Warning: Always run fewer real-time processes than you have processors, unless the tasks are specifically designed to operate in real-time mode. In other words, do not attempt this on a uniprocessor!

Although it delivers very good real-time response, Solaris 2 is *not* a "hard" real-time operating system, in that it does not *guarantee* any specific response time to user or kernel processes. Nonetheless, the "soft" real-time scheduling provided by Solaris 2.5 delivers performance appropriate for many applications such as robotic controls and satellite data capture.

9.7.3 Scheduling Summary

⇒ Use the dispadmin(1) command to modify the scheduler's dispatch tables, especially when batch processing with relatively tight completion requirements.

⇒ Systems that have busy timesharing workloads should increase the maximum quantum from 200 ms to 400 ms on SuperSPARC- or hyperSPARC-based systems, or to 340 ms on UltraSPARC-based systems.

⇒ For systems that are dominated by centralized server processes, such as a timesharing DBMS system, consider launching key processes in the real-time class via the prioctl(1) command.

Table 37. Real-time response and dispatch latency for various platforms on Solaris 2.5

Value	Time (Milliseconds)			
	Minimum	Maximum	Median	Average
SPARCstation 2 (40 MHz CY601)				
Total Response	0.460000	4.860000	0.680000	1.715145
Dispatch Latency	0.290000	4.210000	0.420000	0.346930
SPARCstation 5 (85 MHz MicroSPARC–II)				
Total Response	0.280000	1.410000	0.410000	0.526765
Dispatch Latency	0.180000	0.620000	0.270000	0.281808
Ultra–1 (167 MHz UltraSPARC)				
Total Response	0.070000	0.400000	0.120000	0.124747
Dispatch Latency	0.300000	0.180000	0.080000	0.105173

9.8 SCSI Option Selection

As discussed in section 7.2.4, the SCSI subsystem offers a number of options that can be selected. Under most circumstances, the most suitable options are selected by the system during the initial device probe, but occasionally overriding the defaults as selected by the system or device may be appropriate. Solaris 2 provides a global option configuration parameter called `scsi_options` in the `/etc/system` file that permits selection of most of the interesting SCSI options. The values for `scsi_options` can be found in the file `/usr/include/sys/scsi/conf/autoconf.h`, a portion of which is reproduced here:

```
/*
 * SCSI subsystem options - global word of options are available
 *
 * bits 0-2 are reserved for debugging/informational level
 * bit  3 reserved for a global disconnect/reconnect switch
 * bit  4 reserved for a global linked command capability switch
 * bit  5 reserved for a global synchronous SCSI capability switch
 *
 * the rest of the bits are reserved for future use
 *
 */
#define SCSI_DEBUG_TGT     0x1     /* debug statements in target drivers    */
#define SCSI_DEBUG_LIB     0x2     /* debug statements in library      */
#define SCSI_DEBUG_HA      0x4     /* debug statements in host adapters */

#define SCSI_OPTIONS_DR    0x8     /* Global disconnect/reconnect       */
#define SCSI_OPTIONS_LINK  0x10    /* Global linked commands     */
#define SCSI_OPTIONS_SYNC  0x20    /* Global synchronous xfer capability*/
#define SCSI_OPTIONS_PARITY 0x40   /* Global parity support      */
#define SCSI_OPTIONS_TAG   0x80    /*    "    tagged command support    */
#define SCSI_OPTIONS_FAST  0x100   /*    "    FAST SCSI support   */
#define SCSI_OPTIONS_WIDE  0x200   /*    "    WIDE SCSI support   */
#define SCSI_OPTIONS_FAST20 0x400  /* Global FAST20 SCSI support */
```

As of Solaris 2.5.1, the default value for `scsi_options` is `0x3f8`, which permits devices to select all performance options except fast-20 if they support the features; all debugging options are disabled. The feature mask in `scsi_options` has a global effect: if a feature is disabled here, all host adapters in the system will disclaim the capability during device negotiation, effectively disabling it across the entire system. Extreme care should be exercised when disabling the more basic features, such as disconnect/reconnect, as these can have a serious impact on system performance.

The `scsi_options` variable has historically been most useful for suppressing tagged command support (command queuing). Although most current devices handle command queuing correctly, quite a few devices that still do *not* correctly implement command queuing, and disabling system–wide command queuing is an easy way to isolate the problem. This problem also occasionally afflicts to fast and fast/wide devices, and even to synchronous transfer (these are usually caused by faulty cabling, and manipulation of `/etc/system` is only needed on a temporary basis to isolate the problem).

Sun Product Summary

This appendix contains brief descriptions of various Sun products for those not familiar with the configuration specifics of various systems and expansion products. This is not intended to be an exhaustive treatment; rather it is meant be used in conjunction with the case studies. Consult your vendor for more specific details. The first section describes the most common SPARC systems introduced since 1992.

SPARCstation 10 family—The original multiprocessor capable desktop workstation. A pizzabox enclosure provides space for one, two, or four processors on two MBus modules, four SBus slots, two 3.5" x 1.6" SCSI disk drives, and a floppy disk. The SBus slots are in a two-above-two configuration, permitting the use of double-wide SBus boards. Memory is available from 16MB to 512 MB. The motherboard has two serial ports, basic rate ISDN, fast SCSI-2, and 10baseT ports. The SPARCstation 10 shares model designations with the SPARCstation 20. The model number indicates what type of processors are installed. In a two-digit number, such as Model 50 or Model 51, the tens digit indicates the processor speed (50 MHz in this case), and the ones digit indicates the size of the external cache in megabytes. When a multiprocessor system is configured, the model designation becomes a three-digit number, and the last digit indicates the number of processors. For example, the Model 514 is a quad-processor system with 50 MHz/1 MB SuperSPARC processors, and a Model 712 is a dual-processor system using 75 MHz/1 MB processors.

SPARCstation 20 family—Upgraded packaging for the SPARCstation 10, combined with upgraded internal parts. Like its predecessor, the upgraded system provides space for one to four processors on two MBus modules, four SBus slots, up to 512 MB memory and built-in serial ports, parallel port, 10baseT, and fast SCSI-2. No ISDN is on the newer system. The internal peripheral storage changes two 3.5" x 1" low-profile disks, internal CDROM, and floppy.

SPARCstation 5 family—Uses the same physical packaging as the SPARCstation 20 family with a different motherboard. The SPARCstation 5 uses the MicroSPARC-II processor and offers two serial ports, a parallel port, 10baseT, fast SCSI-2, and three SBus slots. The

SBus boards are three-wide, permitting the use of double-wide SBus boards in either slots 1 and 2, or 2 and 3. Memory is available in configurations from 16 MB to 256 MB.

Ultra–1 family—The first generation of workstations and low-end servers based on the UltraSPARC-I processor. Although their SPARCstation 10 and SPARCstation 20 predecessors have field-replaceable processors, the Ultra–1 family CPUs are soldered down. Confusingly, several varieties exist, differing in subtle but significant ways. The Ultra–1/140 and Ultra–1/170 have three SBus slots, but they are *not* in side-by-side configuration as in the SPARCstation 10 and SPARCstation 20. Consequently, double-wide SBus boards do not fit in these systems. The Ultra–1/140 uses one 143 MHz UltraSPARC-I, and the Ultra–1/170 uses a similar 167 MHz part; both use 512 KB caches. The Ultra–1/140 and Ultra–1/170 have two serial ports, a parallel port, 10baseT , and fast SCSI-2 ports. The similar-looking Ultra–1/170E deletes one SBus slot in favor of a UPA framebuffer slot; only two SBus slots are available. Unlike the Ultra–1/170, the 170E uses 100baseT FastEthernet and fast/wide SCSI-2 instead of 10baseT and fast SCSI-2. All members of the Ultra–1 family have space for 32 MB-1 GB memory, two 3.5" x 1" disks, a floppy, and either a CDROM or a single 8 mm or 4 mm tape drive.

Ultra Enterprise 150—Deskside "tower" packaging for the Ultra–1 family. This system configures an Ultra–1/170 board (i.e., 1 GB memory, three SBus slots, 10baseT, fast SCSI-2, no UPA graphics) in a much larger enclosure. The box has space for a 3.5" x 1" boot disk, CDROM, tape, and twelve 3.5" x 1" data disks in hot pluggable configuration. Some models, notably the Netra *n* NFS server, also include an internal uninterruptible power supply. The data disks can be divided onto two SCSI busses.

Ultra–2 family—The spiritual successor to the SPARCstation 20 family. In a slightly taller package than the Ultra–1, the Ultra–2 offers one or two UPA processor modules; these modules are physically quite different from the MBus modules used in earlier systems. To date no other system shares processor modules with the Ultra–2. These systems offer four SBus slots in the same configuration as the SPARCstation 20 (so double-wide SBus boards do fit and work); in addition, the systems have a UPA framebuffer slot, 64 MB-2 GB memory, two 3.5" x 1" SCSI disks, floppy, and CDROM or low-profile tape drive, along with built-in serial, parallel, 100baseT FastEthernet, and fast/wide SCSI-2. The Ultra–2 model designations are similar to those used on the SPARCstation 10/20. The models are four-digit numbers; the thousands digit indicates the number of processors, and the last three digits indicate the processor speed. The Ultra–2/2200 has two 200 MHz modules, and the Ultra–2/1170 has one 167 MHz module.

The SPARCserver 600MP family was the first multiprocessor server; the design served as the basis for the SPARCstation 10, albeit in a much smaller package. The three members of the 600MP family use the same single processor board but configure it in different packaging. The common processor board is built in a double-high 9U VME form factor and offers space for one to four processors on two MBus modules, 512 MB memory, and four SBus slots. However, the fourth SBus slot and the second MBus slot share the same physical space and cannot both be populated. The SPARCstation 10 uses the same electronics, but a different physical design and is not subject to this limitation. The standard complement of SCSI-2 (not fast), AUI ("thick") Ethernet, and two serial ports are available on the board. The SPARCserver 630MP configures the system board in a three-slot package, leaving only one VME slot for expansion. The 630MP package has physical space for two 5.25" single-ended SCSI disk drives plus a CDROM and a low-profile tape drive. The much larger 670MP package has a twelve-slot card cage, leaving ten slots available for expansion, plus space for three 5.25" disks, CDROM, and tape. Early 670MP systems were offered with an expansion pedestal containing IPI disks. The data center 690MP package configures the system board in a sixteen-slot card cage, combined with space for a multi-tape tray and three trays of 5.25" disks. Early samples were delivered with IPI drives, but most were configured with differential SCSI-2. The 670MP and 690MP have enough room to accept a memory expansion board to expand system memory up to 1 GB.

The SPARCserver 1000 and SPARCserver 1000E are the mid-range members of the SuperSPARC-based server family. The systems have space for four system boards. Each board has space for up to two SuperSPARC processors, up to 512 MB memory, and three SBus slots, along with integrated two serial ports, 10baseT, and fast SCSI-2. A fully configured system includes eight processors, 2 GB memory, and 12 SBus slots. The package also has space for a CDROM, low-profile 4 mm or 8 mm tape drive, and four 3.5" x 1" disk drives. All six internal devices are connected via the onboard SCSI-2 port of the first system board, essentially consuming all of its expansion capability. For additional internal disk space, Sun offered disk boards in the same form factor as the system boards, each including four 3.5" x 1" disks. Expansion disk boards must be connected to SCSI host adapters configured somewhere else in the system, either built into system boards or on SBus boards.

The SPARCcenter 2000 and SPARCcenter 2000E are the enterprise-class SuperSPARC-based servers. Always found in data center racks, these systems have ten slots for system boards. The boards are unique to each model and use a physically different form factor than the SPARCserver 1000/1000E. The larger system boards have space for up to two SuperSPARC processors with caches up to 2 MB, up to 512 MB memory, and four SBus slots. Unlike the smaller sister, the SPARCcenter system boards have no built-in SCSI or Ethernet, although they do have two serial ports. Maximum capacity is 20 processors, 5 GB memory, and 40 SBus slots. The rack is always equipped with a CDROM, configured in a multi-tape tray that fits in the top of the rack. The tape tray has space for three standard full-height 5.25" tape drives such as 4 mm stackers or 8 mm drives. The

CDROM can share space with a half-high tape drive if desired. The entire tape tray must be connected to a single SCSI bus, customarily an FSBE/S is configured in the first SBus slot of the first system board. A fully configured system can accommodate three trays of 5.25" disk drives in the bottom of the rack. Additional disk storage is configured in expansion cabinets of varying configuration.

Cray CS6400—Developed by a division of Cray Research, the CS6400 is a high-end derivative of the SPARCcenter 2000E. Sun has since acquired the business group from Cray, along with the CS6400 design and customer base. The CS6400 is implemented in a data center rack with sixteen XDBus slots. Each system board shares fundamental ASIC components with the smaller SPARCcenter 2000E, but the board is much more extensive. A larger form factor permits each system board to configure up to four SuperSPARC modules, 1 GB memory, and four SBus slots. Maximum configuration is 64 processors, 16 GB memory, and 64 SBus slots.

Ultra Enterprise family—Consisting of the Enterprise 3000, 4000, 5000, and 6000 models. The UE3000 is a deskside enclosure with space for ten 3.5" x 1.6" disks and four system boards. The internal CDROM, tape, and disk drives are connected to the fast/wide SCSI host adapter on the required I/O board. The UE4000 is a deskside enclosure with no internal disks but space for eight system boards. The UE4000 can be rack-mounted using an optional mounting kit. The UE5000 is a UE4000 chassis mounted in a standard Sun system cabinet, and is identical except for some cabling restrictions. The UE6000 is a rack system with space for 16 system boards. System boards can be either CPU/memory boards, SBus I/O boards, or SBus/UPA graphics I/O boards. Any combination can be mixed, subject to obvious minimums of one CPU/memory board, one I/O board, one processor, and 64 MB memory. The Ultra Enterprise family is available with 167 MHz processors equipped with either 512 KB or 1 MB caches. Each CPU/memory board can be equipped with up to two processors and 0-2 GB of memory. The most common SBus I/O board offers three SBus slots on two SBusses plus built-in 100baseT FastEthernet, single-ended fast/wide SCSI-2, and sockets for two 25 MB/sec FibreChannel.

The next section briefly describes SBus boards. The list is not exhaustive; some boards with little or no relevance to servers have been omitted.

FSBE/S (Fast SCSI Buffered Ethernet, SBus)—SBus board with twisted pair 10baseT Ethernet and single-ended fast, narrow 10 MB/sec SCSI-2 interfaces. Ethernet has 128 KB media buffer.

DSBE/S (Differential SCSI Buffered Ethernet, SBus)—SBus board with twisted pair 10baseT Ethernet and differential fast, narrow 10 MB/sec SCSI-2 interfaces. Ethernet has 128 KB media buffer.

SBE/S (SCSI Buffered Ethernet, SBus)—SBus board with single-ended narrow (5 MB/sec) SCSI and Ethernet interfaces. The Ethernet interface has a pigtail that can connect to either twisted pair 10baseT or thick AUI interfaces. Ethernet has 128 KB media buffer.

SOC (serial optical coupler)—SBus board with sockets for two plug-in optical link modules (OLCs). Each OLC provides one 25 MB/sec full-duplex FibreChannel interface.

ATM 1.0—SBus board providing full-duplex 155 Mbit/sec ATM network interface. Available in models for connection to either fibre or Category-5 unshielded twisted pair media.

ATM 2.0—SBus board providing full-duplex 155 Mbit/sec ATM network interface. Available in models for connection to either fibre or Category-5 unshielded twisted pair media. Differs from ATM 1.0 in implementation but not standards compliance.

622 Mbit ATM 2.0—double-wide SBus board providing full-duplex 622 Mbit/sec ATM network interface. Available only with fibre interface.

DWIS/S—SBus board with 20 MB/sec differential fast/wide SCSI-2 interface.

SWIS/S—SBus board with 20 MB/sec single-ended fast/wide SCSI-2 interface.

1055A—SBus board with 5 MB/sec single-ended SCSI-2 interface.

453A—SBus board with thick and thin AUI Ethernet interfaces; only one can be used at a time. Cannot be configured in sun4d or most sun4m systems due to insensitivity to interrupt latency delays.

SQEC/S—SBus board with four twisted pair 10baseT interfaces.

FastEthernet 1.0—SBus board with media independent interface (MII) and Category-5 100baseT interfaces; only one can be used at a time.

FastEthernet 2.0—SBus board with only Category-5 100baseT interface.

FDDI/DX—9U VME board offering dual-attach FDDI interface. Not supported on Solaris 2.

FDDI/S 2.0—SBus board offering single-attach FDDI interface. Uses Sun-developed FDDI chip set. Not supported on Solaris 2.5 or later. Interfaces use MIC connectors.

FDDI/S 3.0—Family of SBus boards offering single-attach and dual-attach fibre FDDI, or single-attach copper FDDI interfaces. All 3.0 boards share software. Single-attach boards are single-wide, dual-attach boards are double-wide (i.e., consume two side-by-side SBus slots). Re-released with upgraded software as the 3.0.1 release. Interfaces use MIC connectors, except for copper, which uses Category -3 twisted pair.

FDDI/S 4.0—Family of SBus FDDI boards with hardware and software slightly upgraded from 3.x. The same models as the 3.0 family are available in 4.0 form. Note that the dual-attach models do not fit in Ultra–1 workstations, because those systems have two SBus slots one above the other, rather than two side-by-side SBus slots as in other platforms. Interfaces use MIC connectors, except for copper, which uses Category -3 twisted pair.

FDDI/S 5.0—Family of SBus boards with software upgraded from FDDI 4.x. The only hardware change is that the dual-attach boards use SC connectors, and thus fit on a single-wide SBus board. FDDI 5.0 software can be used on all members of the 3.0, 4.0, and 5.0 families.

TRI/S—SBus board with 16 Mbit Token Ring interface. Uses DB9 connector. Must have version 3.0.2 hardware and software to operate successfully with sun4d systems.

HSI—9U VME board offering one T1/E1 high-speed synchronous interface for wide-area networking.

HSI/S—SBus board offering four high speed synchronous serial interfaces. The connectors are DB-25. Because the board itself does not have physical space for four DB -25 connectors, the product uses an expansion panel connected to the SBus board via a large six meter cable.

SPC/S—SBus board offering eight RS-232 interfaces and one bidirectional parallel port. All nine interfaces use DB-25 connectors.

ISDN/S—SBus board with single basic rate ISDN interface.

SPRN-400—SBus board with interface for SPARCprinter 1 (12 ppm); also has a bidirectional parallel port interface.

NP20—SBus board with scan-line interface for NeWSprinter 20.

SunVideo—SBus board with dual video RCA inputs and S-VHS input. The DVMA version is capable of 30 frames per second capture with 24-bit color.

SBus Expansion Box—SBus board implementing an SBus bridge. The board (called the Xadapter) has a cable to an external box that contains three expansion SBus slots and provides for two 3.5" x 1.6" SCSI disks. Disk expansion requires a SCSI host adapter configured elsewhere in the system.

SBus Expansion Board—Similar to the SBus Expansion Box in that it uses the same Xadapter SBus card, but instead of housing the expansion SBus slots in a pizzabox, this product locates them on a 9U VME form-factor circuit board. The board is designed to operate in the SPARCserver 600MP family, which has such slots available. The Xboard, as this item is sometimes called, offers four expansion SBus slots. Like the SPARCserver 600MP system board, the Xboard consumes two VME slots.

Index

■ *Index*